ISO 9001:2000 for Small Businesses

About the Author

Ray Tricker (MSc, IEng, FIIE (elec), FCMI, FIQA, FIRSE) is the Principal Consultant of Herne European Consultancy Ltd – a company specialising in Integrated Quality, Safety and Environmental Management Systems and also an established Butterworth-Heinemann author. He served with the Royal Corps of Signals (for a total of 37 years) during which time he held various senior managerial posts culminating in being appointed as the Chief Engineer of NATO's Communication Security Agency (ACE COMSEC).

Most of Ray's work since joining Herne has centered on the European Railways. He has held a number of posts with the Union International des Chemins de fer [e.g. Quality Manager of the European Train Control System (ETCS)] and with the European Union (EU) Commission [for example T500 Review Team Leader, European Rail Traffic Management System (ERTMS) Users Group Project Co-ordinator, HEROE (Harmonisation of European Rail Rules) Project Co-ordinator] and currently (as well as writing books on ISO 9001:2000 for Butterworth-Heinemann!) he is busy assisting small businesses from around the world (usually on a no cost basis) produce their own auditable Quality Management Systems to meet the requirements of ISO 9001:2000. He is also consultant to the Association of American Railroads (AAR) advising them on ISO 9001:2000 compliance and has recently been appointed as UKAS Technical Specialist for the assessment of Notified Bodies for the harmonisation of the trans-European, high speed, rail system.

To Lalita with love – as always

ISO 9001:2000
for Small Businesses

Third edition

Ray Tricker

ELSEVIER
BUTTERWORTH
HEINEMANN

AMSTERDAM • BOSTON • HEIDELBERG • LONDON • NEW YORK • OXFORD
PARIS • SAN DIEGO • SAN FRANCISCO • SINGAPORE • SYDNEY • TOKYO

Elsevier Butterworth-Heinemann
Linacre House, Jordan Hill, Oxford OX2 8DP
30 Corporate Drive, Burlington, MA 01803

First published 1997
Reprinted 1997, 1998, 1999, 2001
Second edition 2001
Reprinted 2001, 2002, 2003
Third edition 2005

British Library Cataloguing in Publication Data
A catalogue record for this book is available from the British Library

Library of Congress Cataloguing in Publication Data
A catalogue record for this book is available from the Library of Congress

ISBN 0 7506 6617 X

For information on all Elsevier Butterworth-Heinemann publications
please visit our website at http://books.elsevier.com

Typeset by Charon Tec Pvt. Ltd, Chennai, India
www.charontec.com
Printed and bound in Great Britain by Biddles Ltd, King's Lynn, Norfolk

Contents

Foreword

During the past decade there has been a growing demand for an assurance of quality before a contract is let. This is not an entirely new concept, for quality has always played an important role in securing new markets as well as retaining those markets that already exist, but without doubt, in these days of competitive world markets, quality assurance has become even more relevant.

To meet this requirement, manufacturers and suppliers have had to recognise the importance of quality and the fact that it can only be achieved through efficient company organisation and a determination by management to meet the increased quality requirements of their potential customers.

This concept is not just related to the larger manufacturing companies and suppliers. It also affects the smaller companies, even those employing only one or two people. In fact, no matter how large or small the company, there has to be an increasing reliance on quality and the recommendations of ISO 9000 in order to meet customers' requirements. In fact, for anyone wanting to sell their product in a multi-national European or American market, the ISO 9000 publications are essential publications. Together they provide a comprehensive set of rules and regulations, specifications and recommendations that enable a manufacturer (or supplier), large or small, to set up workable quality processes and procedures and to operate within their constraints.

Many books have already been written on the topic of Quality Management and ISO 9000, but most of these appear to automatically assume that the reader belongs to a large company who already have an established management system in place. Small to medium size manufacturing companies and/or service industries now need to set up similar systems (but on a smaller scale) and show that they too can work in conformance with ISO 9001:2000.

This book, with its series of examples and audit procedures, attempts to show how a smaller company can benefit from the requirements of ISO 9001:2000 and in so doing, gain entry into more lucrative markets. Its main aim is to enable readers, at very little expense, to set up an ISO 9001:2000 compliant Quality Management System for themselves.

But *ISO 9001:2000 for Small Businesses*, third edn is not **just** a book, it also includes a fully worked, generic Quality Management System that can be customised to suit any company – without having to rely on a specialist or a consultant to complete the task for them.

Prior to the reissue of the ISO 9000 series in 2001, the majority of organisations wrote their Quality Manuals to just show how they met the 20 requirements of the 1994 standard – clause by clause. Although this made it easier for the authors of the manual to show the auditors that all of the requirements of the standard had been met, quite often (especially for very small businesses), the manual was of little use to the organisation itself in actually running their business.

ISO 9001:2000 now requires the Quality Manual to '*include the scope of the system, any justifications for exclusions, refer to established procedures and describe the interaction between processes*'. A Quality Manual that simply echoes the requirements of ISO 9001:2000 will, therefore, not be compliant, as certain sections of the standard's content may not be applicable to a particular organisation. It is essential that an organisation's Quality Manual serves a useful purpose and clearly just paraphrasing ISO 9001:2000's requirements or using an 'off the shelf' generic Quality Manual to show compliance is not the answer **unless**, it has been suitably customised to suit that particular organisation.

The prime aim of this book, therefore, is to help small businesses (who probably will have insufficient time to thoroughly read, understand, extract and implement all of the requirements of ISO 9001:2000) by providing them with a fully worked example. For simplicity my generic QMS is based on one particular type of company (i.e. Stingray – a 'paper producing' company) and this should be used as a template to describe the way that your organisation does business by leaving **out** those bits that are not particularly relevant and/or amplifying/ writing new policies, processes and procedures to cover the organisation-specific areas that I have not covered in my book. To be of any real use, this customisation should be completed on a page by page basis, to suit your own purposes.

 Note: To save you having to copy this QMS 'unlocked', fully accessible, non .pdf, soft copies of all of these files (as well as a selection of audit checklists, etc. from the sister publication 'ISO 9001: 2000 Audit Procedures') are available, on a CD (for a small additional charge) from the author in Word format. See p. xviii for further details.

Historically this is the 3rd edition of *ISO 9001:2000 for Small Businesses* and although the requirements of ISO 9001:2000 have not changed since publication of the 2nd edition in 2000, it was felt that its predecessor (because it was written during the transitional stage between the 1994 and the 2000 standards) made far too much mention and comparisons with the old version of this standard. It also laid insufficient emphasis on the fact that ISO 9001:2000 has now become **the** industry accepted standard for international quality.

Consequently (and with the benefit of three years' field experience of the standard) this book has been completely updated and now includes:

- a thoroughly revised and updated example Quality Manual;
- more detail concerning the relationship of ISO 9001:2000 with other management standards (and the possibility of setting up an Integrated Management System);
- a brief description of the ISO 14001 Environmental Management standard and its association with ISO 9001:2000;
- more detail about the aims, benefits and requirements of ISO 9001:2000;
- reformatted diagrams drawn against a common template;
- a new Appendix providing advice about internal audit programs;
- a new Annex concerning specific ISO 9001:2000 requirements that need to be addressed by Top Management;
- a new Annex briefly describing the requirements for documentation mandated by ISO 9001:2000;
- a new Annex with guidance on how to deal with non-conforming products;
- a new Annex containing advice about customer satisfaction;
- improved advice on how to comply with the requirements of ISO 9001:2000 and the likely documentation that an organisation will need to prove this compliance;
- an enhanced description of the eight quality management principles;
- more detail about TickIT;
- more explanation about the differences between:
  - being certified and being registered
  - being certified and being compliant
  - being certified and being accredited
  - a Quality Manual and a Quality System
  - a Quality Procedure and a Work Instruction
  - a Work Instruction and a Record
- an updated Auditor's Checklist;
- updated Glossary, References, Contacts and Acronyms sections.

Part of the text has also been modified to a Question and Answer type of format to assist understanding of ISO 9001:2000.

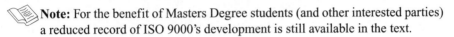 **Note:** For the benefit of Masters Degree students (and other interested parties) a reduced record of ISO 9000's development is still available in the text.

The main parts of the book are as follows:

- Background to ISO 9000;
- Structure of ISO 9001:2000;
- The importance of Quality Control and Quality Assurance;

- Quality Management System;
- Quality organisational structure;
- Example Quality Manual;
- Self-assessment.

For convenience (and in order to reduce the number of equivalent or similar terms) the following, unless otherwise stated, are considered interchangeable terms within this book.

- product – hardware, software, service or processed material;
- organisation – manufacturer and/or supplier.

Preface

With the increased demand for quality in everything that we do or make nowadays has come the need to have some formalised set of rules to work to. Up until a few years ago, however, there were no formalised standards for assuming a manufacturer's (or supplier's) quality. Quality procedures and guarantees were therefore required and the Military – as so often happens in these cases – came to the rescue.

NASA (in their capacity as controlling body for the US Space Program and with their requirement for the highest level of equipment reliability) were the first to produce a set of procedures, specifications and requirements. These become known as Military Specifications (Mil Specs) and manufacturers and suppliers, regardless of their size, were required to conform to these requirements if they wanted to provide equipment for this lucrative military market.

The North Atlantic Treaty Organisation (NATO), under the American influence, then produced a series of quality assurance procedures which were known as the NATO Allied Quality Assurance Publications (AQAPs). These were republished by the British Ministry of Defence (MOD) as the Defence Standard (DEF STAN) 05 series of procedures.

Civilian firms and contractors quickly realised the necessity of ensuring that manufacturers and suppliers should abide to an agreed set of quality standards and the British Standards Institution (BSI) formally adapted the DEF STAN 05 series into a virtually identical set of documents known as the BS 5750 series. This standard was then copied by other nations and a common series of recommendations known as the ISO 9000:1994 series of 'Standards for Quality Assurance' were produced.

Under existing international agreement, all international standards have to be re-inspected five years after publication. In accordance with this agreement, the 1994 versions of ISO 9000 series were revised with more emphasis being placed on the need for customer satisfaction and the use of a more modular, process approach to quality management. The main change caused by this new review process, however, was the amalgamation of the previous (similar) requirements contained in the ISO 9001:1994, ISO 9002:1994 and ISO 9003:1994 standards into a single ISO 9001:2000 standard.

Note: Although not officially referred to as a requirements standard, ISO 9001:2000 does, nevertheless, contain 141 'shalls' and 2 'musts' as opposed to 4 'shoulds' and 1 'could'.

ISO 9001:2000 specifies the national, regional and international accepted procedures and criteria that are required to ensure that products and services meet customers' requirements. It identifies the basic disciplines of a Quality Management System and can be used by manufacturers, suppliers, service industries and end users – large or small – with equal effect.

These processes, procedures, disciplines and criteria can be applied to any firm, no matter its size – whether they employ just a few people or many thousands. It can also be used by companies to set up their own Quality Management System and can form the basis for assessing a manufacturer's Quality Management System (i.e. to ensure that a supplier or service industry has the ability to provide satisfactory goods and/or services).

The aim of ISO 9001:2000 is that it:

- is flexible enough to fit any sort of organisation (the manufacturing emphasis is gone);
- no longer consists of 20 isolated elements;
- has a new quality process management model;
- defines responsibilities and authorities within the process areas;
- has a new emphasis on the identification of stakeholders and how the organisation plans to meet their needs;
- includes quality planning (similar to the automotive industries advanced quality planning shown in QS 9000:1995 'Quality system requirements');
- sets a requirement for the regular review of quality objectives;
- provides a flexible approach to quality documentation;
- provides useful rules for presenting the Quality Manual;
- enables an organisation to assure that its infrastructure is sufficient to meet its quality objectives;
- provides a method for continually reviewing the work environment and its effect on quality;
- emphasises the identification and review of customer needs and expectations;
- needs a formal review of an organisation's ability to meet customer needs;
- emphasises close communications with customers;
- includes process capability studies;
- includes design control based on project management;
- includes expanded validation of design requirements;

- requires configuration management;
- gives a better definition of the function of purchasing and procurement;
- verifies purchased products;
- validates the output of processes within an organisation;
- replaces service requirements with delivery and post delivery service requirements;
- closely integrates with ISO 10012 'Quality Assurance Requirements for Measuring Equipment' concerning the use of measurement and inspection equipment;
- needs process measurements and process audits;
- documents how a product is measured and evaluated using a Quality (Control) Plan;
- includes the requirement for regular revalidation of products or services to ensure that they continue to meet customer expectations;
- requires a formal system of measuring customer satisfaction;
- gives a more aggressive definition of corrective and preventive action;
- requires a formal policy on continuous improvement;
- is in line with other management systems.

Obtaining the customisable Quality Management System

ISO 9000:2001 for Small Businesses is accompanied by a full customisable copy of the QMS files presented in the book, available – at no charge – direct from the author. To obtain copies of these files please send an email to ray@herne.org.uk with 'Small Businesses QMS' in the subject line and provide the following information

- your title and full name
- organisation's name
- full mailing address and postal/zip code
- your email address
- your contact telephone number.

You will be sent, as soon as possible, a key code and instructions by email that will enable you to download a copy of the QMS files in Word format from the author's website. This QMS is provided free of charge and 'as is' by the author. While the original files remain copyright of the author, you we welcome to tailor them to suit the needs of your own organisation's QMS. Please note, however, that the author cannot enter into any further correspondence, or offer any additional support for these freely provided files. Users requiring additional support or information should see below.

Disclaimer

Material provided by this service is provided 'as is' without warranty of any kind, either express or implied. Every effort has been made to ensure accuracy and conformance to standards accepted at the time of publication. The user assumes the entire risk as to the accuracy and the use of this material. This material may be copied and distributed subject to the following conditions:

(1) 'Ray Tricker, ISO 9000:2001 For Small Businesses, Published by Elsevier Butterworth-Heinemann' must be credited as the source of the QMS template;

(2) The QMS document may not be distributed for profit. All trademarks acknowledged.

Obtaining additional material, information and support...

A CD containing a soft copy of the generic Quality Management System featured in ISO 9001:2000 for Small Businesses plus a soft copy of all the check sheets and examples audit forms contained in ISO 9001:2000 Audit Procedures, 2nd edn (Elsevier Butterworth-Heinemann, ISBN 0 7506 661 3) is available from the author for a small additional charge. All of these files can be quickly customised to suit your organisation's business and an ISO 9001:2000 Help Line is also available to purchasers of this CD.

For more information about this and other ISO 9000 consulting services, please visit www.herne.org.uk or e-mail ray@herne.org.uk

Part One

The Background to ISO 9000

In Part One, the necessity and the interoperability of quality standards is discussed, the historical background of ISO 9000 is presented and the basic requirements of ISO 9001:2000 are explained. The UK Government's support of Quality Management Systems is also briefly examined.

1
ISO 9000

1.1 ISO 9000

Wherever you go nowadays, it seems that you are always hearing the word 'quality' especially in relation to the requirements of 'ISO 9000', but even though these have become everyday words, they are often misused, misquoted and misunderstood. But why is this? Well, normally you will find that when most people talk about the quality of an object, they are talking about its excellence, perfection and/or value. In reality, of course, they should be talking about how much it meets its designed purpose and comes up to the manufacturer's or supplier's original specifications. Referring to the quality of a single article is, of course, fairly simple. Problems occur, however, when one has to talk about complex systems. Then it can become very difficult indeed to assess a level of quality.

Quality

"The degree to which a set of inherent characteristics fulfils requirements".

Figure 1.1 The accepted definition of quality

So what exactly is **meant** by the word quality? There are many definitions but the most commonly accepted definition of quality is '*the degree to which a set of inherent characteristics fulfills requirements*'. (ISO DIS 9000:2000).

But customers are not just interested in the level of quality 'intended' by the manufacturer or supplier, they are far more interested in the maintenance of quality level and want an assurance that the product (i.e. hardware, software, service or processed material) that they are buying truly meets the quality standard that they were initially offered and/or recommended.

This customer requirement has, quite naturally, had a sort of knock-on effect which has meant that manufacturers and suppliers (especially in the larger companies) have now had to pay far more attention to the quality of their product than was previously necessary. Organisations have had to set up proper Quality Management Systems in order to control and monitor all stages of the production process **and** they have had to provide proof to the potential customer that their product has the guaranteed – and in some cases certified – quality required by the customer. In other words, the manufacturer or supplier has had

Figure 1.2 Meeting the customer's requirement for quality

to work within a Quality Management System (QMS) in order to provide some degree of quality assurance for their product.

Unfortunately, with the current trend towards microminiaturisation and nano-technology, most modern day products have become extremely complex assemblies of components compared to those which were available a few years ago. This has meant that many more people are now involved in the manufacture and/or supply of a relatively simple object and this has increased the likelihood of a production fault occurring.

In much the same way, the responsibility for the quality of a product or service has also been spread over an increasing amount of people which has meant that the manufacturer's and/or supplier's guarantee of quality has, unfortunately, become less precise.

With the 2004 expansion of the European Union (EU), there is now a potential marketplace of some 450–500 million people. In North America the potential is very similar and selling to these markets has, therefore, become an extremely competitive business and (in order to gain a foothold in these markets) it has meant an increased reliance on internationally recognised quality procedures and recommendations. This is, of course, an area where ISO 9001:2000 has proved its worth.

Figure 1.3 Main producers of national standards within Europe

1.2 Interoperability of standards

Standards, of course, are as international as the markets they serve and currently the main producers of national standards in Western Europe are:

- United Kingdom – British Standards Institution (BSI);
- Germany – Deutsch Institut fur Normung e.v. (DIN);
- France – Association Français de Normalisation (AFNOR).

Outside Europe the most widely used standards come from:

- America – American National Standards Institute (ANSI);
- Canada – Canadian Standards Association (CSA).

There are, of course, others (for example Japan and Saudi Arabia) but Europe and North America are the main two.

Figure 1.4 Main producers of national standards outside Europe

Although these countries publish what are probably the most important series of standards, virtually every country with an industrial base has its own organisation producing its own set of standards. This can obviously lead to a lot of confusion, especially with regard to international trade and tenders. For example, if America were to invite tenders for a project quoting American (ANSI) national standards as the minimum criteria, other countries might find it difficult to submit a proposal, either because they didn't have a copy (or a translation) of the relevant standard, or they wouldn't find it cost effective to retool their entire works in order to conform to the requirements of that particular national standard.

ANSI American National Standards Institute

The situation in Europe has been made even more difficult when the European Union (EU) – in an attempt to stop national standards forming trade barriers to community trade – produced even more regulations!

On the defence electronics side of the fence there is little change. The United Kingdom Ministry of Defence (MOD-UK) use Defence Standards (DEF STANS), the American Division of Defence (DOD) use Military Standards (Mil-Std) and the North Atlantic Treaty Organisation (NATO) use NATO Allied Quality Assurance Publications (AQAPs) and most other nations have their own particular variations.

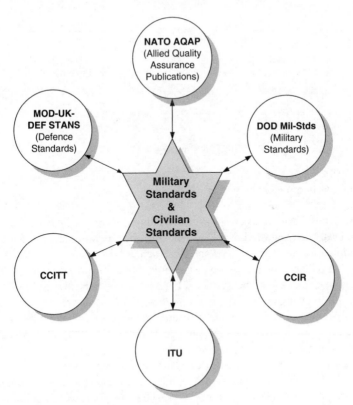

Figure 1.5 Military and civilian standards

From a more civilian point of view the International Telecommunications Union (ITU) Committees (i.e. The International Telegraph and Telephony Consultative Committee (CCITT) and the International Radio Consultative Committee (CCIR)) also publish recommendations.

For this reason there has been a steady growth in international standardisation and ISO, (International Organisation for Standardisation) and the IEC (International Electrotechnical Commission), are now the standards bodies that most countries are affiliated to – via, that is, their own particular National Standards Organisation (NSO).

Like ITU documents, these ISO and IEC standards (ISO is mainly concerned with industrial standards whilst IEC refers to electrical equipment) were initially published as 'recommendations', but they are now accepted as international standards – in their own right.

Figure 1.6 International standards

The standards themselves are drawn up by International Technical Committees which have been approved by ISO or IEC member countries and there are now many hundreds of different ISO and IEC standards available.

But national bodies and national standards cannot dictate customer choice. A product that may legally be marketed need not be of universal appeal. Indeed, where different national standards persist they will do so as a reflection of different market preferences. For industry to survive in this set of 'liberalised' market, therefore, it must have a sound technological base supported by a comprehensive set of internationally approved standards.

Quality has thus become the key word in today's competitive markets and there are now more than 80 countries with similar organisations – most of which are members of ISO and IEC. Figure 1.7 shows the inter-relationship of these standards and committees.

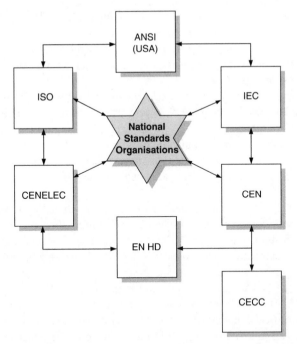

Figure 1.7 Inter-relationship of the standards bodies and committees

1.3 The demand for standardisation of Quality Management Systems

The growing demand for assurance of quality **before** a contract is awarded has reinforced the already accepted adage that quality products play an important role in securing new markets as well as retaining those markets that already exist. Without doubt, in these days of competitive world markets, quality assurance has never been more relevant. No longer can suppliers rely on their reputation alone.

The drive towards quality-led production now means that today's major purchasers are not just **expecting** a quality product but are also **demanding** proof that a company is capable of producing quality products and/or providing quality services. The provision of this proof is normally in the form of an independent third-party certification and this is possibly the single most important requirement for a manufacturer, company or supplier.

Up until the early 1970's, however, there were no viable third-party certification schemes available. But with an increased demand for quality assurance during all stages of the manufacturing processes, came the requirement for manufacturers to work to a recognised set of standards.

Within the United Kingdom the BSI (British Standards Institution) had already published a number of guides to quality assurance (for example BS 4891:1972 – A guide to Quality Assurance) and quickly set about providing an acceptable document that would cover all requirements for a two-party manufacturing or supply contract.

This became the BS 5750 series of standards which were first published in the United Kingdom during 1979. These standards supplied guidelines for internal quality management as well as external quality assurance and they were quickly accepted by manufacturers, suppliers and purchasers as being a reasonable minimum level of quality assurance that they could be expected to work to. The BS 5750:1979 series thus became the 'cornerstone' for national quality.

But in the meantime America had been working on their ANSI 90 series and other European countries were also busily developing their own sets of standards. Quite naturally, however, as the BSI had already produced and published an acceptable standard, most of these national standards were broadly based on BS 5750.

In 1981, the Department of Trade and Industry (DTI) formed a committee called FOCUS to examine areas where standardisation could benefit the competitiveness of British manufacturers and users of high technology – for instance Local Area Network (LAN) standardisation. Owing to the wider international interest concerning quality assurance, ISO then set up a Study Group during 1983 to produce an international set of standards that all countries could use.

This initiative, the Open Systems Interconnection (OSI), ensured that products from different manufacturers and different countries could exchange data and interwork in certain defined areas. In the United States, the Corporation of Open Systems (COS) was formed in 1986 to pursue similar objectives.

1.4 The background to the ISO 9000 set of quality standards

ISO was first established as a United Nations Agency in 1947 and is made up of representatives from more than 90 countries including BSI for the United Kingdom and ANSI for the United States. Over the years the work of ISO has increased considerably and a great number of standards are now available and have already been adopted.

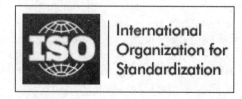

From the consumer's point of view, however, the importance of international (i.e. ISO) standards is that all major agencies are committed to recognising their requirements. Equipment, modules and components can be designed and built so that they will be acceptable to all member countries and in this way interoperability is assured.

1.4.1 What does the term ISO mean?

As the term 'ISO' actually stands for the '*International Organization for Standardization*' one would normally assume that the acronym should be 'IOS'! Apparently there are two reasons why ISO was chosen instead of IOS. The first is that '*iso*' in Greek means '*equal*' (and this mirrors ISO's aim to develop standards that will enable organisations to be on an equal footing and, therefore, conveys the idea of equality). The second (and probably the main reason) is that '*ISO*' is spelt the same (and, therefore, has the same acronym) in most languages spoken by the members of the original organisation.

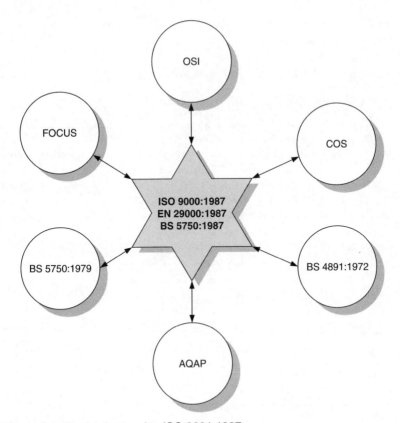

Figure 1.8 The background to ISO 9001:1987

1.4.2 ISO 9000:1987

Similar to quality standards from other countries, ISO's first attempt at producing an international standard for quality management (i.e. the ISO 9000:1987 set of standards) were very heavily based on BS 5750 Parts 1, 2 and 3. They followed the same sectional layout except that an additional section (ISO 9000:1987 Part 0 Section 0.1) was introduced to provide further guidance about the principal concepts and applications contained in the ISO 9000 series.

Table 1.1 Comparison chart of equivalent standards to the ISO 9000:1994 series

Standard no.	Equivalent standard								
	AS	ASQC	BS	CSA	DIN	EN	IEC	JIS	NFX
ISO 9000	AS 3900	ASQC Q90		CSA Q9000	DIN ISO 9000	EN 29000		JIS-Z9900	NFX 50-121
ISO 9000/1		ASQC Q9000-1	BS EN ISO 9000-1		DIN EN ISO 9000 PT1	EN ISO 9000/1			NFX 50-121
ISO 9000/2	AS 3900.2	ASQC Q9000-2							
ISO 9000/3		ASQC Q9000-3	BS 5750 PT13 (1991)	CSA Q9000.3	DIN ISO 9000 PT3	EN 29000 PT3			NFX 50-121/3
ISO 9000/4	AS 3900.4		BS 5750 PT14 (1993)		DIN ISO 9000 PT4	EN 60300 PT1	IEC 300 PT1		
ISO 9001	AS 3901	ASQC Q9001	BS EN ISO 9001	CSA Q9001	DIN EN ISO 9001 DIN ISO 9001	EN ISO 9001		JIS-Z9901	NFX 50-131
ISO 9002	AS 3902	ASQC Q9002	BS EN ISO 9002	CSA Q9002	DIN EN ISO 9002 DIN ISO 9002	EN ISO 9002		JIS-Z9902	NFX 50-132
ISO 9003	AS 3903	ASQC Q9003	BS EN ISO 9003	CSA Q9003	DIN EN ISO 9003 DIN ISO 9003	EN ISO 9003		JIS-Z9903	NFX 50-133
ISO 9004	AS 3904	ASQC Q9004-1		CSA Q9004	DIN ISO 9004	EN 29004		JIS-Z9904	
ISO 9004/1		ASQC Q9004-1	BS EN ISO 9004-1		DIN EN ISO 9004 PT1	EN ISO 9004/1			
ISO 9004/2	AS 3904.2	ASQC Q9004-2	BS 5750 PT8 (1991)	CSA Q9004.2	DIN ISO 9004 PT2	EN 29004 PT2			NFX 50-122-2
ISO 9004/3	AS 3904.3	ASQC Q9004-3							
ISO 9004/4	AS 3904.4	ASQC Q9004-4	BS 7850 PT2 (1994)						

When ISO 9000 was first published in 1987 it was immediately ratified by the UK (under the direction of the Quality Management and Statistics Standards Committee) and republished by the BSI (without deviation), as the new BS 5750:1987 standard for QMSs.

Similarly, on 10 December 1987 the Technical Board of the European Committee for Standardisation (Commission European de Normalisation Electrotechnique – CEN) approved and accepted the text of ISO 9000:1987 as **the** European Standard – without modification – and republished it as EN 29000:1987.

At that time official versions of EN 29000:1987 existed in English, French and German. CEN members were allowed, however, to translate any of these versions into their own language and they then had the same status as the original official versions.

Note: Up-to-date lists and bibliographical references concerning these and other European standards may be obtained on application to the CEN Central Secretariat (Rue Brederode 2, Boite 5, B–1000, Brussels, Belgium) or from any CEN member.

BS 5750:1987 was, therefore, identical to ISO 9000:1987 and EN 29000:1987 except that BS 5750 had three additional guidance sections. Consequently, BS 5750 was not just the British Standard for Quality Management Systems it was also the European **and** the international standard.

1.4.3 ISO 9000:1994

As ISO 9000:1987 became more popular, ISO realised that calling the same document by a variety of different names could cause a certain amount of confusion and so in March of 1994 the ISO 9000:1994 series of Quality Management documents were published.

Although the most notable change between the 1987 and the 1994 versions of the ISO 9000 standard was the streamlining of the numbering system, there were also around 250 other changes, the main ones being that:

- it became an explicit requirement that all members of an organisation (down to supervisory level at least) had job profiles (descriptions) to define their authority and responsibility;
- design reviews were now compulsory throughout the Work Package lifetime;
- documentation control was extended to ensure that all data was kept up to date.

Most of the 250 changes were intended to clarify the standard, making it easier to read. They did not significantly alter the way in which most companies were running their businesses; they simply sought to improve it.

1.5 ISO 9001:2000

1.5.1 Background to the ISO 9001:2000 standard

When ISO 9000 was first released in 1987, it was recognised as being largely incomplete and required the auditors to fill in lots of the gaps. The first revision of ISO 9000 in 1994 got rid of many of these problems. However, an organisation could still conform to the standard **but** at the same time produce substandard products that were of a consistent poor quality! There was clearly a major loophole that enabled organisations to comply with the requirements of ISO 9000:1994 – without having to **improve** their quality!

Some managers also found it extremely difficult to see the real benefit of having to commit more and more manpower and finance in maintaining their ISO 9000 certification. Whilst most organisations accepted that the initial certification process was worthwhile and could result in some very real benefits, these were mainly one-offs and it was felt that once ISO 9000 had been fully adopted within an organisation, these savings could not be repeated. The ISO 9000 certificate had been hanging on the wall in the reception office for many years but third party surveillance visits don't tell the management much more than they already knew from their own internal audits! Quite a few organisations also felt that they had gone well beyond ISO 9000 and apart from associating the organisation with a quality standard, there was little or no actual benefit to be gained from having to continually pay out for re-certification and surveillance fees.

On the other hand, however, BSI frequently come across organisations who initially sought ISO 9000 registration (because it was a requirement to continue business with a client), but having seen the benefits they, in turn, had pushed it on down their own supply chain, thus **increasing** the requirement for ISO 9000 certification.

So as the 1990s progressed, more and more organisations started reaping benefits from the existing ISO 9000:1994 requirements but as the standard became more popular the inadequacies of ISO 9000:1994 became more apparent. For example:

- some organisations did not need to carry out all the 20 elements making up ISO 9000:1994 in order to be a quality organisation;
- the standard was too biased towards manufacturing industries thus making it difficult for service industries to use;
- the requirements were repeated in other management systems, resulting in duplication of effort (e.g. ISO 14001 Environmental Management and BS 8800 Management of Health and Safety);
- many organisations wanted to progress beyond the confines of ISO 9000 towards Total Quality Management (TQM);
- the documents were viewed by many as not being very user-friendly;

- the language used was not clear and could be interpreted in many different ways;
- the standard was very inflexible and could not be tailored to specific industries, etc;
- the standard did not cater for continual improvement;
- the standard did not fully address customer satisfaction.

The reasons went on and on and there was clearly a need for revision.

Fortunately, help was on its way for under existing international agreement, **all** International standards have to be re-inspected, five years after publication, for their continued applicability. In accordance with this agreement, ISO/TC176 (ISO Technical Committee No 176 'Quality Management and Quality Assurance') conducted a global survey of over 1000 users and organisations for their views on ISO 9000:1994 using a questionnaire (produced by ISO member bodies) covering:

- problems with the existing standards;
- requirements for new/revised standards;
- possible harmonisation and interoperability between quality management, environmental management and health & safety standards.

Figure 1.9 The common elements from ISO 9000, BS 8800 and ISO 14001

The primary objective of this exercise was to make ISO 9001:2000:

- more compatible with the other management systems;
- more closely associated to business processes;
- more easily understood;
- capable of being used by all organisations, no matter their size;
- capable of being used by all types of industries and professions (i.e. manu-facturers **and** service providers);
- a means of continually improving quality;
- future proof.

1.5.2 The revision process

The revision process was the responsibility of ISO TC–176. Initial specifications and goals were established following extensive user surveys and these were followed by a user verification and validation process, to ensure that the standards produced would actually meet the requirements of the user.

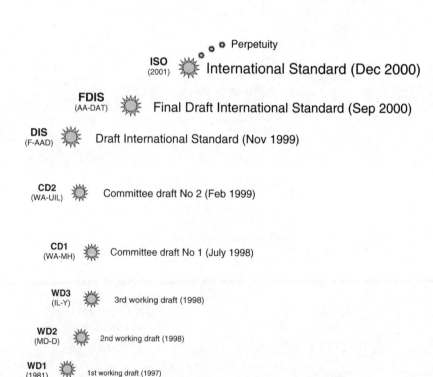

Figure 1.10 The revision process

The program of work was as follows:

4th quarter 1997	1st Working Draft (WD1) for use by TC–176
1st quarter 1998	2nd Working Draft (WD2) for use by TC–176
2nd quarter 1998	3rd Working Draft (WD3) for use by TC–176
July 1998	Committee Draft (CD1) issued for ballot
November 1999	Committee Draft (CD2) issued for ballot
November 1999	Draft International Standard (DIS) for comment and vote by Member Countries (see note)
September 2000	Publication of Final Draft International Standard (FDIS)
December 2000	Publication of International Standard (ISO)

 Note: Once Draft International Standards have been adopted by the technical committees they are then circulated to member bodies for voting. Publication as an International Standard then requires a two-thirds majority of the votes.

1.5.3 Factors considered during the revisions of the standards

Some of the factors considered during the development of the draft standards included:

- the problems with ISO 9001:1994's 20-element model and its current bias towards manufacturing organisations;
- the increased use of the ISO 9000 standards by regulated industries and their subsequent need for change;
- the proliferation of guideline standards in the ISO 9000:1994 family (most of which were not fully used!);
- changed user requirements with more emphasis on meeting customer needs;
- the difficulties that small businesses were having in trying to meet the requirements of the standards;
- the need to be more compatible with other management system standards (e.g. ISO 14001 for environmental management);
- the incorporation of ISO 9000 standards into specific sector requirements standards or documents;
- the adoption of process-oriented management and the need to assist organisations in improving their business performance.

The interest shown by users in improving ISO 9000:1994 was obvious by their response to the questionnaires which resulted in over 6000 comments on each of the first and second sets of committee drafts. The results of the survey clearly showed the need for a revised ISO 9000 standard, which would:

- be split, so that one standard [i.e. ISO 9001:2000 would address requirements, whilst another (ISO 9004:2000) would address the gradual improvement of an organisation's overall quality performance];
- be simple to use, easy to understand and only use clear language and terminology (a definite plus for most readers of current international standards!);
- have a common structure based on a 'process model';
- be capable of being 'tailored' to fit all product and service sectors and all sizes of organisations (and not just the manufacturing industry);
- be more orientated toward continual improvement and customer satisfaction;
- be capable of demonstrating continuous improvement and prevention of non-conformity;
- provide a natural stepping stone towards performance improvement;
- have an increased compatibility with other management system standards;
- provide a basis for addressing the primary needs and interests of organisations in specific sectors such as aerospace, automotive, medical devices, telecommunication and others.

The survey also indicated that organisations were finding it increasingly difficult to do business in the world marketplace without ISO 9000. The growing

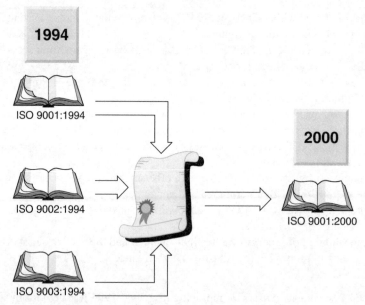

Figure 1.11 Simplified certification with only one standard

confusion about having three quality standards available for certification (i.e. ISO 9001:1994, 9002:1994 and 9003:1994) was also a contributing factor and so it was recommended that the requirements of all three standards be combined into one overall standard (i.e. ISO 9001:2000).

ISO emphasise, however, that the year 2000 revision of the ISO 9000 standards **does not** require the rewriting of an organisation's current QMS documentation! They point out that the major change has been from a 'system based' to a more 'process orientated' management approach, which can be easily addressed by organisations who have a fully documented QMS that already complies with the 1994 standard.

1.5.4 Key changes in the standards

In ISO 9001:2000, the 20 elements contained in section four of ISO 9001:1994 have been replaced by four major sections covering the management of resources, the quality of the product, the maintenance of quality records and the requirements for continual improvement.

Each of the three main standards (i.e. ISO 9000:2000, ISO 9001:2000 and ISO 9004:2000) now have a revised title, which no longer includes the term 'quality assurance'. This has been done in order to reflect the fact that the QMS requirements specified in these standards address the quality assurance of a product as well as customer satisfaction.

They have been designed so that ISO 9000:2000 now includes a description of the basic approach to quality management as well as including a revised

Figure 1.12 How 20 went into 4!

vocabulary to reflect the usage of new and revised terms and associated definitions contained in ISO 9001:2000 and ISO 9004:2000.

ISO 9001:2000 is focused towards '*providing confidence, as a result of demonstration, in product conformance to established requirements*' and includes a clause entitled 'permissible exclusions'. This clause allows organisations to formally 'omit' certain non-applicable requirements of the standard, yet still claim conformance to it. However, only those organisations that can **prove** that the nature of their products, customers and/or the applicable regulatory requirements do not need to meet the full requirements of ISO 9001:2000, are allowed these exclusions. For example, organisations whose products require no design activities (and who would had previously sought ISO 9002:1994 certification) can now claim to be in compliance with ISO 9001:2000 by excluding the requirements for design and/or development.

On the other hand, ISO 9004:2000 is focused towards providing '*benefits for all interested parties through sustained customer satisfaction*'. ISO 9004:2000 also includes the requirements of ISO 9001:2000 in text boxes inserted in appropriate places (which means, I suppose that organisations only need to purchase 9004 and not both of the standards – funny old world!). In addition, ISO 9004:2000 includes an annex giving guidance on '*self-assessment*' to enable an organisation to check the status of their own QMS. This has proved extremely useful for organisations applying for ISO 9001:2000 certification, but who are unsure what additional quality documentation would be required.

ISO 9001:2000 and ISO 9004:2000 have, therefore, been developed as a 'consistent pair' of QMS standards, based on eight quality management principles with a common process-oriented structure and harmonised terminology. They are designed to be used together, or may be used as stand-alone documents, however, only ISO 9001:2000 can be used for certification purposes.

One specific change to ISO 9001:2000 and ISO 9004:2000 that was brought about late in the day concerned the usage of the term 'product'. During the Committee Draft stages, it became apparent that there was a need to have a single word that described an organisation's output as well as the service that it provided. Consequently in the new standards, '*product*' has been defined as '*a process, which uses resources to transform inputs into outputs*' and there are four agreed generic product categories, namely:

- hardware (e.g. engine, mechanical part);
- software (e.g. computer program);
- services (e.g. transport);
- processed materials (e.g. lubricant).

In practice, most products will be combinations of these four generic product categories and whether the combined product is then called hardware, processed material, software or service will depend on the dominant element.

Although upgrading an organisation's QMS to ISO 9001:2000 will be fairly simple for organisations previously certified to ISO 9001:1994, the impact on organisations who were previously only registered to ISO 9002:1994 and 9003:1994 (i.e. organisations not involved in the design and manufacture of a product) have inevitably proved to be more difficult as greater documentation is now required (in order to demonstrate why service and design functions do not apply to their organisations) and more detailed records are required.

1.5.5 What are the aims, benefits, main changes and new requirements of ISO 9001:2000?

1.5.5.1 What are the aims of ISO 9001:2000?

The aim of ISO 9001:2000 is to assist users to produce a QMS that is capable of being:

(1) Flexible

- it is flexible enough to fit any sort of organisation (the manufacturing emphasis is gone);
- it provides a flexible approach to quality documentation;
- it includes quality planning similar to other associated standards (e.g. ISO 13484:2004);
- it is in line with other management systems.

(2) Structured

- no longer consists of 20 isolated elements;
- has a new quality process management model;
- includes process capability studies;
- relies on process measurements and process audits;
- includes design control based on project management;
- includes expanded validation of design requirements;
- requires configuration management;
- documents how a product is measured and evaluated using a Quality (Control) Plan.

(3) Customer orientated

- has a new emphasis on the identification of stakeholders and how the organisation plans to meet their needs;
- emphasises close communications with customers;
- requires a formal system of measuring customer satisfaction;

- emphasises the need to identify and review customer requirements and expectations;
- replaces service requirements with delivery and post-delivery service requirements.

(4) Verification and validation
- verifies purchased products;
- validates the output of processes within an organisation;
- includes the requirement for regular revalidation of products and/or services to ensure that they continue to meet customer expectations.

(5) Corrective action
- gives a more assertive definition of corrective and preventive action.

(6) Continuous improvement
- provides for continually reviewing the work environment and its effect on quality.

(7) Workforce
- defines responsibilities and authorities within the process areas;
- enables an organisation to assure that its infrastructure is sufficient to meet its quality objectives.

(8) Reviews
- sets a requirement for the regular review of quality objectives;
- requires a formal policy on continuous improvement.

1.5.5.2 What are the advantages of ISO 9001:2000?

With the publication of ISO 9001:2000, there is now a single quality management 'requirements' standard that is applicable to all organisations, products and services. It is the only standard that can be used for the certification of a QMS and its generic requirements can be used by any organisation to:

- address customer satisfaction;
- meet customer and applicable regulatory requirements;
- enable internal and external parties (including certification bodies) to assess the organisation's ability to meet these customer and regulatory requirements.

1.5.5.3 What are the benefits of the revised standards?

The major benefits associated with the new standards include its:

- applicability to all product categories, regardless of sector and/or size of an organisation;
- capability of being used (as the basis) for other product sector systems (e.g. medical devices, telecommunications, automotive, etc.);
- compatibility with other management systems (e.g. such as ISO 14000);
- emphasis on continual improvement;
- emphasis on customer satisfaction;
- move toward improved organisational performance;
- need for less documentation;
- pivotal part in integrated management;
- process approach;
- understandability and ease of use;
- use of one standard (i.e. ISO 9001) to cover the requirements and another (i.e. ISO 9004) to provide guidance.

1.5.5.4 What are the main changes?

The main changes caused by the introduction of 9001 and 9004 as a consistent pair of QMS standards are:

- a considerable reduction in the amount of required documentation;
- the introduction for the need to monitor customer satisfaction (as a measure of system performance);
- the introduction of organisational self-assessment as a driver for improvement;
- their consideration of the benefits and needs of all interested parties;
- their continual improvement process;
- their increased emphasis on the role of top management especially its commitment to:
  - the development and improvement of the QMS;
  - the consideration of legal and regulatory requirements;
  - the establishment of measurable objectives for relevant functions and levels;
- their increased compatibility with other management systems (e.g. ISO 14001);
- their logical structure;
- their new process-oriented structure;
- their reference to quality management principles;
- their terminology (providing easier interpretation).

1.5.5.5 What new requirements have been introduced?

Main new requirements include the:

- analysis of collected data to evaluate the performance of the QMS;
- consideration of statutory and regulatory requirements;
- establishment of measurable objectives at relevant functions and levels;
- increased attention to availability of resources;
- increased emphasis on the role of top management;
- need to determine training objectives and effectiveness;
- need to monitor customer satisfaction as a measure of system performance;
- requirement for continual improvement;
- requirement to measure (and monitor) system and processes as well as product.

1.5.5.6 What are the main advantages to organisations using ISO 9001:2000?

Many companies stipulate that their suppliers are ISO 9000 compliant; therefore, once you're certified, your opportunities will increase. What's more…

- profitability increases;
- market share expands;
- customer satisfaction increases;
- operating costs dramatically reduce;
- demand for your products and services are heightened;
- employees experience better working conditions.

1.5.6 Certification registration and accreditation

Following consultation between ISO/TC 176, the International Accreditation Forum (IAF) and the ISO Committee on Conformity Testing (ISO/CASCO), it was agreed that those organisations who had previously used ISO 9002:1994 and ISO 9003:1994 would be allowed to work to this new international standard by reducing the scope of their conformance. For example, when a customer needs a particular type of product and/or service that does not necessarily require all the QMS requirements, then they can be excluded. This exclusion can be made, **provided** that the organisation does not reduce the actual scope of its QMS or exclude any QMS requirements that affect the organisation's ability to provide a conforming product and/or service. All exclusions need to be defined in the organisation's Quality Manual and by definition, reducing the scope of conformance does not absolve the organisation from providing a product and/or service which meets customer requirements.

As previously mentioned, the 2000 revision is also an attempt to harmonise the common quality management elements of ISO 9000 with those contained in the

ISO 14001 environmental management system standard and, to some degree, the health and safety requirements of standards such as BS 8800. The overall intention is to enable an organisation to run one management system that addresses quality, the environment **and** health and safety.

It has to be said, however, that much of the old standard has been preserved and the revisions that have been made have been aimed mainly at closing the gap between ISO 9000, QS 9000 for the automotive industry and TR 9000 for the telecommunications industry and ISO 13485 for the medical industry etc.

1.5.6.1 What is the difference between being certified and being registered?

Actually there is no difference! In some countries companies/organisations will say that they are certified, in others they will say that they are registered – but it means the same thing.

1.5.6.2 What is the difference being certified and being compliant?

When an organisation claims that they are ISO 9000 certified or registered, they mean that a Notified Body (that is, an independent registrar) has audited their QMS, certified that it meets the requirements of ISO 9001:2000, given them a written assurance that ISO's quality management system standard has been met and registered their organisation as having been certified.

On the other hand, when an organisation says that they are ISO 9000 'compliant', they usually mean that they have met ISO's quality system requirements but have **not** been formally certified by an independent registrar. In effect, they are self-certified and whilst this is perfectly acceptable for many organisations, especially the smaller ones, an official certificate issued by an independent registrar does tend to carry more weight in the market place.

Note: As ISO 9001:2000 is a process standard (and not a product standard), when a company says that they are certified or compliant, they are **not** saying that their products and/or services meet the ISO 9000 requirements.

1.5.6.3 What is the difference between being certified and being accredited?

Registrars, audit and certify organisations who wish to become ISO 9000 registered. Accreditation Bodies, like UKAS (United Kingdom Accreditation Service), on the other hand, evaluate and accredit the registrars. In effect accreditation bodies audit the auditors and certify that the registrars are competent and authorised to issue ISO 9001:2000 certificates in specified business sectors.

1.5.7 The 'consistent pair'

ISO 9001:2000 and ISO 9004:2000 have been developed together – with the same sequence and structure – in order to form a 'consistent pair' of quality management standards. Their primary aim is to give ISO 9000 a more global applicability, to relate modern quality management to the actual processes and activities of an organisation and to promote continual improvement and achievement of customer satisfaction.

These two international standards are designed to be used together, but can also be used independently. ISO 9001:2000 specifies the **requirements** for a QMS (that can be used for internal application, certification, or contractual purposes), ISO 9004:2000 gives **guidance** on a wider range of objectives aimed at improving an organisation's overall performance. ISO 9004:2000 is **not**, however, meant as a guideline for implementing ISO 9001:2000 **neither** is it intended for certification or contractual use. Both standards are based on eight quality management principles, which reflect best management practices.

1.5.8 Quality management principles

The eight quality management principles defined in ISO 9000:2000 *Quality Management Systems – Fundamentals and vocabulary* can be used by senior management as a basis for improving their organisation's performance. They have been derived from the collective experience and knowledge of the international experts making up the technical committee responsible for developing and maintaining ISO 9000 (i.e. ISO-TC 176).

Note: ISO 9000:2000 also provides examples of the benefits that can be derived from the use of these eight principles and some of the actions that managers could typically take in applying them to improve their organisations' performance.

Principle 1 Customer focus

> Organisations depend on their customers and therefore should understand current and future customer needs, should meet customer requirements and strive to exceed customer expectations.

Key benefits:
- Better use of the organisation's resources.
- Enhanced customer satisfaction.
- Flexible and fast response to market opportunities.
- Improved customer loyalty.

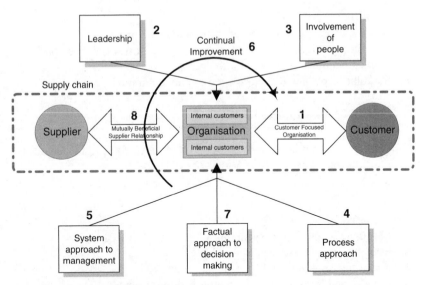

Figure 1.13 The process model

- Increased revenue and market share.
- Repeat business.

Principle 2 Leadership

> Leaders establish unity of purpose and direction of the organisation. They should create and maintain the internal environment in which people can become fully involved in achieving the organisation's objectives.

Key benefits:
- Better communication levels throughout the organisation.
- Better understanding of the reasons for achieving the organisation's goals and objectives.
- Evaluation of activities.
- Minimising the possibilities for error.

Principle 3 Involvement of people

> People at all levels are the essence of an organisation and their full involvement enables their abilities to be used for the organisation's benefit.

Key benefits:

- Helping people to be motivated, committed and involved.
- Inspiring people to continually improve on their organisation's objectives.
- Making people accountable for their own performance.
- Stimulating people to always aim for continual improvement.

Principle 4 Process approach

A desired result is achieved more efficiently when activities and related resources are managed as a process.

Key benefits:

- Lower costs and shorter cycle times.
- Effective use of resources.
- Improved, consistent and predictable results.
- Focused and prioritised opportunities for improvement.

Principle 5 System approach to management

Identifying, understanding and managing interrelated processes as a system contributes to the organisation's effectiveness and efficiency in achieving its objectives.

Key benefits:

- Being able to focus effort on the key processes.
- Being better able to achieve desired results.
- Integration and alignment of business processes.
- Promoting confidence (to interested parties) about the organisation's effectiveness, efficiency and capability.

Principle 6 Continual improvement

Continual improvement of the organisation's overall performance should be a permanent objective of the organisation.

Key benefits:

- Coordination of all improvement possibilities and activities.
- Improving the organisational capability.
- Providing the flexibility to react to opportunities quickly.

Principle 7 Factual approach to decision making

> Effective decisions are based on the analysis of data and information.

Key benefits:
- Ability to review, challenge and change opinions and decisions.

Principle 8 Mutually beneficial supplier relationships

> An organisation and its suppliers are interdependent and a mutually beneficial relationship enhances the ability of both to create value.

Key benefits:
- Ability to react quickly to a changing market and/or customer needs and expectations.
- Costs optimised.
- Possibilities for creating value for both parties.
- Resources used to their best advantage.

1.5.9 What has happened to other standards previously based on ISO 9000:1994?

During its lifetime, the 1994 version of ISO 9000 was frequently used as the generic template for other industry management system standards. The problem with using ISO 9001:1994, however, was that because it was a requirements based quality management system (primarily designed for manufacturers) it was not entirely suitable for all industries. As a result, these other industries found that they had to leave out some of the requirements of this standard whilst, at the same time, include additional topics that were specific to their own particular industry.

By the end of the 1990's there were a growing number of these 'ISO 9000 equivalent standards' and standards for telecommunications (TL 9000), the automotive industry (QS 9000) and medical devices (ISOs 13485 and 13488:1966) were widely used. To simplify matters, it was agreed that part of ISO TC-176's work in upgrading the 1994 standard would, therefore, be to take these 'sons of 9000' into consideration and try to produce one standard that would cover virtually all industries – not just one for the manufacturers of a product.

Currently, although there are still a number of these other industry standards available, they are all gradually being rewritten around the requirements and recommendations of ISO 9001:2000 and the following is a selection of some of the most important ones.

1.5.9.1 Telecommunications industry

TL 9000 (*Quality management standard for the telecommunication sector*) is a set of quality system requirements for the telecommunications industry which were originally developed by the QuEST Forum (Quality Excellence for Suppliers of Telecommunications Leadership) and was first published in November 1999. It has now been updated to conform to ISO 9001:2000.

The purpose of TL 9000 is to provide a quality management system for the design, development, production, delivery, installation and maintenance of telecommunication products and services, using ISO 9000 as the base with certain specific additions. It applies to all suppliers of telecommunications hardware, software and services and – as it is totally compatible with existing ISO 9000 protocols – registration to TL 9000 reduces the need to meet other telecommunication quality management standards.

The three registration options (or any combination of these three) being offered are:

- TL 9000 – H (Hardware quality system requirements and metrics);
- TL 9000 – S (Software quality system requirements and metrics);
- TL 9000 – V (Services quality system requirements and metrics).

Further information about the QuEST Forum is available from their website (www.questforum.org) or from the American Society for Quality at www.asq.or.

1.5.9.2 Automotive industry

QS-9000 (*Quality System Requirements QS-9000*) is a common supplier quality standard for the Daimler Chrysler Corporation, Ford Motor Company and General Motors Corporation. It is based on the 1994 edition of ISO 9001, but contains additional requirements that are particular to the automotive industry.

QS-9000 applies to all suppliers of production materials, production and service parts, heat treating, painting and plating and other finishing services for the 'Big Three' and its requirements are divided into three sections, as follows:

- Section 1: Common requirements – the exact text of ISO 9001 with the addition of automotive/heavy trucking requirements;
- Section 2: Additional requirements – requirements beyond the scope of ISO 9001, common to all three manufacturers;
- Section 3: Customer specific sections – requirements unique to Ford, General Motors, or Chrysler.

Being specific to the automotive industry, additional documentation is required for the QS 9000 program and consist of:

- QS-9000 Quality System Requirements;
- Advanced Product Quality Planning and Control Plan (APQP);

- Failure Mode and Effects Analysis (FMEA);
- Measurement Systems Analysis;
- Fundamental SPC;
- Production Part Approval Process (PPAP) manual and the
- Quality System Assessment (QSA) manual.

When ISO 9001:2000 was released it was realised that this standard with its process orientated approach more closely met the requirements of the automotive industry and so a working party was set up to amend QS 9000. This resulted in the publication of ISO/TS 16949:2002 (*Quality management systems – Particular requirements for the application of ISO 9001:2000 for automotive production and relevant service part organizations*) which, in conjunction with ISO 9001:2000, now defines the quality management system requirements for the design and development, production and, when relevant, installation and service of automotive-related products.

ISO/TS 16949:2002 was released in March 2002 and provides a supplier to vehicle manufacturers with a QMS that is recognised by all of the IATF (International Automotive Task Force). The Big Three (as part of IATF) have agreed to adopt ISO/TS 16949:2002 as the minimum qualifying standard for suppliers to vehicle manufacturers and as from 14th December 2006 the current QS-9000 standard (which includes text from the old ISO 9000:1994) will cease to exist.

More information on ISO/TS 16949:2002 is available from the following websites:

- IATF Oversight Organization at www.iaob.org
- Automotive Industry Action Group at www.aiag.org (which also contains information on qualified registrars)
- Chrysler Group suppliers hg3@daimierchrysier.com
- Ford Motor suppliers rhopkins@ford.com
- General Motors 103114.2516@compuserve.com

1.5.9.3 Medical devices

ISO 13485:2003 (*Medical devices – Quality management systems – Requirements for regulatory purposes*) is intended for the medical device industry, regardless of the type and/or size of the organisation. The standard specifies the requirements for a quality management system and is aimed at ensuring that all medical devices manufactured and/or provided by an organisation continue to meet customer and regulatory requirements applicable to those medical devices.

As patient safety is involved, **all** of the requirements of ISO 13485:2003 are mandatory and as this standard differs from ISO 9001:2000 by including some additional requirements that are intended only for medical devices and excluding some ISO 9001:2000's requirements that are inappropriate. One major change is that rather than targeting customer satisfaction – as the new ISO 9001 does – ISO 13485 targets customer requirements. Because of these exclusions, an organisation that is registered to ISO 13485:2003 **cannot** also claim conformity to ISO 9001:2000 unless their QMS also covers the excluded ISO 9001:2000 requirements.

For further details about ISO 13485:2003 contact one of the following:

- The Medical Device Manufacturers' Association mdmainfo@medical-devices.org
- Medicines and Healthcare products Regulatory Agency (MHRA) info@mhra.gsi.gov.uk
- Food and Drug Administration (FDA) www.fda.gov.

1.5.9.4 Testing and calibration laboratories

ISO/IEC 17025:2000 (*General requirements for the competence of testing and calibration laboratories*) was produced as a result of EN 45001 and ISO/IEC Guide 25 and contains requirements for all test and calibration laboratories wishing to demonstrate that they are technically competent and operate an acceptable quality system.

The standard is applicable to all laboratories (regardless of size) and laboratories meeting this standard are certified as being able to produce test and calibration results which are mutually acceptable between countries. The standard has two main requirement clauses, Clause 4 (which specifies the management requirements) and Clause 5 which specifies the technical requirements.

Clause 4 has been written around the 1994 version of ISO 9000 and emphasises the need for:

- a quality manual (containing quality policy statement, supporting procedures and a formalised document control system – so very much the same as ISO 9001:2000);
- procedures for the review of requests, tenders and contracts;
- purchase control (including subcontractor management);
- corrective and preventative action (including control of non-conforming product and cause analysis);
- control of records (particularly technical records);
- regular internal and management audits.

Clause 5 is specifically aimed at testing and calibration laboratories and covers additional items such as:

- competence of personnel performing the tests and calibrations;
- laboratory facilities (accommodation, infrastructure and environmental conditions);

- test and calibration methods (plus method evaluation);
- control of data (in particular computer software);
- control of equipment (records, maintenance plan, transportation etc.);
- measurement traceability (calibration of test equipment, reference standards);
- sampling plan;
- reporting the results of testing and calibrations (test reports, calibration certificates and test reports).

This standard is currently being updated to comply with the basic management system requirements of ISO 9001:2000.

1.5.9.5 Petroleum, petrochemical and natural gas industries

PD ISO/TS 29001:2003 (*Petroleum, petrochemical and natural gas industries – Sector specific quality management systems – Requirements for product and service supply organizations*) is another new Technical Specification that has recently been developed by ISO as a quality management system for these particular industries.

As with all QMSs, the aim is for continual improvement and this specification is no different except, in this particular case, continual improvement is focused on:

- defect prevention;
- reduction of variation and waste in the supply chain;
- reduction of variation and waste from service providers.

The requirements specified in PD ISO/TS 29001:2003 are supplementary to ISO 9001 and have been developed separately to ensure that the requirements for the design, development, production, installation and service of products are clear and auditable. The standard also helps to guarantee a global consistency and improved assurance in the quality of goods and services supplied from providers – the failure of which could have severe ramifications for the companies and industries involved.

Further details concerning this Technical Specification are available from the Association for Petroleum and Explosives Administration (APEA) via admin@apea.org.uk.

1.5.9.6 Aerospace

AS/EN/JIS Q 9100:2001 (*Quality Management Systems – Aerospace – Requirements*) is an international aerospace standard for quality assurance in design, development, production, installation and servicing. ASQ 9100 certification can be obtained by companies specialising in design and manufacture of equipment, aircraft accessory supply, airport and airline operations, spares supply and maintenance, flight operations or cargo handling. An increasing number of major aerospace contractors (e.g. Boeing, Rolls Royce Allison, GEAE, NASA and Honeywell etc.) are now encouraging suppliers to use ASQ 9100, which is boosting ('propelling' one might even say!) its use throughout the industry.

For further details about the requirements of AS 9100, try the American Society for Quality (ASQ) website at www.asq.org.

1.5.9.7 Computer software

ISO/IEC 90003:2004 (*Software engineering – Guidelines for the application of ISO 9001:2000 to computer software*) provides guidance for organisations using ISO 9001:2000 to purchase, supply, develop, operate and maintain computer software and related support services. It is suitable for all software that is:

- part of a commercial contract with another organisation;
- a product available for a market sector;
- used to support the processes of an organisation;
- embedded in a hardware product, or
- related to software services.

ISO/IEC 90003:2004 itself is independent of the technology, life cycle models, development processes, sequence of activities and business structure used by an organisation. It does not add to or otherwise change the requirements of ISO 9001:2000 and the guidelines provided are not intended to be used as assessment criteria in quality management system registration/certification.

1.5.9.8 Food and drink industry

ISO 15161:2001 (*Guidelines on the application of ISO 9001:2000 for the food and drink industry*) is aimed at organisations involved in all aspects of this industry sector, including sourcing, processing and packaging food and drink products.

The standard provides guidelines for the food and drink industry for implementing a QMS based on ISO 9001:2000 and provides information on the possible interactions between ISO 9000 and the Hazard Analysis and Critical Control Point (HACCP) system for food safety requirements.

This International Standard is not intended for certification, regulatory or contractual use.

1.5.9.9 Education

IWA 2:2003 (*Quality management systems – Guidelines for the application of ISO 9001:2000 in education*)

International Workshop Agreement IWA 2:2003 provides guidelines for the application of ISO 9001:2000 in educational organisations providing educational products. These guidelines do not add to, change or modify the requirements of ISO 9001:2000 and are not intended for use in contracts for compliance assessments or for certification.

Each clause of ISO 9001:2000 is included before the corresponding text of IWA 2:2003. The whole text of ISO 9004:2000 is also included to provide a complete vision of the continual performance improvement of organisations.

1.5.9.10 Iron ore industry

ISO/TR 13352:1997 (*Guidelines for interpretation of ISO 9000 series for application within the iron ore industry*) was written around the old procedural based 1994 version of ISO 9000 with certain additions that were specific for the mining and quarrying (iron ore) industry.

It is currently being updated to comply with the basic management system requirements of ISO 9001:2000.

1.5.9.11 TickIT

TickIT procedures relate directly to the requirements set out in ISO 9001:2000 and similar to this standard, certification is conducted by an independent third party certification body using specialist auditors trained by the International Register of Certificated Auditors (IRCA) with the support of the British Computer Society. A successful audit by a TickIT-accredited certification body results in the award of a certificate of compliance to ISO 9001:2000, endorsed with a TickIT logo.

TickIT is supported by the UK and Swedish software industries with the aim of stimulating software system developers to think about:

- what quality really is in the context of the processes of software development;
- how quality may be achieved;
- how quality management systems may be continuously improved.

Through the following objectives:

- to improve market confidence in a third party QMS certification through software sector accredited certification bodies;
- to improve professional practice amongst software sector QMS auditors;
- to publish authoritative guidance material (i.e. *the TickIT Guide*) for use by all stakeholders.

TickIT, therefore, provides software developers with an accredited quality certification scheme that meets the special needs of the industry, enjoys the confidence of professional staff and commands respect from purchasers and suppliers. It applies to all types of information system suppliers (software houses and in-house developers) which involve software development processes. TickIT disciplines are also relevant to the development of embedded software.

Within the UK, TickIT is recognised by all Government departments and major purchasers and it is compatible with European requirements for accredited quality system certification. World-wide, over 1400 TickIT certificates have now been issued and currently, 50% of all new certificates are being granted to organisations outside the United Kingdom.

For more information about this scheme, contact the TickIT Office at BSI (Floor 8E), 389 Chiswick High Road, London W4 4AL.

Tel: + 44(0) 20 8996 7427

Fax: + 44(0) 20 8996 7429

e-mail: **tickit@bsi-global.com**

1.5.9.12 The future evolution of ISO 9000

To ensure that the current ISO 9000 family can continue to benefit from new developments within the quality management field, ISO/TC-176 continuously monitor the use of the ISO 9000 standards.

Similar to other ISO standards, ISO 9000:2000 is due to be reviewed every five years and so a new version might well be published during 2008 (i.e. five years after ISO 9001:2000 became the mandatory standard for quality management). As well as customer feedback, ISO have stated that this review will take into consideration all of the other system specific industrial standards and specifications and be aimed at producing a more generic standard.

1.5.10 Are there any other standards based on ISO 9001:2000?

Well, yes . . . there is BS 7799 which provides a specification for the design, development and implementation of an information security management system – just as ISO 9001 does for a QMS. This standard recognises that information is a significant asset to any organisation and, therefore, it needs to be carefully managed. It also recognises the risks associated with software copies and records and, as well as having to accurately identify its information assets, an organisation must also ensure that the security of this information is maintained.

As an information security management standard, BS 7799 is designed to help anyone who is responsible for initiating, implementing and/or maintaining security within an organisation. It provides a comprehensive set of controls for best practice in information security. It was first published in 1995 with the purpose of:

- providing a common basis for developing organisational security standards and an effective security management practice;
- providing confidence in inter-organisational dealings;

and the preservation of:

- confidentiality;
- integrity – safeguarding the accuracy and completeness of information and processing methods;
- availability – ensuring that authorised users have access to information and associated assets when required.

The 1999 revision took into account recent developments in the application of information processing technology (in particular networks, communications and information security) and now addresses all types of information that is stored electronically and/or transmitted electronically, such as through the Internet and other telecommunications channels. This standard also covers data that is written, mailed or on film.

There are definite parallels between BS 7799 and ISO 9000 and so the aim of the 2002 revision of BS 7799 was to bring it into line with ISO 9001:2000 and other management system standards. The latest revision even includes the plan-do-check-act model.

1.5.11 What is the ISO 9000 family?

The three main standards which make up the ISO 9000 family areas follows:

Figure 1.14 The ISO 9001:2000 family

Standards and guidelines	Purpose
ISO 9000:2000 *Quality Management Systems – Fundamentals and vocabulary* (Supersedes ISO 8402:1995 *'Quality Management and Quality Assurance – Vocabulary'* and ISO 9000-1:1994 *'Quality Management and Quality Assurance Standards – Guidelines for selection and use'*).	Establishes a starting point for understanding the three standards. Describes the fundamentals for QMSs and defines the fundamental terms and definitions used in the ISO 9000 standards.
ISO 9001:2000 *Quality Management Systems – Requirements* (Superseding ISO 9001:1994 *'Quality Systems – Model for quality assurance in design, development, production, installation and servicing'*; ISO 9002:1994 *'Quality Systems – Model for quality assurance in production, installation and servicing'*; and ISO 9003:1994 *'Quality Systems – Model for quality assurance in final inspection and test'*).	This is the requirement standard you use to assess your ability to meet customer and applicable regulatory requirements and thereby address customer satisfaction. It is now the **only** standard in the ISO 9000 family against which third-party certification can be carried.
ISO 9004:2000 *Quality Management Systems – Guidelines for performance improvements* (Superseding ISO 9004-1:1994 *'Quality Management and Quality System Elements – Guidelines'*).	This guideline standard provides guidance for continual improvement of your quality management system to benefit all parties through sustained customer satisfaction.

Note: Whilst the term 'ISO 9001' has only one very specific meaning (i.e. it refers to the ISO 9001:2000 requirements standard), the term 'ISO 9000' can be taken two ways. In its broadest sense, it can mean all of the ISO 9001:2000 family (i.e. ISO 9000:2000, ISO 9001:2000, ISO 9004:2000 and ISO 19001). In its narrow sense, the term ISO 9000 can refer only to the ISO 9000:2000 standard (which talks about definitions and vocabulary!). In trying to make their definitions easier to understand, ISO have unfortunately introduced a little bit of added confusion!

These three standards are then supported by:

ISO 19011:2002 *Guidelines on Quality and/or Environmental Management Systems Auditing* (currently under development) (Superseding ISO 10011:1990 *'Guidelines for Auditing Quality Systems: 1991 Guidelines for Auditing Quality Systems – Qualification criteria for quality system auditors'*; ISO 10011-3:1991 *'Guidelines for Auditing Quality Systems – Management of audit programs'*, as well as ISO 14010:1996 *'Guidelines for Environmental Auditing – General principles'*; ISO 14011:1996 *'Guidelines for Environmental Auditing – Audit procedures – Auditing of environmental management systems'* and ISO 14012:1996 *'Guidelines for Environmental Auditing – Qualification criteria for environmental auditors'*).	For auditing. ISO 19011:2002 provides guidance on the principles of auditing, managing audit programmes, conducting quality management system audits and environmental management system audits, as well as guidance on the competence of quality and environmental management system auditors. It is applicable to all organisations needing to conduct internal or external audits of quality and/or environmental management systems or to manage an audit programme.

(*continued*)

ISO 10005:1995, *Quality Management – Guidelines for quality plans*	For Quality Plans. Provides guidelines to assist in the preparation, review, acceptance and revision of quality plans.
ISO 10006:1997, *Quality Management – Guidelines to quality in project management*	For project management. Guidelines to help you ensure the quality of both the project processes and the project products.
ISO 10007:1995, *Quality Management – Guidelines for configuration management*	For configuration management. Gives you guidelines to ensure that a complex product continues to function when components are changed individually.
ISO/DIS 10012, *Quality assurance requirements for measuring equipment – Part 1: Metrological confirmation system for measuring equipment*	For measurement systems. Gives you guidelines on the main features of a calibration system to ensure that measurements are made with the intended accuracy.
ISO 10012-2:1997, *Quality assurance for measuring equipment – Part 2: Guidelines for control of measurement of processes*	For measurement systems. Provides supplementary guidance on the application of statistical process control when this is appropriate for achieving the objectives of Part 1.

(*continued*)

ISO 10013:1995, *Guidelines for developing quality manuals*	For quality documentation. Provides guidelines for the development, and maintenance of quality manuals, tailored to your specific needs.
ISO/TR 10014:1998, *Guidelines for managing the economics of quality*	For managing the economics of quality. Provides guidance on how to achieve economic benefits from the application of quality management.
ISO 10015:1999, *Quality Management – Guidelines for training*	For training. Provides guidance on the development, implementation, maintenance and improvement of strategies and systems for training that affects the quality of products.

1.5.12 Integrated Management Systems

ISO 9001:2000 is intended to be compatible with other management system standards in particular, those relating to environmental management, occupational health & safety and financial management, etc. With this in mind TC/176 when producing ISO 9001:2000 have made sure that the requirements of ISO 14001 '*Environmental Management Systems – Specifications with guidance for use*' have been carefully considered and a very good degree of compatibility now exists between these two standards.

 Note: For a brief description of ISO 14001 see Appendix 1 to this Chapter.

Thus, although ISO 9001:2000 does not include any requirements that are specific to ISO 14001 (or, indeed, any of the other management systems) it does, nevertheless, allow an organisation to align and integrate its own QMS with other (related) management system requirements. In some cases, it may even be possible for an organisation to adapt its existing management system(s) in order to establish a QMS that complies with the requirements of ISO 9001:2000.

Both from a financial and a business perspective the advantages to be gained from combining the management systems for quality, environment, and health and safety into just one basic, integrated management system are well worth pursuing – especially considering the natural similarity between a company's business processes and procedures for each of these three systems (for example, the document control process shown in the Quality Manual will be the same as that for the other two systems).

Other than economy of scale and unnecessary duplication, the three main reasons for integrating the systems together are:

- ease of use – one simple arrangement that is used frequently by staff will become far more familiar than three disconnected systems, used periodically;
- reduced amount of internal auditing – and advantages gained by using different departments to audit each other (e.g. the quality department can audit the environmental department etc.);
- reduction in certification costs – as there now only needs to be one assessment and surveillance.

Without doubt, an Integrated Management System (IMS) – based on a process structure that reflects an organisation's business model – is the way forward and many organisations have seen the light.

Note: There are a number of texts on this topic (e.g. those published by BSI in its IMS series).

1.5.13 ISO 9000:2000

To ensure a more harmonised approach to standardisation and the (hopeful!) achievement of coherent terminology within the ISO 9000:2000 family, the development of ISO 9000:2000 was completed in parallel with ISO 9001:2000, ISO 9004:2000 and all other existing and planned management standards.

ISO 9000:2000 now includes a revision of the previous ISO 8402:1995 *Quality Management and Quality Assurance – Vocabulary* standard, provides a more formal approach to the definition of terms, specifies terminology for QMSs and will assist:

- those concerned with enhancing mutual understanding of the terminology used in quality management (e.g. suppliers, customers, regulators);
- those internal or external to the organisation who assess the QMS or audit it for conformance to the requirements of ISO 9001:2000 (e.g. auditors, regulators, independent Registrar and/or Notified Body);
- those internal or external to the organisation who give advice on QMSs appropriate to that organisation;
- developers of related standards.

Figure 1.15 The way to ISO 9000:2000

Figure 1.16 The way to ISO 9001:2000

ISO 9000:2000 also provides an introduction to the fundamentals of QMSs and following publication of this standard, ISO 8402:1995 was withdrawn.

1.5.14 ISO 9001:2000

The previous ISO 9001:1994, ISO 9002:1994 and ISO 9003:1994 family of standards have now been consolidated into a single revised ISO 9001:2000 standard.

With the publication of ISO 9001:2000, there is now, therefore, a single quality management '**requirements**' standard that is applicable to all organisations, products and services. It is the **only** standard that can be used for the certification of a QMS and its generic requirements can be used by **any** organisation to:

- address customer satisfaction;
- meet customer and applicable regulatory requirements;

Figure 1.17 The basic process

- enable internal and external parties (including certification bodies) to assess the organisation's ability to meet these customer and regulatory requirements.

For certification purposes, an organisation will have to possess a documented management system which takes the inputs and transforms them into targeted outputs. Something that effectively:

- says what they are going to do;
- does what they have said they are going to do;
- keep records of everything that they do – especially when things go wrong.

The basic process to achieve these targeted outputs will encompass:

- the client's requirements;
- the inputs from management and staff;
- documented controls for any activities that are needed to produce the finished article;
- and, of course, delivering a product or service, which satisfies the customer's original requirements.

The adoption of a QMS has to be a strategic decision for any organisation and the design and implementation of their QMS will be influenced by its varying needs, objectives, products provided, processes employed and the size and

Figure 1.18 The four major generic business processes of ISO 9001:2000

structure of that organisation. As ISO are quick to point out, however, it is not the intention of ISO 9001:2000 to insist on a uniform structure to a QMS or uniformity of documentation. The QMS requirements specified in this standard should always be viewed as complementary to the product technical requirements.

This latest revision process has made ISO 9001:2000 into a far more generic standard than the previous 20-element ISO 9001:1994 structure. It adopts the process management approach widely used in business today and more clearly addresses the QMS requirements for an organisation in order to demonstrate its capability of meeting customer requirements. It is now also more compatible (indeed linked with) the ISO 14001 standard for environmental management and includes the relevant managerial requirements found in national/international health and safety management standards.

As previously mentioned, the ISO 9001:2000 standard is the **only** standard within the 2000 edition to which an organisation can be certified. It includes all the key points from the previous 20 elements of ISO 9001:1994, but integrates them into four major generic business processes, namely:

- management responsibility (policy, objectives, planning, system, review);
- resource management (human resources, information, facilities);
- product realisation (customer, design, purchasing, production, calibration);
- measurement, analysis and improvement (audit, process/product control, improvement).

The new structure of ISO 9001:2000 is shown in Tables 1.2–1.6.

Table 1.2 The structure of ISO 9001:2000 – Sections 1–4

Section	Sub section	Sub-sub section	Title
1			**Scope**
	1.1		General
	1.2		Application
2			Normative reference
3			Terms and definitions
4			Quality Management System
	4.1		General requirements
	4.2		Documentation requirements
		4.2.1	General
		4.2.2	Quality Manual
		4.2.3	Control of documents
		4.2.4	Control of records

Table 1.3 The structure of ISO 9001:2000 – Section 5

Section	Sub section	Sub-sub section	Title
5			Management responsibility
	5.1		Management commitment
	5.2		Customer focus
	5.3		Quality policy
	5.4		Planning
		5.4.1	Quality objectives
		5.4.2	Quality management system planning

(*continued*)

Table 1.3 *(continued)*

Section	Sub section	Sub-sub section	Title
	5.5		Responsibility, authority, communication
		5.5.1	Responsibility and authority
		5.5.2	Management representative
		5.5.3	Internal communication
	5.6		Management review
		5.6.1	General
		5.6.2	Review input
		5.6.3	Review output

Table 1.4 The structure of ISO 9001:2000 – Section 6

Section	Sub section	Sub-sub section	Title
6			Resource management
	6.1		Provision of resources
	6.2		Human resources
		6.2.1	General
		6.2.2	Competence, awareness, training
	6.3		Infrastructure
	6.4		Work environment

Table 1.5 The structure of ISO 9001:2000 – Section 7

Section	Sub section	Sub-sub section	Title
7			Product realisation
	7.1		Planning of product realisation
	7.2		Customer-related processes
		7.2.1	Determination of requirements related to the product

(continued)

Table 1.5 *(continued)*

Section	Sub section	Sub-sub section	Title
		7.2.2	Review of requirements related to the product
		7.2.3	Customer communication
	7.3		Design and development
		7.3.1	Design and development planning
		7.3.2	Design and development input
		7.3.3	Design and development outputs
		7.3.4	Design and development review
		7.3.5	Design and development verification
		7.3.6	Design and development validation
		7.3.7	Control of design and development changes
	7.4		Purchasing
		7.4.1	Purchasing process
		7.4.2	Purchasing information
		7.4.3	Verification of purchased product
	7.5		Production and service provision
		7.5.1	Control of production and service provision
		7.5.2	Validation of processes for production and service provision
		7.5.3	Identification and traceability
		7.5.4	Customer property
		7.5.5	Preservation of product
	7.6		Control of measuring and monitoring device

Table 1.6 The structure of ISO 9001:2000 – Section 8

Section	Sub section	Sub-sub section	Title
8			Measurement, analysis and improvement
	8.1		General
	8.2		Monitoring and measurement
		8.2.1	Customer satisfaction
		8.2.2	Internal audit
		8.2.3	Monitoring and measurement of processes
		8.2.4	Monitoring and measurement of product
	8.3		Control of non-conforming product
	8.4		Analysis of data
	8.5		Improvement
		8.5.1	Continual improvement
		8.5.2	Corrective action
		8.5.3	Preventive action

1.5.15 Process approach

Any activity that receives inputs and converts them to outputs can be considered as a process. Often, the output from one process will directly form the input into the next process.

For organisations to function effectively, they will have to identify and manage numerous interlinked processes. This systematic identification and management of the processes employed within an organisation (and particularly the interactions between such processes) is referred to as the 'process approach'.

Throughout ISO 9001:2000, the requirement for continuous improvement is frequently (and heavily) emphasised. 'Continual improvement' (i.e. in the

Figure 1.19

Figure 1.20 Continual improvement

context of ISO 9001:2000) requires an organisation to concentrate on continually increasing the effectiveness and efficiency of its business processes whilst carrying out the policies and objectives of that organisation. With a well structured, planned process, continual improvement will respond to the growing needs and expectations of customers and ensure a dynamic evolution of the Quality Management System.

The following process model (shown in Figure 1.21) seeks to show how the four major sections of ISO 9001:2000 (i.e. management responsibility, resource management, product realisation and measurement, analysis and improvement) interrelate and how the improvement processes continuously revolve around all other aspects of quality management.

Continual improvement is assured by utilisation of the PDCA model developed by ISO (see Figure 1.20 above).

For clarity, the QMS requirements and management responsibilities can be combined as shown in Figure 1.22.

Organisations seeking to change over an existing ISO 9000:1994 QMS to the 2000 edition are referred to Figure 1.23 below that shows the correlation between the key elements from ISO 9001:1994 and the clauses of ISO 9001:2000.

Note: If your current Quality Management System is successfully implemented, satisfies the needs and objectives of your organisation, reflects the way your organisation works, addresses all of the new requirements, no changes are required. However, if your current documented system does **not** address all of the new requirements, additional documentation may be necessary.

Figure 1.21 The ISO 9000:2000 process model

Figure 1.22 Quality Management System requirements and management responsibilities

1.5.16 Planning an organisation's business processes

All businesses are made up of a series of processes which, when placed together, make the business operate. In a similar manner, ISO 9001:2000 is based around

| COMPARISON BETWEEN ISO 9001:1994 AND ISO 9001:2000 ||
ISO 9001:1994	ISO 9001:2000
1. Scope	1
2. Normative reference	2
3. Definitions	3
4. Quality system requirements	
4.1 Management responsibility	
4.1.1 Quality policy	5.1, 5.3, 5.4.1
4.1.2 Organisation	
4.1.2.1 Responsibility & authority	5.5.1
4.1.2.2 Resources	5.1, 6.1, 6.2.1, 6.3
4.1.2.3 Management representative	5.5.2
4.1.3 Management review	5.6.1, 5.6.2, 5.6.3, 8.5.1
4.2 Quality system	
4.2.1 General	4.1, 4.2.1, 4.2.2, 5.1, 5.4.1
4.2.2 Quality system procedures	4.2.1
4.2.3 Quality planning	5.4.2, 6.2.1, 7.1
4.3 Contract review	5.2, 7.2.1, 7.2.2, 7.2.3
4.4 Design control	7.2.1, 7.3.1, 7.3.2, 7.3.3, 7.3.4, 7.3.5, 7.3.6, 7.3.7
4.5 Document & data control	4.2.1, 4.2.3
4.6 Purchasing	7.4.1, 7.4.2, 7.4.3, 7.4.4
4.7 Control of customer-supplied product	7.5.4
4.8 Product identification & traceability	7.5.3
4.9 Process control	6.3, 6.4, 7.1, 7.5.1, 7.5.2, 8.2.3
4.10 Inspection & testing	7.1, 7.4.3, 7.5.1, 7.5.3, 8.1, 8.2.4
4.11 Control of inspection, measuring and test equipment	7.6
4.12 Inspection & test status	7.5.3
4.13 Control of non-conforming product	8.3
4.14 Corrective & preventive action	8.4, 8.5.2, 8.5.3
4.15 Handling, storage, packaging, preservation & delivery	7.5.1, 7.5.5
4.16 Control of quality records	4.2.4
4.17 Internal quality audits	8.2.2, 8.2.3
4.18 Training	6.2.1, 6.2.2
4.19 Servicing	7.1, 7.5.1
4.20 Statistical techniques	8.1, 8.2.3, 8.2.4, 8.4

Notes
1.   Reference numbers are given in numerical order, not in order of significance.
2.   The clause numbers in ISO 9001:2000 are as follows:
     5.x.x - Management Responsibility
     6.x.x - Resource Management
     7.x.x - Product Realisation
     8.x.x - Measurement, Analysis and Improvement

Figure 1.23 Correlation between the clauses of ISO 9001:1994 and ISO 9001:2000

Figure 1.24

four generic business processes, these being management responsibility, resource management, product and/or service realisation and measurement, analysis and improvement. All processes within businesses will contain an element of these four business processes.

Processes are the keys to providing a clear understanding of what an organisation does and the quality controls it has in place to control their business activities. ISO 9001:2000 recommends the use of 'processes' to define how resources and activities are combined, controlled and converted into deliverables. As shown in Table 1.7, there are three types of processes associated with an organisation's QMS.

Table 1.7 Core Business and supporting processes

Core Business Process	Describing the end-to-end activities involved in an organisation manufacturing or supplying a deliverable.
Primary supporting processes	The basic set of activities which, when combined into a logical sequence, takes you from receipt of an order (or marketing opportunity) through to the realisation of the finished product or service.
Secondary supporting processes	Those activities that are vital to attaining the desired levels of quality but which are seen as supporting the primary supporting processes.

Figure 1.25 The integration of business and quality

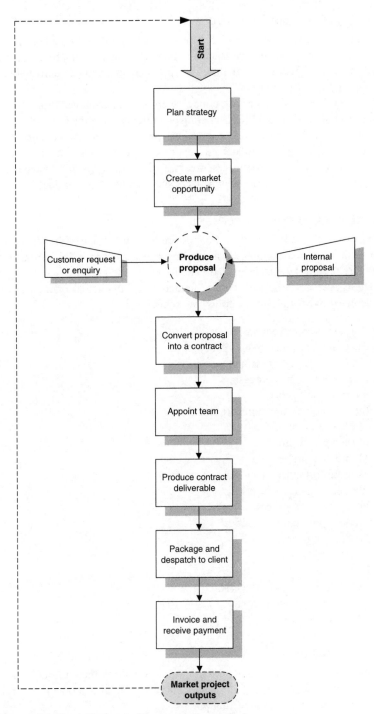

Figure 1.26 Core Business Process – Example A

1.5.16.1 Core Business Process

A company's organisational processes making up their QMS normally comprise a Core Business Process supplemented by a number of supporting processes which describe the infrastructure required to produce the contact deliverable (or market opportunity) on time.

The Core Business Process describes the end-to-end activities involved in producing a contract deliverable or marketing opportunity. It commences with the definition of corporate policy and ends when the product is manufactured and/or marketed. Marketing and product information is then used to plan future strategies.

A process owner with full responsibility and authority for managing the process and achieving process objectives should always be nominated.

1.5.16.2 Supporting processes

The Core Business Process may then (depending on the size of the business) be supplemented by a number of supporting processes that describe the infrastructure required to produce a deliverable on time.

These business processes could (depending on the actual organisation) be made up of one (or all) of the following processes:

- Continual improvement process;
- Customer communications process;
- Customer needs assessment process;
- Document control process;
- Internal audit process;
- Internal communications process;
- Market research process;
- Measurement process;
- Monitoring process;
- Non-conformance management process;
- Planning process;
- Product design process;
- Product protection process;
- Production process;
- Purchasing process;
- Record keeping process;
- Regulatory research process;
- Service provision process;
- Training process.

Primary supporting processes

All businesses revolve around taking inputs and putting them through a series of activities that turn them into useful outputs, be that a product or service. These activities are the supporting processes.

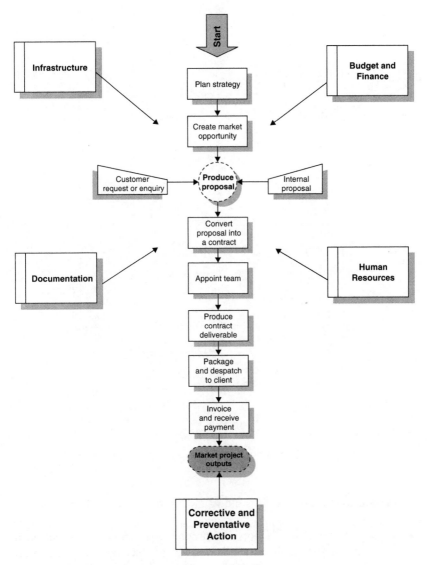

Figure 1.27 Supporting processes

Of course the only way to ensure repeat orders is to control the quality of not only the deliverable but also the organisation itself. Consequently, it is essential that you define your quality policy and objectives for each supporting process.

For each process within the flowchart there needs to be an organisational documentation detailing:

- **objective** – what the process aims to achieve;
- **scope** – what the process covers;

Figure 1.28 Flowchart showing typical primary supporting process

- **responsible owner** – who is ultimately responsible for implementing the process;
- **policy** – what the organisation intends doing to ensure quality is controlled;
- **key performance indicators** – those items of objective evidence that can be used as a way of monitoring performance of the process;
- reference to **supporting system documentation** (QPs and WIs).

Secondary supporting processes

In addition to primary supporting processes there may also be a number of **secondary supporting processes** that run in parallel with and support the primary supporting processes. These secondary supporting processes are equally important as they control all other activities that may influence the quality of the product.

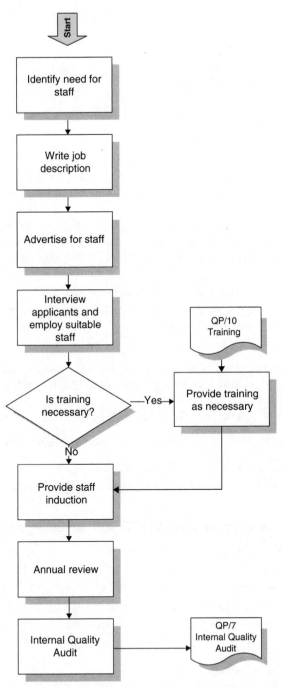

Figure 1.29 An example of a secondary supporting process flowchart for the identification, provision, management and support of staff

Secondary supporting processes may include such things as:

- identification and provision of suitable staff;
- management and support of staff;
- identification and provision of information;
- identification and provision of materials;
- identification and provision of equipment and facilities;
- management of the QMS;
- continual improvement.

The purpose of secondary supporting processes is to document those activities that are essential for supporting and achieving the primary supporting processes. An example of a secondary supporting process is shown in Figure 1.28.

These secondary-supporting processes will have an identical structure to the primary supporting processes, and will also have their own associated supporting documentation (e.g. Quality Procedures (QPs) and Work Instructions (WIs)).

1.5.16.3 Interrelationship of process documentation

All processes are documented so as to provide a complete picture of how to perform the activity to a consistent level of quality. The level of detail varies depending whether it is a:

- **Process** – an outline of its objective, scope and key performance indicators;
- **Quality Procedure** – an enlargement of the process explaining how it is controlled;
- **Work Instruction** – the 'fine print' required to perform a specific activity.

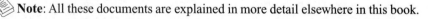 **Note**: All these documents are explained in more detail elsewhere in this book.

Note: By using a matrix such as that shown in Figure 1.30, it is possible to identify the parts of ISO 9001:2000 which are met by each process.

1.5.17 Brief summary of the ISO 9001:2000 standard

ISO 9001:2000 is made up of eight sections which are summarised below.

Section 1 – Scope

This short section explains what the standard covers and emphasises its primary objective of achieving customer satisfaction by meeting customer requirements. In this context, customer satisfaction is achieved through the:

- effective application of a QMS;
- process for continual improvement of that system;
- prevention of non-conformity.

Figure 1.30 The inter-relationship of documented processes within QPs/WIs

Section 2 – Normative reference

Another short section directs the reader to other standards that form a **mandatory** input to ISO 9001:2000. In this instance the only reference is 'ISO 9000:2000, *Quality Management Systems – Fundamentals and vocabulary*'.

Section 3 – Terms and definitions

This third section explains how the standard is based on the supply chain shown in the Figure 1.31.

Figure 1.31 The supply chain

Section 4 – Quality management system

This basically states that an organisation **shall** have a documented QMS that defines the processes necessary to ensure that the product conforms to customer requirements. This QMS must be implemented, maintained and, most importantly, continually improved by the organisation.

This section also clearly states the types of documentation required to comply with the standard, as follows:

- **Quality Manual** – establishing and maintaining an organisational 'Rule Book';
- **Control of documents** – establishing and maintaining a documented procedure for the control of QMS documents;
- **Quality records** – controlling and maintaining quality records;
- **System level procedures** – used to detail the activities needed to implement the QMS;
- **Procedures** that clearly describe the sequence of processes necessary to ensure the conformity of a product or service;
- **Instructions** that describe the physical operating practices and controls within each process.

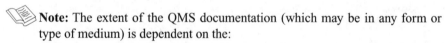 **Note:** The extent of the QMS documentation (which may be in any form or type of medium) is dependent on the:

- size and type of the organisation;
- complexity and interaction of the processes;
- competency of personnel.

Section 5 – Management responsibility

This section consists of the majority of the old ISO 9001:1994 management responsibility and quality requirements all rolled together. It is broken down into the following sub-sections that cover the requirements for:

- **Management commitment** – top (i.e. senior) management committing, fully, to the development and improvement of the QMS. (Without their commitment the system will fall at the first hurdle);
- **Customer focus** – determining, fully understanding and documenting customer requirements; ensuring compliance with identified statutory legislation (e.g. EC Directives, other national and international standards etc.);
- **Quality policy** – ensuring that it is appropriate for the purpose, understood by everyone and reviewed for continued suitability;
- **Planning** – clearly stating management's quality objectives and policy on quality in an established, fully documented, QMS;
- **Administration** – identifying and planning the activities and resources required to achieve quality objectives;

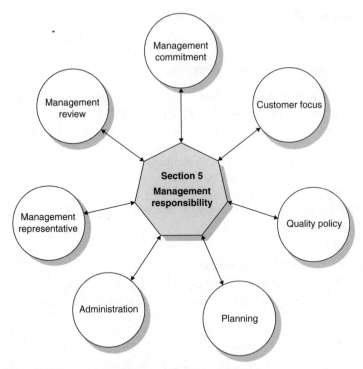

Figure 1.32 Section 5 – Management responsibility

- **Management representative** – appointing someone (or some people) to be responsible for the implementation and improvement of the organisation's QMS;
- **Management review** – carrying out regular reviews of the QMS to ensure it continues to function correctly (and to identify areas for improvement).

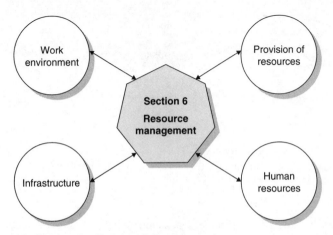

Figure 1.33 Section 6 – Resource management

Section 6 – Resource management

This section covers resources with regard to training, induction, responsibilities, working environment, equipment requirements, maintenance etc. It is broken down into the following sub-sections:

- **Provision of resources** – identifying the resources required to implement and improve the processes that make up the QMS;
- **Human resources** – assigning personnel with regard to competency, education, training, skill and/or experience;
- **Infrastructure** – identifying, providing and maintaining the workspace, facilities, equipment (hardware and software) and supporting services to achieve conformity of product;
- **Work environment** – identifying and managing the work environment (e.g. health and safety, ambient conditions etc.).

Section 7 – Product realisation

Section 7 absorbs most of the 20 elements of the old ISO 9000:1994 standard, including process control, purchasing, handling and storage and measuring

Figure 1.34 Section 7 – Product realisation

devices. This section is broken down into a number of sub-sections that cover the requirements for:

- **Planning of realisation processes** – clearly defining and documenting the processes used to ensure reliable and consistent products (e.g. verification and validation activities, criteria for acceptability and quality records etc.);
- **Customer-related processes** – identifying customer, product, legal and design requirements;
- **Design and development planning** – controlling the design process (e.g. design inputs, outputs, review, verification, validation and change control);
- **Purchasing** – having documented processes for the selection and control of suppliers and the control of purchases that affect the quality of the finished product or service;
- **Production and service provision** – having documented instructions that control the manufacture of a product or delivery of a service;

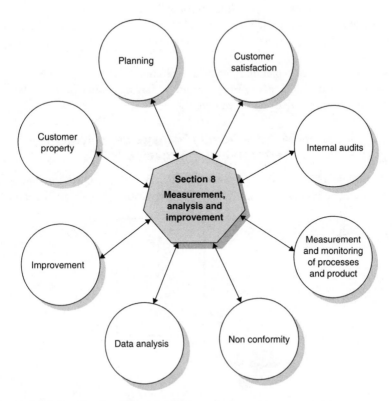

Figure 1.35 Section 8 – Measurement, analysis and improvement

- **Customer property** – identifying, verifying, protecting and maintaining customer property provided for use or incorporation with the product;
- **Control of monitoring and measuring devices** – their control, calibration and protection.

Section 8 – Measurement, analysis and improvement

This section absorbs the former inspection and measurement control sections of ISO 9001:1994 and includes requirements for:

- **Planning** – defining the requirements for measurement analysis and improvement (including statistical analysis);
- **Customer satisfaction** – monitoring customer satisfaction (and dissatisfaction) as a measurement and improvement of the QMS;
- **Internal audits** – conducting periodic internal audits to confirm continued conformity with ISO 9001:2000;
- **Monitoring and measurement of processes and product** – defining processes to monitor the performance of the QMS and the products and services delivered by the organisation;
- **Non-conformity** – controlling non-conformity and its rectification;
- **Data analysis** – collecting and analysing statistical data obtained from the organisation's measuring and monitoring activities to find areas of improvement;
- **Improvement** – planning for continual improvement of the QMS;
- **Corrective and preventive action** – having available procedures to address corrective and preventive action.

1.5.18 ISO 9004:2000 Quality Management Systems – guidelines for performance improvement

ISO 9004:2000 provides guidance on all aspects of a QMS (including the processes for continual improvement) that contribute to the satisfaction of an

ISO 9004:2000

Figure 1.36 The reason for ISO 9004:2000

organisation's customers and other interested parties. The guidance provided in this standard is generic and is applicable to all organisations, regardless of the type, size and the product provided. It is based on sound quality management principles that provide an understanding of quality requirements and their application to improve the performance of an organisation.

ISO 9004:2000, therefore, is aimed at improving an organisation's overall quality performance and provides a stepping stone to Total Quality Management (TQM). In the words of the standard, '*ISO 9004:2000 is, therefore, designed to go beyond quality management requirements and provide organisations with guidelines for performance improvement through sustained customer satisfaction*'. In doing so it:

- provides guidance to management on the application and use of a QMS to improve an organisation's overall performance;
- is recommended as a guide for organisations whose management wishes to move beyond the minimum requirements of ISO 9001:2000 in pursuit of increased performance improvement;
- defines the minimum QMS requirements needed to achieve customer satisfaction by meeting specified product requirements;
- can also be used by an organisation to demonstrate its capability to meet customer requirements.

 Note: ISO 9004:2000 is **not** a guideline for **implementing** ISO 9001 and is **not** intended for certification, regulatory or contractual use.

1.6 Certification

1.6.1 Who can certify an organisation?

There are a number of companies (i.e. Notified Bodies and/or Registrars) available to carry out ISO 9001:2000 certification (e.g. TÜV, BSI, SGS Yarsley, etc.) and it really depends on where your organisation's main market is going to be as to which one you eventually choose.

BSI is the recognised world leader in setting quality and safety standards for industry. BSI's main offices are in London which, in addition to conference rooms that host ISO committees, has a huge administration block for the update and dissemination of standards. They also have a large library containing copies of all the BS, EN, IEC, ISO and ANSI standards together with the majority of all the other industrial and management standards. BSI Inc is a separate company under US law with 11 regional offices and a corporate office in Reston, VA. They recently acquired CEEM (the Center for Energy and Environmental Management that was founded in Fairfax, VA, in 1979) and is now located in their Reston offices. As well as providing the usual certification services, BSI

Inc (through CEEM) provide training in all ISO 9000/14000 topics including BSI's well-established Quality Managers' and Lead Auditors' courses.

1.6.2 What is required for certification?

A fully documented, auditable QMS that is totally supported by senior management and one that is implemented throughout the organisation.

The QMS shall consist of:

- a **Quality Manual** – describing how an organisation meets the requirements of ISO 9001:2000 (objectives, goals, roles, organisation and responsibilities, etc.);
- **Processes** – describing the end-to-end activities involved in project management;
- **Quality Procedures** – describing the method by which the processes are managed;
- **Work Instructions** – describing how individual tasks and activities are carried out.

 Note: Organisations that previously used ISO 9002:1994 and ISO 9003:1994 are allowed to be certified to ISO 9001:2000 through 'permissible exclusions' of the standard's requirement – i.e. by omitting those requirements that do not apply to their particular organisation. Organisations revising their quality policy for the first time (i.e. in order to meet ISO 9001:2000 requirements) are advised to pay particular attention to clauses 4.2.3 (c), (d) and (g).

1.6.3 Who will be responsible for quality within an organisation?

ISO 9001:2000 requirement:

'5.5.2 Management representative
Top management shall appoint a member of management who, irrespective of other responsibilities, shall have responsibility and authority that includes:

- *ensuring that processes needed for the quality management system are established, implemented and maintained;*
- *reporting to top management on the performance of the quality management system, and any need for improvement;*
- *ensuring the promotion of awareness of customer requirements throughout the organisation;*

- *liaison with external parties on matters relating the quality management system'.*

An organisation, therefore, needs a Quality Manager who has the full support of senior management. They need to appoint someone who is fully versed in the requirements of ISO 9001:2000 and who is capable of acting as a catalyst and management coach. This post will initially have to be full-time whilst the organisation is setting up their QMS, but (dependent on the size of the company) could probably reduce to part-time following certification.

The Quality Manager's prime qualities should include:

- approachability;
- an ability to establish two-way communication with all levels of the company personnel.

The Quality Manager shall report to the Managing Director and must be independent of all responsibilities that may adversely affect quality performance.

1.7 Assistance (in the UK) for obtaining a Quality Management System

1.7.1 Government assistance

Following publication of the White Paper entitled 'Standards, Quality and International Competitiveness' and via its National Quality Campaign, the UK Government are also promoting the wider use of quality control, quality assurance and QMSs within industry.

As part of this National Quality Campaign, the UK Government – in this case the Department of Trade and Industry (DTI) – offers assistance to small and medium-sized companies in order to 'bring awareness of quality through the application of modern quality management techniques'.

1.7.1.1 DTI Business Links

Currently, over 100 Business Links (see *Yellow Pages*) are now open to help small and medium companies to cut costs, to grow, increase sales and export. They are also there to help companies operate at the leading edge of design, quality and delivery and to face the challenge of international competition. The President of the Board of Trade has stated that the object of Business Links is to pool the important support services in an area to improve the effectiveness and quality of support to customers. They are places where services are tailored to fit individual customers' needs and where trust is built through a long-term relationship with a personal business adviser.

Business Link services include personal business advisers who work with a company over time and put together a package of support; access to specialist counsellors in design, exports and innovation and technology; information and advice on grants; finance and taxation; consultancy; health checks and diagnostics services; export services; and training courses.

1.7.1.2 National Quality Information Centre

The National Quality Information Centre (NQIC) was set up in 1984, in consultation with the DTI, to provide an information source on standards, training courses and quality generally and to assist the DTI's National Quality Campaign. It is run by the Institute of Quality Assurance (IQA) with the aim of assisting industry and commerce in obtaining information about how to improve quality in their activities and the products and services they provide.

The Centre's main commercial services, in addition to enquiries, are its bibliography or abstracts service, quality journals from the American Society for Quality Control and European Organisation for Quality. The Centre plans to open a library in the near future for the benefit of those wishing to carry out serious study.

For further details contact:

The National Quality Information Centre
Tel: 020 7245 6722
Fax: 020 7245 6755
www.iqa.org/info/information.html

1.7.2 Assistance for the smaller company

Most small firms are either unable or unwilling to undertake the complicated procedures required to achieve certification and registration to ISO 9000. With this in mind, BSI launched (in 1994) a low-cost, no-fuss BSI/QA Small Business Service. A customer service helpline is also available to provide assistance.

Further details of this facility are available from:

BSI Customer Services and Information
Tel: 020 8996 7000
Fax: 020 8996 7001
www.bsi.org.uk

1.7.3 Assistance in setting up a Quality Management System in America

Assistance in setting up a QMS in America may be obtained from two standards bodies. The American Society for Quality (ASQ) are responsible for quality management systems and standards whilst the American Society Testing & Materials (ASTM) responsibilities lie in the provision of quality statistics for the implementation of Total Quality Management (TQM).

1.7.3.1 American Society for Quality

The American Society for Quality (ASQ) provides:

- guidelines for the selection and use of the appropriate internal quality management and external quality assurance standards. This includes clarification of the relationships and differences between the principal quality concepts;
- guidelines and recommendations for the implementation and development of quality management and quality systems;
- assistance on the particular vocabulary used within the quality management and quality assurance fields (i.e. supplying specific terms applicable to the preparation and use of quality management and quality assurance standards);
- details of all elements that should be considered in quality systems within a laboratory.

Further details are available from:

American Society for Quality (ASQ)
Tel: 001 414 272 8575
www.asq.org

1.7.3.2 American Society Testing & Materials

The American Society Testing & Materials (ASTM) provide individual case studies to illustrate examples of how to establish and maintain Total Quality Control (TQC). In addition, ASTM are able to provide statistics for the application of Total Quality Management (TQM) and the latest information on standardisation, particularly with emphasis on documentation planning and control. Further details are available from:

American Society Testing & Materials (ASTM)
Tel: 001 610 832 9585
www.astm.org

Part One has explained the background to the ISO 9000 standards, its requirements and recommendations. It has described how ISO 9001:2000 can be used to the best advantage and it has shown how much importance is being placed on companies (large and small) in having ISO 9001:2000 certification or possessing an effective QMS that ensures they work in conformance with that standard.

In Part Two the structure of the ISO 9000:2000 series is explained and the various clauses and elements making up ISO 9001:2000 are reviewed.

Appendix A to Chapter 1 ISO 14001 – Environmental Management System

What is the difference between ISO 9000 and ISO 14000?

Whilst both of these standards are effectively 'generic management system standards', the ISO 9000 family is primarily concerned with 'quality management' and:

- what the organisation does to fulfil the customer's quality requirements;
- how it meets the applicable regulatory requirements;
- how it enhances customer satisfaction;
- how it achieves continual improvement of its performance, product and/or serve.

On the other hand, the ISO 14000 family is an Environmental Management System (EMS) that is aimed at continually reducing pollution (through the more efficient and responsible use of raw materials and the minimisation of energy usage and waste) and is concerned with how an organisation:

- minimises harmful effects on the environment caused by its activities;
- achieves continual improvement of its environmental performance.

Although ISO 14001 does not set performance requirements (such as emission limits) it does provide a mandatory, auditable, framework for an Environmental Management System. In quite a number of areas, these requirements are similar to those of ISO 9000 and other management systems (e.g. TL 9000, QS 9000, ISO 13485 and ISO/IEC 17025 etc.) and currently work is under way to produce an integrated management system involving quality, environmental as well as safety management.

The main difference between ISO 14001 and these other standards, however, is that organisations must have procedures to identify, examine and evaluate all the environmental aspects of its activities, products and services. Whilst the standard doesn't actually specify the depth of the evaluation or the methodology (the only requirement is that *the methodology should be appropriate!*) it does, however, suggest the use of Critical Path Project Management (CPPM), Life Cycle Assessment (LCA) or other methodologies, such as mass-balance, assessment of environmental loads, etc.

EMS

An EMS is a continual cycle of planning, implementing, reviewing and improving the processes and actions that an organisation undertakes to meet its business and environmental goals. Most EMS's are built on the ISO 9001:2000 PDCA (Plan, Do, Check, Act) model which leads to continual improvement based upon:

- planning, including identifying environmental aspects and establishing goals [PLAN];
- implementing, including training and operational controls [DO];
- checking, including monitoring and corrective action [CHECK]; and
- reviewing, including progress reviews and acting to make needed changes to the EMS [ACT].

Although ISO 14001 does not specifically require an organisation to have an 'Environmental Manual' it does ask them to document their 'core system requirements' (which is almost the same as them needing to have a systems manual – and so there is little difference between this and any of the other management systems really). There is also no need to appoint a separate EMS representative and frequently this position is combined with that of the Quality Manager or the Health and Safety Manager.

Organisations do, however, have to demonstrate that they have an auditable, *fully documented, management program in place to meet their declared objectives* and they need to have *an established system for controlling any environmental impacts caused by new or modified developments, products, services or processes* and that this program should cover all aspects of emergency responsibilities and emergency planning. Other changes include:

(1) Document Control – and the specific requirement:

- for controlling documents by date;
- care and status over legal documents;
- retention of obsolete documents (providing it is absolutely clear that they are obsolete and will not be used for current operational controls).

(2) Records – an additional requirement to maintain records to demonstrate that the organisation's objectives and targets have been met.

(3) Management review – and the specific requirement to '*address the possi-ble need for changes to the policy and objectives*'.

Note: Unlike ISO 9001:2000, there is no requirement to audit the system for effectiveness.

(4) Environmental management system audit – and the establishment of an audit program to demonstrate that an organisation's EMS complies with its stated requirements and complies with the environmental policy.

ISO 14001:1996 replaced BS 7750:1994 (*Environmental Management Systems*) and is supported by a range of related standards (see Table A1 below) to pro-vide guidance on auditing, qualification criteria, environmental labelling and life-cycle assessment.

Table A1 The most important environmental standards

ISO/IEC guide 66:1999	General requirements for bodies operating assessment and certification/registration of environmental management systems (EMS)
ISO 14001:1996	Environmental management systems – Specification with guidance for use
ISO 14004:1996	Environmental management systems – General guidelines on principles, systems and supporting techniques
ISO 14015:2001	Environmental management – Environmental assessment of sites and organisations (EASO)
ISO 14031:1999	Environmental management – Environmental performance evaluation – Guidelines
ISO/TR 14032:1999	Environmental management – Examples of environmental performance evaluation (EPE)
ISO 14040:1997	Environmental management – Life cycle assessment – Principles and framework
ISO 14041:1998	Environmental management – Life cycle assessment – Goal and scope definition and inventory analysis

(*continued*)

Table A1 *(continued)*

ISO 14042:2000	Environmental management – Life cycle assessment – Life cycle impact assessment
ISO 14043:2000	Environmental management – Life cycle assessment – Life cycle interpretation
ISO/TR 14047:2003	Environmental management – Life cycle impact assessment – Examples of application of ISO 14042
ISO/TR 14049:2000	Environmental management – Life cycle assessment – Examples of application of ISO 14041 to goal and scope definition and inventory analysis
ISO 14050:2002	Environmental management – Vocabulary
ISO/TR 14061:1998	Information to assist forestry organisations in the use of Environmental Management System standards ISO 14001 and ISO 14004
ISO/TR 14062:2002	Environmental management – Integrating environmental aspects into product design and development
ISO 19011:2002	Guidelines for quality and/or environmental management systems auditing

EMAS

In support of ISO 14001 is the Eco-Management and Audit Scheme (EMAS) for registering verified industrial sites, whose aim is to improve the quality of environmental management throughout industry in Europe, by assisting companies to develop environmental policies, implement them and establish a continuous programme of improvement. Companies are encouraged to communicate their progress to the general public and participation in the scheme which (as well as bringing valuable cost benefits) helps to improve relations with customers, investors and insurers and provide better control of raw materials and energy.

The EMAS scheme has proved that the adoption of an environmentally friendly process can help reduce some of the costs associated with environmental damage such as high insurance premiums or massive clean-up operations.

To become a member of this scheme, an organisation must demonstrate their compliance with existing industry pollution control measures and have in place a programme of continuous improvement that is in excess of the legal minimum. Organisations must also:

- have an environmental policy for the whole organisation;
- complete an environmental review that covers all aspects of the industrial site they seek to register;
- have in place an environmental programme with pre-determined objectives;
- produce an environmental management system defining their operating procedures for the policy and programme;
- complete an environmental audit cycle, to provide regular updates on progress;
- produce an environmental statement of progress for circulation to the general public;
- be validated by an independent verifier.

Obtaining EMAS registration can be quite expensive (especially for small businesses) but assistance is available via the Small Company Environmental and Energy Management Scheme (SCEEMAS) which has been set up by the UK Department of the Environment to assist the production of an EMS. This scheme meets some of the costs involved for companies involved in manufacturing, waste disposal, recycling, mining, quarrying or power generation.

Euro Info Centres (EICs) have also been set up to help industrial SMEs make the first move towards EMAS registration. Their Eco Management Guide is a well thought out publication which provides arguments, technical information, a short test to confirm an organisation's readiness and suitability for EMAS registration. The EIC also have available audit checklists to enable organisations to analyse their EMS against the EMAS requirements.

Further information about the EMS and the various schemes mentioned in this Annex are available from:

Eco-Management and Audit Scheme
www.emas.org.uk

Envirowise
http://www.envirowise.gov.uk/
Envirowise is a government funded programme that offers UK businesses free, independent, confidential advice and support on practical ways to ensure compliance with environmental legislation, increase profits, minimise waste and reduce environmental impact.

US Environmental Protection Agency
ems@epa.gov

This Web site provides information and resources related to Environmental Management Systems for businesses, associations, the public as well as state and federal agencies.

BSI Business Centre
www.iso14000-iso14001-environmental-management.com

The Department of Trade and Industry
www.dti.gov.uk/sectors_environment.html

Part Two

The Structure of ISO 9001:2000

In Part One we looked at the background to the ISO 9000 standard, its requirements and recommendations.

In Part Two the structure of ISO 9001:2000 is explained and details provided of the various clauses and elements contained in the ISO 9001:2000 sections are reviewed.

2

The structure of ISO 9001:2000

Although the formal procedures contained in ISO 9001 are mainly used by larger companies, there is absolutely no reason why smaller companies cannot adapt these procedures to suit their own purposes.

For example, ISO 9001:2000 Section 7.3 states that '*an organization shall plan and control the design and development of a product*'. Perhaps your company does not have a design office and this activity is achieved by an individual. Although all of the requirements of Section 7.3 are probably inappropriate, the procedures are still the same – so why not use them!

A detailed description of the main sections making up ISO 9001:2000 now follows.

2.1 Section 1 – Scope

2.1.1 Section 1.1 General

Section 1.1 General requirements	The organisation shall demonstrate its ability to: • consistently provide a product that meets customer and regulatory requirements; • enhance customer satisfaction through the application of their QMS.

This short section contains an explanation of the contents of the standard and states the basic requirements for achieving customer satisfaction through the effective application of a Quality Management System (QMS).

 Note: In this international standard the word 'product' applies only to the product intended for (or required by) a customer, product or service.

2.1.2 Section 1.2 Application

Section 1.2 Permissible exclusions	If there are clauses that an organisation does not need to meet in order to fulfil the requirements of this standard, these clauses may be excluded. They may be due to: • the nature of the product; • customer requirements; • applicable regulatory requirements.

Section 1.2 emphasises that all the requirements of this International Standard are generic and are applicable to all organisations regardless of type, size and product provided.

If any of the requirements contained in Section 7 cannot be applied owing to the nature of the organisation, then provided that the exclusion(s) do not affect the organisation's ability, or responsibility to provide a product that fulfils customer and/or applicable regulatory requirements, then it can be considered an exclusion.

For example, if the organisation manufactures a product that does not have any design and development input, then Clause 7.3.2 is not really relevant.

A reduction in the scope of the ISO 9001:2000 requirements is also permitted for those organisations that were previously registered to ISO 9002:1994 and ISO 9003:1994 and this is achieved by omitting requirements that do not apply to their particular organisation.

In all cases, they may be excluded **provided** that the reason(s) why they are not entirely applicable to that particular organisation are fully documented in the organisation's Quality Manual.

Note: The **only** clauses that may be excluded from ISO 9001:2000 are those from Section 7.

2.2 Section 2 – Normative reference

Section 2 Normative reference	This section lists standards that form a **mandatory** input to ISO 9001:2000.

This short section requires an organisation to take into consideration ISO 9000:2000: *Quality Management Systems – Fundamentals and vocabulary*, when applying ISO 9001:2000.

2.3 Section 3 – Terms and definitions

Section 3 Terms and definitions	In addition to those terms defined within ISO 9000:2000, an organisation shall make a note of the specific terms used to describe the supply chain.

This section covers the specific use of terminology to describe the supply chain.

The word 'product' is defined so as to cover all manufacturing and service outputs and so, whenever the term 'product' occurs, it can also mean 'service'.

In this particular ISO standard, the definition of a product is '*the result of a process*'. A product may be defined as:

- hardware;
- software;

Figure 2.1 The supply chain

- services;
- processed materials.

The definition of a supply chain is shown in Figure 2.1.

Note: Most products are, of course, combinations of one of these four generic product categories and whether the combined product is then called hardware, processed material, software or service depends on the dominant element. For example, if the product were an 'automobile', it would consist of hardware (e.g. tyres), processed materials (e.g. fuel, cooling liquid), software (e.g. engine control software, driver's manual), and service (e.g. operating explanations given by the salesman).

2.4 Section 4 – Quality Management System

Section 4 of ISO 9001:2000 covers the requirements for all organisations to establish, document, implement, maintain and continually improve a QMS in accordance with the requirements of this standard.

It is broken down into the following sub clauses:

- **Quality Manual** – establishing and maintaining an organisational 'Rule Book';
- **Control of documents** – establishing and maintaining a documented procedure for the control of QMS documents;
- **Quality records** – controlling and maintaining quality records.

Note: The extent of the QMS documentation (which may be in any form or type of medium) is dependent on the:

- size and type of the organisation;
- complexity and interaction of the processes;
- competency of personnel.

Figure 2.2 Quality Management System

Note: The term 'Organisation' replaces the term 'Supplier' (previously used in ISO 9001:1994) and refers to the unit to which this International Standard applies. In addition, the term 'Supplier' – now replaces the term 'Subcontractor'.

2.4.1 Section 4.1 General requirements

Section 4.1 General requirements	The organisation shall establish, document, implement, maintain and continually improve a QMS, that ensures and covers: • identification of processes; • their operation and control; • the availability of resources and information; • measurement, monitoring, analyse and support; • achievement of planned results; • continual improvement; • management (in accordance with the requirements of ISO 9001:2000).
Proof	A definition of the processes necessary to ensure that a product conforms to customer requirements which is capable of being implemented, maintained and improved.

The management of any organisation will rely on a number of different management disciplines, the most important of which, is quality management. As this is the core of all organisational structures, the activities and processes that affect performance improvement will need to be described and defined by management. They will also need to ensure that they are clearly understood by the whole workforce, monitored (i.e. to evaluate improvement on a continuing basis) and managed. Self-assessment can be a very useful tool to evaluate improvement and ISO 9004:2000 helps organisations by providing an annex containing 'Guidelines for self-assessment'.

Note: For the assistance of small businesses, I have also included a section (see Part Seven) on 'self-assessment' which includes check sheets against the requirements of ISO 9001:2000 and examples of Stage Audit checklists.

An organisation's self-assessment should be completed on a regular basis. Indeed, the use of self-assessment methodology can provide an overall view of the performance of the organisation and the degree of maturity of its QMS. It can also help to identify areas that need improving and determine priorities.

2.4.2 Section 4.2 Documentation requirements

2.4.2.1 Section 4.2.1 General

Section 4.2 General documentation requirements	The QMS documentation shall include: • a Quality Manual; • specific statements regarding quality policy and quality objectives; • documented procedures that clearly describe the sequence of processes necessary to ensure the conformity of the product; • documented instructions to ensure the effective operation and control of the processes; • quality records.

As ISO 9001:2000 is a generic requirements standard it doesn't state exactly what an organisation's quality documentation should look like. It merely provides details of the mandatory requirements and then leaves it up to the organisation to determine the appropriate documentation to suit their own size and type of business. This is a good point to be remembered by small businesses who, whilst wanting to 'work in conformance with the requirements of ISO 9001:2000' do not necessarily see the **need** for their system to be certified against that standard.

Thus the QMS documentation and records can be in any form or in any media provided that they meet:

- the needs of that particular organisation;
- customer and contractual requirements;
- the relevant international, national, regional and industry sector standards;
- the relevant statutory and regulatory requirements.

2.4.2.2 Section 4.2.2 Quality Manual

Section 4.2.2 Quality Manual	The organisation shall: • establish and maintain a Quality Manual; • include details of any ISO 9001:2000 exclusions; • include details of associated documented procedures; • indicate the sequence and interaction of processes.
Proof	A document which describes an organisation's quality policies, procedures and practices that makes up their Quality Management System.
Likely documentation	A controlled document (i.e. Quality Manual) containing everything related to quality control and quality assurance within an organisation.

One of the requirements of ISO 9001:2000 (see Section 4.2.1) is to define the documentation required to support an organisation's QMS. The primary purpose of this quality documentation is to express the quality policy and describe the QMS. This documentation serves as the basis for implementing and maintaining the system and should be capable of controlling the effective operation of the QMS.

Details of the quality documentation are usually found in an organisation's Quality Manual, which will provide information about all of the quality policies, processes, and their associated Quality Procedures (QPs) and Work Instructions (WIs). Depending on the size of the organisation, the Quality Manual will also, probably, include standard formats for data collection, data reporting and quality records. It will also have to show (and justify) if certain requirements from ISO 9001:2000 have been omitted.

There are no set rules about what should or should not be included in a Quality Manual. It all rather depends on the structure and business of the organisation concerned. As a Quality Consultant, I always recommend that organisations address **each** requirement contained in ISO 9001:2000 separately, and in turn, to ensure that none of the essential (i.e. mandatory requirements) are left out. As previously described, organisations are allowed to leave out the non-relevant sections of ISO 9001:2000 **provided**, that is, that the relevant detail and reasons are included in the organisation's Quality Manual. At Part Six I have provided a complete example of a Quality Manual together with a number of example QPs and WIs which can be used as a template for your own Quality Manual.

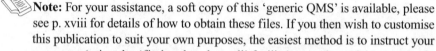

Note: For your assistance, a soft copy of this 'generic QMS' is available, please see p. xviii for details of how to obtain these files. If you then wish to customise this publication to suit your own purposes, the easiest method is to instruct your computer (using the 'find and replace all' facility) to replace 'Stingray QMC' with your own company's name. Each section of the Quality Manual and **all** of the QPs and WIs should then be read and carefully modified so that it reflects your own company's business.

If you require further assistance please feel free to contact me at 'ray@herne.org.uk'.

2.4.2.3 Section 4.2.3 Control of documents

Section 4.2.3 Control of documents	The organisation shall instigate a documented procedure for the quality control of documents. This procedure shall include processes for: • controlled distribution of documents; • approval of documents prior to issue; • review, updating and re-approval of documents; • identifying the current revision status of documents; • ensuring that only relevant versions of applicable documents are available at points of use; • ensuring that documents remain legible, readily identifiable and retrievable; • identifying, distributing and controlling documents from an external source; • controlling obsolete documents.
Proof Likely documentation	A documented procedure. • Document control procedures; • Work Instructions.

ISO 9001:2000 requires an organisation to establish and maintain procedures for the control of all their documents and data (i.e. hard copy as well as electronic media) especially those relating to quality assurance and quality control. Indeed, where the term '*documented procedure*' appears within ISO 9001:2000, this requires the procedure to be *established, documented, implemented and maintained*.

All documentation used by the organisation in support of its QMS and/or the execution of a contract (e.g. specifications, customer orders, plans, drawings, manuals, operating procedures, national and international standards and codes of practice etc.) must be controlled to ensure that:

• they are issued to the appropriate personnel;
• they are revised and reissued as necessary;
• all obsolete versions are removed from the point of use.

Value of documentation

Documentation enables communication of intent and consistency of action. It is therefore a necessary element within a QMS and its use contributes to:

• achievement of product quality and quality improvement;
• provision of appropriate training;

- ensured repeatability and traceability;
- provision of objective evidence;
- evaluation of the effectiveness of the system.

The production of documentation should not be an end in itself but should be a value-adding activity.

Quality Manual

Normally the Quality Manual and it associated processes, procedures, plans and instructions are maintained by the Quality Manager who ensures that the appropriate items, at the correct revision levels, are issued (or at least made available) to all who need them within the organisation.

Support documentation

National and international standards, codes of practice and so on should (in large organisations) normally be maintained by the General Manager and/or the Engineers who would then be responsible for ensuring that the appropriate documents are available within the organisation and that they are issued at the correct revision levels. External suppliers of documentation should be contacted on a regular basis to ascertain that the documents held remain current.

Document distribution

The distribution of standard documents should be controlled and recorded on distribution lists, which also show the current issue status. A master list of all documents should be maintained which clearly shows the current status of each document. This list needs to be available at all locations where operations effective to the functioning of the QMS are performed and this distribution list needs to be reviewed and updated as changes occur and all invalid and/or obsolete documents/data must be immediately removed.

Document changes

All changes (e.g. modified wording, new procedures to be adopted etc.) that need to be made to a previously issued document or data should, ideally, be approved by the same person who performed the original review and approval. Where appropriate, the nature of the change should be indicated on the document and master copies of the revised documents retained as records of the changes.

Contract documents

Each contract should have a separate file which contains all the relevant information applicable to that contract.

2.4.2.4 Section 4.2.4 Control of records

Section 4.2.4 **Control of records**	The organisation shall establish a documented procedure for the: • control; • maintenance; • identification; • storage; • retrieval; • protection; • retention time; • disposition; of all quality records.
Proof	A documented procedure.
Likely documentation	• Record keeping procedures.

The question is often asked, why bother to keep records?

Nothing is worse than ordering a product or service, finding a firm to meet the delivery time, but then not being able to use it because the relevant documentation (for example a specific working instruction), has still to arrive. It is, therefore, vitally important for the supplier to ensure that the documentation for the assembly, installation, commissioning and operation of a deliverable are provided to the purchaser well before delivery and that these are both comprehensive and clear.

The progress of a product throughout its life cycle, its many maintenance cycles, during storage and operational use etc. will doubtless produce a considerable amount of records. Product improvement relies heavily on the availability of records such as the results of previous audit reports, customer feedback and failure reports gathered in the design office and from the shop floor. From a contract point of view, the maintenance of a complete historical record of all the alterations made to a contract, concessions allowed, variations permitted by the purchaser and specifications changed need to be recorded. Indeed it is usually a contract requirement for organisations to have available, at all times, sufficient records to be able to demonstrate that their products continue to comply with the relevant contract requirements and specifications. Quality records that can be analysed to provide inputs for corrective and preventive action, process improvements etc. are also very important to the quality of the product.

The above are only a few of the examples which show why records should be maintained and ISO 9001:2000 makes it a mandatory requirement that all records that are required for the QMS **shall** be controlled.

2.5 Section 5 – Management responsibility

This section contains the majority of the old ISO 9001:1994 management responsibility and quality requirements all rolled together. It is broken down into the following sub-clauses that cover the requirements for:

- **Management commitment** – top (i.e. senior) management committing, fully, to the development and improvement of the QMS. (Without their commitment the system will fall at the first hurdle);
- **Customer focus** – determining, fully understanding and documenting customer requirements; ensuring compliance with identified statutory legislation (e.g. EC Directives, other national and international standards etc.);
- **Quality policy** – ensuring that it is appropriate for the purpose, understood by everyone and reviewed for continued suitability;
- **Planning** – clearly stating management's quality objectives and policy on quality in an established, fully documented, QMS;
- **Responsibility, authority and communication** – identifying and planning the activities and resources required to achieve quality objectives. Appointing

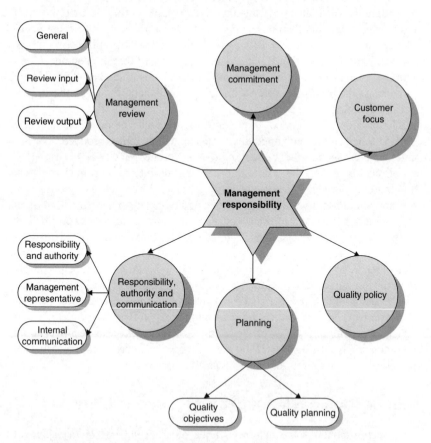

Figure 2.3 Management responsibility

someone (or some people) to be responsible for the implementation and improvement of the organisation's QMS;

- **Management review** – carrying out regular reviews of the QMS to ensure it continues to function correctly (and to identify areas for improvement).

2.5.1 Section 5.1 Management commitment

Section 5.1 Management commitment	Management shall demonstrate their commitment to developing and improving their QMS by: • conducting regular management reviews; • establishing organisational objectives and quality policies; • ensuring the availability of necessary resources; • ensuring everyone is aware of the importance of meeting customer, regulatory and legal requirements.
Proof	A description of management responsibility and quality requirements. A written demonstration of an organisation's commitment to sustainable quality management.
Likely documentation	A Quality Manual containing: 1. A high-level policy statement concerning organisational objectives and quality policies. 2. A list of Government regulatory, legal and customer-specific requirements. 3. Procedures describing: • resource management; • contract review procedures; • management reviews; • financial business plan(s).

Top management should always try to create an environment where people are fully involved and in which their QMS can operate effectively. They should use the principles of quality management as a basis for:

- establishing the organisation's quality policies and quality objectives;
- ensuring that customer requirements are recognised;
- ensuring that processes are available (and implemented) that enable customer requirements to be fulfilled and quality objectives to be achieved;
- ensuring that an effective QMS is established, implemented and maintained to achieve these objectives;
- ensuring the availability of necessary resources;
- comparing the achieved results against the quality objectives that were set by top management;

- evaluating the ongoing effectiveness of their organisation's quality policies and quality objectives;
- deciding on actions for improvement;
- defining responsibilities and authorities – e.g. the person or persons responsible for managing, performing and verifying that the end product meets the organisation's quality requirements;
- nominating a management representative (or representatives – depends on the size of the organisation) for quality matters.

2.5.2 Section 5.2 Customer focus

Section 5.2 Customer focus	Customer needs and expectations shall be: • determined; • converted into requirements; • fulfilled.
Proof	Auditable proof that all of the customer's requirements are (and have been) fully met.
Likely documentation	Procedures describing: • resource management; • contract review procedures; • management reviews; • financial business plan(s).

To satisfy customer requirements, organisations must fully understand the customer's current (and future) needs and expectations. In an ideal world, of course, management should always attempt to exceed their customers' needs and expectations and in so doing, stand to gain follow-on orders. To define customer and end-user needs and expectations, an organisation should:

- identify its customers (including potential customers);
- determine the customer's key product characteristics;
- identify and assess market competition;
- identify opportunities and weaknesses;
- define financial and future competitive advantages;
- ensure that the organisation has sufficient knowledge of the statutory and regulatory requirements (and is capable of implementing them);
- identify the benefits to be achieved from exceeding compliance;
- identify the role of the organisation in the protection of community interests.

In addition to their customers' needs and expectations, organisations may also have a number of other 'interested parties' whose needs and expectations will also have to be addressed. For quality management purposes, these interested parties may include:

- people within the organisation;
- owners, partners, investors and shareholders;
- suppliers;
- the general public.

The needs and expectations of these interested parties will be similar to the customers **except** that they will be more directed to recognition, work satisfaction, competencies and development of knowledge. Involving motivated people in the finalisation of a product can be a key to success!

2.5.3 Section 5.3 Quality policy

Section 5.3 Quality Policy	The organisation's quality policy shall be: • controlled; • appropriate; • committed to meeting requirements; • communicated and understood throughout the organisation; • capable of continual improvement; • a framework for establishing and reviewing quality objectives; • regularly reviewed.
Proof	A description of how an organisation approaches quality and how they ensure that this approach is appropriate for both customer and their own organisation.
Likely documentation	• A high-level managerial statement on an organisation's quality policy containing clear responsibilities, training and resources required for each organisational activity.

Quality policies and quality objectives need to be established in order to provide a general focus for the organisation. Policies and objectives determine the intended results and assist the organisation in applying its resources to achieve these results.

First step

The first step that an organisation must take is to define and document its quality management policy. That is, produce a mission statement that covers the organisation's objectives for quality and its commitment to quality. This quality policy must be relevant to the company's organisational goals and take into account the expectations and needs of the customer. The organisation then needs to ensure that its quality management policy is understood and implemented by all staff members and use it to provide confidence that the application of management (as described in the Quality Manual) is efficient, comprehensive and effective in ensuring that the organisation delivers the right product:

- on time;
- to the agreed specifications;
- within budget.

The purpose and benefits of establishing a quality policy and quality objectives

The organisation's quality policy should always be to achieve 'sustained, profitable growth by providing products which consistently satisfy the needs and expectations of its customers'. This level of quality can be achieved by adopting a system of procedures that reflect the competence of the organisation to existing customers potential customers and independent auditing authorities and which is aimed at:

- maintaining an effective QMS that complies with ISO 9001:2000;
- achieving and maintaining a level of quality which enhances the organisation's reputation with customers;
- ensuring compliance with all the relevant statutory and safety requirements;
- endeavouring, at all times, to maximise customer satisfaction with the products provided by the organisation.

Quality policy structure

Summarised, the quality management policy shall include the requirement that:

- clear responsibilities for each activity and development task are identified;
- each organisational activity is defined and controlled by a Quality Process, Quality Procedure (QP) or Quality Plan;
- staff are trained to the requirements listed in the company's Quality Manual;
- compliance with company procedures detailed in the Quality Manual and associated Quality Plans are audited;
- remedial action is taken whenever appropriate;
- the QPs contained in the Quality Manual and associated Quality Plans themselves are regularly reviewed.

Quality Management System review

One of the responsibilities of top management is to carry out regular systematic evaluations of their organisation's QMS to confirm its continued suitability, adequacy, effectiveness and efficiency with regard to their organisation's quality policy and objectives. This review should include the need to adapt and respond to changing needs, customer expectations, the market it serves and include details of any remedial actions that are required.

2.5.4 Section 5.4 Planning

Section 5.4 Planning	Quality planning shall be documented and shall include: • quality objectives; • resources.
Proof	Planned resources and infrastructure etc. to meet an organisation's overall business objectives.
Likely documentation	• Quality Manual.

Having defined its overall business objectives, the organisation is then in a position to define its quality objectives and to plan the resources etc. that they will need to meet these objectives.

2.5.4.1 Section 5.4.1 Quality objectives

Section 5.4.1 Quality objectives	Quality objectives shall: • be established; • be measurable; • be consistent with quality policy; • include a commitment for continual improvement; • cover product requirements.
Proof	Quality objectives that Top Management expect to achieve within each function and level of the organisation.
Likely documentation	• Policy statements defining the objectives of the company and those responsible for achieving these objectives.

 Note: Normally these will be found in the Quality Manual.

The overall quality objectives of the organisation need to be firmly established during the planning stage and then circulated to all personnel involved so that they can easily translate them into individual (and achievable) contributions. These objectives should be periodically reviewed and should:

- be relevant to the various levels and functions within the organisation;
- be consistent with the organisation's quality policy;
- be capable of being measured.

They should consider:

- current and future requirements;
- the markets served;
- the output from management previous reviews;
- current product and process performance;
- the required (and anticipated) levels of satisfaction of all interested parties.

2.5.4.2 Section 5.4.2 Quality management system planning

Section 5.4.2 Quality management system planning	Quality planning shall be documented and shall: • meet the requirements contained in section 4.1; • QMS processes; • identification of resources; • requirements for continual improvement; • requirements for change control.
Proof	The identification and planning of activities and resources required to meet an organisation's quality objectives.
Likely documentation	• Processes and procedures used by senior management to define and plan the way that their organisation is run.

Having defined its quality objectives, the next step will be to plan how to meet these objectives (i.e. the processes, resources, responsibilities, methodologies, procedures etc. that will be needed). As ISO is quick to point out 'Quality planning is an integral part of the QMS' and so organisations should take into careful consideration the:

- needs and expectations of the customers;
- required product performance;
- previous experiences and lessons learned;
- improvement opportunities;
- risk assessment;
- performance indicators;
- results of reviews and the need for change control;
- the need for documentation and records.

Customer satisfaction and quality can only be achieved by operating in accordance with the documented QMS. Specific customer requirements need to be identified and documented during the contract review process and these requirements need to be communicated and achieved in order to ensure customer satisfaction.

2.5.5 Section 5.5 Responsibility, authority and communication

Section 5.5 Responsibility, authority and communication	Administration of the QMS shall be documented and shall cover: • responsibilities and authorities; • management representative's duties; • internal communication.
Proof	How the organisation documents and administers its QMS.
Likely documentation	• A Quality Manual containing everything related to quality controls within the organisation.

Management need to define and implement their QMS so that it provides confidence that the organisation can satisfy the needs and expectations of interested parties and in such a way that is consistent with the organisation's size, culture and products.

The following sub-sections describe how an organisation's QMS should be administered.

2.5.5.1 Section 5.5.1 Responsibility and authority

Section 5.5.1 Responsibility and authority	The organisation shall define and communicate throughout the organisation: • functions and their interrelationships; • responsibilities and authorities.
Proof	The definition of the roles, responsibilities, lines of authority, reporting and communication relevant to quality.
Likely documentation	• Job descriptions and responsibilities; • organisation charts showing lines of communication.

The QMS is effectively the organisation's rule book. As such it has to be accepted and implemented by everyone. There needs to be a feeling of involvement **and** commitment in achieving the organisation's quality objectives, from top management right down to the newest employee. Personnel need, however, to know exactly what they are responsible for and so management must clearly define functions, levels of responsibility and authority for all personnel, in order to implement and maintain their QMS effectively and efficiently.

It is essential that top management ensures that the responsibilities, authorities (and their relationship) for documenting, planning and implementing the QMS are defined and communicated throughout the organisation.

Top management should continually review the organisation's resources to ensure that adequate staff, equipment and materials are available to meet customer requirements. All staff should be allocated authority to perform their allocated responsibilities and they should have a share in the responsibility for identifying non-compliance or possible improvements and recording these instances so that that corrective action can be taken, both to rectify the immediate situation and to prevent recurrence.

2.5.5.2 Section 5.5.2 Management representative

Section 5.5.2 Management representative	The organisation shall appoint a member who, irrespective of all other duties, is responsible for: • establishing, administering and maintaining the QMS processes; • advising top management on the performance of and improvements to the organisation's QMS; • promoting awareness of customer requirements; • liaising with external parties on all matters relating to the organisation's QMS.
Proof	The identification and appointment of a 'Quality Manager' with overall responsibility for the organisation's QMS.
Likely documentation	• Job description and responsibilities; • organisation charts showing lines of communication.

Whilst top management can all agree that they going to have a QMS, they need to nominate someone from within management (and at managerial level) with responsibility and authority to see its successful implementation. This person (usually referred to as the Quality Manager) is responsible for:

- ensuring that the organisation's QMS is (at all times) relevant, effective and appropriate – usually achieved by completing internal quality audits (see 8.2.2).
- ensuring that the organisation meets the customer's quality requirements;
- ensuring that all personnel are aware and capable of meeting and (when required) administering the organisation's quality processes;
- producing and maintaining the quality documentation (i.e. procedures and instructions) required for those processes;
- managing, performing and verifying that the end product meets the company's quality requirements;
- supplying regular reports to top management on the performance of the QMS and making recommendations for its improvement;
- liaising with external parties on all matters relating to the QMS.

2.5.5.3 Section 5.5.3 Internal communication

Section 5.5.3 Internal communication	The details of the organisation's QMS processes shall be given to all those responsible for their effectiveness.
Proof	Confirmation that the requirements of an organisation's QMS are communicated throughout the company.
Likely documentation	• Notice boards; • in-house journals/magazines; • audio-visual; • e-information. Also: • team briefings; • organisational meetings.

To ensure the continued effectiveness of the organisation's QMS, it is important that everyone involved in the implementation of the system is aware of the Quality Processes that have been agreed by management. It is the responsibility of the Quality Manager (as management's representative) to inform everyone about the requirements, objectives and accomplishments of and from the Quality Processes. There are no set rules about how this sort of information should be distributed; it really depends on how the organisation is set up. Choices can include (but not necessarily be restricted to) team briefings, organisational meetings, notice boards, in-house journals/magazines, audio-visual and other forms of e-information systems.

2.5.6 Section 5.6 Management review

Section 5.6 Management review	The QMS shall be regularly reviewed to ensure its continued suitability, effectiveness and adequacy. Opportunities for improvement shall be assessed and records of all reviews shall be maintained.
Proof	How Top Management reviews the QMS.
Likely documentation	Procedures concerning: • process and product performance; • audits of process, product and service; • customer feedback; • corrective and preventive action; • supplier performance; • record keeping.

Although, when first written, an organisation's QMS is assumed to cover all eventualities, doubtless there are parts of the system that will need further definition.

ISO 9001:2000 has recognised this possibility and has made it a mandatory requirement for top management to complete a review of their organisation's QMS (for continued suitability and effectiveness) on a bi-annual basis. Records of these reviews should be retained and details of all actions agreed, allocated and minuted.

The objective of these management reviews is to establish that the QMS:

- is achieving the expected results;
- meets the organisation's requirements;
- conforms to the requirements of ISO 9001:2000;
- continues to satisfy the customers needs and expectations;
- is functioning in accordance with the established operating procedures;
- is capable of identifying irregularities, defects and/or weaknesses in the system (and to evaluate possible improvements).

During the review, management will also review:

- the effectiveness of previous corrective actions;
- the adequacy and suitability of the QMS for current and future operations of the organisation;
- any complaints received, identify the cause and recommend corrective action if required;
- previous internal and external audits and identify any areas of recurring problems or potential improvements;
- reports of non-conforming items and trend information to identify possible improvements.

Evaluation and auditing

When evaluating a QMS, there are four basic questions that should be asked in relation to every process being evaluated.

- is the process identified and appropriately described?
- are responsibilities assigned?
- are the procedures implemented and maintained?
- is the process effective in providing the required results?

There are three basic types of audit to choose from:

- **First-party audits** – conducted by, or on behalf of, the organisation itself for internal purposes and which can form the basis for an organisation's self-declaration of conformity.
- **Second-party audits** – conducted by customers of the organisation or by other persons on behalf of the customer.
- **Third-party audits** – conducted by external independent audit service organisations. Such organisations, usually accredited, provide certification or registration of conformity with requirements such as those of ISO

9001:2000. (See ISO 9001:2000 Section 8.2.2 Internal audit for further information).

2.5.6.1 Section 5.6.1 General

Section 5.6.1 General	The QMS shall be subject to regular reviews to evaluate the: • need for changes; • effectiveness of the organisation's quality policies; • effectiveness of the organisation's quality objectives.
Proof	How Top Management reviews the QMS to ensure its continued suitability, adequacy and effectiveness, in the context of an organisation's strategic planning cycle.
Likely documentation	• Management review; • QMS audit procedures.

Management need to establish a process for periodically reviewing the organisation's QMS to ensure that it continues to meet the requirements of ISO 9001:2000, agrees with the organisation's policies and objectives and continues to provide customer satisfaction. Current performance, client feedback and opportunities for improvement all need to be evaluated and possible alterations have to be made to the relevant quality documentation analysed.

It is essential that records are retained of all these management reviews and that any change that might have an effect on existing work practices is subjected to a change control procedure.

2.5.6.2 Section 5.6.2 Review input

Section 5.6.2 Review input	The input to management reviews shall include results from: • earlier management reviews (e.g. follow-up actions); • previous internal, third-party and external audits; • customer feedback; • process performance; • product conformance; • preventive and corrective actions; • changes that could affect the QMS and recommendations for improvement.
Proof	How a Top Management review of the QMS is completed.
Likely documentation	• Results of audits, customer feedback, analysis of product conformance with process and procedural rules, corrective and preventive action reports and supplier performance records.

For completeness, inputs to management reviews should include everything concerned with the performance, conformance and improvement of the product. The review body should evaluate new technologies, statutory conditions, regulatory changes and environmental conditions for their affect on their product. Inputs would include, but are not restricted to:

- results from previous internal, customer and third-party audits;
- analysis of customer feedback;
- analysis of process performance;
- analysis of product conformance;
- the current status of corrective and preventive actions;
- the results of self-assessment of the organisation;
- supplier performance.

2.5.6.3 Section 5.6.3 Review output

Section 5.6.3 Review output	Management reviews shall be aimed at: • improving the organisation's overall QMS and its processes; • improving the product; • enhancing customer satisfaction; • confirming the resources required.
Proof **Likely documentation**	How the results of management reviews of the QMS are documented. • Minutes of the meetings where the overall running of the company is discussed.

The aim of completing management reviews is to provide a continuing record of the organisation's capability to produce quality products that meet the quality objectives, policies and requirements (contained in their QMS) and which continue to provide customer satisfaction.

Review output should be centred on:

- improved product and process performance;
- conformation of resource requirements and organisational structure;
- meeting market needs;
- risk management;
- change control;
- continued compliance with relevant statutory and regulatory requirements.

The actual management review process should also be evaluated to confirm its continued effectiveness and a complete record of all reviews must be retained for future use.

2.6 Section 6 – Resource management

This section covers resources with regard to training, induction, responsibilities, working environment, equipment requirements, maintenance etc.

It is broken down into the following sub-sections that cover the requirements for:

- **Provision of resources** – identifying the resources required to implement and improve the processes that make up the QMS;
- **Human resources** – assigning personnel with regard to competency, education, training, skill and experience;
- **Infrastructure** – identifying, providing and maintaining the workspace, facilities, equipment (hardware and software) and supporting services to achieve conformity of product;
- **Work environment** – identifying and managing the work environment (e.g. health and safety, ambient conditions etc.).

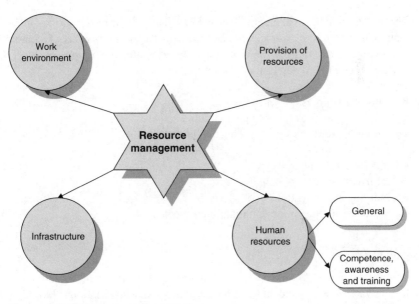

Figure 2.4 Resource management

2.6.1 Section 6.1 Provision of resources

Section 6.1 Provision of resources	The organisation shall provide resources to: • implement, maintain and continually improve their QMS and its processes; • enhance customer satisfaction; • meet customer requirements.
Proof	How resource needs (i.e. human, materials, equipment, and infrastructure) are identified with regard to training, induction, responsibilities, working environment, equipment needs, maintenance, etc...
Likely documentation	• Quality Plans; • Quality Procedures; • Work Instruction.

The organisation needs to identify and make available all the resources (e.g. information, infrastructure, people, work environment, finance, support etc.) required to implement and improve their QMS and its associated quality processes.

Resources can include (but not be limited to):

• natural resources;
• tangible resources (e.g. support facilities);
• intangible resources (e.g. intellectual property);
• future resources;
• organisational resources;
• information management systems;
• training and education;
• resources to encourage continual improvement.

Suppliers

A complete historical record should be maintained by an organisation to register any variations to the contract, any concessions made, variations allowed by the purchaser and specifications altered. The design office often carries out this activity.

In a similar manner, suppliers must provide the purchasers with an assurance that they are capable of continuing to supply logistic support for the lifetime of the product. This logistic support may include the provision of spares, updating of documentation, details of product improvement etc., depending upon the purchaser's requirements.

2.6.2 Section 6.2 Human resources

Section 6.2 Human resources	The organisation shall establish procedures for: • the assignment of personnel; • training, awareness and competency.
Proof **Likely documentation**	How human resources to implement and improve the QMS are identified. • Quality Plans; • Quality Procedures; • Work Instructions.

The organisation needs to identify and make available human resources to implement and improve their QMS and comply with contract conditions. Consideration must be given to their competency for the job that they are selected to complete and the possible requirements for additional training.

2.6.2.1 Section 6.2.1 General

Section 6.2.1 General	Assigned personnel shall be: • competent; • educated and trained; • skilled and experienced.
Proof **Likely documentation**	How an organisation assigns personnel. • Job descriptions and responsibilities; • training records; • staff evaluations; • Quality Plans, QPs and WIs identifying human resources required to complete a task.

Human resources are the principal method of achieving product completion and customer satisfaction. The old adage 'a happy worker is a good worker' still stands true in this age of information technology and with the increased training and education opportunities currently available, highly motivated, well qualified personnel are at a premium. To employ and retain the right sort of person for the job, management must, when determining the resources required, adequately define their responsibilities and authorities, establish their individual and team objectives and encourage recognition and reward. They must also:

• consider career planning and On-The-Job training (OJT);
• encourage innovation and effective teamwork;
• make use of information technology;
• measure people satisfaction.

2.6.2.2 Section 6.2.2 Competence, awareness and training

Section 6.2.2 Competence, awareness and training	The organisation shall: • identify the requirements for training personnel; • provide appropriate training; • evaluate the effectiveness of the training provided; • maintain records of all training.
Proof **Likely documentation**	Documents showing how an organisation assigns personnel to specific tasks. System level procedures for: • training; • staff evaluations; • review of work assignments and staff assessments; • records.

The organisation is responsible for ensuring that all personnel are trained and experienced to the extent necessary to undertake their assigned activities and responsibilities effectively. Thus, whenever training needs have been identified, top management should endeavour to make the relevant training available and full records must be maintained of all training undertaken by employees.

Most organisations will recruit employees who are already well qualified and quite capable of meeting the relevant technical, skill, experience and educational requirements of the organisation. There will still, however, be a need for some additional system or contract-specific training and all staff have a responsibility for identifying and recommending the training needs of others and for ensuring that all employees allocated specific tasks are suitably qualified and experienced to execute those tasks.

It is very important that an organisation's staff receive sufficient training to enable them to carry out their functions. Organisations should, therefore, determine the competence levels required, assess the competence of its people and develop plans to close any gaps. Then, based on an analysis of the present and expected needs of the organisation (compared with the existing competence of its people and the requirements of related legislation, regulation, standards, and directives) determine the type and amount of training required.

Training plan

Training should cover the organisation's policies and objectives and, as well as having introductory programmes for new people, there should also be available periodic refresher programmes for people already trained. The training should emphasise the importance of meeting requirements and the needs of customers and other interested parties. It should also include an awareness of the consequences to the organisation and its people of failing to meet the requirements.

A typical training plan would include:

- training objectives;
- training programmes and methodologies;
- the training resources needed;
- identification of necessary support;
- evaluation of training in terms of enhanced competence of people;
- measurement of the effectiveness of training and the impact on the organisation.

2.6.3 Section 6.3 Infrastructure

Section 6.3 Infrastructure	The organisation shall identify, provide and maintain the necessary: • *workspace and associated facilities;* • *equipment, hardware and software;* • *supporting services.*
Proof	How an organisation defines, provides and maintains the infrastructure requirements to ensure product conformity.
Likely documentation	• Policies, procedures and regulatory documents stating organisation and customer requirements; • budget and financial documents; • maintenance plans; • project plans identifying the human resources required to complete the task.

Depending on the size of the organisation and the products that it is offering, the infrastructure (e.g. workspace and facilities) required may include plant, hardware, software, tools and equipment, communication facilities, transport and supporting services.

The organisation should define, provide, develop, implement, evaluate and consider its requirements in terms of product performance, customer satisfaction and controlled improvement.

2.6.4 Section 6.4 Work environment

Section 6.4 Work environment	The organisation shall identify and manage the work environment required to achieve conformity of product.
Proof	How an organisation defines and organises its work environment.
Likely documentation	• Environmental procedures; • project plans; • budgetary processes; • legal processes and procedures.

An organisation's work environment is a combination of human factors (e.g. work methodologies, achievement and involvement opportunities, safety rules and guidance, ergonomics etc.) and physical factors (e.g. heat, hygiene, vibration, noise, humidity, pollution, light, cleanliness and air flow). All of these factors influence motivation, satisfaction and performance of people and as they have the potential for enhancing the performance of the organisation, they must be taken into consideration by the organisation when evaluating product conformance and achievement.

2.7 Section 7 – Product realisation

This section absorbs most of the 20 elements of the old ISO 9000:1994 standard, including process control, purchasing, handling and storage, and measuring devices. It is broken down into a number of sub-sections that cover the requirements for:

- **Planning of realisation processes** – clearly defining and documenting the processes used to ensure reliable and consistent products (e.g. verification and validation activities, criteria for acceptability and quality records etc.);

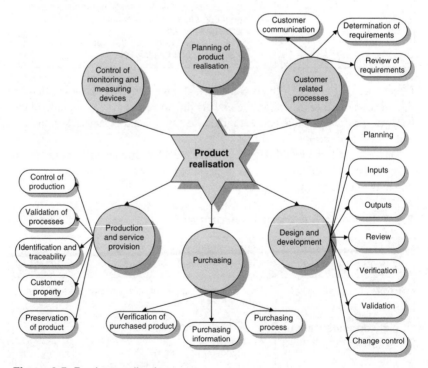

Figure 2.5 Product realisation

- **Customer-related processes** – identifying customer, product, legal and design requirements;
- **Design and development** – controlling the design process (e.g. design inputs, outputs, review, verification, validation and change control);
- **Purchasing** – having documented processes for the selection and control of suppliers and the control of purchases that affect the quality of the finished product or service;
- **Production and service provision** – having documented instructions that control the manufacture of a product or delivery of a service as well as identifying, verifying, protecting and maintaining customer property provided for use or incorporation with the product;
- **Control of monitoring and measuring devices** – their control, calibration and protection.

2.7.1 Section 7.1 Planning and realisation

Section 7.1 Planning and realisation	The organisation shall plan and develop the processes needed for product realisation. These shall include: • product, contract quality objectives and requirements; • product processes and their associated documentation, resources and facilities; • verification, validation, monitoring, inspection and test requirements; • criteria for acceptability; • details of the records that are required.
Proof	The availability of documented plans for processes that are required to realise a product – and the sequences in which they occur.
Likely documentation	• Process models (flow charts) showing the sequence of activities that an organisation adopts in order to produce a product; • documented QPs and WIs to ensure that staff work in accordance with stipulated requirements; • records that prove the results of process control.

A process can be represented as a flow of activities consisting of three separate elements as shown in Figure 2.6.

Realisation processes result in the products of an organisation. Support processes include all the other management processes that are necessary to the organisation, but do not directly add any value. To ensure product realisation, therefore, consideration should be given to desired outputs, process steps, activities, workflow, control measures, training needs, equipment, methodologies, information, materials and other resources. In fact, anything that might have an effect on the output.

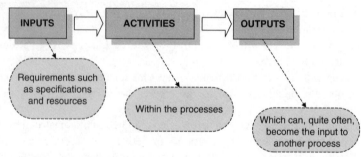

Figure 2.6 Planning realisation processes

Identification of processes

The organisation needs to identify the processes required to realise products that satisfy the requirements of customers and a plan has to be defined to manage these processes, especially their input and output stages. The documentation that describes how the QMS processes are applied for a specific product, project or contract is usually contained in a separate Quality Plan.

In ISO 9001:2000 the organisation is recommended to identify and plan all of the production, installation and servicing processes that directly affect quality. Procedures should be available to ensure that these processes are completed under controlled conditions especially with respect to special processes such as those for defining work to be carried out where no previous procedure exists.

Process planning

Special equipment or environmental conditions; compliance with relevant standards (national, European and international); criteria for workmanship (e.g. written standards, representative samples or illustrations) need to be planned. Procedures must be available to ensure that there is an appropriate system for the maintenance of equipment to ensure a continuing process capability. Records of all these procedures and processes must be maintained, controlled and fully documented.

Indeed, all productive work should be planned and undertaken in accordance with the organisation's procedures and any specific documents that have been detailed for that particular contract (e.g. contract specifications).

2.7.2 Section 7.2 Customer-related processes

Section 7.2 Customer-related processes	The organisation shall establish procedures for the: • identification of customer requirements; • review of product requirements; • customer communication.
Proof	The identification, review and interaction with customers and customer requirements.
Likely documentation	• Quality Manual; • Quality Plans.

Before entering into a contract situation, an organisation needs to find out exactly what the customer wants in terms of product specification, availability, delivery, support etc. It also needs to confirm that it has sufficient resources to complete the contract and is capable of satisfying the customer's requirements, in full.

2.7.2.1 Section 7.2.1 Determination of requirements related to the product

Section 7.2.1 Determination of requirements related to the product	The organisation shall determine: • product requirements specified by the customer; • product requirements not specified by the customer; • regulatory and legal product requirements.
Proof	How an organisation determines and implements customer, product and regulatory requirements.
Likely documentation	• Formal contracts; • contract review specifications and procedures; • regulatory and legal product requirements.

On receipt of an order and/or contract, the organisation should thoroughly review it to ensure:

• customer requirements are fully understood and documented;
• the organisation has the ability to meet the customer's requirements;
• any differences between a quotation and the order are identified and resolved.

The customer's requirements can include many elements (e.g. product, options, delivery method, terms of contract, method of payment etc.) and the organisation's ability to meet these requirements will rely on:

• people and their skills, experience and motivation;
• production tools and equipment;
• raw materials;

- stock availability;
- information, drawings and instructions.

Once the organisation has successfully proved to the customer that their QMS is acceptable (see preceding paragraphs), the next step is to commence contract negotiations.

2.7.2.2 Section 7.2.2 Review of requirements related to the product

Section 7.2.2 **Review of requirements related to the product**	Prior to submission of a tender or acceptance of a contract, the organisation shall ensure that: • product requirements have been defined; • contract requirements have been fully established; • all requirements differing from those previously expressed are resolved; • the organisation has the ability to meet defined requirements.
Proof	How an organisation reviews product and customer requirements to check that they can actually do the job.
Likely documentation	• Contract review procedures; • project plans showing lines of communication with the customer.

Most organisations will offer their standard products in a catalogue for the customer to make a selection from. These products will be identified against a design specification and normally be accompanied by a picture and/or technical description. Most organisations will also usually be willing to provide system-specific products to suit individual customer requirements. These specialist service requirements will differ from one customer to another (and from one contract to another) and will, therefore, possibly need to be covered by an individual tender, quotation and/or contract.

The contract document

The contract will specify which part of ISO 9001:2000 is to be used, what portions can be deleted and what additional conditions have to be inserted. The contract will also specify the use of quality plans, quality programs, quality audit plans and other relevant technical specifications.

Once the customer has accepted a proposal, or an order is placed, it should be recorded and reviewed in order to establish that the requirements of the order are adequately defined and documented. Any differences from the proposal should be resolved and the organisation should have established that they are fully capable of meeting and satisfying the customer's requirements. Most of the larger organisations will rely on some form of computerised order processing system to ensure rapid fulfilment of customer orders. Whilst this is a preferred method, it is not an essential ISO 9001:2000 requirement.

Contract signature

Before signature, both parties must thoroughly review the contract and be absolutely sure that:

- the QMS requirements are fully understood;
- all the requirements, clauses and provisions are complete, unambiguous, mutually acceptable (considering the economics and risks in their respective situations);
- the requirements are adequately documented and defined;
- the organisation is able to meet all the contractual requirements.

Where product requirements are changed, the organisation shall ensure that the relevant documentation is amended and that the relevant personnel are made aware of the changed requirements. Where the customer provides no documented statement of requirement, the customer requirements must be confirmed before acceptance.

Any requirement differing from those in the original enquiry or tender should be resolved at this stage and it must be confirmed that all the contractual requirements can be met.

Servicing

Most service practices will vary widely between suppliers, distributors and users. If servicing is to be provided, or is required as part of the contract, then the supplier must establish procedures for controlling and authenticating the quality of the service performed and ensure that they meet the required standards.

2.7.2.3 Section 7.2.3 Customer communication

Section 7.2.3 Customer communication	The organisation shall have procedures available to: • provide customers with product information; • handle, customer enquiries, contracts or order handling including amendments; • cover customer feedback and/or customer complaints.
Proof	How an organisation communicates (i.e. liaises) with their customers, keeps them informed (of product progress etc.) and handles their enquiries and complaints.
Likely documentation	Project plans showing lines of communication with the customer.

The need to maintain open lines of communication with the customer cannot be over-emphasised and procedures should be put in place to ensure that the customer is kept fully up-to-date with the progress of their product/contract and that all customer comments and complaints are dealt with in a speedy and effective manner.

2.7.3 Section 7.3 Design and development

Section 7.3 Design and development	The organisation shall develop procedures for design and development: • planning; • inputs; • outputs; • review; • verification; • validation; • change control.
Proof	The availability of a process to control design and development stages within an organisation.
Likely documentation	• Processes and procedures for design and development; • design plans and development plans.

Design is usually meant to mean the production of something new, although it can, in many circumstances, be a variation of an existing product or service. It could, therefore, be a new product or it could be a system made up of a variety of products. Either way, a process or design plan needs to be developed that confirms:

• what the customer needs;
• what the boundaries are (e.g. customer requirements);
• how the organisation is going to achieve it;
• how long it will take;
• who will undertake the task;
• who will check and verify the product.

2.7.3.1 Section 7.3.1 Design and development planning

Section 7.3.1 Design and development planning	The organisation shall plan and control the design and development of the product through all processes. This planning shall include: • stage reviews; • verification and validation activities; • identification of responsibilities and authorities; • management of the interfaces between different groups that may be involved; • provision of effective communication; • clarity of responsibilities; • product and planning review procedures.
Proof	How an organisation goes about planning and controlling the design and development of a product.
Likely documentation	• Design and development plans; • processes and procedures for design and development; • risk assessment; • job descriptions and responsibilities.

The best production methods cannot compensate for an inadequate or mediocre design! Quality cannot be an 'add on'; it has to be designed into a product before it is manufactured and the only way of achieving that is through careful planning and controlled documentation throughout the design stage.

Whether the responsibility for the design of a product rests purely with the supplier, the purchaser, or is a joint function, it is essential that the designer is fully aware of the exact requirements of the project and has a sound background knowledge of all the proper standards, information and procedures that will be required.

Functions of the design office

The functions of the design office are extremely important for they will not only influence the maintenance of quality throughout the manufacturing process, but also play a major part in setting the quality level of the final product. If there is no quality control in the drawing office, what chance is there of ever having quality on the shop floor? When the engineers are trying to manufacture something to a set of drawings that have countless mistakes on them, how on earth can they be expected to produce an acceptable item!

 Note: The same applies to the production of a service.

Thus, in close co-operation with the marketing, sales and manufacturing sections, the design office prepares business and performance specifications, sets target dates, provides technical specifications, reviews drawings, produces overall schemes to the estimating section, discusses these schemes with the manufacturing section and develops the design in conjunction with other supplier functions.

Design criteria

Design criteria will have to be clarified, documented and recorded in the design plan and used for reference throughout the design process. The level of detail on the design plan will vary depending upon the type and size of system, but at all times it should contain sufficient detail to control the design process in accordance with the customer's requirements. Where items require interpretation (e.g. positioning, practicality, maintainability, etc.) they will need to be reviewed prior to design finalisation.

2.7.3.2 Section 7.3.2 Design and development inputs

Section 7.3.2 Design and development inputs	Product requirement inputs shall be defined, documented and include: • functional and performance requirements; • regulatory and legal requirements; • information derived from previous similar designs; • other requirements essential for design and development.
Proof	How an organisation identifies the requirements to be met by a product.

Likely documentation	• Project Plans detailing:
	  • policies;
	  • standards;
	  • specifications and tolerances;
	  • skill requirements;
	• regulatory and legal requirements;
	• information derived from previous (similar) designs or developments;
	• environmental requirements;
	• health and safety aspects.

Following initial contract approval, details of all the relevant standards, specifications and specific customer requirements that are going to be used during production will have to be identified and steps taken to ensure that they are available. Procedures will have to be established and maintained in order to make certain that the functions of the design office are in agreement with the specified requirements. Any incomplete, ambiguous or conflicting requirements must be resolved at this stage and revisions of the specification reviewed and agreed by both parties.

The design input items are documented on the design plan and reviewed by the designer prior to commencing design process. Where ambiguity exists, the designer will need to clarify this with customer and document the results.

Design input may consist of:

• national/international codes of practice;
• customer supplied documents, drawings, specifications and samples;

- statutory regulations;
- previous and/or similar designs.

Process inputs for product design and/or development can be divided into three categories:

1. **internal** – policies, standards, specifications, skill and dependability requirements, documentation and data on existing products and outputs from other processes;
2. **external** – customer or marketplace needs and expectations, contractual requirements, interested party specifications, relevant statutory and regulatory requirements, international or national standards, and industry codes of practice;
3. **other** – operation, installation and application, storage, handling, maintenance and delivery, physical parameters and environment and disposal requirements.

Staff

All staff performing productive work should be capable of undertaking their tasks correctly. Guidance concerning tasks may be available from training, experience, detailed instructions, comparison with examples; or a mixture of these. Detailed instructions are normally required where their absence could adversely affect the quality and acceptability of the product. Other items that need controlling (especially those that ensure that acceptable products are produced) include:

- tools;
- production equipment;
- production environment.

Special processes

ISO 9001:2000 requires an approved control system for 'special processes' that cannot easily be inspected on completion of the product (e.g. welding). The simplest means to ensure that they are correct each time is by experimenting, and then documenting the successful process (personnel, equipment, materials, sequence and environment). The process can then be repeated each time the product is required. Production of a reject then becomes an improbability but not, unfortunately, an impossibility!

Process control and instructions

As part of a contract, the supplier may be required to identify (and plan) any production and/or installation process that directly affects quality and (in particular) any special process that may only become apparent after production and/or when the product is used. These plans and instructions should be included in any representative samples that are provided.

Marketing implications

It would be totally unproductive for an organisation to make something (e.g. a product or a system), find that it is not required by anyone and consequently be unable to sell it! For this reason most organisations have a separate marketing section who are responsible for determining the need for a product or service and for estimating the market demand.

Customer requirements

Customer requirements will specify and detail the way the work is to be performed, the standard of workmanship and the degree of quality assurance that they require. The marketing section must be capable of translating the user requirements into technical language that will be sufficient to enable the design staff to convert the requirements into practical designs and specifications that enable production, testing, maintenance and servicing to be technically and economically possible.

The customer's technical requirements should include:

- performance and environmental characteristics – specific use, reliability etc.;
- sensory characteristics – style, colour, taste, smell;
- installation configuration or fit;
- standards, specifications and specific user requirements;
- packaging;
- quality assurance.

Market readiness

In order for the management to always be aware of their organisation's market readiness, the marketing section (in close co-operation with the design and manufacturing sections) needs to define and review market readiness, field support and production capability.

Components, parts and materials

Although the design office needs to be free to be creative, it is also imperative that they maintain a close relationship with the manufacturing section so that they can be aware of **their** exact requirements, **their** problems and **their** component preferences etc. It can be so easy for the design office to work in splendid isolation, make arbitrary decisions, select components that **they** think are suitable, but then find that the size and tolerance is completely inappropriate for the manufacture of that device.

The design office must have available complete listings of all the appropriate components, parts and materials, their reliability, availability, maintainability, safety, acceptability and adequacy. They must be aware of recent developments, new technologies and advances in both materials and equipment that are available on the market and applicable to that particular product.

Specifications and tolerances

Tolerances should never be unduly restrictive for this could create problems with respect to machine capabilities or require operator skills (and time) far beyond those, which are really essential. Tolerance specifications should also be flexible enough to allow for interchangeability of material where necessary.

Health and safety

As health and safety has now become a mandatory requirement of ISO 9001:2000, designers should be even more aware of the implications of the statutory national, European and international legal requirements for health and safety as they could well place constraints on their designs.

These regulations will not just be concerned with the condition and safety of the material but will also provide measures for overcoming the possibility of danger to persons and property when the material is being used, stored, transported or tested. All aspects of a product or service should be identified with the aim of enhancing product safety and minimising product liability. This can be achieved by:

- identifying the relevant safety standards that make a product or service more effective;
- carrying out design evaluation tests and prototype testing for safety;
- analysing instructions, warnings, labels and maintenance manuals etc. to minimise misinterpretation;
- developing a means of traceability to allow a product to be recalled if safety problems are discovered.

Note: Currently there are no ISO approved standards for Occupational Health & Safety (OH&S) management systems. In January 1997, ISO's Technical Management Board (TMB) shelved the possibility of ISO developing OH&S standards along the lines of ISO 9000. At that time, the TMB noted that the outcome of the international workshop on OH&S management system standardisation held by ISO on 5–6 September 1996 in Geneva indicated that there was little support from the main stakeholders for ISO to develop standards in this field. The question was revisited with the same outcome some three years later. At the time of writing this third edition of *ISO 9001:2000 for Small Business*, the situation is still uncertain. Such standards have, however, been developed at a national level (e.g. in Australia, Canada, the United Kingdom and the USA etc.).

Computers

Nowadays, of course, most design offices have computers to record and store their information on plus disc retrieval systems that enable regular updating and amendment of data. This updated information is then available for use with standard software programs and Computer Aided Design (CAD) packages to produce accurate information either by list, graph or drawing.

2.7.3.3 Section 7.3.3 Design and development outputs

Section 7.3.3 Design and development outputs	The organisation shall ensure that: • design output meets design input requirements; • sufficient information is available for production and service operations; • product acceptance criteria have been met; • the characteristics of the product that are essential to its safe and proper use have been defined.
Proof **Likely documentation**	How an organisation ensures that the design output meets the design input requirements. • Drawings; • schematics; • schedules; • system specifications; • system descriptions, etc.

All documentation associated with the design output (e.g. drawings, schematics, schedules, system specifications, system descriptions, etc.) needs to:

- be produced in accordance with agreed customer requirements;
- be reviewed (by another designer who has not been associated with the initial design) to ensure that it meets the design input;
- identify all of the characteristics which are critical to the effective operation of the designed system;
- be reviewed and approved by the customer prior to use.

Design office responsibilities

Another responsibility of the design office is to maintain a link with the production department so that they can assist in the analysis of failures, swiftly produce solutions and forestall costly work stoppages. This is often referred to as 'design output' and is covered by the activities of the 'internal audit' system that is required to ensure that the design output meets the specified requirements of the design input through design control methods such as:

- undertaking qualification tests and demonstrations;
- comparing the new design with a similar proven design;
- ensuring that it conforms to appropriate regulatory (for example safety) requirements; whether or not these have been stated in the input documentation;
- identifying those characteristics of the design that are crucial and establishing that these characteristics meet the design input criteria.

Examples of the output from design and/or development activities include:

- product specifications;
- training requirements;
- methodologies;
- purchase requirements;
- acceptance criteria.

Inspection and test status

Once products have been inspected, there needs to be a method for easily identifying them as being either acceptable or unacceptable. This can be achieved in many ways, including:

- marking;
- stamping;
- labelling;
- segregating;
- associated documents;
- test reports;
- physical location.

2.7.3.4 Section 7.3.4 Design and development review

Section 7.3.4 Design and development review	The organisation shall complete systematic reviews to: - evaluate the ability of the product to fulfil requirements; - identify problems; - propose follow-up actions.
Proof	How an organisation ensures that it is capable of meeting product requirements.
Likely documentation	- Design process review procedures; - procedures detailing how changes are made to designs and how they are approved, recorded and distributed; - management reviews and audit procedures; - records.

Design process control

The process of translating the design input into design and developed output is primarily controlled by the design review, which ensures that:

- adherence to contractual and statutory requirements has been fully met;
- all alternative design concepts and items have been considered;

- all potential design problems have been identified and evaluated;
- all calculations have been correctly performed and re-checked;
- the suitability of the designed item/system with respect to environmental and operating conditions has been considered;
- the compatibility with existing (or proposed) items or systems is assured;
- the designed item or system is maintainable;
- all necessary working documents (e.g. calculations, notes, sketches, etc.) accompany the design output documentation.

The majority of design activities can be verified during the design process review and a record maintained of all the items that have been considered together with their results. Whenever possible the use of computers is recommended for verifying designs and currently there are many proprietary brands being marketed.

Final verification of the design is usually completed during final inspection and test and the designer is responsible for specifying and supplying any inspections or tests that are required during system installation to practically verify the design.

Design process review

When designing and/or developing products or processes, as well as ensuring that the needs of all interested parties are satisfied, the organisation will have to take into consideration life cycle costs, environmental requirements, Reliability, Availability, Maintainability and Safety (RAMS) requirements and ergonomic considerations.

A risk assessment (using risk assessment tools such as Failure Mode and Effects Analysis (FMEA), Fault Tree Analysis (FTA), reliability assessment, simulation techniques etc.) will be needed to assess the potential for, and the effect of, possible failures in products and/or processes and the results used to define and implement preventive actions to mitigate identified risks.

Periodic reviews

Periodic reviews should be completed throughout the design process (for example, preliminary, intermediate and final) with the aim of:

- confirming design and/or development objectives are being met;
- evaluating potential hazards and/or modes of failure found in product use;
- evaluating life-cycle product performance data;
- evaluating the impact of the product on the environment;
- ensuring all other viable paths have been considered;
- confirming that all statutory requirements have been considered and are complied with;
- ensuring that there is adequate supporting documentation available to define the design and how the product or service is to be used and maintained.

The tests should include:

- the evaluation of the performance, durability, safety, reliability and maintainability of the product under expected storage and operational conditions;
- inspection procedures to verify that all design features are as they were originally intended and that all authorised design changes have been carried out and that these have been properly recorded;
- validation of computer systems and associated software.

Participants in such reviews should include representatives of functions concerned with the design and/or development stage(s) being reviewed and the results of the reviews and subsequent follow-up actions need to be recorded.

2.7.3.5 Section 7.3.5 Design and development verification

Section 7.3.5 Design and development verification	The organisation shall verify that: • design output meets the design and development inputs; • the results of the verification have been recorded.
Proof	How an organisation ensures that product specifications are fulfilled and that the finalised product meets the original input requirements.
Likely documentation	• Design process review procedures; • procedures for periodic reviews; • records.

ISO 9001:2000 requires an organisation to verify that design outputs meet the design input specifications and that they meet the needs of the customer. In particular, verification of engineering designs (prior to construction, installation or application) software outputs (prior to installation or use) and direct customer services (prior to their widespread introduction) can prove very beneficial to an organisation! The aim should be to generate sufficient data through these verification activities to enable design and development methodologies and decisions to be reviewed.

Design verification and review is another form of periodic evaluation and uses one of the following methods:

- **alternative calculations** – to verify the precision of the original calculations and their analysis;
- **comparison** – with other similar designs;
- **third party evaluation** – to verify that the original calculations and/or other design activities have been correctly carried out;
- **feedback** – from previous designs and experience;

- **information** – gained during manufacture, assembly, installation, commissioning, servicing and field use;
- **customer** – feedback (i.e. asking the customer);
- **testing** – by model or prototype.

2.7.3.6 Section 7.3.6 Design and development validation

Section 7.3.6 Design and development validation	The organisation shall validate that the: • product is capable of meeting the requirements for its intended use; • results of the validation have been recorded.
Proof	How an organisation ensures that the design is actually capable of doing the intended job.
Likely documentation	• Procedures for in-process inspection and testing; • final inspection and test procedures; • records.

As design work is normally performed in accordance with the customer's instructions, it is sometimes difficult for an organisation to validate the end product. In these situations, the organisation will normally only be required to validate that the design meets the customer's requirements. Installed systems will then need to be inspected and tested to ensure compliance and customer satisfaction and acceptance and it is only **then** that the design can be finally validated.

In-process inspection and testing

Items that have been produced in accordance with an organisation's documented processes generally pass through a number of stages. Rather than leaving inspection and testing to when the last stage has been completed, it is more cost effective to check the items as they progress through the various stages of their production and/or installation. These are called 'in-process inspections' and their objective is to identify rejects and inadequate processes as they happen and not at the end of a job lot.

The organisation must, therefore, establish effective stages of inspection, define the type of inspection to be performed and clarify the acceptance/rejection criteria. All the in-process inspections should be documented, and any faulty items must be identified and segregated.

Final inspection and testing

Once again, the principle of final inspection is similar to an in-process inspection, i.e. to identify acceptable products from faulty products, record the results and confirm the acceptance/rejection decision.

The tests will normally include the:

- evaluation of the performance, durability, safety, reliability and maintainability of the product under expected storage and operational conditions;
- inspection procedures to verify that all design features are as they were originally intended and that all authorised design changes have been carried out and that these have been properly recorded;
- validation of computer systems and associated software.

Note: Wherever applicable, validation should be completed prior to the delivery or implementation of the product. If this isn't possible or impractical, then partial validation should be performed to the extent applicable.

2.7.3.7 Section 7.3.7 Control of design and development changes

Section 7.3.7 Control of design and development changes	The organisation shall: • identify, document and control all design and development changes; • evaluate the effect of these changes; • verify, validate and approve these changes before implementation.
Proof	How changes to a design are identified, evaluated, recorded and approved.
Likely documentation	• Change control procedures; • design process review procedures; • management reviews and audit procedures; • records.

Throughout the design and development phase, there are likely to be a number of changes, alterations, modifications and improvements made to the design of the product and its development processes. It is essential that:

- these are identified, documented and controlled;
- the effect of the changes on constituent parts and delivered products is evaluated;
- the changes are verified, validated and approved before implementation.

All changes to the design criteria (input and/or output) should be subject to strict documentation control and should be reviewed and verified by the designer and/or the customer, prior to incorporation within the design. All changes need to be subject to an agreed change control procedure to ensure that the changes have been fully evaluated, agreed (or concessions made) and that only the latest versions of design documents are available in work places. It is essential that the results of the review of changes and subsequent follow up actions are always documented.

It is essential that all of the design documentation, drawing and notes etc. are retained in a design project file so that it can be made immediately available and can be produced for reviews etc. The design output should be reviewed and approved by top management before being provided to the customer for approval and use.

2.7.4 Section 7.4 Purchasing

Section 7.4 Purchasing	The organisation shall have documented procedures for: • purchasing control; • purchasing information; • verification of purchased product.
Proof	How an organisation controls the purchase of materials, products and services from suppliers and third parties.
Likely documentation	• Documented procedures for the evaluation of suppliers; • documented procedures for the evaluation of a purchased product or service.

When an organisation has to purchase products, materials and/or services from suppliers who have not been previously specified in a contract or by a customer, they are normally selected on their ability to meet the organisation's requirements given due consideration to the quality, statutory obligations, timescale and cost. A list of approved suppliers and subcontractors needs to be maintained by the organisation and this should contain the following information:

• previous performance in supplying to similar specifications and requirements;
• stocking of high-volume standard items conforming to relevant national and/or international standards (or supplied with a statement of conformity);
• compliance with an approved third-party product or quality registration scheme;
• recommendation by other similar purchasers or manufacturers of equipment;
• trial order and evaluation of performance.

Purchasing process

The organisation should have available a process to ensure appropriate selection, evaluation and control of all purchased products. All supplies and subcontracts should be subject to an authorised purchase order that provides full details of the type and extent of supply.

2.7.4.1 Section 7.4.1 Purchasing process

Section 7.4.1 Purchasing process	The organisation shall have procedures to: • ensure purchased product conforms to purchase requirements; • evaluate, re-evaluate and select suppliers.
Proof	The controls that an organisation has in place to ensure purchased products and services are of an acceptable standard.
Likely documentation	• Approved list of suppliers; • supplier evaluations; • purchasing procedures; • purchase orders.

Purchasing processes and procedures

The organisation is responsible for producing purchasing processes and procedures that include:

- identification of requirements;
- selection of suppliers;
- quotations and tenders;
- purchase price;
- order forms;
- verification of purchased products;
- non-conforming purchased products;
- contract administration and associated purchase documentation;
- supplier control and development;
- risk assessment.

Suppliers

Having identified their suppliers (usually selected from previous experience, past history, test results on similar projects or published experience from other users) an organisation should establish a system by which the supplier/subcontractor is clearly advised exactly what is required, and by when. This is often achieved by use of a purchase order system.

Subcontractors

If a supplier uses subcontractors, it is important that they can be relied on to produce a quality product, have the ability to meet subcontractual requirements, (including quality assurance) and do not reduce the quality of the final product. The supplier (who is normally referred to as the prime contractor) must ensure that all items purchased from a subcontractor are covered by a purchasing document. This document will contain details of the product ordered, type, class, style, grade and the title/number/issue of the relevant standard, specification, drawing, inspection instruction etc. that it must conform to. The prime contractor should ensure that subcontractors have their own QMS and that the purchased product or service is satisfactory.

2.7.4.2 Section 7.4.2 Purchasing information

Section 7.4.2 Purchasing information	Purchasing documents shall describe: • the product to be purchased; • requirements for approval or qualification of product, service, procedure, process, equipment and personnel; • QMS requirements.
Proof	The details that need to be provided by an organisation when placing an order with a supplier.
Likely documentation	• Approved list of suppliers; • supplier evaluations; • purchasing procedures; • purchase orders; • stock control procedures.

A process should be established to ensure that purchasing documents contain sufficient details about:

- the product to be purchased;
- the necessary approval and qualification requirements (i.e. procedures, processes etc.) for product, equipment and personnel;
- the QMS requirements;
- agreement on quality assurance – whether the prime contractor can completely rely on the subcontractor's quality assurance scheme or whether some (or all) of the product will have to be tested by the prime contractor or via a third party;
- agreement on verification methods by the purchaser at source or on delivery; whether this should be by sample or on a 100% basis; whether this inspection should be at the prime contractor's or the subcontractor's premises;
- settlement of quality disputes – who, how, when and where.

2.7.4.3 Section 7.4.3 Verification of purchased product

Section 7.4.3 Verification of purchased product	The organisation shall establish procedures to verify that the purchased product meets specified purchase requirements.
Proof	The controls that an organisation has in place to ensure that products and services provided by suppliers meet their original requirements.
Likely documentation	• Approved list of suppliers; • supplier evaluations; • purchasing procedures; • purchase orders; • stock control procedures.

It is essential that all goods and services received from a third party are checked to confirm that they are those that were ordered, the delivery is on time and that they are of good quality. The amount of inspection will depend on how critical the supplied goods and service is to the end product and the amount of inspection should be compatible with the risk or inconvenience if the item is later found to be faulty.

A consumable item (e.g. low-cost items such as lights bulbs, duplicating paper etc.) are normally only checked for correct identity, correct quantity and any signs of damage. It would be unwise to perform detailed inspections on these items which, if found to be faulty, could be replaced within a short time at little comparative expense. Conversely, detailed inspections should always be performed on major components, as, if they are faulty, the rectification could be expensive and time-consuming.

It should also be appreciated that the worst possible time to identify an item as a reject is when it is handed over to the final customer. If the product (or its components) can be checked at earlier stages, it is time well spent.

In-inspection

Receiving or in-inspection should be documented to confirm that it has taken place and that the goods or services are deemed fit for use in the next stage of the process. This may often be by a completing goods received note, or marking the supplier's delivery note. The delivery should also be checked against the purchase order to ensure that it is complete. Should the inspection identify the delivery as reject, the items should be segregated, labelled or identified to avoid them being used in error.

Goods inwards

In industry there are very few suppliers who are not actually purchasers themselves. Even the largest companies have to obtain consumables, components and sometimes complete assemblies from a subcontractor at some stage or other and therefore the quality of the supplier's final product, to a considerable degree, depends on the quality of the subcontractor's goods.

To be certain that the items purchased, or obtained, from a third party are up to the required standard, the prime contractor will have to set up some kind of quality inspection, unless that is, the supplier himself operates a fully satisfactory and recognised QMS.

The term 'goods inwards' describes the procedures designed to cover this type of inspection and it is a very important quality assurance function.

Inspection and testing

It is the prime contractor's responsibility to ensure that inspection and tests are always performed on all incoming goods and that no incoming material is used or processed until it has been inspected or otherwise verified to confirm that it is up to the specified requirements.

The prime contractor will have to show in their Quality Plan exactly how this is to be achieved and precisely what inspections and tests are to be carried out to confirm quality. It is then up to the purchaser to decide if this is enough or whether they would like to see additional or supplementary inspections carried out. The amount of inspection will, of course, vary according to the degree of control exercised by the subcontractor, their past performance and records – for example, are they assessed to ISO 9001:2000, etc.

This inspection should complement and be in addition to the existing quality control procedures and must be clearly laid down. Records should detail who actually carried out the inspection that released the product, the assembly line and despatch services. The inspection must:

- consider that all incoming material where quality is unproved should remain suspect until proven as satisfactory;
- ensure that written control procedures are available to establish a product has:
    - not been inspected;
    - been inspected and approved or;
    - been inspected and rejected;
- ensure that any defective material that is received from a third party is subject to the same controls as defective material that may occur in their own production.

Inspection procedures

Ineffective or incomplete control usually leads to costly defects. The prime contractor must, therefore, ensure that all manufacturing operations are carried out under strictly controlled conditions. These conditions should be covered by work instructions that define the manufacturing process, suitable manufacturing equipment and if a special working environment is required.

Workmanship criteria will have to be fully documented using either written standards, photographs, sketches or representative samples.

Control of quality

The choice of how quality is controlled and the type of inspection is normally left up to the prime contractor who may decide on a stage inspection, sampling inspection, final inspection or perhaps even a combination of all methods as being more appropriate. The method chosen should, however, cover every phase of manufacture, assembly and installation and the instructions should include the following details:

- identification of material;
- detailed operations to be performed;
- tools or test equipment required;
- requirements for operational checks, calibration and equipment availability;
- methods of inspection;
- environmental conditions to be maintained during operation or inspection;
- criteria for passing or failing the test;
- sampling techniques and related decision criteria if applicable.

Non-compliance

Inspection and testing is normally carried out on completion of installation and maintenance activities, with results being documented. If items fail to comply with agreed contract criteria, then they should either be repaired, replaced or identified for subsequent evaluation and decision. All repaired items need to be re-inspected to ensure their acceptability prior to being used.

2.7.5 Section 7.5 Production and service provision

Section 7.5 Production and service provision	The organisation shall have procedures for the control of: • production and service operations; • validation of processes; • identification and traceability; • customer property; • preservation of product.
Proof	The availability of a process to cover all production and service operations.
Likely documentation	Documented: • Processes; • Quality Procedures; • Work Instructions.

A documented process needs to be agreed and implemented by the organisation to cover all production and service operations.

2.7.5.1 Section 7.5.1 Control of production and service provision

Section 7.5.1 Control of production and service provision	The organisation shall have the following available: • information concerning product characteristics; • appropriate work instructions; • suitable production equipment; • measuring and monitoring devices and facilities; • processes to cover the release, delivery and post-delivery activities.
Proof Likely documentation	The availability of all relevant information concerning control production and service operations. • Procedures; • project plans; • resources.

The organisation should identify the requirements for product realisation and ensure that it has:

- the ability to comply with contractual requirements;
- the ability to train and have available competent people;
- a viable system for communication;
- a process for problem prevention.

2.7.5.2 Section 7.5.2 Validation of processes for production and service provisions

Section 7.5.2 Validation of processes for production and service provisions	The organisation shall define validation arrangements for: • review and approval of processes; • approval of equipment; • qualification of personnel; • use of defined methodologies and procedures; • requirements for records; • re-validation.
Proof Likely documentation	How an organisation identifies processes which cannot be verified by subsequent monitoring/testing/inspection (including the validation of these processes to demonstrate their effectiveness). Documented: • Processes; • Quality Procedures; • Work Instructions.

Where the resulting output cannot be verified by subsequent measurement or monitoring (and where deficiencies may become apparent **only** after the product is in use or the service has been delivered), the organisation needs to validate any production and/or service processes to demonstrate the ability of the processes to achieve their planned results.

The organisation should have procedures available to ensure that these processes are completed under controlled conditions especially with respect to special processes, and for defining work to be carried out where no previous procedure exists.

Note: Design verification is a process whose purpose is to examine design outputs and to use objective evidence to confirm that outputs meet design input requirements. Your purpose here is to see whether your design outputs meet your organisation's design goals. **Design validation** is a process whose purpose is to examine products and to use objective evidence to confirm that these products meet customer needs and expectations. Your purpose here is to see whether your product does what your customer or user wants it to do under real-world conditions.

2.7.5.3 Section 7.5.3 Identification and traceability

Section 7.5.3 Identification and traceability	The organisation shall have procedures available for: • identification of product; • product status; • traceability.
Proof	How the status of a product is identified during all stages of its production/delivery.
Likely documentation	Documented: • Processes; • Quality Procedures; • Work Instructions.

ISO 9001:2000 recommends organisations maintain documented procedures for identifying products (hardware, software, documents and/or data) throughout all stages of production, delivery, receipt and installation. This process should be documented and reviewed for its continued applicability on a regular basis.

If required, organisations can also establish a system for identifying individual products or batches.

As previously mentioned (see Goods inwards in Section 2.7.4.3) all received goods should be inspected, their status defined and be located in stores. Non-conforming items should be placed in a reject area or marked as 'reject for review'. The status of work in progress should be clearly indicated by markings or associated documentation recording the inspections undertaken and their acceptability.

2.7.5.4 Section 7.5.4 Customer property

Section 7.5.4 Customer property	The organisation shall: • retain records of all customer provided material; • protect and maintain all customer provided property.
Proof	How an organisation looks after property that has been provided by a customer.
Likely documentation	A documented procedure for the control of customer property.

Customer supplied products are goods which have been provided by the customer (or his agent), normally free of charge, for incorporation into the product. The existence of 'free issue' products will only be relevant to certain organisations. However, it should be remembered that items returned to the organisation for repair or rectification are also within this category.

Any goods received from customers need to be visually inspected at the receipt stage and any undeclared non-conformance immediately reported to the customer.

The organisation should ensure that all property belonging to the customer (including its intellectual, property rights) is protected and that care is taken to ensure that it is well maintained, used in accordance with the manufacturer's instructions and safeguarded at all times.

Should the items become lost, damaged or unserviceable, while in the organisation's control, the problem should be recorded and the customer advised.

Purchaser supplied product

In some circumstances material, sub assemblies or components may have been supplied to the organisation by the purchaser as part of the contract. In these cases it is important that the organisation has a goods inward inspection process to assure themselves that the item they are receiving is the correct one, has not been damaged in transit and is suitable for its purpose.

Note: 'Customer property' can include 'intellectual property'!

2.7.5.5 Section 7.5.5 Preservation of product

Section 7.5.5 Preservation of product	The organisation shall have procedures available for identifying, handling, packaging, storing and protecting products during internal processing and delivery to their intended destination.
Proof	How an organisation looks after its own products.
Likely documentation	• Product approval procedures; • procedures which ensure the safety and protection of products.

Part numbers and labels

A manufacturer's/supplier's part number or description label should identify any material or equipment that cannot be obviously identified. This identification can be on the packaging or on the item itself and should remain in place for as long as possible provided it does not hamper effective use of the item. If items have a serial number then this number should also be recorded.

Product protection

All materials and goods that are received, whether they are the property of the organisation or others, should, as far as practicable, be protected and their quality preserved until such time as they are transferred to a customer, disposed of to a third party or utilised. The overall objective should be to prevent deterioration and damage whilst in storage, or in the process of transportation, installation, commissioning and/or maintenance. Written instructions and procedures for the handling, identification and storage of materials, components, parts, sub assemblies and completed items will have to be established and made available. These instructions must contain details of quarantine areas or bonded stores, how they should be used, together with methods of cleaning, preserving and packaging.

Documented procedures

As previously mentioned, ISO 9001:2000 recommends organisations to maintain documented procedures for identifying products (e.g. hardware, software, documents and/or data) throughout all stages of production, delivery, receipt and installation. If required, organisations can also establish a system for identifying individual products or batches and consider the need for any special requirements (i.e. associated with software, electronic media, hazardous materials, specialist personnel and products or materials) arising from the nature of the product which are unique or irreplaceable.

In some cases (e.g. toxic contamination), in order to prevent damage and deterioration of the product (and harm to the product user!), it might even be necessary to refer to another document, regulation or standard to ensure that the items are correctly handled, stored and delivered.

Storage

All QMS standards emphasise the importance of having satisfactory storage facilities and stipulate that these must be available for **all** materials, consumables, components, sub assemblies or completed articles. In a similar manner, the standards specify that materials should always be properly stored, segregated, handled and protected during production so as to maintain their suitability.

The supplier will thus have to provide secure storage areas or stock rooms so that the materials can be isolated and protected (e.g. from harmful environments) pending use or shipment. Storage areas will have to be protected and kept tidy and the supplier must ensure that material only leaves the storage areas when it has been properly authorised.

Procedures for rotation of stock will need to be established and special consideration should always be given to items with limited shelf life and items that might require special protection during transit or storage. This is usually referred to as deterioration control. Where corrosive or toxic materials are stored in quantity, these items must be kept in a separate storage area.

Delivery

The supplier must make arrangements to ensure that the quality of the product is protected following final inspection and test. Where contractually specified, this protection can even be extended to include delivery to the final destination. Some of the factors that should be considered by suppliers when delivering their product to the purchaser are:

- the nature of the material;
- the type(s) of transport to be used;
- environmental conditions during transit;
- time in transit;
- handling methods en route;
- storage en route and at the destination.

2.7.6 Section 7.6 Control of measuring and monitoring devices

Section 7.6 Control of measuring and monitoring devices	The organisation shall ensure that all measuring and monitoring devices are: • calibrated and adjusted periodically or prior to use; • traceable to international or national standards; • safeguarded from adjustments that would invalidate the calibration; • protected from damage and deterioration during handling, maintenance and storage.
Proof	The controls that an organisation has in place to ensure that equipment (including software) used for proving conformance to specified requirements is properly maintained.
Likely documentation	• Equipment records of maintenance and calibration; • Work Instructions.

The control of measuring and test equipment (whether owned by the supplier, on loan, hired or provided by the purchaser), should always include a check that the equipment is exactly what is required, has been initially calibrated before use, operates within the required tolerances, is regularly recalibrated and that facilities exist (either within the organisation or via a third party) to adjust, repair or recalibrate as necessary.

In particular, measuring and monitoring devices that are used to verify process outputs against specified requirements need to be maintained and calibrated against national and international standards. The results of all calibrations carried out must be retained and the validity of previous results re-assessed if they are subsequently found to be out of calibration.

All production and measuring equipment that is held needs to be well-maintained, in good condition and capable of safe and effective operation within a specified tolerance of accuracy. Test and measuring equipment should be regularly inspected and/or calibrated to ensure that it is capable of accurate operation, by comparison with external sources traceable back to national standards. Any electrostatic protection equipment that is utilised when handling sensitive components should be regularly checked to ensure that it remains fully functional.

Control of inspection, measuring and test equipment

All production equipment including machinery jigs, fixtures, tools, templates, patterns and gauges should always be stored correctly and satisfactorily protected between use to ensure their bias and precision. They should be verified or recalibrated at appropriate intervals. Special attention should be paid to computers if they are used in controlling processes and particularly to the maintenance and accreditation of any related software.

Software

Software used for measuring and monitoring of specified requirements should be validated prior to use.

 Note: also see ISO 10012:1992 *'Quality Assurance Requirements for Measuring Equipment – Metrological confirmation system for measuring equipment'*.

Calibration

Without exception, all measuring instruments can be subject to damage, deterioration or just general wear and tear when they are in regularly use in workshops and factories. The organisation's QMS should take account of this fact and ensure that **all** test equipment is regularly calibrated against a known working standard held by the manufacturer.

Of course, calibrating against a standard is pretty pointless if that particular standard cannot be relied upon and so the 'workshop standard' must also be calibrated, on a regular basis, at either a recognised calibration centre or at the UK Physical Laboratory (or similar) against one of the national standards.

The supplier's QMS will thus have to make allowances for:

- the calibration and adjustment of all inspection, measuring and test equipment that can affect product quality;
- the documentation and maintenance of calibration procedures and records;
- the regular inspection of all measuring or test equipment to ensure that they are capable of the accuracy and precision that is required;
- the environmental conditions being suitable for the calibrations, inspections, measurements and tests to be completed.

The accuracy of the instrument will depend very much on what items it is going to be used to test, the frequency of use of the test instrument, industry standards of acceptability, etc. and the organisation will have to decide on the maximum tolerance of accuracy for each item of test equipment.

Calibration methods

There are various possibilities, such as:

- send all working equipment to an external calibration laboratory;
- send one of each item (i.e. a 'workshop standard') to a calibration laboratory, then sub-calibrate each working item against the workshop standard;
- testing by attributes – i.e. take a known 'faulty' product, and a known 'good' product; and then test each one to ensure that the test equipment can identify the faulty and good product correctly.

Calibration frequency

The calibration frequency depends on how much the instrument is used, its ability to retain its accuracy and how critical the items being tested are. Infrequently used instruments are often only calibrated prior to their use whilst frequently used items would normally be checked and re-calibrated at regular intervals depending, again, on product criticality, cost, availability etc. Normally 12 months is considered as about the maximum calibration interval.

Calibration ideals

- Each instrument should be uniquely identified, allowing it to be traced.
- The calibration results should be clearly indicated on the instrument.
- The calibration results should be retained for reference.
- The instrument should be labelled to show the next 'calibration due' date to easily avoid its use outside of the period of confidence.
- Any means of adjusting the calibration should be sealed, allowing easy identification if it has been tampered with (e.g. a label across the joint of the casing).

• If the instrument is found to be outside of its tolerance of accuracy, any items previously tested with the instrument must be regarded as suspect. In these circumstances, it would be wise to review the test results obtained from the individual instrument. This could be achieved by compensating for the extent of inaccuracy to decide if the acceptability of the item would be reversed.

2.8 Section 8 – Measurement, analysis and improvement

This section absorbs the former inspection and measurement control sections of ISO 9001:1994.

This part of the standard absorbs the former inspection and measurement control sections of ISO 9001:1994. It includes requirements for:

• **General** – defining the requirements for measurement analysis and improvement (including statistical analysis);
• **Monitoring and measurement** – monitoring customer satisfaction/dissatisfaction as a measurement and improvement of the QMS. Conducting periodic internal audits to confirm continued conformity with ISO 9001:2000 and defining processes to monitor the performance of the QMS and the products and services delivered by the organisation;
• **Control of non-conforming product** – controlling non-conformity and its rectification;

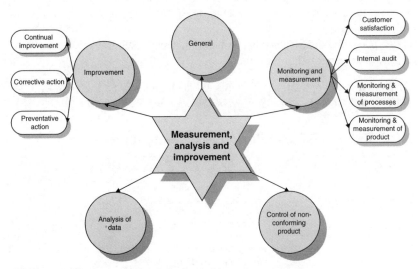

Figure 2.7 Measurement, analysis and improvement

- **Analysis of data** – collecting and analysing statistical data obtained from the organisation's measuring and monitoring activities to find areas of improvement;
- **Improvement** – planning for continual improvement of the QMS, including having available procedures to address corrective and preventive action.

2.8.1 Section 8.1 General

Section 8.1 General	The organisation shall define the activities needed to measure and monitor: <ul><li>product conformity;</li><li>product improvement.</li></ul>
Proof	Documented procedures to ensure product conformity and product improvement.
Likely documentation	Procedures for: <ul><li>product conformity;</li><li>product improvement;</li><li>statistical process review.</li></ul>

Under ISO 9001:2000 the organisation is required to determine and implement procedures to ensure product and QMS conformity and improvement.

The use of statistical techniques can help to understand the variability of a product and in so doing, help organisations to solve problems and improve efficiency. Basically, statistical techniques:

- make better use of available data to assist in decision making;
- help to measure, describe, analyse, interpret and model variability;
- help to provide a better understanding of the nature, extent and causes of variability;
- help to solve and even prevent problems that may result from such variability;
- promote continual improvement.

Details of the application of statistical techniques are given in ISO TR 10017:1999 – *Guidance on Statistical Techniques for ISO 9001:1994.*

2.8.2 Section 8.2 Monitoring and measurement

Section 8.2 Monitoring and measurement	The organisation shall have procedures available to: <ul><li>ensure customer satisfaction;</li><li>control internal audits;</li><li>ensure effective monitoring and measurement of product and processes.</li></ul>
Proof	The analysis of customer satisfaction and the control of products and processes.
Likely documentation	<ul><li>Procedures for inspection and measurement.</li></ul>

To enable an organisation to measure customer satisfaction, evaluate its product and the efficiency of its processes, they need to establish a method to monitor, measure, collect, analyse and record the relevant data using statistical or other appropriate techniques such as:

- customer satisfaction measurement;
- internal audits;
- financial measurements;
- self-assessment methodologies.

Collection of this data should not be purely for the accumulation of information. This process should always be aimed at progressive improvement of the organisation's QMS. The results of this analysis will then be one of the inputs to the management review process.

2.8.2.1 Section 8.2.1 Customer satisfaction

Section 8.2.1 Customer satisfaction	The organisation shall monitor customer satisfaction and/or dissatisfaction.
Proof	The processes used to establish whether a customer is satisfied with a product.
Likely documentation	Procedures for: • customer feedback; • change control; • customer complaints.

The organisation should establish processes to gather, analyse and make effective use of all customer-related information as one of the measurements of performance of their QMS. This information can come from many sources such as:

- customer requirements and contract information;
- feedback from the delivery of a product;
- market needs;
- service delivery data;
- information relating to competition.

The organisation's process should address conformance to requirements, meeting the needs and expectations of customers, price and delivery of product and overall customer satisfaction. Examples of sources of information on customer satisfaction include:

- customer complaints;
- direct communication with customers;
- questionnaires and surveys;
- focus groups;

- reports from consumer organisations;
- reports in various media;
- sector studies.

2.8.2.2 Section 8.2.2 Internal audit

Section 8.2.2 Internal audit	The organisation shall plan and conduct periodic internal audits to determine whether the QMS: • continues to conform to the requirements of ISO 9001:2000; • has been effectively implemented and maintained. The organisation shall plan the audit programme taking into account: • the status and importance of the activities and areas to be audited; • the results of previous audits. The organisation shall have a documented procedure which includes: • the responsibilities and requirements for conducting audits; • the scope, frequency, methodologies used; • the method for recording results and reporting to management.
Proof	The in-house checks made to determine if the QMS is: • functioning properly; • continues to comply with the requirements of ISO 9001:2000.
Likely documentation	• Audit procedures; • audit schedules; • audit plans, check sheets and records.

An organisation should establish an internal audit process to assess the strengths and weaknesses of its QMS, to identify potential danger spots, eliminate wastage and verify that corrective action has been successfully achieved. The internal audit process should also be used to review the efficiency and effectiveness of other organisational activities and support processes including:

- existence of adequate documentation;
- effective implementation of processes;
- identification of non-conformance;
- documentation of results;
- competence of personnel;
- opportunities for improvement;
- capability of processes;

- use of statistical techniques;
- use of information technology;
- analysis of quality cost data;
- assigned responsibilities and authorities;
- performance results and expectations;
- adequacy and accuracy of performance measurement;
- improvement activities;
- relationships with interested parties, including internal customers.

To be effective, an 'internal audit' must be completed by trained personnel and where possible by members of the quality control staff – provided, that is, that they are not responsible for the quality of that particular product and they are **not** associated with the activity being audited. In addition to documenting non-conformances, internal audit reporting should also indicate areas for improvement (with recommendations), as well as areas of outstanding performance.

There are three basic types of audit to choose from:

- **First-party audits** – conducted by, or on behalf of, the organisation itself for internal purposes and can form the basis for an organisation's selfdeclaration of conformity.
- **Second-party audits** – conducted by customers of the organisation or by other persons on behalf of the customer.
- **Third-party audits** – conducted by external independent audit service organisations. Such organisations, usually accredited, provide certification or registration of conformity with requirements such as those of ISO 9001:2000.

It is essential that management shall take timely corrective action on all deficiencies found during the audit. Follow-up actions should include the verification of the implementation of corrective action, and the reporting of verification results.

Financial approach

As part of their overall management system, organisations should establish a methodology for linking financial considerations with the QMS. This could include:

- prevention, appraisal and failure costs analysis;
- costs of conformance and non-conformance;
- life-cycle approach.

Self-assessment

Organisations should consider establishing and implementing a self-assessment process. The range and depth of the assessment should be planned in relation to the organisation's objectives and priorities. Self-assessment can be a very useful tool to evaluate improvement and ISO 9004:2000 helps organisations by providing an annex containing '*Guidelines for self-assessment*'. For the assistance of small businesses, I have also included a section (see Part Seven) on 'self assessment' which includes check sheets against the requirements of ISO 9001:2000 and examples of Stage Audit checklists.

2.8.2.3 Section 8.2.3 Monitoring and measurement of processes

Section 8.2.3 Monitoring and measurement of processes	The organisation shall measure and monitor QMS processes to ensure they: • meet customer requirements; • satisfy their intended purpose.
Proof	The methods used to check if processes continue to meet their intended purpose.
Likely documentation	• Audit schedules, plans, check sheets and records; • processes for product assessment, failure cost analysis, conformity, non-conformity, life cycle approach, self-assessment; • compliance with environmental and safety policies, laws, regulations and standards; • procedures for testing and monitoring processes.

The organisation should identify measurement methodologies, perform measurements to evaluate their process performance and use the results obtained to improve the product realisation process. Examples where process performance measurements can be used to improve processes include:

- timeliness;
- dependability;
- reaction time of processes and people to special internal and external requests;
- cycle time or throughput;
- effectiveness and efficiency of people;
- utilisation of technologies;
- cost reduction.

2.8.2.4 Section 8.2.4 Monitoring and measurement of product

Section 8.2.4 Monitoring and measurement of product	The organisation shall: • monitor and measure the characteristics of a product; • document evidence of conformity with the acceptance criteria; • indicate the authority responsible for release of product; • not release the product until all the specified activities have been satisfactorily completed.
Proof	How an organisation ensures that product characteristics meet customer's specified requirements.
Likely documentation	• Audit schedules; • audit plans, check sheets and records; • approval procedures for product acceptance; • processes for failure cost analysis, conformity, non-conformity, life cycle approach, self-assessment; • compliance with environmental and safety policies, laws, regulations and standards; • procedures for testing and monitoring processes; • performance and product measurement procedures; • supplier approval procedures.

The organisation should establish, specify and plan their measurement requirements (including acceptance criteria) for its products taking into consideration the:

- location of each measurement point in its process sequence;
- characteristics to be measured at each point;
- documentation and acceptance criteria to be used;
- equipment and tools required;
- inspections and tests that need to be witnessed or performed by the customer, statutory and/or regulatory authorities;
- possible requirements for qualified third parties to perform type testing, in-process inspections, product verification and/or product validation;
- necessary qualification requirements of material, product, process, people or the QMS;
- requirements for final inspection;
- outputs of the measurement process of the product;
- conformance to customer, statutory and regulatory requirements.

Typical examples of product measurement records include:

- inspection and test reports;
- material release notices;

- certificates as required;
- electronic data.

To be of any use it is very important that the inspection and test status of a product is immediately clear. The QMS will have to show exactly how this will be achieved (using such methods as markings, stamps, tags, labels, routing cards, inspection records, test software, physical location or other suitable means) to indicate the conformance or non-conformance of the product, and whether it has been inspected and approved, or inspected and rejected.

Production control

To reduce the possibility of manufacturing or design errors causing production line and product delays, the quality status of the product, process, material or environment must be checked at various stages during the production sequence. The use of control charts, statistical sampling procedures and plans are some of the techniques that are used for production and process control.

Product testing

Product testing (i.e. final inspection and testing), are methods of testing whether the product is acceptable or not. These methods have to be developed by the supplier in conjunction with the purchaser and should be included in the suppliers QMS, Quality Manual and/or Quality Plan. These methods would normally contain:

- confirmation that all the relevant inspections and tests have been carried out during manufacture, are fully documented and are recorded in accordance with the Quality Plan or agreed procedure;
- details of the acceptance and rejection criteria that are to be used;
- the measurement and acceptance criteria;
- the quantity to be inspected;
- the sampling plan;
- who is to complete the inspection processes;
- details of the equipment that requires statistical analysis.

Special processes

Occasionally during manufacture, the supplier will be required to perform an inspection on components or activities that cannot normally be verified or inspected at a later stage. The purpose of these inspections is to detect, at an early stage, non-conforming material. If these inspections are required, then the prime contractor will have to establish 'special manufacturing processes' (such as welding, forging, plastic and wood fabrication, heat treatment and the application of protective treatments) and inspection and testing processes (such as temperature and humidity cycling, vibration, radiography, magnetic particle inspection, penetrant inspection, ultrasonic inspection, pressure testing, chemical and spectrographic analysis and salt spray tests).

2.8.3 Section 8.3 Control of non-conforming product

Section 8.3 Control of non-conforming product	The organisation shall define procedures to ensure that: • products which do not conform to requirements are prevented from unintended use or delivery; • non-conforming products that have been corrected are re-verified to demonstrate conformity; • non-conforming products detected after delivery or use are either corrected or removed from service.
Proof	The methods used to prevent the use or delivery of non-conforming products as well as their storage and disposal.
Likely documentation	• Documented procedure to identify and control the use and delivery of non-conforming products. • Approval procedures. • Quarantine procedures. • Change control procedure. • Corrective and preventive action.

Material control and traceability

To ensure that a non-conforming or hazardous product is not delivered by mistake to a customer, the organisation must establish and maintain procedures for identifying the product (from drawings, specifications or other documents), during all stages of production, delivery and installation. This also ensures that all parts of the product are capable of being traced and recalled if necessary.

Control of non-conformity

To cover the possibility of confusing an acceptable quality product with a defective, non-conforming or unacceptable product (and accidentally using this material or despatching it to the purchaser!), all non-conforming articles **must** be clearly identified and kept completely separate from **all** other acceptable (conforming) products. Non-conforming products can then be:

• documented and steps taken to see that they do not occur again;
• reworked so that they meet the specified requirement;
• accepted with or without repair by concession;
• regraded for possible use elsewhere;
• rejected or scrapped.

Since most production processes inevitably yield some kind of defective material, the organisation must investigate methods for preventing this from happening again and arrange for their immediate disposal. The most obvious method of disposing of a non-conforming material is to scrap it. First making sure, of course, that it cannot be confused with any other material or accidentally used again!

Whatever the choice, details about the non-conformance must be fed back into the system so that action (where economically feasible) can be taken to establish and correct the cause of the non-conformance and hopefully prevent its recurrence.

Supplier responsibility

BS 6143–2:1990 'Guide to the Economics of Quality – Prevention, appraisal and failure model' provides detailed information concerning the procedures that should be adopted. In precis form they stipulate that the supplier must:

- investigate the cause of any non-conforming product and have a corrective course of action available to prevent its recurrence;
- analyse all processes, work operations, concessions, quality records, service reports and customer complaints to eliminate the causes of non-conforming products;
- initiate preventive actions;
- change any designs, specifications or work methods that may be unsatisfactory; ensure that the responsibilities for corrective action are clearly assigned to personnel and that these responsibilities are carried out correctly;
- apply controls to ensure that corrective actions are taken and that the existing (as well as the modified) work, methods and designs are effective and suitable;
- implement and record changes in procedures that result from this corrective action.

BS 6143–2:1990 emphasises that this control of quality is not only limited just to the design, manufacture or installation facilities under the supplier's direct control. They also extend to those services, parts, materials or products that are provided by subcontractors. In some circumstances, if a subcontractor's work is found to be unsatisfactory this could mean dispensing with that particular subcontractor and having to find another one. This can, however, cause additional problems such as finding another one capable of supplying the same service and the materials before the lack of those materials (or service) causes product delays.

Permanent changes

If there are any permanent changes resulting from this corrective action, then they should be recorded in work instructions, manufacturing processes, product specifications and in the organisation's QMS. In some cases it might even be necessary to revise the procedures used to detect and eliminate potential problems.

2.8.4 Section 8.4 Analysis of data

Section 8.4 Analysis of data	The organisation shall collect data for the analysis of: • customer satisfaction; • conformance to product requirements; • characteristics and trends (and opportunities) for preventive action.
Proof	The methods used to review data that will determine the effectiveness of the QMS.
Likely documentation	Data or statistics produced as a result of audits, customer satisfaction surveys, complaints, non-conformances, supplier evaluations, etc.

Customers may often require confirmation that the organisation is capable of continuing to produce a quality article or process. One of the methods frequently used to provide this sort of confirmation is statistical analysis. Nowadays there are many methods of statistically analysing whether the product is:

- what the market requires;
- the correct design;
- derived from a reliable specification and one that can be relied upon to last the test of time (i.e. durability);
- subject to the correct process control and capabilities;
- covered by relevant quality standards, specifications and plans.

Statistical analysis

Statistical analysis can also include data analysis, performance testing and defect analysis. Other forms of analysis are design process review and design verification. Statistical analysis is, of course, a subject on its own and vast amounts of information about statistical methods, reliability and maintainability data are readily available. An exceedingly good overview of Statistical Analysis is provided in *Statistical Process Control* by John Oakland and other sources of information such as *Quality and Standards in Electronics* (details of which are provided in the reference section).

With the use of statistical methodologies, the organisation should analyse data in order to assess, control, and improve the performance of processes and products and to identify areas for improvement. Analysis of data can help determine the cause of many problems and the results of this analysis can be used to determine:

- trends;
- operational performance;
- customer satisfaction and dissatisfaction;

- satisfaction level of other interested parties;
- effectiveness and efficiency of the organisation;
- economics of quality and financial and market-related performance;
- benchmarking of performance.

Records

In order that the statistical significance of a failure can be properly assessed and that the correct retrospective action may be taken, it is essential that the design section has access to all the records and other pertinent data failure reports gathered in the design office and on the shop floor.

The storage, maintenance and analysis of reliability data will require the design section to follow the progress of the product throughout its productive life cycle, through its many maintenance cycles and take due note of any customer comments. The compilation and retention of design office reliability data is not only very important, but essential to the reliability of the product and the manufacturing facility.

Storage of records

Storage facilities should be available to ensure that all stored records are identifiable and retrievable and that the storage areas are free from damp and other agents which could cause premature deterioration. If records are maintained on computer magnetic media, then these should be subject to 'back-up' at regular intervals, with the 'back-up' information being stored in a protected location to ensure security from loss or damage of active data. All records are normally retained for a minimum of two years after contract completion.

2.8.5 Section 8.5 Improvement

Section 8.5 Improvement	The organisation shall have procedures available for: • planning for continual improvement; • corrective action; • preventive action.
Proof	How an organisation controls corrective and preventive actions and how they ensure the continual improvement of their product.

Likely documentation	• Documented procedures for:
	  • corrective action;
	  • preventive action;
	  • product/process improvement;
	  • customer complaints/feedback.
	• Non-conformity reports;
	• management reviews;
	• staff suggestions scheme.

The organisation shall plan and manage the processes, policies and objectives that are required for the continual improvement of their QMS as well as their products using audit results, analysis of data, corrective and preventive action and management reviews.

Non-conformity

Once non-conforming items have been recognised, they should be identified by location, associated documents, or specific markings in order to prevent their inadvertent use. All non-conforming items and customer complaints should be subject to review and rectification by nominated personnel. The type and extent of non-conformity needs to be documented in order to establish trends and identify possible areas for improvement.

Corrective action

The corrective action required to prevent recurrence should be evaluated, documented, and its effective implementation monitored. All rectification should subsequently be re-inspected to ensure complete customer satisfaction.

Preventive action

All employees should be encouraged to suggest improvements in methods, materials, suppliers and subcontractors and organisations should have an established procedure for review of all activities in order to identify and evaluate all possible improvements in methods/materials and its procedures.

2.8.5.1 Section 8.5.1 Continual improvement

Section 8.5.1 Continual improvement	The organisation shall plan, manage and ensure the continual improvement of their QMS.
Proof	How an organisation goes about continually improving its QMS.
Likely documentation	<ul><li>Procedures, minutes of meetings (where improvement to the organisation's business is discussed);</li><li>management reviews.</li></ul>

The organisation should continually seek to improve its processes and procedures (rather than just waiting for a problem to come along) and have available documented procedures to identify, manage and improve them. Such actions would include the following:

- defining, measuring and analysing the existing situation;
- establishing the objectives for improvement;
- searching for possible solutions;
- evaluating these solutions;
- implementing the selected solution;
- measuring, verifying, and analysing results of the implementation;
- formalising changes.

2.8.5.2 Section 8.5.2 Corrective action

Section 8.5.2 Corrective action	The organisation shall have documented procedures for: • identifying non-conformities (including customer complaints); • determining the causes of non-conformity; • evaluating the need for action to ensure non-conformities do not recur; • implementing corrective action; • recording results; • reviewing corrective action taken.
Proof	What an organisation does in order to identify and put right non-conformities.
Likely documentation	• Process for eliminating causes of non-conformity; • documented complaints; • complaints procedure; • staff suggestions scheme.

The organisation should plan and establish a process for corrective action, the results of which shall be included in the management review process. The input information for this activity can derive from a number of sources such as:

- customer complaints;
- non-conformance reports;
- outputs from management review;
- internal audit reports;
- outputs from data analysis;
- relevant QMS records;
- outputs from satisfaction measurements;
- process measurements;
- results of self-assessment.

The corrective action process should include:

- a definition of the causes of non-conformances and defects;
- elimination of causes of non-conformances and defects;
- appropriate actions to avoid recurrence of problems;
- a record of the activity and results.

The necessity for corrective action should be evaluated in terms of the potential impact on operating costs, costs of non-conformance, performance, dependability, safety and customer satisfaction.

Concessions and approvals

No matter how much an organisation may pay attention to the control of quality and no matter how hard they try to avoid problems with both manpower and the product, all too often things go wrong. There could, for instance, be a problem in the production shop, an accident could happen, piece-part material could be damaged or a mistake could be made by an engineer when reading a drawing or setting up an electrical or electronic machine. Or the print shop could print the deliverable incorrectly or leave out sections.

In all of these cases there has to be a recognised method of accepting the problem instead of just trying to hide the blunder through either unofficial 'modifications' or, even worse, trying to cover it up! As the saying goes 'honesty is always the best policy' and in any case, 'Murphy's Law' says that more than likely the hidden 'repairs' will be found out and the manufacturer will consequently lose his customer's trust and any chance of follow on orders.

Concession scheme

The machinery for overcoming these problems is called the 'concession scheme'. This will normally consist of a form that has to be completed by the manufacturer/supplier **and** the customer. Details of each document, component, sub assembly, defect or mistake that is identified has to be recorded together with the action that was taken to rectify, scrap, modify or accept the problem.

The Quality Plan will indicate the acceptance or rejection criteria that will be adopted. It will describe compulsory methods that must be taken to mark imperfect or faulty material and indicate how they should be separated from any other material before it is scrapped, reworked or repaired.

If the problem is the result of a faulty design or specification that originated from the purchaser any problems must of course be referred back to them. If the fault is found to be the fault of the purchaser (e.g. unsatisfactory design) the manufacturer/supplier may, of course, be able to insist on having an exgratia payment to overcome the problem. If the problem originated from the manufacturer/supplier, then the purchaser is perfectly within his rights to insist on a reduction in the agreed price.

In cases where a subcontractor requests a concession, then the prime contractor has to carry out a full investigation and agree to the subcontractor's proposal before asking the purchaser to consider the request.

A concession system is a very important part of the supplier/purchaser relationship. It also promotes better discipline within the factory, shows up reoccurring problem areas and ensures that the supplier's standard of workmanship is maintained.

Defects and defect reports

One of the requirements of the QMS is that signatures shall be required from inspectors at each stage of the production to show that the product is of the required standard and assured quality.

When an item fails to meet these criteria, then the inspector must submit a defect report, showing exactly what is defective, how it affects the product and, where possible, what steps can be taken to overcome these failures in future productions.

Bonded store

Owing to the possibility of having unacceptable goods inside their premises, the manufacturer must also set up some kind of 'bonded store' where all incoming material is placed pending inspection.

Even when goods have left the bonded store it is still necessary to have some form of marking (e.g. labels or tags) to distinguish between those awaiting inspection, those inspected and accepted, and those rejected and awaiting return.

2.8.5.3 Section 8.5.3 Preventive action

Section 8.5.3 **Preventive action**	The organisation shall have documented procedures for: <ul><li>*identifying potential non-conformities;*</li><li>*implementing preventive action;*</li><li>*recording and reviewing all preventive action taken.*</li></ul>
Proof	The proactive methods an organisation employs to prevent non-conformities from happening in the first place.
Likely documentation	<ul><li>Process for the prevention of non-conformity;</li><li>complaints procedure;</li><li>staff suggestions scheme.</li></ul>

The organisation should use preventive methodologies such as risk analysis, trend analysis, statistical process control, fault tree analysis, failure modes and effects and criticality analysis to identify the causes of potential non-conformances. Examples of sources are:

- customer needs and expectations;
- market analysis;
- management review output;
- outputs from data analysis;
- satisfaction measurements;
- process measurements;
- systems that consolidate many sources of customer information;
- relevant QMS records;
- results of self-assessment;
- processes that provide early warning of approaching out-of-control operating conditions.

Preventive actions should be considered for inclusion in the management review process.

 Note: Corrective actions are steps that are taken to remove the causes of existing non-conformities, while preventive actions are steps that are taken to remove the causes of potential non-conformities. Corrective actions address actual problems, ones that have already occurred, while preventive actions address potential problems, ones that haven't yet occurred. In general, the corrective action process is a problem solving process, while the preventive action process is a risk analysis process.

Part Two has provided a complete overview and explanation of the various sections and subsections making up ISO 9001:2000.

In Part Three we shall look at some of the benefits of Quality Control and Quality Assurance from the point of view of the manufacturer, supplier, purchaser and/or end user.

Part Three

The Importance of Quality Control and Quality Assurance

In Parts One and Two of this book, the recommendations, background and the various uses of ISO 9001:2000 were explained. In Part Three the reader is introduced to the requirements and benefits of quality control and quality assurance from the point of view of the manufacturer and the supplier as well as the purchaser and/or end user.

The significance and the types of specifications are explained, manufacturer's and purchaser's responsibilities are defined and a thorough review of quality during a product's life cycle enables the reader to appreciate the costs and associated benefits of quality.

 Note: Although I have written Part Three primarily from the point of view of a manufactured product, it is equally applicable for the production of a document, report or any other form of deliverable.

3
Quality control and quality assurance

The international definition of 'Quality' as stated in ISO 9000:2000 is '*the degree to which a set of inherent characteristics fulfils requirements.*'

But what of quality assurance and quality control?

Although the terms 'quality assurance' and 'quality control' are both aimed at ensuring the quality of the end product, they are in fact two completely separate processes.

3.1 Quality control

The definition of quality control (QC) is '*that part of quality management focussed on fulfilling quality requirements*' (ISO 9000:2000). In other words, the operational techniques and activities that are used to fulfil the requirements for quality.

It is the amount of supervision that a product is subjected to so as to be sure that the workmanship associated with that product meets the quality level required by the design. In other words, it is the control exercised by the manufacturer to certify that **all** aspects of their activities during the design, production, installation **and** in-service stages are to the desired standards.

Figure 3.1 Quality control

Quality control is exercised at all levels, and, as all personnel are responsible for the particular task they are doing, they are **all** quality controllers to some degree or other.

Section Leaders or Managers, because of their positions and responsibilities, have more control over their own particular process and therefore have more control over the final quality. It is true, therefore, to say that all personnel are quality controllers and that Section Heads are the Principal Quality Controllers, within their own particular organisation.

3.2 Quality assurance

Quality assurance (QA) is '*that part of quality management focussed on providing confidence that quality requirements are fulfilled*' (ISO 9000:2000). In other words, all those planned and systematic actions necessary to provide adequate confidence that a product or service will satisfy given requirements for quality.

- 'Quality': is fitness for intended use;
- 'Assurance': is a declaration given to inspire confidence in an organisation's capability;
- 'Quality assurance': in a product (or service), by consistently achieving stated objectives is, therefore, a declaration given to inspire confidence that a particular organisation is capable of consistently satisfying need as well as being a managerial process designed to increase confidence.

Quality assurance ensures that a product has achieved the highest standards and that its production, modification or repair (in the case of a manufactured item) has been completed in an efficient and timely manner.

The purpose of quality assurance is, therefore:

- to provide assurance to a customer that the standard of workmanship within a contractor's premises is of the highest level and that all products

Figure 3.2 Quality assurance

leaving that particular firm are above a certain fixed minimum level of specification;
- to ensure that production standards are uniform between divisions/sections and remain constant despite changes in personnel.

In a nutshell, quality assurance is concerned with:

- an agreed level of quality;
- a commitment within a company to the fundamental principle of consistently supplying the right quality product;
- a commitment from a customer to the fundamental principle of only accepting the right quality product;
- a commitment within all levels of (contractor and or customer) to the basic principles of quality assurance and quality control.

The main benefits of quality assurance are:

- an increased capability of supplying a product which consistently conforms to an agreed specification;
- a reduction in manufacturing and production costs because of less wastage and fewer rejects;
- a greater involvement and motivation within an organisation's workforce;
- an improved customer relationship through fewer complaints, thus providing increased sales potential.

3.3 Specifications

Without proper specifications it is impossible to expect a manufacturer or supplier to produce an article, equipment or system that completely satisfies the purchaser's requirements. Equally, if the manufacturer and/or supplier does not work within laid down specifications they will be unable to produce something that comes up to the purchaser's required standard.

If a manufacturer does not meet required specifications, then the part, equipment or system will not work as expected or the components will be the wrong dimensions and not fit properly etc. Worst of all, the article will not be exactly what the purchaser wanted.

The importance of specifications is, therefore, very much the responsibility of the purchaser **as well as** the manufacturer/supplier.

3.3.1 The significance of specifications

Specifications always form the basis of a contract and as such they need to be a comprehensive and precise description of exactly what the purchaser requires. The document must, therefore, avoid ambiguous words, mixed systems of units (e.g. metric and imperial) and, in particular, avoid over specification such as listing extremely close tolerances with respect to dimensions, colour, surface finishes and/or performance which are liable to increase the cost of the product unnecessarily.

Specifications can be very simple and just covered by a few words, or they can be extremely rigid and run into many volumes. It all depends on the size of the assignment and the level of accuracy that the purchaser requires.

3.3.2 Types of specification

There are three main ways in which the purchaser's requirements can be specified: general specifications, overall performance specifications and standard specifications. Although slightly different in content, each of these specifications closely examines the procedures used by the manufacturer.

3.3.2.1 General specification

A general specification requires the purchaser to produce a detailed written description of the article, its construction, the materials to be used and the level

Figure 3.3 Types of specification

of performance that it is required to provide. It is usually written by a member of the design team and then passed to an experienced engineer (independent of that particular design team) for final vetting and approval.

To avoid any problems later on, specifications must always guard against using such words as 'suitable', 'appropriate' or 'conventional'. In a similar manner, inclusion of 'possible alternatives' and 'by agreement' clauses should also be avoided.

If in-house specifications are produced in quantity, it is essential that any amended specification is published and immediately issued to all concerned. To make life simpler and avoid future problems, it is equally important that these amendments are numbered, dated and the recipients are made to destroy all previous copies and issues.

3.3.2.2 Overall performance specification

An overall performance specification tells the manufacturer in comprehensive terms exactly what the purchaser is looking for. The obvious disadvantage of this method is that it leaves the design of the product completely up to the manufacturer. This can often lead to arguments later on especially when the purchaser realises that the product is either too big, too small, the wrong shape, not up to (or exceeding) his engineering requirements and, as frequently happens, is far more expensive than the purchaser really intended.

3.3.2.3 Standard specification

A standard specification is a list that describes, **in detail**, the items or materials that are to be used in the manufacture of the product.

Obviously, without any real experience it would take a purchaser a long time to compile such a list or even be able to express – in technical terms – exactly what he wants. To overcome these problems, National Standards Organisations (NSOs) publish lists of all the materials and sub assemblies commonly used by manufacturers.

In the United Kingdom (UK) the British Standards Institution (BSI) have produced these lists in the BS 9000 series (**not** to be confused with ISO 9000!). In Europe they are made available by the CENELEC Electronic Components Committee (CECC) and internationally by the Quality Assessment System for Electronic Components (IECQ).

3.3.3 Manufacturer's responsibilities

The manufacturer's prime responsibility must always be to ensure that anything **and everything** leaving their factory conforms to the specific requirements of the purchaser – particularly with regard to quality.

The simplest way of doing this is for the manufacturer to ensure that their particular office, production facility or manufacturing outlet fully complies

Figure 3.4 Manufacturer's responsibilities

with the requirements of the quality standards adopted by the country in which they are manufacturing and the country to whom they intend supplying the component, equipment or system.

To do this they must of course first be aware of the standards applicable to that country, know how to obtain copies of these standards, how to adapt them to their own particular environment and how to get them accepted by the relevant authorities.

Although an organisation can set out to abide by accepted standards, unless they achieve this aim they will fail in their attempt to become a recognised manufacturer of quality goods. The main points that they should note are:

- that all managerial staff, from the most junior to the most senior, must firmly believe in the importance of quality control and quality assurance and understand how to implement them;
- that managerial staff **must** create an atmosphere in which quality assurance rules are obeyed and not simply avoided just because they are inconvenient, time consuming, laborious or just too boring to bother with;
- that there has to be an accepted training scheme to ensure that all members of the firm are regularly brought up to date with the ongoing and the latest requirements of quality assurance;

- that there must be a quality assurance team available to oversee and make sure that quality control and quality assurance are carried out at all times and **at all levels**, within their premises.

In addition, the manufacturer will have to provide proof that they are supplying a quality product. This is actually a 'measurement of their quality control' and usually takes the form of a supplier's evaluation, surveillance and/or audit.

National and international QMSs will also require the manufacturer to establish and maintain a fully documented method for the inspection of their system for quality control. Procedures must be developed and identified for classifying lots, cataloguing characteristics, selecting samples and rules for acceptance and/or rejection criteria, together with procedures for segregating and screening rejected lots.

3.3.4 Purchaser's responsibilities

Quite a number of problems associated with a product's quality are usually the fault of the purchaser! Obviously the purchaser can only expect to get what he ordered. It is, therefore, extremely important that the actual order is not only correct, but also provides the manufacturer with all the relevant (and accurate) information required to complete the task.

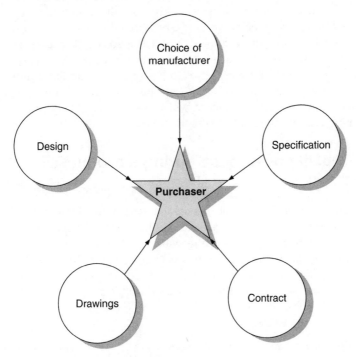

Figure 3.5 Purchaser's responsibilities

There is little point in trying to blame the manufacturer when an article doesn't come up to expectation because of an unsatisfactory design provided by the purchaser. In certain cases (for example when the requirements of the item cannot easily be described in words), it could be very helpful if the purchaser was to provide a drawing as a form of graphic order. In such cases, this drawing should contain all the relevant details such as type of material to be used, the material's grade or condition, the specifications that are to be followed and, where possible, the graphic order/drawing should be to scale.

If this approach proves impractical, then the order would have to include all the relevant dimensional data, sizes, tolerances etc., or refer to one of the accepted standards.

Having said all that, it must be appreciated that the actual specification being used is also very important for it sets the level of quality required and, therefore, directly affects the price of the article. Clearly, if specifications are too demanding then the final cost of the article will be too high. If specifications are too vague or obscure, then the manufacturer will have difficulty in assembling the object or may even be unable to get it to work correctly.

The choice of manufacturer is equally important. It is an unfortunate fact of life that purchasers usually consider that the price of the article is the prime and (in some cases), even the only consideration. Buying cheaply is obviously **not** the answer because if a purchaser accepts the lowest offer all too often he will find that delivery times are lengthened (because the manufacturer can make more profit on other orders), the article produced does not satisfy his requirements and worst of all, the quality of the article is so poor that he has to replace the device well before its anticipated life cycle has been completed.

If a manufacturer has received official recognition that the quality of his work is up to a particular standard, then the purchaser has a reasonable guarantee that the article being produced will be of a reasonable quality – always assuming that the initial order was correct!

3.4 Quality assurance during a product's life cycle

As shown in Figure 3.6, the life of a product is made up of five stages. Each of these stages has specific requirements that need to be correctly managed and which need to be regulated by quality controls.

As quality assurance affects the product throughout its life cycle, it is important that quality assurance procedures are introduced for design, manufacturing and acceptance stages, as well as in service utilisation.

3.4.1 Design stage

'Quality must be designed into a product before manufacture or assembly' (ISO 9004:2000).

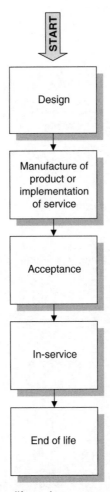

Figure 3.6 Quality assurance life cycle

Throughout the design stage of a product or service, the quality of that design must be regularly checked. Quality procedures have to be planned, written and implemented so as to predict and evaluate the fundamental and intrinsic reliability of the proposed design.

It doesn't matter whether the responsibility for the design of a product rests purely with the supplier, the purchaser, or is a joint function. It is essential that the designer is fully aware of the exact requirements of the project and has a sound background knowledge of the relevant standards, information and procedures that will have to be adopted during the design stages.

This is extremely important, because the actions of the design office will not only influence the maintenance of quality during manufacture, but also play a

Figure 3.7 Quality assurance during a product's life cycle

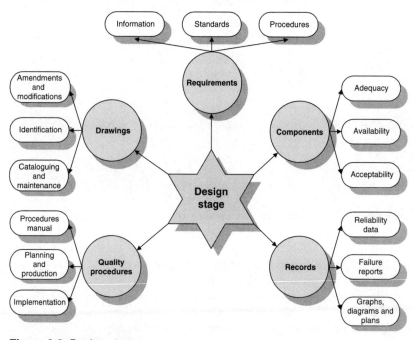

Figure 3.8 Design stage

major part in setting the quality level of the eventual product. If there is no quality control in the drawing office, there is little chance of there ever being any on the shop floor. When the engineers are trying to manufacture something (or a technician is attempting to assemble a system or module) to a set of drawings that have countless mistakes on them, what chance is there of them ever being able to produce an acceptable item!

These problems, although not specifically stipulated in ISO 9001:2000 should, nevertheless be addressed. The design office (or team) should produce some sort of 'Procedures Manual' which lists and describes the routine procedures that are required to turn a concept into a set of functional drawings.

These procedures will cover such activities as the numbering of drawings, authorisation to issue amendments and modifications, how to control changes to drawings, the method of withdrawing obsolete drawings and the identification, cataloguing and maintenance of drawings.

In addition to these procedures, the design office will also have to provide a complete listing of all the relevant components, availability, acceptability and adequacy and be aware of all the advances in both materials and equipment that are currently available on today's market which are relevant to the product.

It is imperative that the design team maintains a close relationship with the manufacturing division throughout these initial stages so as to be aware of their exact requirements, their problems, their choice of components etc., assist in the analysis of failures, swiftly produce solutions and forestall costly work stoppages. One of the main problems to overcome is the ease with which the design office can make an arbitrary selection, but then find that the size and tolerance is completely inappropriate for the manufacturing or assembly process.

In order that the statistical significance of a particular failure can be assessed and correct retroactive action taken, it is essential that the design team has access to all the records, failure reports and other data as soon as it is available within the design office or shop floor.

The storage, maintenance and analysis of reliability data will require the design team to follow the progress of the product throughout its productive life cycle, its many maintenance cycles and to take due note of customers' comments.

The compilation and retention of design office reliability data is not only very important, but also essential to the reliability of the product and the manufacturing facility.

Nowadays, of course, most large design offices are computerised and use processors to store their records on discs so that these records can be continually updated and amended. This information (data) can then be used with standard software such as Computer Aided Design (CAD) programs and computer aided design facilities to produce lists, graphs and drawings. The possibilities are almost endless but there are associated problems such as security against virus attack and computer crashes.

3.4.2 Manufacturing stage

'Manufacturing operations must be carried out under controlled conditions' (ISO 9004:2000).

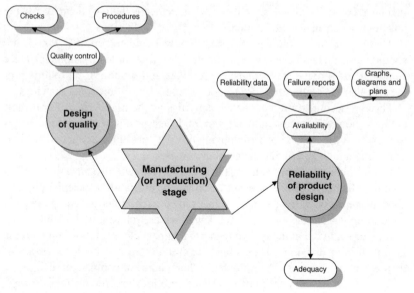

Figure 3.9 Manufacturing stage

During all manufacturing processes (and throughout early in-service life), the product must be subjected to a variety of quality control procedures and checks in order to evaluate the degree of quality.

One of the first things that must be done is to predict the reliability of the product's design. This involves obtaining sufficient statistical data so as to be able to estimate the actual reliability of the design before a product is manufactured.

All the appropriate engineering data has to be carefully examined, particularly the reliability ratings of recommended parts and components. The designer then extrapolates and interpolates this data and uses probability methods to examine the reliability of a proposed design.

Design deficiencies such as assembly errors, operator learning, motivational or fatigue factors, latent defects and improper part selection are frequently uncovered during this process.

3.4.3 Acceptance stage

'The Quality of a product must be proved before being accepted' (ISO 9004:2000).

'The outputs of design and development shall be provided in a form that enables verification against the design and development input and shall be approved prior to release' (ISO 9001:2000 clause 7.3.3).

During the acceptance stage, the product is subjected to a series of tests designed to confirm that the workmanship of the product fully meets the levels

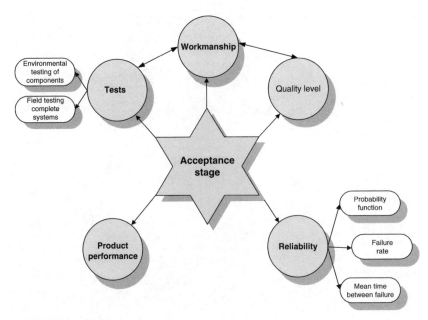

Figure 3.10 Acceptance stage

of quality required, or stipulated by the user and that the product performs the required function correctly. Tests will range from environmental tests of individual components to field testing complete systems.

Three mathematical expressions are commonly used to measure reliability and each of these expressions can be applied to a part, component assembly or an entire system. They are, Probability Function (PF), Failure Rate (FR) and Mean Time Between Failures (MTBF).

3.4.4 In-service stage

'Evaluation of product performance during typical operating conditions and feedback of information gained through field use improves product capability' (ISO 9004:2000).

During the in-service stage the equipment user is, of course, principally concerned with system and equipment reliability.

Although reliability is based on the product's generic design (and can be easily proved by statistics), its practical reliability is often far less design dependent. This difference can be due to poor or faulty operating procedures, operating the system beyond its design capability or operational abuses (e.g. personal, extended duty cycles, neglected maintenance, training etc.). Each of these hazards can damage individual components and sub assemblies and each will, in turn, reduce the product's dependability.

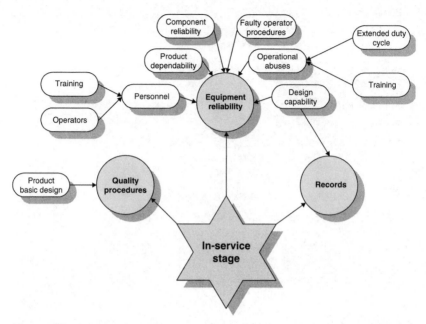

Figure 3.11 In-service stage

It is interesting to note that according to studies completed by the British Chartered Management Institute at the turn of the century, the maintenance technician (or engineer) still remains the primary cause of reliability degradations during the in-service stage. The problems associated with poorly trained, poorly supported, or poorly motivated maintenance personnel with respect to reliability and dependability requires careful assessment and quantification.

The most important factor that affects the overall reliability of a modern product, nevertheless, is the increased number of individual components that are required in that product. Since most system failures are actually caused by the failure of a single component, the reliability of each individual component must be considerably better than the overall system reliability.

Information obtained from in-service use and field failures are enormously useful (always assuming that they are entirely accurate, of course!) in evaluating a product's performance during typical operating conditions. But the ain reason for accumulating failure reports from the field is to try to improve the product. This can be achieved by analysing the reports, finding out what caused the failure and taking steps to prevent it from recurring in the future.

Because of this requirement, quality standards for the maintenance, repair and inspection of in-service products have had to be laid down in engineering standards, handbooks and local operating manuals (written for specific items and equipment). These publications are used by maintenance engineers and should always include the most recent amendments. It is **essential** that quality assurance personnel also use the same procedures for their inspections.

3.5 Benefits and costs of quality assurance

'An effective QMS should be designed to satisfy the purchaser's conditions, requirements and expectations whilst serving to protect the manufacturer's best interests' (ISO 9004:2000).

In practice, some quality assurance programmes can be very expensive to install and operate, particularly if inadequate quality control methods were used previously. If the purchaser requires consistent quality he must pay for it, regardless of the specification or order which the manufacturer has accepted. However, against this expenditure must always be offset the savings in scrapped material, rework and general problems arising from lack of quality.

From a manufacturer's point of view there is a business requirement to obtain and maintain the desired quality at an optimum cost. The following represent some of the additional expenses that can be incurred:

- salaries for the quality assurance team, planners, quality supervisors, calibration/test equipment staff and Quality Managers;
- training for the quality assurance team;
- visits by the quality assurance staff to other companies, subcontractors and the eventual consumer, for evaluation and audit of their facilities and products;
- test equipment of a recognised type, standard and quality; regularly maintained and calibrated by an accredited calibration centre;
- better storage facilities.

But why bother with 'quality assurance'?! It is all very expensive to set up and extremely expensive to run – is it really worth it?!

The short answer is, '**yes**'.

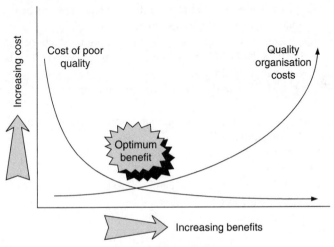

Figure 3.12 Quality Management System costs

In order to be part of this enormous European and world market, manufacturers, suppliers **and** sole traders must not merely be aware of the requirements and need for quality assurance, they must also be able to prove that they are capable of constantly producing a quality product that is as good as, if not better, than any others available.

Hopefully they will take pride in producing an item of equipment or system that operates correctly and which will fully satisfy the purchaser – as opposed to something that goes wrong as soon as it is switched on. There will not be many reorders for that model!

Insisting on an assurance of quality has got to save money in the long run. It ensures that manufacturing design features are more dependable and efficient, and built-in quality at every stage will obviously reduce wastage and increase customer satisfaction.

3.6 Costs of quality failure

With an effective QMS in place, the manufacturer will achieve increased profitability and market share and the purchaser can expect reduced costs, improved product fitness for role, increased satisfaction and, above all, growth in confidence.

3.6.1 The manufacturer

Lack of quality control and quality assurance can cause the manufacturer to:

- replace scrapped material or have to rework unsatisfactory material;
- re-inspect and reprocess material returned as unsatisfactory by the purchaser;
- lose money by having to send staff to the purchasers premises to sort out their complaints of unsatisfactory labour;
- lose money through a major quality failure halting production;
- lose money through field repairs, replacements and other work having to be carried out under warranty;
- lose money by having to carry out investigations into claims of unsatisfactory work;
- lose money by having to investigate alternative methods of producing an article without quality failures;
- lose their image and reputation;
- lose market potential;
- have to acknowledge complaints, claims, liabilities and be subject to waste of human and financial resources;

But most of all …

- lose customers!

3.6.2 The purchaser

By not insisting that the manufacturer abides by a set of recognised quality standards, the purchaser can be involved in:

- delays in being able to use the product and the possibility of the purchaser losing orders because of it;
- possible increases in their organisation, operation, maintenance downtime and repair costs;
- dissatisfaction with goods and services;
- health and safety aspects (now a mandatory requirement of ISO 9001:2000);
- lack of confidence in the manufacturer.

So far we have detailed some of the requirements and benefits of quality control and quality assurance from the point of view of the manufacturer, supplier, purchaser and the end user. Terms have been explained and specifications defined.

Having discussed the pros and cons of an efficient quality system, in Part Four we will see how by adopting a properly structured Quality Management System we can meet these requirements.

Part Four

Quality Management System

In Part Four, the basic requirements of a Quality Management System are discussed and the reader is shown how an organisation's Quality Management System becomes the documented proof of a firm's commitment to quality management. The reader is shown how a Quality Management System can be structured to an organisation's particular type of business and how a Quality Management System will cover such functions as customer liaison, design, purchase, subcontracting, manufacturing, training and installation.

4
Quality Management System

4.1 Quality Management System – requirements

'A Quality Management System is a management system to direct and control an organisation with regard to quality.' (ISO 9000:2000).

It is an organisational structure of responsibilities, activities, resources and events that together provide procedures and methods of implementation to ensure the capability of an organisation to meet quality requirements.

Figure 4.1 Quality Management System

Having seen in Part Three the advantages and benefits of quality control and quality assurance, what about the Quality Management System (QMS) that needs to be set up so as to adapt and instigate these procedures?

4.1.1 Basic requirements of a Quality Management System

To be successful, an organisation, large and small, must:

- be able to offer services that satisfy a customer's expectations;
- agree with the relevant standards and specifications of a contract;
- be available at competitive prices; **and**
- supply at a cost that will still bring a profit to that organisation.

They must, above all, provide a quality product that will promote further procurement and recommendations.

So how can your organisation become a quality organisation? Well, I can assure you that it is not just a case of simply claiming that you are a reliable organisation and then telling everyone that you will be able to supply a reliable product or service! Nowadays, especially in the European and American markets, purchasers are demanding proof of these claims. Proof that you are the organisation that **they** should be dealing with.

How can anyone supply this proof? Well, up until the end of 1994 the standard that was most often called up in UK contracts was BS 5750:1987. Within the Single European Market, tenders required the equivalent European Union (EU) standard EN 29000:1987 or the equivalent International standard (ISO 9000:1987). In America these are included in the ASQC Q90 series.

Nowadays, of course, these requirements are covered under the common ISO 9001:2000 and ISO 9004:2000 standards (see Part One). These standards provided the requirements and guidelines for organisations wishing to establish their own QMS and in doing so control the quality of their organisation – from within their organisation.

You may also find that some contracts stipulate that the product '*must comply with the requirements of (such and such) a standard*' (for example, for a British component manufacturer it might be BS 3934:1992 'Mechanical standardisation of semiconductor devices', or ANSI A137-1:1988 'Ceramic Tiles').

But perhaps we are moving on too fast. Before an organisation is even **qualified** to tender for a contract to produce something, they must first **prove** their organisation capability by showing that they can operate a Quality Management System.

To satisfy these requirements an organisation's QMS has to encompass all the different levels of quality control that are required during the various stages of design, manufacture and acceptance of a product and be capable of guaranteeing quality acceptance.

Figure 4.2 Quality Management System – organisational structure

These requirements are covered by national, European and international standards. But although these standards may vary slightly from country to country, basically they are very similar and cover the following topics:

- organisational structure;
- measurement of quality assurance;
- the contract;
- design control;
- purchasing and procurement;
- production control;
- product testing;
- handling, storage, packaging and delivery;
- after sales service.

4.2 Quality Management System principles

The first thing that ISO 9000 requires is for an organisation to set up and fully document their position with regard to quality assurance. These documents comprise the organisation's QMS and describe their capability for supplying goods and services that will comply with laid down quality standards. It contains a general description of the organisation's attitude to quality assurance and specific details about the quality assurance and quality control from within that organisation.

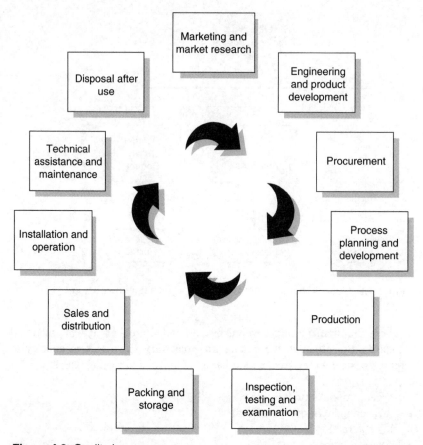

Figure 4.3 Quality loop

To be successful an organisation must be able to prove that they are capable of producing the component, product or service to the customer's complete satisfaction so that it conforms exactly to the purchaser's specific requirements and that it is always of the desired quality.

An organisation's QMS is, therefore, the organisational structure of responsibilities, procedures, processes and resources for carrying out quality management and as such must be planned and developed in order to be capable of maintaining a consistent level of quality control.

The QMS must be structured to the organisation's own particular type of business and should consider all functions such as customer liaison, designing, purchasing, subcontracting, manufacturing, training, installation, updating of quality control techniques and the accumulation of quality records. In most organisations this sort of information will normally be found in the organisation Quality Manual.

The type of QMS chosen will, of course, vary from organisation to organisation depending upon its size and capability. There are no set rules as to exactly

Figure 4.4 Some of the determinants and measurements of the quality of a service. (Figures 4.4 and 4.5 are extracts from BS 4778:1979 which have been reproduced with the kind permission of BSI. Although the 1979 edition has been superseded these figures are included here since they illustrate the concept.)

how these documents should be written. However, they should – as a minimum requirement – be capable of showing the potential customer exactly how the manufacturer or supplier is equipped to achieve and maintain the highest level of quality throughout the various stages of design, production, installation and servicing.

As an example, some of the determinants and measures of the quality of a service are shown in Figure 4.4 whilst those effecting the quality of a product are shown in Figure 4.5.

4.3 Quality Management System approach

Customers require products that continually meet their needs and expectations and in order to be profitable, an organisation must be able to offer products that continually achieve customer satisfaction and satisfy their customers' requirements. As well as providing a framework for providing customer satisfaction, a QMS also provides confidence (to the organisation and to its customers) that the organisation is capable of providing products that consistently fulfil

Figure 4.5 Some of the determinants and measurements of the quality of a product

requirements. This is achieved by:

- determining the needs and expectations of the customer;
- establishing the quality policy and quality objectives of the organisation;
- determining the processes and responsibilities necessary to attain the quality objectives;
- establishing measures for the effectiveness of each process towards attaining the quality objectives;
- applying the measures to determine the current effectiveness of each process;
- determining means of preventing non-conformities and eliminating their causes;
- looking for opportunities to improve the effectiveness and efficiency of processes;
- determining and prioritising those improvements which can provide optimum results;

- planning the strategies, processes and resources to deliver the identified improvements;
- implementing the plan;
- monitoring the effects of the improvements;
- assessing the results against the expected outcomes;
- reviewing the improvement activities to determine appropriate follow-up actions.

Any organisation that adopts the above approach will create confidence in the capability of its processes and the reliability of its products. It will also provide a basis for continual improvement and can lead to increased customer satisfaction.

4.3.1 What is a quality system?

In terms of the ISO standard, 'quality system' and 'Quality Management System' mean one and the same thing. A 'quality system', however, is neither a manual (i.e. a document) nor a computer program (which is an information system as opposed to being a real quality system), it is a system that contains all the things that are used to regulate, control, and improve the quality of your products and/or services. It is a network of interrelated processes with each process being made up of people, work, activities, tasks, records, documents, forms, resources, rules, regulations, reports, materials, supplies, tools, equipment etc. that are required to transform inputs into outputs.

4.3.2 What is the difference between a quality manual and a quality system?

Basically, a quality manual is all about paperwork and is just a document whereas a quality system is about a network of processes. Your quality manual is **not** supposed to be your system, it merely documents your quality system.

4.4 Quality Management System structure

An organisation's QMS defines the policy, organisation and responsibilities for the management of quality within that organisation.

   It ensures that all activities comply with an agreed set of rules, regulations and guidelines and that the end product (i.e. the deliverable) conforms to the customer's (i.e. the user's) contractual requirements.

Figure 4.6 ISO 9001:2000 Quality Management System structure

4.4.1 QMS documentation

'A QMS can only be effective if it is fully documented, understood and followed by all' (ISO 9000:2000).

Within the ISO 9001:2000 quality model, there are four levels of documentation and these are structured as shown in Figure 4.6 above.

When trying to work out which processes should be documented, the organisation may wish to consider factors such as:

- effect on quality;
- risk of customer dissatisfaction;
- statutory and/or regulatory requirements;
- economic risk;
- competence of personnel;
- complexity of processes.

Where it is found necessary to document processes, a number of different methods (such as graphical representations, written instructions, checklists, flow charts, visual media, or electronic methods) can be used.

Table 4.1 QMS documentation

Level 1	Quality Manual	The main policy document that establishes the QMS and how it meets the requirements of ISO 9001:2000.
Level 2	Processes	The Core Business Process plus Supporting Processes that describe the activities required to implement the QMS and to meet the policy requirements made in the Quality Manual.
Level 3	Quality Procedures	A description of the method by which quality system activities are managed.
Level 4	Work Instructions	A description of how a specific task is carried out.

4.5 Quality Manual

The Quality Manual is at the very heart of an organisation's Quality Management System and describes the interrelationships between:

- **A Process** – an outline of its objective, scope and key performance indicators;
- **Quality Procedures** – an enlargement of the process explaining how it is controlled;
- **Work Instructions** – the 'fine print' required to perform a specific activity.

It is the main policy document that establishes the QMS and how it meets the requirements of ISO 9001:2000. It provides general information on the system (i.e. objectives, goals, roles, organisation and responsibilities).

The Quality Manual (see example in Part Six) is the formal record of that organisation's QMS. It:

- is a rule book by which an organisation functions;
- is a source of information from which the client may derive confidence;
- provides consistent information, both internally and externally, about the organisation's QMS;
- is a means of defining the responsibilities and inter-related activities of every member of the organisation;
- is a vehicle for auditing, reviewing and evaluating the organisation's QMS.

To be effective, the Quality Manual:

- will have to include a firm statement of the organisation's policy towards quality control;

Figure 4.7 Quality Manual

- must contain details of their quality assurance section, its structure and organisation, together with a description of their responsibilities;
- must indicate quality assurance training programmes etc.

The Quality Manual will describe how the organisation:

- documents and records inspections;
- how their goods inwards facility operates;
- how they monitor quality.

The Quality Manual will identify the organisation's business-critical processes and their associated Quality Procedures (QPs) and Work Instructions (WIs). The Quality Manual will also provide examples of the various forms and documentation used by the manufacturer – such as production control forms, inspection sheets and documents used to purchase components from subcontractors.

For a complete description and guidance on how to develop a Quality Manual, the reader is referred to ISO 10013 – Guidelines for developing Quality Manuals.

4.6 Processes

Processes describe the activities required to implement the QMS and to meet the policy requirements set out in the Quality Manual.

Typically, the organisational processes making up a company's QMS will normally comprise a Core Business Process supplemented by a number of supporting processes which describe the infrastructure required to produce the contract deliverable (or market opportunity) on time and within budget. These processes consist of:

Table 4.2 Core Business and supporting processes

Core Business process	Which describes the end-to-end activities involved in producing a contract deliverable or marketing opportunity. It commences with the definition of corporate policy and ends when the product is manufactured and marketed. The Core Business Process is then supplemented by a number of supporting processes that describe the infrastructure required to manufacture (or supply) the product on time.
	Note: All businesses revolve around taking inputs and putting them through a series of activities that turn them into useful outputs, be that a product or service. These activities are the supporting processes.
Primary supporting processes	The basic set of activities which, when combined into a logical sequence, takes you from receipt of an order (or marketing opportunity) through to the realisation of the finished product or service.
Secondary supporting processes	The purpose of secondary supporting processes is to document those activities that are essential for supporting and achieving the primary supporting processes. Secondary supporting processes will have an identical structure to the primary supporting processes, and will also have their own associated supporting documentation [e.g. Quality Procedures (QPs) and Work Instructions (WIs)]. Secondary supporting processes may include such things as: • identification and provision of suitable staff; • management and support of staff; • identification and provision of information; • identification and provision of materials; • identification and provision of equipment and facilities; • management of the QMS; • continual improvement.

 Note: A process owner with full responsibility and authority for managing the process and achieving process objectives should be nominated.

For each process there will be an organisation document detailing:

- **Objective** – what the process aims to achieve;
- **Scope** – what the process covers;
- **Responsible owner** – who is ultimately responsible for implementing the process;
- **Policy** – what the organisation intends doing to ensure quality is controlled;
- **Key performance indicators** – those items of objective evidence that can be used as a way of monitoring performance of the process;
- **Cross reference** to supporting system documentation (QPs and WIs).

All processes should be documented to give a complete picture of how to perform the activity to a consistent level of quality. The level of detail varies from:

- **Process** – an outline of its objective, scope and key performance indicators;
- **Quality Procedures** – an enlargement of the process explaining how it is controlled;
- **Work Instructions** – the 'fine print' required to perform a specific activity.

4.7 Quality Procedures

QPs are formal documents that describe the method by which the Core Business and supporting processes are managed. They describe how the policy objectives of the Quality Manual can be met in practice and how these processes are controlled. They contain the basic documentation used for planning and controlling all activities that impact on quality.

There are two types of procedures namely:

- system level procedures that are used to detail the activities needed to implement the QMS;
- procedures that describe the sequence of processes necessary to ensure the conformity of a product or service.

4.7.1 What documented procedures are required by ISO 9001:2000?

In section 4.2.2 of ISO 9001:2000, the standard requires the organisation to: *'establish and maintain a quality manual that includes the documented procedures established for the quality management system'*.

There is no restriction about how many of these documented procedures an organisation should have to cover, ISO 9001:2000 does, however, contain a mandatory requirement for formal documented procedures to be produced for the:

1. Control of documents (4.2.3);
2. Control of quality records (4.2.4);

3. Internal audits (8.2.2);
4. Control of non-conforming products (8.3);
5. Corrective actions (8.5.2);
6. Preventative actions (8.5.3).

 Note: Where the term 'documented procedure' appears within this International Standard, this means that *the procedure has to be established, documented, implemented and maintained.*

By implication documented procedures should also be included for:

1. Customer Communications (7.2.3)
   (which states: *'The organisation shall determine and implement effective arrangements for communication with customers'*).

2. Purchasing process (7.4.1)
   (which states: *'Criteria for selection, evaluation and re-evaluation shall be established'*).

 Note: Procedures can take any suitable form. They can be a narrative, a flow chart, a process map, or indeed any other suitable structure. As long as the procedure is effective, it really doesn't matter what it looks like.

4.8 Work Instructions

WIs describe in detail how individual tasks and activities are to be carried out, e.g. what is to be done, by whom and when it has to be completed.
Work Instructions describe:

- the physical operating practices and controls within each process;
- in detail, how individual tasks and activities are to be carried out.

In other words what is to be done, by whom and when.
They provide examples of the various forms and documentation used by the manufacturer or supplier. For instance:

- production control forms;
- inspection sheets;
- documents used to purchase components from subcontractors.

 Note: Work Instructions, similar to the remainder of the QMS documentation, can take any appropriate form. However, one of the best ways to document a work instruction is probably to use a flow chart associated with a form which can then become a record once they are filled in.

4.8.1 What is the difference between a Work Instruction and a record?

Work Instructions describe how tasks should be done and are used before the task is performed. Records document how tasks were actually done and are used after the task has been performed. Work Instructions come before the fact, while records come after the fact.

4.9 Quality Plan

When complex assemblies or multi-part contracts are required, separate instructions may have to be included in the Quality Manual in order to cover individual parts of the contract. These types of instructions are called Quality Plans.

The accepted definition (as provided in ISO 9000:2000) of a Quality Plan is that it is '… *a document specifying which procedures and associated resources shall be applied, by whom and when to a specific project, product, process or contract*'. In setting out the specific quality practices, resources and sequence of activities a Quality Plan, therefore, ensures that specific requirements for quality are appropriately planned and addressed. It should state its purpose, to

Figure 4.8 Quality Plan

what it applies its quality objectives (in measurable terms), specific exclusions and, of course, its period of validity.

Quality Plans describe how the QMS is applied to a specific product or contract. They may be used to demonstrate how the quality requirements of a particular contract will be met, and to monitor and assess adherence to those requirements. While a Quality Plan usually refers to the appropriate parts of the Quality Manual, it can be used in conjunction with a QMS or as a stand-alone document.

Quality Plans provide a collated summary of the requirements for a specific activity. They include less information than the organisation's QMS but, with all the detail brought together, the requirement for performance should be more readily understandable and the risk of non-conformance and misinterpretation of intentions should be reduced.

Quality assurance for the manufacture of complex assemblies can be very difficult to stipulate in a contract especially if the most important inspections have to be left until the assembly is almost complete – and by which time many of the sub assemblies and components will have become almost inaccessible! In these cases it is essential for the organisation's Quality Manager to develop and produce a Quality Plan that details all the important information that has to be provided to the shop floor management.

The Quality Plan will cover all of the quality practices and resources that are going to be used, the sequence of events relevant to that product, the specific allocation of responsibilities, methods, QPs and WIs, together with the details of the testing, inspection, examination and audit programme stages.

The Quality Plan should, nevertheless, be flexible and written in such a way that it is possible to modify its content to reflect changing circumstances.

At all work places, QPs and WIs must be readily available. These will include the specifications that must be obeyed, particulars of the drawings, documentation, tools and gauges that are going to be used, the sampling method, the tests which have to be made, the test specifications and procedures, the acceptance/rejection criteria – and so on.

The main requirement of a Quality Plan, however, is to provide the customer (and the workforce) with clear, concise instructions and guidance as well as the appropriate inspection methods and procedures; the results of inspections (including rejections) and details of any concessions issued for rework or repair. All these must be clearly recorded and available for a purchaser's future (possible) examination.

A well thought out Quality Plan will divide the project, service, product or assembly work into stages, show what type of inspection has to be completed at the beginning, during, or end of each stage and indicate how these details should be recorded on the final document. The Quality Plan should be planned and developed in conjunction with design, development, manufacturing, sub-contract and installation work and ensure that all functions have been fully catered for.

One of the main objectives of quality planning is to identify any special or unusual requirements, processes, techniques including those requirements that are unusual by reason of newness, unfamiliarity, lack of experience and/or absence of precedents. As ISO 9004:2000 points out, if the contract specifies that Quality Plans are required, then these Quality Plans should fully cover the following areas and ensure that:

- design, contract, development, manufacturing and installation activities are well documented and adequate;
- all controls, processes, inspection equipment, fixtures, tooling, manpower resources and skills that an organisation must have to achieve the required quality, have been identified, recorded and the necessary action taken to obtain any additional components, documentation etc. that is required;
- quality control, inspection and testing techniques (including the development of new instrumentation) have been updated;
- any new measurement technique (or any measurement involving a measurement capability that exceeds the known state of the art) that is required to inspect the product, has been identified and action taken to develop that capability;
- standards of acceptability for all features and requirements (including those which contain a subjective element) have been clearly recorded;
- compatibility of design, manufacturing process, installation, inspection procedures and applicable documentation have been assured well before production begins;
- as each special requirement is identified, the means for testing and being able to prove successfully that the product or service is capable of successfully complying with the requirements has to be considered.

The integration of special or unusual requirements into the QMS must be carefully investigated, planned and documented.

As a Quality Plan is effectively a sub set of the actual Quality Manual. The layout of the Quality Plan is very similar to that of the Quality Manual and refers (other than system-specific QPs and WIs) normally to the QPs and Work Instructions contained in that Quality Manual.

The following briefly describes how each of the ISO 9000 elements is covered in a Quality Plan.

4.9.1 Management responsibility

The Quality Plan should show who is responsible for:

- ensuring activities are planned, implemented, controlled and monitored;
- communicating requirements and resolving problems;
- reviewing audit results;

Figure 4.9 Management responsibility

- authorising exemption requests;
- implementing corrective action requests.

   Where the necessary documentation already exists under the present QMS, the Quality Plan need only refer to a specific situation or specification.

4.9.2 Contract review

Contract review should cover:

- when, how and by whom the review is made;
- how the results are to be documented;
- how conflicting instructions or ambiguities are resolved.

4.9.3 Design control

Design control should indicate:

- when, how and by whom the design process, validation and verification of the design output is carried out, controlled and documented;
- any customer involvement;
- applicable codes of practice, standards, specifications and regulatory requirements.

4.9.4 Document and data control

Document and data control should refer to:

- what is provided and how it is controlled;
- how related documents will be identified;
- how and by whom access to the documents can be obtained;
- how and by whom the original documents are reviewed and approved.

4.9.5 Purchasing

Under the heading of purchasing the following should be indicated:

- the important products to be purchased;
- the source and requirements relating to them;
- the method, evaluation, selection and control of subcontractors;
- the need for a subcontractor's Quality Plan in order to satisfy the regulatory requirements applicable to purchase products/services.

4.9.6 Customer supplied product

Customer supplied products should refer to:

- how they are identified and controlled;
- how they are verified as meeting specified requirements;
- how non-conformance is dealt with.

4.9.7 Product identification and traceability

If traceability is a requirement then the plan should:

- define its scope and extent (including how services/products are identified);
- indicate how contractual and regulatory authority traceability requirements are identified and incorporated into working documents;
- indicate how records are to be generated, controlled and distributed.

4.9.8 Process control

Process control may include:

- the procedures/instructions;
- process steps;
- methods to monitor and control processes;
- service/product characteristics.

The plan could also include details of:

- reference criteria for workmanship;
- special and qualified processes;
- tools, techniques and methods to be used.

4.9.9 Inspection and testing

Inspection and testing should indicate:

- any inspection and test plan;
- how the subcontractors' product shall be verified;
- the location of inspection and test points;
- procedures and acceptance criteria;
- witness verification points (customers as well as regulatory);
- where, when and how the customer requires third parties to perform:
  - type tests;
  - witness testing;
  - service/product verification;
  - material, service/product, process or personnel certification.

4.9.10 Inspection, measuring and test equipment

Inspection, measuring and test equipment should:

- refer to the identity of the equipment;
- refer to the method of calibration;
- indicate and record calibration status and usage of the equipment;
- indicate specific requirements for the identification of inspection and test status.

4.9.11 Non-conforming service/product

Under the heading of non-conforming service/product, an indication should be given:

- of how such a service/product is identified and segregated;
- the degree or type of rework allowed;
- the circumstances under which the supplier can request concessions.

Details should also be provided with respect to:

- corrective and preventive action;
- handling, storage, packaging, preservation and delivery.

4.9.12 Other considerations

Quality Plans should:

- indicate key quality records (i.e. what they are, how long they should be kept, where and by whom);
- suggest how legal or regulatory requirements are to be satisfied;
- specify the form in which records should be kept (e.g. paper, microfilm or disc);
- define liability, storage, retrievability, disposition and confidentiality requirements;
- include the nature and extent of quality audits to be undertaken;
- indicate how the audit results are to be used to correct and prevent recurrence of deficiencies;
- show how the training of staff in new or revised operating methods is to be completed.

Where servicing is a specified requirement, suppliers should state their intentions to assure conformance to applicable servicing requirements, such as:

- regulatory and legislative requirements;
- industry codes and practices;
- service level agreements;
- training of customer personnel;
- availability of initial and ongoing support during the agreed time-period;
- statistical techniques, where relevant.

 Note: For further information I would recommend looking at ISO 10005:1995 which provides the reader with guidance on how to produce Quality Plans as well as including helpful suggestions on how to maintain an organisation's quality activities.

4.10 Quality records

Quality records provide objective evidence of activities performed or results achieved.

Records of QMS inspections and tests concerning the design, testing, survey, audit and review of a product or service are the evidence that a supplier is capable of and is indeed meeting the quality requirements of the customer.

Records such as QMS audit reports, calibration of test and measuring equipment, inspections, tests, approvals, concessions, etc., ensure that an organisation is capable of proving the effectiveness of their QMS.

Records, therefore, are important parts of quality management and the QMS will have to identify exactly what type of record is to be made, at what stage of

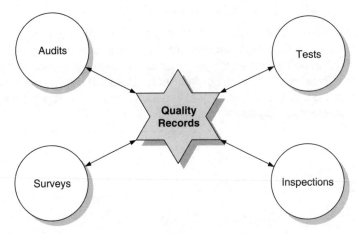

Figure 4.10 Quality records

the production process they should be made and who should make them etc. To be of any real value it is essential that these records are covered by clear, concise instructions and procedures. Above all, the storage of records should be systematic and capable of being easily and quickly accessed.

Having agreed and decided on the necessity for records, the next step is to:

- establish methods for making changes, modifications, revisions and additions to these records;
- establish methods for accounting for the documents;
- show their retention time;
- lay down methods for the disposal of those that are superseded or become out of date;
- show how they should be stored.

These procedures would be written up as QPs and will normally form part of the Quality Manual. WIs should also be available to show how important it is to keep records of defects, diagnosis of their causes and details of the correct-ive action that was carried out together with the success or failure of this cor-rective action.

If this information is stored in a computer, then it is essential that the integrity of that system **must** also be satisfactorily assured.

The retention of records is an aspect that is far too often overlooked by organisations. Records are very important, not only from an historical point of view, but also as a means to settling disputes about bad workmanship, identifying faults and settling production problems whether this be internally, by the supplier, or externally, by the organisation.

In Part Four of this book we have addressed the basic requirements for a Quality Management System and shown how ISO 9000 can be structured to suit a particular business or profession.

In Part Five, quality control techniques, the organisational structure and the duties of quality assurance personnel plus their resources are discussed.

Part Five _____
Quality Organisational Structure

Having seen the basic requirements for a Quality Management System, Part Five will cover quality control techniques, organisational structure and duties of quality staff.

Then in Part Six a complete example of a Quality Manual is provided which can be easily customised to suit any organisation's business.

5
Quality organisational structure

As previously described in Chapter 4, the QMS is an organisation's rulebook which defines the policy, organisation and responsibilities for the management of quality within an organisation. The following tables are an indication of the sort of tasks that senior management would be responsible for in a typical organisation (see Table 5.1 below).

For a manufacturing organisation, these responsibilities will then probably be further subdivided as shown in Table 5.2 overleaf:

Table 5.1 Organisational responsibilities – senior management

Title	Responsibility
Managing Director	• Establish, document and define the organisation's policy and objectives; • approve the QMS; • management reviews; • design control.
Quality Manager	• Internal audit; • resolution of QMS discrepancies; • control & maintenance of the QMS; • quality documentation & (quality) change control procedures; • quality training.
Financial Director	• Control of budget and finance; • supplier selection and purchasing; • contract management, control and review; • management & co-ordination of sales and support functions.

Table 5.2 Organisational responsibilities – others

General Manager	• Planning and co-ordination; • design control; • estimating; • project management; • control of contract documentation; • supplier selection & purchasing; • definition of installation, inspection, test & maintenance requirements; • training.
Business Development Manager	• Sales; • estimating; • new product identification & evaluation; • system design.
Sales Managers	• Quotations; • contract review and order processing; • sales order processing.
Support Manager	• Control of production and measuring equipment; • maintenance of support stores; • processing of sales orders; • purchasing.
Engineers	• Installation, repairs, testing and maintenance activities; • control of equipment and materials allocated.
Warehouse	• Stock control; • stock replenishment; • protection and preservation of stock; • receiving inspection; • packaging and despatch.
Administration	• Sales database administration; • checking of sales orders; • allocation of order reference numbers.

5.1 Management

The main requirement of the organisation's management is that they establish, define and document their organisation's policy, objectives and commitments to quality. This documented system is then presented as a Quality Manual, quality programme, or as a controlled documented system.

Whatever system is chosen, the document must include details of the organisation's Quality Management System (QMS) and the aims, policies, organisation

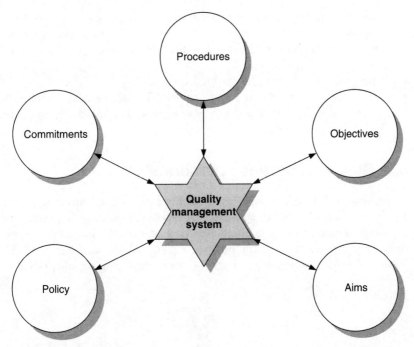

Figure 5.1 Quality organisational requirements

and procedures that are essential to demonstrate that they are in agreement
with the requirements of ISO 9001:2000.

 Note: Suppliers having difficulty in establishing their own particular level of
managerial responsibility with regard to organisation quality assurance should
obtain a copies of BS 6143:1992 'Guide to the economics of quality' Parts 1
and 2. These standards are available from the BSI and are a user-friendly
guide to:

- the costs for continuous improvement and Total Quality Management
  (TQM) (Part 1);
- the costs of defect prevention and a study of the various activities and
  losses due to internal or external failures (Part 2).

Having established their overall position, the management will then have to:

- develop, control, co-ordinate, supervise and monitor their corporate
  quality policy and ensure that this policy is understood and maintained
  throughout the organisation;

- ensure that the organisation's QMS always meets the requirements of the national, European or international standards that that particular organisation has chosen to work to and where this fails to happen, see that corrective actions are carried out;
- define objectives such as fitness for use;
- ensure that the performance, safety and reliability of a product or service is correct and make sure that the costs associated with these objectives are kept to a reasonable figure.

5.2 Quality assurance personnel

As previously described in Part Three, quality assurance is concerned with a consistency of quality and an agreed level of quality. To achieve these aims the organisation must be firmly committed to the fundamental principle of consistently supplying the right quality product. Equally, a purchaser must be committed to the fundamental principle of only accepting the right quality product.

Figure 5.2 Quality assurance – typical organisation structure

Thus, a commitment within all levels of an organisation (manufacturer, supplier or purchaser), to the basic principles of quality assurance and quality control is required. It is, therefore, essential that a completely separate and independent division is formed to deal solely with quality matters. In a large company the organisation and duties of this section would usually look something like that shown in Figure 5.2.

5.2.1 Quality manager

The first requirement is for the organisation to nominate an individual who will be solely responsible to top management for the implementation and maintenance of the QMS. This person is called the 'Quality Manager'.

The Quality Manager will answer directly to the Managing Director and will be responsible for all matters regarding the quality of the end product together with the activities of **all** sections within the organisation's premises.

In small organisations this requirement might even be part of the General Manager's duties, but regardless of who it may be, it is essential that this person must be someone who is completely independent of any manufacturing, production or user function and has a thorough working knowledge of the requirements and recommendations of ISO 9000.

In addition, owing to the importance of quality assurance, it is essential that the Quality Manager is fully qualified (both technically and administratively) and can quickly exert (show) his position and authority.

As can be seen from Figure 5.3, the Quality Manager's job is usually a very busy one (even in a small organisation!) and the Quality Manager's responsibilities are spread over a wide area which covers all of the organisation's operations.

5.2.1.1 General functional description

The Quality Manager is responsible for ensuring that the organisation's QMS is defined, implemented, audited and monitored in order to ensure that the organisation's deliverables comply with both the customer's quality and safety standards together with the requirements of ISO 9001:2000.

5.2.1.2 Tasks

The Quality Manager reports directly to the General Manager and his tasks will include:

- ensuring the consistency of the organisation's QMS;
- ensuring compliance of the organisation's QMS with ISO 9001:2000;
- maintenance and effectiveness of the organisation's QMS;
- ensuring that the quality message is transmitted to and understood by everyone.

Figure 5.3 Responsibilities of the Quality Manager

5.2.1.3 Responsibilities

The Quality Manager is responsible for:

- ensuring that the Quality Manual and individual Quality Plans are keptup to date;
- assisting and advising with the preparation of the organisation's procedures;
- producing, reviewing and updating the organisation's QMS;
- ensuring compliance with the organisation's QMS by means of frequent audits;
- maintaining the organisation's quality records;
- producing, auditing and maintaining division, section and project Quality Plans;
- identifying potential/current problem areas within the organisation's life cycle through analysis of organisation error reports;
- holding regular division quality audits.

5.2.1.4 Co-ordination

The Quality Manager shall:

- act as the focal point for all of the organisation's quality matters within the organisation;
- co-ordinate and verify that all internal procedures and instructions are in accordance with the recommendations of ISO 9001:2000;
- operate the QMS as described in the Quality Manual and ensure that its regulations are observed.

Above all the Quality Manager must always ensure that the customer's interests are protected. Even if this means, at times, that he and his division become very unpopular with the rest of the organisation and sometimes they even have to assume the mantel of organisation 'scapegoat'!

5.2.2 Chief Quality Assurance Inspector

There may be more than one Chief Quality Assurance Inspector (QAI) in an organisation depending upon its size and activities.

The duties of the Chief QAI are to:

- plan, co-ordinate and supervise all pre-shop, in-process, and out-going inspections within their area of responsibility;
- ensure that the product or service is in agreement with the customers' requirements and conform to the established quality standards and specifications;
- be responsible for scheduling and controlling inspections, designating inspection stations, setting up local inspection procedures and statistical inspection controls;
- oversee the maintenance of inspection records, control charts and the preparation of inspection reports;
- ensure that all test equipment is maintained, properly calibrated and readily available at all inspection stations;
- be responsible for reviewing the maintenance of quality inspection stations;
- co-ordinate on-the-job and cross training within sections;
- establish and maintain inspection systems and controls to determine the acceptability of a completed product;
- be responsible for detecting deficiencies during manufacture, initiate corrective actions where applicable and prevent defects;
- compile quality and feedback data, quality history and statistical results to help quality control development, refinement and management;
- advise management and key maintenance personnel on all aspects concerning quality trends.

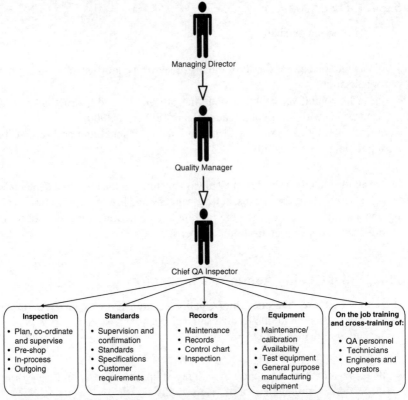

Figure 5.4 Responsibilities of the Chief Quality Assurance Inspector

5.2.3 Section Quality Assurance Inspectors

Two assurers are normally nominated for each section, a principal and an alternate. The principal is always the assurer, the alternate assumes the duties when asked to do so by the principal and during the absence of the principal. When not engaged on QA duties, the QAIs are employed on normal everyday activities.

The task of the Section QAI is to:

- review (and make recommendations) to the Chief QAI on all things concerning engineering change proposals, waivers, deviations and substitution of parts, materials, equipment and processes;
- compile quality feedback data and quality history sheets;
- supply technical data and assistance to the design office.

Internal audits

Surveillance or audit visit

Supplier evaluation

QA measurement

Figure 5.5 Responsibilities of the Section Quality Assurance Inspectors

5.2.4 Quality assurance personnel

Quality assurance personnel are members of the organisation judged competent to carry out quality assurance duties. They are nominated by the Quality Manager in consultation with the QAIs and are directly responsible to the Quality Manager when engaged in QA work.

Quality assurance personnel are:

- not to allow their own judgement to be influenced by others;
- not to allow equipment to leave the premises below the desired standard;
- to ensure – by close liaison with Section Heads – that a section's work is not unreasonably delayed because of quality assurance;
- to ensure that when a job (system, module or equipment etc.) fails their inspection that the respective Section QAI is informed and that the Section Head (and engineer responsible) are made fully aware of the reasons for the failure;
- to advise the Section QAI of any problems associated with quality assurance, particularly anything that is likely to effect production or harmony between any of the sections and the quality assurance division.

5.2.5 Quality assurance resources

It is not enough for management to supply just the personnel for a quality assurance section. Resources, appropriate for the implementation of the quality policies, must also be available.

These shall include:

- management budget;
- design and development equipment;
- manufacturing equipment;
- inspection, test and examination equipment;
- instrumentation and computer software.

Parts One to Five have provided complete details of the background and requirements of ISO 9001:2000. Having understood this material, it is now time to move on to the next stage – to design your own Quality Management System!

Part Six contains a complete example of a Quality Management System which can be used as a template to design your own Quality Management System.

Part Six

Example Quality Management System

Prior to the reissue of the ISO 9000 series in 2001, the majority of organisations wrote their Quality Manuals to show how they met the 20 individual requirements of the 1994 standard. Although this made it easier for the manual's authors to show the auditors that all of the requirements of the standard had been covered, quite often (especially in a very small business), the manual was of little use to the organisation itself in actually running their own business.

ISO 9001:2000 now requires the Quality Manual to '*include the scope of the system, any justifications for exclusions, refer to established procedures and describe the interaction between processes*'. A Quality Manual that simply echoes the requirements of ISO 9001:2000 will, therefore, **not** be compliant, as certain sections of the standard's content may not be applicable.

The Quality Manual should serve a useful purpose and so simply paraphrasing ISO 9001:2000's requirements will not represent the best approach. Thus, an organisation should no longer use an 'off the shelf' generic Quality Manual to show compliance **unless**, it has been **suitably customised** to suit that particular organisation.

The whole reason for my book is to try to help small businesses (who probably have insufficient time to thoroughly read, understand, extract and implement all of the requirements of ISO 9001:2000 – and who quite likely cannot afford to employ a consultant to do the job for them) with a fully worked example. Although this generic QMS is based on one particular type of company (i.e. Stingray who are a 'paper producing' company) it can be used as a template to describe the way that your particular organisation does business by leaving out those bits that are not particularly relevant to you and/or amplifying/writing new policies, processes and procedures to cover the organisation-specific areas that I have not covered in my book.

Although a lot of consultants say that there is now no need to address each requirement, clause by clause, I tend to disagree because if you are having to identify the requirements that are not applicable to your organisation (i.e. the 'exclusions') and **then** say why they are permitted exclusions, surely there is less chance of missing a possible sub-requirement by actually listing all of them and showing whether they are applicable or not?! If you are having to describe the interaction between processes (which probably result from different requirements or sub-requirements scattered within ISO 9001:2000), then why not list them all, so as to ensure that you don't miss any? I have sought ISO's advice on this matter and they said that '*Although ISO 9001:2000 does not state that there needs to be any reference to the requirements of the standard, if an organisation chooses to list all of the requirements, then that is its choice*'.

As I understand it, the Quality Manual should be an overview of the organisation's QMS and show how the organisation runs its business. The Manual is primarily intended for the Managing Director (to document his policy for running that organisation), the Quality Manager (to give him a set of rules with which to ensure that the organisation meets the policy requirements of the MD) and the auditors (to quickly identify which of the standard's requirements are applicable to that organisation and how they have been met). Depending on the individual organisation, therefore, the Quality Manual could be just a few A4 sheets of paper simply listing the exclusions, procedures and interaction of processes. Or, similar to my generic example, it could be more of a reference document aimed at assisting internal and external auditors in understanding the organisation's policies and how it completes its business – as well as providing a checklist for the Quality Manager.

The same thing can be said about the Quality Procedures contained in Part 3. These again are meant as examples of the sort of QPs that will be needed by an organisation to show how they implement their policies and processes. They are based around Stingray (who are a paper producing consultancy as opposed to a manufacturing facility) and the intention is that purchasers/users of my book can take these QPs and then modify, adjust and customise them to replicate what they actually do.

For example, the Document Control procedure, whilst covering the requirements for a very large organisation would probably be over the top for a small organisation. You **do**, however, need to have some form of document control and at the very least be able to identify where your documents are located or where they are saved on the server. You may also want to show who is responsible for these documents, their revision status and their date of issue. In some circumstances (especially when dealing with foreign countries) you might even need to know who was responsible for translating a specific document.

One of the main advantages of ISO 9001:2000 is that it encourages organisations to develop systems that are **specifically** tailored to their own needs. The QMS is an integral part of the business processes but you should not lose sight of the fact that it still has to meet the requirements of ISO 9001:2000.

ISO 9001:2000 for Small Businesses (Third Edition) is meant to save you time from having to constantly refer to the standard to see that you have covered everything. My generic example covers **all** of the standard's requirements and similar to the actual standard itself, the intention is that organisations pick and choose what bits they need for themselves.

 Note: To save you having to copy this QMS 'unlocked', fully accessible, non .pdf, soft copies of all of these files (as well as a selection of audit checklists etc. from the sister publication *ISO 9001:2000 Audit Procedures*) are available, on a CD (for a small additional charge) from the author in Word format. See p. xviii for further details.

Stingray Management Services Ltd

Quality Management System
Part 1 – Quality Manual

This Quality Manual has been issued on the authority of the Managing Director of Stingray Management Services Ltd for the use of all staff, subcontractors, clients and/or regulatory bodies to whom Stingray Management Services Ltd may be required to provide such information to.

Approved

.... **Date:** 1st January 2005......

Ray Rekcirt
Managing Director
Stingray Management Services Ltd

Document Control Sheet

Abstract

The Stingray Management Services Ltd Quality Management System is divided into four parts. This Quality Manual is Part 1 and describes the policies adopted by Stingray Management Services Ltd. It defines:

- the overall Quality Management System adopted by Stingray Management Services Ltd;
- the organisation that has been developed to implement that Quality Management System;
- the associated documentation (e.g. Quality Processes, Quality Procedures and Work Instructions) that have been designed to enable Stingray Management Services Ltd to carry out the Quality Management System.

The Quality Processes designed to meet these policies are contained in Part 2 and the details of the Quality Procedures and Work Instructions are in Parts 3 and 4.

Attachments

Attachment	Description
Annex A	Stingray organisation and responsibilities
Annex B	ISO 9001:2000 cross-check
Annex C	List of Quality Procedures
Annex D	Abbreviations, Acronyms and References

QMS revision history

No.	Chapter	Amendment details	Date
01.00	All	First published version in accordance with ISO 9001:1994	28.06.93
01.01	3	Inclusion of new chapter for customer satisfaction	05.04.94
01.02	4.2.3	Procedure for the control of documents changed	23.12.95
01.03	All	Minor editorial revisions of all sections and annexes	30.07.96
02.00	All	Second published version to conform to ISO 9001:2000	31.12.00
02.01	5	Management responsibility procedure updated to cover new (i.e. Fuels) Division	01.01.02
02.02	All	Minor editorial changes following three years' experience of ISO 9001:2000	01.01.05

Contents

List of illustrations

List of tables

Stingray Management Services Ltd – Policy statement

Within Stingray Management Services Ltd (Stingray) we are committed to provide products and services, which meet the customers' specified contractual requirements.

Stingray recognises that in order to provide and maintain a consistently high quality in the work it undertakes, an effective Quality Management System is necessary so as to ensure that proper communication, work control and accountable records are generated for all work undertaken. We are totally committed to setting and achieving quality standards that are capable of meeting (in **all** respects) the specified requirements and reasonable expectations of our customers.

It is the policy, therefore, of Stingray to control and conduct its business of producing and implementing integrated management services by means of a formalised system of modern quality management. This quality management shall be in accordance with the quality system requirements specified in ISO 9001:2000.

This Quality Manual defines Stingray's Quality Management System which has been established and adopted as the means for achieving these declared objectives and which is detailed in the sections below.

All members of Stingray staff are charged with promoting these aims and are required to familiarise themselves with the contents of this Quality Manual and to observe and implement the systems and procedures defined in the performance of their work. Everyone connected with Stingray Management Services Ltd shall be supported according to their individual needs for personal development.

The Quality Manager based at the Stingray main office is my appointed management representative responsible for monitoring and ensuring the correct and effective implementation of Stingray's Quality Management System as a whole.

Ray Rekcirt
Managing Director
Stingray Management Services Ltd

Mission Statement

'To deliver effective, evidence-based management systems in accordance to the recommendations of ISO 9001:2000 and other industry equivalent standards'

1 Quality assurance at Stingray

This Quality Manual has been issued on the authority of the Managing Director of Stingray Management Services Ltd (Stingray) for the use of all staff, sub-contractors, clients or regulatory bodies to whom Stingray Management Services Ltd may be required to provide such information.

This Quality Manual defines:

- the overall quality policy adopted by Stingray;
- the organisation that has been developed to implement this quality policy;
- the documentation (i.e. Quality Processes, Quality Procedures & Work Instructions) that has been designed to enable Stingray to carry out that policy.

Other than the permissible exclusions shown in the relevant parts of the text, Stingray's Quality Manual conforms to the requirements of ISO 9001:2000 (Ref 1). It takes into consideration the requirements of Stingray's Memorandum and Articles of Association (Ref 3), together with all other applicable national, European and international standards and procedures [e.g. ACP8 and ACP9 (Refs 4 and 5) written for the aircraft industry]. If there are any discrepancies between the Stingray Quality Manual and these other directives/standards, the requirements of the Stingray Quality Manual shall prevail.

Changes in the organisation of Stingray or the environment, in which it operates, may necessitate modifications, amendments, insertions and/or deletions to the overall quality management adopted by Stingray and its associated documentation (e.g. Quality Processes, Quality Procedures and Work Instructions). The contents of this Quality Manual may, therefore, be altered on an as required basis. All changes shall be subject to QP/1 – Document Control. Changes shall be deemed operational following approval by the authorised person(s) and published as updated sections of the Quality Manual.

Certain technical terms and usage in this Quality Manual, although only reflecting the masculine gender, are, in fact, the parlance of the field and should be interpreted to apply equally to both sexes.

1.1 Company profile

Stingray Management Services Ltd (Stingray) is a Private Limited Company specialising in the production of integrated quality management systems for Small and Medium sized Enterprises (SME) as well as Large Multinational Organisations (LMO). All deliverables are designed and supplied to the highest standards and conform to the relevant international and European standards.

Stingray's aim is to produce everything that you want in support of your company's Quality Management System (QMS). Stingray provides advice and guidance on **all** quality matters. We can produce either complete QMSs, Quality Manuals, Quality Processes, Quality Procedures, Work Instructions or technical books to suit individual customer requirements. Stingray also provides qualified advice on environmental requirements (particularly those for the electronic industry) and are experts in fuel conservation, management and safety issues.

Stingray controls and conducts its business of producing and implementing integrated management systems by means of a formalised system of modern quality management which is in accordance with the quality system requirements and recommendations specified in the ISO 9001:2000.

At Stingray, we believe that it is important to develop a good working relationship with our customers at every level, ensuring that they receive a quality product and service. Nothing is considered too small. Indeed Stingray have become renowned for assisting the smaller company (who rarely possess a quality infrastructure) in establishing their own Quality Management System in accordance with ISO 9001:2000 and working towards becoming an ISO 9001:2000 certified company.

1.2 Costs

Each deliverable budget is carefully prepared taking into account the type of product and the market to which it is aimed. Emphasis is placed on producing a quality product at a realistic cost thereby giving the customer value for money.

1.3 Stingray Management Services Ltd – organisational chart

Figure 6.1.1 Stingray Management Services Ltd – organisational chart

1.4 Quality policy and objectives

1.4.1 Policy

Stingray shall define and manage the processes necessary to ensure that all project deliverables conform to customer requirements. As a means of continually improving project performance, Stingray shall establish a QMS covering the requirements of ISO 9001:2000. This QMS shall be implemented, maintained, continually improved and have the full support of top management.

Stingray shall prepare procedures that describe the processes required to implement the QMS. These shall include:

- Core Business Processes and Supporting Processes;
- Quality Procedures that describe the methods adopted to manage the Core Business Process and Supporting Processes;
- Work Instructions that describe the operating methods, practice and control of the Core Business Process and Supporting Processes.

1.4.2 Objectives

The main objective of the Stingray QMS is to ensure that company activities, whether they are organisational (e.g. management and infrastructure) or technical (e.g. specification work, testing and simulation) comply with the Quality Manual and its associated Quality Plans.

1.5 Implementation

Quality management at Stingray is based on the Quality Management System described in ISO 9001:2000. The purpose of the Stingray QMS is to define the policy, organisation and responsibilities for the management of quality within Stingray.

The most important aspects of Stingray's QMS are to be found in the Stingray Quality Manual (i.e. this document) which describes, in detail, how the main elements of ISO 9001:2000 are catered for. The Quality Manual is then supported by individual Quality Plans (for each section or major contract/document) which in turn are supported by Quality Processes, Quality Procedures and Work Instructions.

All Stingray personnel shall have access to a copy of this Quality Manual (see Section 3.10 page 239) and as part of personnel induction training, the objectives of the manual shall be explained to them by the Stingray Quality Manager.

1.5.1 Overall responsibility

The responsibility of ensuring that Stingray has a quality policy and for ensuring that an organisation with the necessary resources is in place to implement the policy, lies with the Managing Director.

1.5.2 Responsibility for quality system

The Managing Director has appointed the Quality Manager to have overall responsibility for implementing and maintaining the Stingray quality system. As Quality Manager he has the responsibility and the authority to ensure that adequate processes, procedures, plans and instructions are drawn up so as to provide a common approach to quality assurance throughout Stingray and to ensure that the quality system is continuously monitored and improved by means of internal audits and management reviews.

1.5.3 Responsibility for contract quality

The responsibility for the development of contract quality rests with Stingray's Managing Director via the Company Managers.

1.5.4 Responsibility for product quality

The responsibility for ensuring that the product conforms to the defined quality requirements in this manual lies with **all** Stingray personnel.

1.5.5 Responsibility for subcontractor(s) quality

Specialised areas of operation and technical expertise may be required to meet the needs of Stingray. In many cases these shall have to be provided externally via a subcontractor. These subcontractors will need to supply and prove that their QMS is in accordance with the requirements of the principles of ISO 9001:2000.

1.6 Registrations and approvals held

Stingray is a Registered Organisation certified by an Accredited Certification Body and verified as having quality documentation and effective practices in operation which are in accordance with the requirements of the international Quality System ISO 9001:2000.

2 Stingray's Management System

2.1 Requirements

Stingray's QMS is the organised structure of responsibilities, activities, resources and events that together provide procedures and methods of implementation to ensure the capability of Stingray meets the quality requirements of our customers.

Stingray has to develop, establish and implement a Quality Management System in order to ensure that the overall objectives and policies stated in Stingray's Memorandum of Articles and Association are met.

To achieve these requirements, Stingray involves all phases of a quality loop (see Figure 6.1.2) that is derived from the requirements of ISO 9001:2000 and covers the initial identification of the requirement to the final satisfaction of the customer's needs and expectations.

Within Stingray an effective QMS ensures that all activities are fully understood, controlled and documented and that everyone knows exactly what they are supposed to be doing and how they should be doing it.

There are four main requirement sections making up the ISO 9001:2000 standard ranging from how to control a design process to how to audit an activity – but the most important element is the first one which demands that **everyone** shall be involved in quality in order for it to succeed and that it **must** be management led and that there **must** be a commitment to quality – **at the highest level**.

Figure 6.1.2 Quality loop

Within Stingray we have this commitment. It stems from Stingray's decisions in this respect and manifests itself throughout Stingray's management, at all levels.

2.2 Organisational goals

The primary goal of Stingray shall, at all times, be the quality of the end product and service. To succeed, Stingray must be able to offer products and services that:

- meet the need, use and purpose as defined in Stingray's Memorandum and Articles of Association;
- satisfy the customer's requirements and expectations;
- comply with applicable international, European and national quality standards and specifications.

In order to meet these objectives, Stingray shall organise itself in such a way that the technical, administrative and human factors affecting the quality of Stingray products and services are always under control.

It is **imperative** that this control is orientated to the reduction, elimination and – of paramount importance – the prevention of quality deficiencies. The Stingray QMS, therefore, has to be developed and implemented for the purpose of accomplishing the objectives set out in Stingray's Memorandum and Articles of Association.

Above all (and to achieve maximum effectiveness) it is essential that the Stingray QMS is designed so that it is appropriate to the type of contract and services being offered by Stingray.

Demonstration of the continued success of the QMS shall be achieved via regular audits and reviews.

2.3 Purpose

The purpose of a QMS is to ensure that the end product (i.e. the deliverable) conforms to the customer's (i.e. user's), contractual requirements.

Stingray's QMS, therefore, involves all Stingray's functions, wherever and however instigated (e.g. Director level, Section Manager level, etc.) that directly, or indirectly, affect Stingray deliverables and contracts.

In essence, Stingray's QMS essentially consists of the documented rules, procedures and instructions prepared in accordance with ISO 9001:2000. These are stated in the Quality Manual (QM) as well as the associated Core Business Process (CP), Supporting Processes (SPs), Quality Procedures (QPs) and Work

Instructions (WIs). The Stingray audit team (consisting of the Managing Director, Quality Manager and Company Secretary) plus Section Manager may decide if additional documents are required for individual sections. In these cases, the requirement for an additional document shall be clearly stated and rules developed. This following section of the manual describes Stingray's quality policy for meeting the requirements of ISO 9001:2000.

3 Quality policy

3.1 Introduction

This section of the manual defines the Stingray quality policy and outlines the main responsibilities for its implementation.

3.2 Quality Management System requirements

'A Quality Management System (QMS) is the organised structure of responsibilities, activities, resources and events that together provide procedures and methods of implementation to ensure the capability of an organisation meets the quality requirement of the client.' (ISO 10011:2002).

Quality is an objective concept. It is something that the whole workforce can understand and measure and for which they accept responsibility.

As an indicator, some of the determinants and measures of Stingray's quality of a service are shown in Figure 6.1.3 below, whilst those appertaining to the quality of a product are shown in Figure 6.1.4.

3.3 Company requirements

As described in the company policy statement, within Stingray we are totally committed to setting and achieving quality standards that will enable the company to provide its customers with a high quality product and service.

To meet this commitment, Stingray shall develop and maintain a QMS that meets the requirements and the recommendations of ISO 9001:2000.

Total Quality Management (TQM) shall be applied to every aspect of our activity and quality shall be the responsibility of everyone, in every activity, throughout Stingray.

To achieve these objectives, everyone's involvement and commitment is vital in adhering to the system adopted and in fully appreciating their quality responsibilities. Everyone connected with Stingray shall be supported according to their individual needs for personal development, training and facilities.

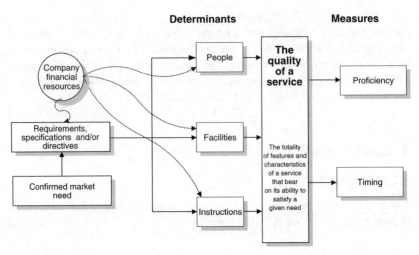

Figure 6.1.3 Some of the determinants and measurements of the quality of a service

3.4 Company quality policy

Quality management within Stingray is based on the quality system described in Section 4 of ISO 9001:2000. The purpose of the quality system is to define the policy, organisation and responsibilities for the management of quality within Stingray.

Quality management forms an integral part of our overall company management and the role of quality management within our company is an essential requirement. It provides confidence that application of company management (as described within this Quality Manual) is efficient, comprehensive and effective in ensuring that every stage of the product (or service) development is delivered:

- on time;
- to the agreed product specifications;
- within budget.

The main objective of Stingray's QMS is to ensure that all activities, whether they are managerial (e.g. organisation) or technical (e.g. specification work) comply with the Quality Manual and it is incumbent on all staff to have a day-to-day responsibility for ensuring conformance to the requirements and rules as stated in this Quality Manual.

Figure 6.1.4 Some of the determinants and measurements of the quality of a product

In cases of non-compliance (e.g. if part of the specified work is not carried out in accordance with the product and/or service requirements) a problem solving process shall be executed by the first responsible manager. This process shall include the location of root causes, remedial action, review of Stingray's QMS and, if necessary, its adjustment and modification.

The Quality Manager plays an important part in this process. His role will be to suggest alternative solutions and help the First Line Manager to take the necessary remedial action. If no effective corrective action is taken, the Quality Manager has the duty to inform the Managing Director.

Summarised, Stingray's QMS shall ensure:

- clear responsibilities for all activities and tasks;
- confirmation that all activities are defined and controlled by a Quality Procedure or Work Instruction;

- staff are trained to the requirements listed in the Quality Manual and contract Quality Plans;
- compliance with Stingray's Quality Procedures detailed in the Quality Manual and Contract Quality Plans are audited;
- remedial action is taken whenever appropriate;
- the Quality Processes, Quality Procedures, Work Instructions (contained in the Quality Manual) and contract Quality Plans themselves are regularly reviewed.

3.5 Adherence to standards

Stingray's Quality Manual is based on the requirements of ISO 9001:2000 and takes into consideration the requirements of all other applicable national, European and international standards, procedures and directives. If there are any discrepancies between Stingray's Quality Manual and these other directives/standards, the requirements of Stingray's Quality Manual shall prevail.

3.6 Purpose of a Quality Management System

The purpose of having a QMS is to ensure that the end product or service conforms to the customer's (i.e. user's) contractual requirements. Stingray's Quality Management System, therefore, involves all Stingray functions, wherever and however instigated that directly, or indirectly, affect deliverables and contracts.

Demonstration of the continued success of our Quality Management System shall be achieved via regular audits and reviews (for details see QP/6 – Internal Quality Audits).

3.7 Quality in performance

The system adopted by Stingray to achieve quality in performance with accountability is based on the following four main items or activities:

1. **Quality Manual** – the Quality Manual (as the primary control document) which defines the policy, processes, responsibilities, procedures, etc. that are to be used;
2. **Quality Manager** – the appointment of a Quality Manager within a defined organisational structure, who is responsible for operating the system and ensuring that the Quality Manual and its associated documentation is fully and effectively implemented;
3. **Documented Processes and Procedures** – the use of documented processes and procedures to define all activities which could lead to variability of

execution with consequent loss of quality attainment, performance or safety if not rigorously controlled;

4. **Quality Management System reviews** – regular reviews of the Quality Manual (and its supporting documentation) together with auditing its effective implementation to ensure that the most suitable and effective methods and procedures are still prescribed and used.

3.8 Organisational goals

The primary goal of Stingray shall be, at all times, to ensure that the quality of the product and/or service:

- satisfies the customer's requirements and expectations;
- meets the need, use and purpose as defined in the approved product and/or service specifications;
- complies with the requirements of ISO 9001:2000;
- complies with applicable international, European and national quality standards, specifications and directives.

In order to meet these objectives, Stingray has to be organised in such a way that the technical, administrative and human factors affecting the quality of Stingray products and services are always under control. It is imperative that this control is orientated to the reduction, elimination and – very importantly – the prevention of quality deficiencies.

A Stingray QMS, therefore, has to be developed and implemented for the purpose of accomplishing the objectives set out above.

To achieve maximum effectiveness, it is essential that this QMS is designed so that it is appropriate to the type of contract and services being offered by Stingray.

3.9 Structure for quality management

Stingray's QMS defines the policy, organisation and responsibilities for the management of quality within Stingray. It ensures that all activities comply with an agreed set of rules, regulations and guidelines and that the end product or service (i.e. the deliverable) conforms to the customer's (i.e. the user's) contractual requirements. A QMS can only be effective if it is fully documented, understood and followed by all.

Within the ISO 9001:2000 Quality Model, there are four levels of documentation, and these are structured as shown in Figure 6.1.5.

Figure 6.1.5 Quality Management System

The Stingray QMS relies on the eight quality management principles contained in ISO 9001:2000 to provide and enable a continual improvement of our business and our overall efficiency and to make us capable of responding to customer needs and expectations. These eight principles are:

1. **Customer focused organisation** – Stingray depends on our customers and is committed to understanding, anticipating and responding to every customer requirement with product and service excellence.
2. **Leadership** – leaders establish unity of purpose and directions create the environment in which people can become fully involved in achieving Stingray's objectives.
3. **Involvement of people** – Stingray have created an environment, which makes every employee a team member and encourages participation in achieving our goals.
4. **Process approach** – the desired result is achieved by relating resources and activities to managed processes.

5. **System approach to management** – identifying, understanding and managing a system of interrelated processes for a given objective contributes to the effectiveness and efficiency of Stingray.
6. **Continual improvement** – continual improvement is a permanent objective of Stingray.
7. **Factual approach to decision-making** – effective decisions are based on the logical and intuitive analysis of data and information.
8. **Mutually beneficial supplier relationships** – mutually beneficial relationships between Stingray and its suppliers enhance the ability of both organisations to create value.

Table 6.1.1 QMS documentation

Level 1	Quality Manual	The main policy document that establishes Stingray's QMS and how it meets the requirements of ISO 9001:2000
Level 2	Processes	The Core Business Process plus Supporting Processes that describe the activities required to implement the QMS and to meet the policy requirements made in the Quality Manual
Level 3	Quality Procedures	A description of the method by which quality system activities are managed
Level 4	Work Instructions	A description of how a specific task is carried out (supplemented by drawings, blueprints, forms, checklists, records and flowcharts)

3.9.1 QMS document control

One copy of the QMS shall be held on the server. For control purposes, the Quality Manager shall have sole access to this file and it is the Quality Manager's responsibility to modify, update, amend and approve these documents as required. In all cases, the procedures and instructions contained in this controlled copy shall be official company policy.

Uncontrolled copies of the Quality Manual (including Quality Procedures and Work Instructions) shall be available to all staff via a link on Stingray's Intranet Home Page. Uncontrolled copies (stamped 'Uncontrolled copy' across the title page) may be provided to outside organisations, or individuals, for publicity or information purposes (these copies will **not** be automatically updated).

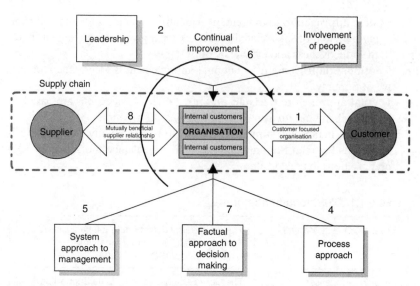

Figure 6.1.6 The eight principles of ISO 9001:2000 expressed diagrammatically

Staff shall be informed by e-mail when a controlled copy has been amended, it will include a request for all uncontrolled copies to be destroyed. All staff will reply by e-mail to the Quality Manager stating that they have complied with the request.

3.10 The Quality Manual

The Quality Manual is a statement of the managerial policy and the objectives for each element of ISO 9001:2000. For Stingray this is included in Section 4 and, having been established in response to the specified system requirements, it provides a statement of commitment to customers (or external approval and/or regulatory bodies) to which Stingray may be required to provide such information.

Stingray's Quality Manual describes a number of systematic controls and procedures for the staff in fulfilling their duties and responsibilities. It defines the lines of traceability, accountability and responsibility and whilst it exists primarily as an internal management control document, the Quality Manual also provides a definitive statement of the policy, objectives, operating systems, processes and procedures established by Stingray. The system recognises the established elements of modern formalised quality management as

Figure 6.1.7 Stingray's Quality Manual

expressed in national and international standards and as appropriate to the nature of the work undertaken.

3.11 Quality Processes

Stingray's QMS is founded on the requirements of ISO 9001:2000, with a common structure based on a Core Business Process (CP) (describing the end-to-end activities involved in Stingray's project management and the production of contract deliverables) supplemented by a number of Supporting Processes (SPs) which describe the infrastructure required to complete Stingray's projects on time and within budget.

To ensure achievement of process objectives, a process owner with full responsibility and authority for managing the process and achieving process objectives is nominated.

From the initial identification of the task through to the final customer satisfaction all steps in Stingray's Core Business Process are supported by Quality Procedures that ensure that all activities are fully understood, controlled and documented and that everyone knows exactly what they are supposed to be doing and how they should be doing it.

Current Stingray processes are listed in Part 2 of the QM.

3.12 Quality Procedures

Quality Procedures (QPs) form the bulk of Stingray's QMS and describe how the policy objectives of the Quality Manual can be met in practice and how these processes are controlled. A list of the current Stingray Quality Procedures is shown in Annex C to this Quality Manual.

QPs shall cover all the applicable elements of ISO 9001 and shall detail procedures that concern Stingray's actual method of operation. They shall be used for planning and controlling all activities that impact on quality.

Each QP shall cover an easily identifiable and separate part of the quality system and shall be capable of being easily traced back to the policies dictated by senior management.

QPs should not normally include technical requirements or specialist procedures required for the manufacture of a product. This type of detail will generally be included in a Work Instruction.

The generation and control of QPs is defined in QP/2 – Production of a Quality Document. In addition to a descriptive title and a file number, each procedure is dated and is subject to regular review (during an internal audit) for possible updating. These documented procedures are made available as uncontrolled

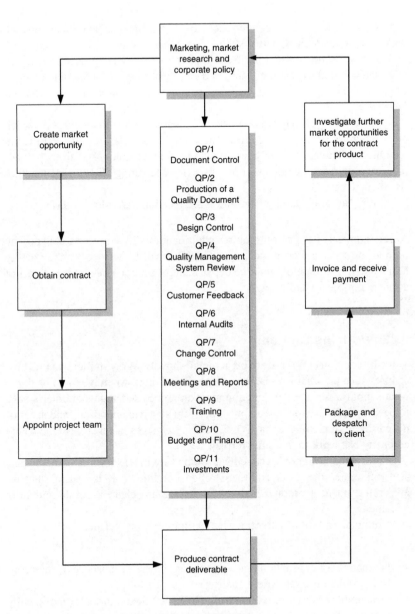

Figure 6.1.8 Stingray's Core Business Process

copies via a link on Stingray's Intranet Home Page and can be used as separate documents outside the Quality Manual in places of work.

A number of forms are used in the application of certain procedures, which mainly relate to the communication of data or instructions for keeping records. Copies of theses forms are included in the relevant procedures and Work Instructions.

Some procedures may contain data or information, the knowledge of which must remain restricted to Stingray. These procedures shall not be included in the Quality Manual, beyond their title and reference number. If these procedures are required for contractual purposes, the Managing Director must authorise their release.

Current Stingray Quality Procedures are listed in Part 3 to the QMS.

 Note: If a particular project requires additional quality controls for a specific product or service then project specific QPs shall be written by the Quality Manager (in conjunction with the department or section concerned) as part of a separate project Quality Plan.

3.13 Work Instructions

Work Instructions (WIs) describe, in detail, how Stingray implements its procedures such as, what is to be done, who should do it, when it should be done, what supplies, services and/or equipment are to be used and what criteria have to be satisfied. They describe how to perform specific operations and are produced for all of the relevant activities of Stingray so as to ensure that the whole company can work to the same format.

In order that Stingray Management can be sure that everything is being carried out under the strictest of controlled conditions, it is crucial that all WIs referring to a product activity or service are clear, accurate and fully documented.

In summary a Work Instruction shall, as a minimum, define:

- the manner of production (and installation) where the absence of such controls would adversely affect quality;
- measurable criteria for workmanship to ensure the required level of quality is being adhered to;
- monitoring and quality control requirements;
- the approval processes by which compliance can be identified;
- who can carry out this procedure.

The generation and control of WIs is defined in QP/2 – Production of a Quality Document. In addition to a descriptive title and a file number, each instruction is dated and is subject to regular review (during an internal audit) for possible updating. These documented instructions are made available as uncontrolled copies and can be used as separate documents outside the Quality Manual in places of work (see QP-01 'Document Control').

Current Stingray WIs are listed in Part 4 of the QMS.

 Note: If a particular project demands further detail then project specific Work Instructions shall be created. These project specific WIs shall appear in the Quality Plan applicable to that particular project.

Figure 6.1.9 Inter-relationship of documented processes with QPs and WIs

3.14 Records

Records provide objective evidence of and demonstrate conformance to specified requirements contained in the QMS. Normally records are retained for five years – except as required by local or national law.

3.15 Project quality plans

For larger and more complex projects/contracts, project-specific Quality Plans may have to be produced. These are effectively a subset of the QM and describe additional procedures and controls that will have to be applied. The production of these Quality Plans shall be co-ordinated between the Quality Manager and Project/Contract Manager concerned.

4 Quality Management System (ISO 9001:2000 – 4)

Subsequent sections of this QM are modelled on ISO 9001:2000 and describe the arrangements or systems that have been established to meet the specified requirements of this standard. As far as possible, the following sections (i.e. 4–8) have been structured in a similar manner to those in ISO 9001:2000 (i.e. each section, sub-section, etc. directly corresponds in terms of number and content with the ISO equivalent number). The correspondence between the Quality Manual and the requirements of ISO 9001:2000 is shown at Annex B.

Conformance with ISO 9001:2000

Other than the permissible exclusions shown in the relevant parts of the text and at Annex B, Stingray's QMS conforms to the requirements specified in ISO 9001:2000.

Quality Manual administration

The Quality Manager shall review the effectiveness and suitability of the Quality Manual at least twice a year. Where the system is found to be ineffective as a result of changed requirements, amendments shall be made to the QM.

Confidentiality

This QM is the intellectual property of Stingray and may not be copied in whole or part, or transmitted to any third party without the express written permission of the Quality Manager.

4.1 General requirements (ISO 9001:2000 – 4.1)

Stingray shall define and manage the processes necessary to ensure that all project deliverables conform to customer requirements.

As a means of continually improving project performance, Stingray shall:

- establish a QMS covering the requirements of ISO 9001:2000;
- prepare procedures that describe the processes required to implement the QMS.

4.2 Documentation requirements (ISO 9001:2000 – 4.2)

4.2.1 General (ISO 9001:2000 – 4.2.1)

Stingray QMS documentation shall include:

- statements regarding quality policy and quality objectives;
- documented procedures, that clearly describe the sequence of processes necessary to ensure conformance with ISO 9001:2000;
- documented instructions to ensure the effective operation and control of processes and quality records.

4.2.2 Quality Manual (ISO 9001:2000 – 4.2.2)

1. Stingray policy and objectives

Stingray shall establish and maintain a QM, which shall include:

- details of any ISO 9001:2000 exclusions;
- details of associated documented procedures;
- their sequence and interaction.

2. Responsibilities

The Quality Manager is responsible for overseeing the operation of the QMS; for ensuring that the QM is fully and effectively implemented and for co-ordinating the writing as well as the availability of the necessary processes, procedures and instructions.

3. Implementation

QP/4 – Quality Management System Review.

4.2.3 Control of documents (ISO 9001:2000 – 4.2.3)

1. Stingray policy and objectives

Stingray shall establish QMS level procedures for controlling documents required for the operation of the QMS. These procedures shall ensure that:

- documents are approved for adequacy prior to release;
- documents are reviewed, updated as necessary and re-approved;
- relevant versions of documents are available at locations where activities essential to the effective functioning of the QMS are performed;
- obsolete documents are removed from all points of issue and use, or otherwise controlled to prevent unintended use;
- any obsolete documents retained for legal or knowledge-preservation purposes are suitably identified.

A master list identifying the current revision status of documents shall be established and be readily available to preclude the use of invalid and/or obsolete documents.

Documents shall be legible, readily identifiable and retrievable. Applicable documents of external origin shall be identified and recorded (see 4.2.4).

2. Responsibilities

The Quality Manager (in consultation with the Company Secretary) is responsible for the overall planning of document control procedures throughout Stingray.

3. Implementation

QP/2 – Production of a Quality Document.
QP/7 – Change Control.

4.2.4 Control of quality records (ISO 9001:2000 – 4.2.4)

1. Stingray policy and objectives

Stingray shall maintain quality records appropriate to the company to demonstrate conformance to the requirements and the effective operation of the QMS. Stingray shall establish and maintain QMS level procedures for the identification, storage, retrieval, protection, retention time, and disposition of quality records.

2. Responsibilities

The Quality Manager (in consultation with the Company Secretary) is responsible for maintaining quality records demonstrating conformance to the requirements and the effective operation of the QMS.

3. Implementation

QP/1 – Document Control.
QP/2 – Production of a Quality Document.
QP/7 – Change Control.

5 Management responsibility (ISO 9001:2000 – 5)

5.1 Management commitment (ISO 9001:2000 – 5.1)

1. Stingray policy and objectives

Stingray top management (Managing Director, Quality Manager and Company Secretary) shall demonstrate their commitment by:

- establishing the quality policy and quality objectives (also see 5.3 and 5.4.1);
- carrying out regular management reviews of the QMS and its associated documentation aimed at ensuring the continual improvement of the system (also see 5.6);
- ensuring the availability of necessary resources (also see 6.1);
- ensuring adequate focus on customer requirements throughout Stingray;
- ensuring that all staff are aware of the importance of meeting customer, regulatory and legal requirements.

2. Responsibilities

The Stingray Executive Board is responsible for demonstrating their commitment to quality and for supporting management in achieving that commitment.

3. Implementation

The Stingray QM sections 5–8 together with its supporting annexes.

5.2 Customer focus (ISO 9001:2000 – 5.2)

1. Stingray policy and objectives

With the overall aim of achieving customer satisfaction, Stingray shall ensure that:

- customer needs and expectations are determined and converted into requirements;
- customer requirements are fully understood and met (also see 7.2.1);
- customer satisfaction is enhanced.

2. Responsibilities

Top management has overall responsibility for establishing, implementing and maintaining this activity.

3. Implementation

Stingray QMS Part 1 (i.e. this Quality Manual).

5.3 Quality policy (ISO 9001:2000 – 5.3)

1. Stingray policy and objectives

Stingray shall establish its quality policy and ensure that it:

- is appropriate for the needs of Stingray and its customers;
- includes a commitment to meeting requirements and continual improvement;
- provides a framework for establishing and reviewing quality objectives;
- is communicated, understood and implemented throughout Stingray;
- is regularly reviewed for continuing suitability.

2. Responsibilities

Top management has overall responsibility for establishing, implementing and maintaining this activity.

3. Implementation

Stingray QM Section 1.4.
QP/2 – Production of a Quality Document.

5.4 Planning (ISO 9001:2000 – 5.4)

5.4.1 Quality objectives (ISO 9001:2000 – 5.4.1)

1. Stingray policy and objectives

Stingray shall establish quality objectives at each relevant function and level. These quality objectives shall be consistent with the quality policy and the commitment to continual improvement. Quality objectives shall include those needed to meet product and service requirements.

2. Responsibilities

Top management has overall responsibility for establishing, implementing and maintaining this activity.

3. Implementation

Stingray QM Section 1.4.
QP/2 – Production of a Quality Document.

5.4.2 Quality Management System planning (ISO 9001:2000 – 5.4.2)

1. Stingray policy and objectives

Stingray shall identify and plan the activities and resources needed to achieve quality objectives. This planning shall be consistent with other requirements of the QMS and the results shall be documented.
   Planning shall cover the:

- processes required in the QMS (and any reduction in scope of this international standard);
- realisation processes and resources needed, identifying quality characteristics at different stages, to achieve the desired results;
- verification activities, criteria for acceptability and the quality records needed.

Planning shall ensure that organisational change is conducted in a controlled manner and that the QMS is maintained during this change.

2. Responsibilities

Top management has overall responsibility for establishing, implementing and maintaining this activity.

3. Implementation

Stingray QM Sections 1.4, 2.1 and 2.2.
SP/1 – Compliance and Approval.
QP/2 – Production of a Quality Document.

5.5 Responsibility, authority and communication (ISO 9001:2000 – 5.5)

5.5.1 Responsibility and authority (ISO 9001:2000 – 5.5.1)

1. Stingray policy and objectives

Stingray shall define the roles and their interrelations, responsibilities and authorities in order to facilitate effective quality management and this information shall be communicated throughout Stingray. Organisational freedom necessary to perform tasks that affect quality shall be defined.

2. Responsibilities

Top management has overall responsibility for establishing, implementing and maintaining this activity.

3. Implementation

Stingray QM, Annex A – Duties and responsibilities.

5.5.2 Management representative (ISO 9001:2000 – 5.5.2)

1. Stingray policy and objectives

The Managing Director shall appoint a member of the management who, irrespective of other responsibilities, shall have defined authority that includes:

- ensuring that the Stingray QMS is implemented and maintained in accordance with the requirements of this international standard;
- reporting to top management on the performance of the QMS, including needs for improvement;
- ensuring awareness of customer requirements throughout Stingray;
- liaising with external parties on matters relating to the Stingray QMS.

2. Responsibilities

The Quality Manager reports to the Managing Director and is independent of all contractual and project responsibilities that may adversely affect quality performance. He is responsible for ensuring that the QM and its associated CPs, SPs, QPs and WIs (making up the Stingray QMS) are kept up-to-date and are administered and implemented correctly and efficiently according to the quality policy laid down by the Managing Director.

The Quality Manager has the overall responsibility for ensuring that the policies set out in this QMS are understood, implemented and maintained at all levels in the organisation and that the company works towards achieving its vision and key objectives.

The Quality Manager represents Stingray in all matters relevant to the QMS as established by customer, regulatory and ISO 9001:2000 requirements. He is responsible for ensuring that the system is effectively implemented and maintained, and reports on the performance of the QMS at management review meetings.

The Quality Manager is the prime point of liaison with certification bodies and customers' quality management representatives.

3. Implementation

Details of the Quality Manager's duties and responsibilities are included at Annex A to the QM.

5.5.3 Internal communication (ISO 9001:2000 – 5.5.3)

1. Stingray policy and objectives

Stingray shall establish and maintain procedures for internal communication between the various levels and functions regarding the QMS and its effectiveness.

2. Responsibilities

The Quality Manager has overall responsibility for establishing, implementing and maintaining this activity.

3. Implementation

QP/9 – Training.

5.6 Management review (ISO 9001:2000 – 5.6)

5.6.1 General (ISO 9001:2000 – 5.6.1)

1. Stingray policy and objectives

Stingray shall establish a process for the periodic review of the QMS. It shall be reviewed to ensure its continuing suitability, adequacy and effectiveness.

The review shall evaluate the need for changes to Stingray's QMS, including policy and objectives and continues to provide customer satisfaction.

2. Responsibilities

The Quality Manager (in consultation with the Company Secretary) is responsible for ensuring that quality records are maintained in a systematic and presentable form.

All staff are responsible for ensuring that they provide the necessary records as required from their involvement in implementing the quality systems.

3. Implementation

QP/4 – Quality Management System Review.

5.6.2 Review input (ISO 9001:2000 – 5.6.2)

1. Stingray policy and objectives

The review input of the QMS shall include (but not be limited to):

- results and follow-up actions from earlier management reviews;
- results of previous internal, customer and third party audits;
- self-assessment results;
- analysis of customer feedback;
- analysis of process performance;
- analysis of product conformance;
- the current status of preventive and corrective action;
- supplier performance;
- changes that could affect the QMS;
- recommendations for improvement.

2. Responsibilities

The Quality Manager (in consultation with the Company Secretary) is responsible for ensuring that quality records are maintained in a systematic and presentable form.

All staff are responsible for ensuring that they provide the necessary records as required from their involvement in implementing the quality systems.

3. Implementation

QP/4 – Quality Management System Review.
QP/2 – Production of a Quality Document.

5.6.3 Review output (ISO 9001:2000 – 5.6.3)

1. Stingray policy and objectives

The output of the management review shall include:

- improved product and process performance;
- confirmation of resource requirements and organisational structure;
- market needs;
- risk management;
- change control;
- continued compliance with the relevant statutory and regulatory requirements.

Results of management reviews shall be recorded (see 4.2.4).

2. Responsibilities

The Quality Manager (in consultation with the Company Secretary) is responsible for ensuring that quality records are maintained in a systematic and presentable form.

All staff are responsible for ensuring that they provide the necessary records as required from their involvement in implementing the quality systems.

3. Implementation

QP/4 – Quality Management System Review.

6 Resource management (ISO 9001:2000 – 6)

6.1 Provision of resources (ISO 9001:2000 – 6.1)

1. Stingray policy and objectives

Stingray shall determine and provide in a timely manner, the resources needed to establish and maintain (and continually improve) their QMS so as to enhance customer satisfaction by meeting customer requirements.

2. Responsibilities

The Managing Director (assisted by the Quality Manager, Company Secretary and the Section Managers) has overall responsibility for establishing, implementing and maintaining this activity.

3. Implementation

QP/9 – Training.
QP/10 – Budget and Finance.

6.2 Human resources (ISO 9001:2000 – 6.2)

6.2.1 General (ISO 9001:2000 – 6.2.1)

1. Stingray policy and objectives

Stingray shall only assign personnel who are competent (e.g. education, training, skills and experience, etc.). Their responsibilities shall be defined in Annex A to this Quality Manual.

2. Responsibilities

The Managing Director (assisted by the Quality Manager, Company Secretary and the Section Managers) has overall responsibility for establishing, implementing and maintaining this activity.

3. Implementation

SP/2 Subcontractors and Suppliers.
QP/9 – Training.
QP/10 – Budget and Finance.

6.2.2 Competence, awareness and training (ISO 9001:2000 – 6.2.2)

1. Stingray policy and objectives

Stingray shall establish and maintain system level procedures to:

- determine competency and training needs;
- provide training to address identified needs;
- evaluate the effectiveness of training at defined intervals;
- maintain appropriate records of education, training, skills, and experience (see 4.2.4);
- ensure that the necessary expertise and levels of skills, etc. are available to handle the expected workload and range of activities.

Stingray shall establish and maintain procedures to make its employees at each relevant function and level aware of:

- the importance of conformance with the quality policy, and with the requirements of the Quality Management System;
- the significant impact of their work activities on quality, actual or potential;
- the benefits of improved personal performance;
- their roles and responsibilities in achieving conformance with the quality policy and procedures and with the requirements of the Quality Management System;
- the potential consequences of departure from specified procedures.

2. Responsibilities

Section Managers are responsible for ensuring that appropriate training is carried out and that all staff involved in their projects are aware of the requirements, rules and procedures to which they are to conform and against which they will be audited.

The Quality Manager is responsible for providing internal training in the QMS.

3. Implementation

QP/9 – Training.

6.3 Infrastructure (ISO 9001:2000 – 6.3)

1. Stingray policy and objectives

Stingray shall determine, provide and maintain the infrastructure to achieve product requirements regarding (but not limited to) the following:

- workspace and associated facilities;
- hardware and software;
- tools and equipment;
- communication facilities;
- supporting services.

2. Responsibilities

The Company Secretary (in consultation with the Quality Manager) has overall responsibility for establishing, implementing and maintaining this activity.

3. Implementation

QP/4 – Quality Management System Review.
QP/6 – Internal Quality Audits.
QP/8 – Meetings and Reports.
QP/10 – Budget and Finance.

6.4 Work environment (ISO 9001:2000 – 6.4)

1. Stingray policy and objectives

Stingray shall define and manage those human and physical factors of the work environment required to achieve conformity of product.
This shall include:

- health and safety conditions;
- work methods;
- work ethics;
- ambient working conditions.

2. Responsibilities

Section Managers have overall responsibility for establishing, implementing and maintaining this activity.

3. Implementation

HSE relevant documents.

7 Product realisation (ISO 9001:2000 – 7)

7.1 Planning of realisation processes (ISO 9000:2000 – 7.1)

1. Stingray policy and objectives

Processes that are necessary to realise the required product and their sequence and interaction shall be determined, planned and implemented taking into consideration the outputs from quality planning (see 5.4.2).
Stingray shall ensure these processes are operated under controlled conditions and produce outputs, which meet customer requirements. Stingray shall

determine how each process affects the ability to meet product requirements and shall:

- establish methods and practices relevant to these processes, to the extent necessary, to achieve consistent operation;
- determine and implement the criteria and methods to control processes, to the extent necessary, to achieve product conformity with the customer requirements;
- verify and validate that processes can be operated to achieve product conformity with customer requirements;
- determine and implement arrangements for measurement, monitoring and follow-up actions, to ensure processes continue to operate to achieve planned results and outputs (see 8);
- ensure the availability of the information and data necessary to support the effective operation and monitoring of the processes;
- maintain as quality records the results of process control measures, to provide evidence of effective operation and monitoring of the processes (see 4.2.4).

2. Responsibilities

Top management has overall responsibility for establishing, implementing and maintaining this activity.

3. Implementation

CP/1 – Core Business Process.
SP/1 – Compliance and Approval.
SP/2 – Subcontractors and Suppliers.
QP/3 – Design Control.

7.2 Customer-related processes (ISO 9000:2000 – 7.2)

7.2.1 Determination of requirements related to the product (ISO 9001:2000 – 7.2.1)

1. Stingray policy and objectives

Stingray shall establish a process for identifying customer requirements that determine the:

- completeness of the customer's product and/or service requirements;
- requirements not specified by the customer but necessary for fitness for purpose;
- statutory, regulatory and legal requirements;

- specific customer requirements for availability, delivery and support of product and/or service.

2. Responsibilities

The Managing Director (assisted by the Quality Manager, Company Secretary and the Section Managers) has overall responsibility for establishing, implementing and maintaining this activity.

3. Implementation

CP/1 – Core Business Process.
SP/1 – Compliance and Approval.
SP/2 – Subcontractors and Suppliers.
QP/3 – Design Control.
QP/5 – Customer Feedback.

7.2.2 Review of requirements related to the product (ISO 9000:2000 – 7.2.2)

1. Stingray policy and objectives

The customer requirements, including any requested changes, shall be reviewed before a commitment to supply a product is provided to the customer (e.g. submission of a tender, acceptance of a contract or order) to ensure that:

- customer requirements are clearly defined for product and/or service;
- where the customer provides no written statement of requirement, the customer requirements are confirmed before acceptance;
- contract or order requirements differing from those previously expressed (e.g. in a tender or quotation), are resolved;
- Stingray has the ability to meet the customer requirements for the product and/or service.

The results of the review and subsequent follow-up actions shall be recorded (see 4.2.4) and the information disseminated to all the relevant personnel.

2. Responsibilities

Section Managers have overall responsibility for establishing, implementing and maintaining this activity.

3. Implementation

CP/1 – Core Business Process.
QP/1 – Document Control.
QP/3 – Design Control.
QP/7 – Change Control.

7.2.3 Customer communication (ISO 9000:2000 – 7.2.3)

1. Stingray policy and objectives

Stingray shall determine and implement arrangements for customer communication with the overall aim of meeting customer requirements. Stingray shall define communication requirements relating to:

- product information;
- enquiries and order handling, including amendments;
- customer complaints and actions relating to non-conforming product (see 8.3 and 8.5.2);
- customer responses relating to product performance (see 7.3.2 and 8.2.1).

2. Responsibilities

The Managing Director (in consultation with the Quality Manager, Company Secretary and the Section Managers) has overall responsibility for establishing, implementing and maintaining this activity.

3. Implementation

QP/5 – Customer Feedback.

7.3 Design and development (ISO 9000:2000 – 7.3)

7.3.1 Design and development planning (ISO 9001:2000 – 7.3.1)

1. Stingray policy and objectives

Stingray shall plan and control the design and development of a product, which shall include:

- stages of the design and development process;
- required review, verification and validation activities;
- responsibilities and authorities for design and development activities.

Interfaces between different groups involved in design and development shall be managed to ensure effective communication and clarity of responsibilities.

Planning output shall be updated, as the design and development progresses.

2. Responsibilities

Section Managers have overall responsibility for establishing, implementing and maintaining this activity.

3. Implementation

CP/1 – Core Business Process.
SP/1 – Compliance and Approval.
QP/3 – Design Control.
QP/6 – Internal Quality Audits.
QP/7 – Change Control.
QP/8 – Meetings and Reports.

7.3.2 Design and development inputs (ISO 9001:2000 – 7.3.2)

1. Stingray policy and objectives

Stingray shall define and record the requirements to be met by the product and/or service (see 4.2.4). These shall include:

- functional and performance requirements from customer or market;
- applicable statutory, regulatory and legal requirements;
- applicable environmental requirements;
- requirements derived from previous similar designs;
- any other requirements essential for design and development.

These inputs shall be reviewed for adequacy and incomplete, ambiguous or conflicting requirements shall be resolved.

2. Responsibilities

Section Managers have overall responsibility for establishing, implementing and maintaining this activity.

3. Implementation

CP/1 – Core Business Process.
QP/3 – Design Control.

QP/6 – Internal Quality Audits.
QP/7 – Change Control.
QP/8 – Meetings and Reports.

7.3.3 Design and development outputs (ISO 9001:2000 – 7.3.3)

1. Stingray policy and objectives

Design and development output shall:

- meet the design and development input requirements;
- contain or make reference to product and/or service acceptance criteria;
- define the characteristics of the product that are essential to its safe and proper use;
- be approved before being released.

2. Responsibilities

Section Managers have overall responsibility for establishing, implementing and maintaining this activity.

3. Implementation

CP/1 – Core Business Process.
QP/3 – Design Control.
QP/6 – Internal Quality Audits.
QP/7 – Change Control.
QP/8 – Meetings and Reports.

7.3.4 Design and development review (ISO 9001:2000 – 7.3.4)

1. Stingray policy and objectives

At suitable stages, systematic reviews of design and development shall be conducted to:

- evaluate the ability of a product to fulfil requirements for quality;
- identify problems;
- propose follow-up actions.

Participants of these reviews shall include a representative from the design stage being reviewed.

Results of the reviews and subsequent follow-up actions shall be recorded (see 4.2.4).

2. Responsibilities

Section Managers have overall responsibility for establishing, implementing and maintaining this activity.

3. Implementation

CP/1 – Core Business Process.
SP/1 – Compliance and Approval.
QP/2 – Production of a Quality Document.
QP/3 – Design Control.
QP/6 – Internal Quality Audits.
QP/8 – Meetings and Reports.

7.3.5 Design and development verification (ISO 9001:2000 – 7.3.5)

1. Stingray policy and objectives

A verification process shall be planned and implemented to ensure that the design and development output meets the design and development input. The results of the verification and subsequent follow-up actions shall be recorded (see 4.2.4).

2. Responsibilities

Section Managers have overall responsibility for establishing, implementing and maintaining this activity.

3. Implementation

CP/1 – Core Business Process.
SP/1 – Compliance and Approval.
QP/3 – Design Control.
QP/6 – Internal Quality Audits.
QP/7 – Change Control.
QP/8 – Meetings and Reports.

7.3.6 Design and development validation (ISO 9001:2000 – 7.3.6)

1. Stingray policy and objectives

Prior to the delivery or implementation of the product and/or service, design and development validation shall be performed to confirm that resultant product and/or service is capable of meeting the particular requirements for a specific intended customer use.

Wherever applicable, validation shall be defined, planned and completed prior to the delivery or implementation of the product and/or service. Where it is impossible to undertake full validation prior to delivery or implementation, partial validation of the design or development outputs shall be undertaken to the maximum extent practical.

The results of the validation and subsequent follow-up actions shall be recorded (see 4.2.4).

2. Responsibilities

Section Managers have overall responsibility for establishing, implementing and maintaining this activity.

3. Implementation

CP/1 – Core Business Process.
SP/1 – Compliance and Approval.
QP/3 – Design Control.
QP/6 – Internal Quality Audits.
QP/7 – Change Control.
QP/8 – Meetings and Reports.

7.3.7 Control of design and development changes (ISO 9001:2000 – 7.3.7)

1. Stingray policy and objectives

Stingray shall identify, document and control all design and development changes and shall evaluate the effect of these changes and/or modifications on:

- the interaction between the elements of the design and development;
- the interaction between the component parts of the resulting product and/or service;

- existing products and/or services and upon post-delivery product operations;
- the need for carrying out re-verification or re-validation for all or part of the design and development outputs.

The results of the review of changes and subsequent follow-up actions shall be recorded (see 4.2.4).

2. Responsibilities

Section Managers have overall responsibility for establishing, implementing and maintaining this activity.

3. Implementation

CP/1 – Core Business Process.
SP/1 – Compliance and Approval.
QP/3 – Design Control.
QP/6 – Internal Quality Audits.
QP/7 – Change Control.

7.4 Purchasing (ISO 9001:2000 – 7.4)

7.4.1 Purchasing process (ISO 9001:2000 – 7.4.1)

1. Stingray policy and objectives

Although the majority of purchases only concern stationery and the maintenance/improvement of IT facilities, Stingray, nevertheless, needs to control its purchasing processes to ensure that the purchased product conforms to Stingray's requirements. The type and extent of methods to control these processes shall be dependent on the effect of the purchased product upon the final product.

Stingray shall evaluate and select suppliers based on their ability to supply products in accordance with Stingray's requirements. Evaluation, re-evaluation and selection criteria for suppliers shall be established. The results of evaluations and subsequent follow-up actions shall be recorded (see 4.2.4).

The Stingray system for control of all purchased goods or subcontracted services shall ensure those products or services purchased and received conform to specified requirements and include provision for the assessment of suppliers and subcontractors. It shall also establish rules for the specification of requirements for purchased documents and the verification of goods and services received.

2. Responsibilities

The Company Secretary (assisted by the Section Managers and the Quality Manager), has overall responsibility for establishing, implementing and maintaining this activity.

3. Implementation

SP/2 – Subcontractors and Suppliers.
QP/1 – Document Control.
QP/10 – Budget and Finance.
Individual (i.e. sectional) subcontract assessment procedures according to product and/or contract.

7.4.2 Purchasing information (ISO 9001:2000 – 7.4.2)

1. Stingray policy and objectives

Purchasing documents shall contain information clearly describing the product and/or service ordered, including where appropriate:

- requirements for approval or qualification of product and/or service, procedures, processes, equipment and personnel;
- any QMS requirements.

Stingray shall ensure the adequacy of specified purchase requirements prior to release.

2. Responsibilities

The Company Secretary (assisted by the Section Managers and the Quality Manager), has overall responsibility for establishing, implementing and maintaining this activity.

3. Implementation

SP/2 – Subcontractors and Suppliers.
QP/1 – Document Control.
QP/10 – Budget and Finance.

Individual (i.e. sectional) subcontract assessment procedures according to product and/or contract.

7.4.3 Verification of purchased product (ISO 9001:2000 – 7.4.3)

1. Stingray policy and objectives

Stingray shall determine and implement the procedures necessary for verification of purchased product (see 8.2.4).

Where Stingray or its customer proposes to perform verification activities at the supplier's premises, Stingray shall specify the required verification arrangements and method of product release in the purchasing documents.

2. Responsibilities

The Company Secretary (assisted by the Section Managers and the Quality Manager), has overall responsibility for establishing, implementing and maintaining this activity.

3. Implementation

SP/2 – Subcontractors and Suppliers.
QP/1 – Document Control.
QP/7 – Change Control.
QP/10 – Budget and Finance.
Individual (i.e. sectional) subcontract assessment procedures according to product and/or contract.

7.5 Production and service provision (ISO 9001:2000 – 7.5)

7.5.1 Control of production and service provision (ISO 9001:2000 – 7.5.1)

1. Stingray policy and objectives

Stingray shall plan and control production and service operations, including those undertaken after initial delivery, through:

- the availability of information and specifications that clearly define the characteristics of the product that is to be achieved;
- the availability of Work Instructions for those activities where they are necessary for the achievement of conformity of products;

- the use and maintenance of suitable production, installation, and maintenance equipment (see 6.3);
- the availability of monitoring and measuring equipment;
- the implementation of suitable monitoring and measuring activities (see
  8.2.3 and 8.2.4);
- suitable methods for release and delivery and/or installation of product
  and/or service.

2. Responsibilities

Top management, assisted by Section Managers, has overall responsibility for
establishing, implementing and maintaining this activity.

3. Implementation

Stingray QMS Part 3 – Quality Procedures.
Stingray QMS Part 4 – Work Instructions.
QP/1 – Document Control.
QP/7 – Change Control.

7.5.2 Validation of processes for production and service provision (ISO 9001:2000 – 7.5.2)

1. Stingray policy and objectives

As Stingray's product is exclusively management system documents and
reports, this section is **not** applicable to Stingray's business.

7.5.3 Identification and traceability (ISO 9001:2000 – 7.5.3)

1. Stingray policy and objectives

Stingray shall have procedures for identifying the status of a product with
respect to required measurement and verification activities and, where traceability is a requirement, Stingray shall identify the product throughout all
processes. In particular this shall apply to the component parts of the product
where their interaction affects conformity with requirements.

2. Responsibilities

Top management, assisted by Section Managers, has overall responsibility for
establishing, implementing and maintaining this activity.

3. Implementation

QP/1 – Document Control.
QP/6 – Internal Quality Audits.
QP/7 – Change Control.

7.5.4 Customer property (ISO 9001:2000 – 7.5.4)

1. Stingray policy and objectives

Stingray shall ensure that all customer property while it is under Stingray's supervision or being used by Stingray is identified, verified, stored and maintained. Any customer property that is lost, damaged or otherwise found to be unsuitable for use shall be recorded and reported to the customer (see 7.2.3).

 Note: Customer property may include intellectual property e.g. information provided in confidence.

2. Responsibilities

Top management, assisted by Section Managers, has overall responsibility for establishing, implementing and maintaining this activity.

3. Implementation

QP/1 – Document Control.
QP/5 – Customer Feedback.
QP/6 – Internal Quality Audits.
QP/8 – Meetings and Reports.

7.5.5 Preservation of product (ISO 9001:2000 – 7.5.5)

1. Stingray policy and objectives

Stingray shall ensure that during internal processing and final delivery of product to the intended destination that the identification, packaging, storage, preservation, and handling do not affect conformity with product requirements. This shall also apply to parts or components of a product and elements of a service.

Product release/delivery shall not proceed until all the specified activities have been satisfactorily completed and the related documentation is available and authorised.

2. Responsibilities

The Company Secretary, assisted by Section Managers, has overall responsibility for establishing, implementing and maintaining this activity.

3. Implementation

Stingray QMS Part 3 – Quality Procedures.
Stingray QMS Part 4 – Work Instructions.
QP/1 – Document Control.

7.6 Control of monitoring and measuring devices (ISO 9001:2000 – 7.6)

1. Stingray policy and objectives

As Stingray's product is exclusively management system documents and reports this section is **not** applicable to Stingray's business.

8 Measurement, analysis and improvement (ISO 9001:2000 – 8)

8.1 General (ISO 9001:2000 – 8.1)

1. Stingray policy and objectives

Stingray shall define, plan and implement measurement, monitoring, analysis and improvement processes to ensure that the QMS, processes and products conform to requirements and shall ensure that:

- the type, location, timing and frequency of measurements and the requirements for records are defined (see 4.2.4);
- the effectiveness of measures implemented is periodically evaluated.

Stingray shall identify and use appropriate statistical tools and the results of data analysis and improvement activities shall be an input to the management review process (see 5.6).

2. Responsibilities

Top management, assisted by Section Managers, has overall responsibility for establishing, implementing and maintaining this activity.

3. Implementation

QP/6 – Internal Quality Audits.
QP/8 – Meetings and Reports.

8.2 Monitoring and measurement (ISO 9001:2000 – 8.2)

8.2.1 Customer satisfaction (ISO 9001:2000 – 8.2.1)

1. Stingray policy and objectives

Stingray shall monitor customer satisfaction and/or dissatisfaction as one of the measurements of performance of the QMS. The methods and measures for obtaining and utilising such information and data shall be defined.

2. Responsibilities

Top management, assisted by Section Managers, has overall responsibility for establishing, implementing and maintaining this activity.

3. Implementation

QP/5 – Customer Feedback.
QP/7 – Change Control.

8.2.2 Internal audit (ISO 9001:2000 – 8.2.2)

1. Stingray policy and objectives

Stingray shall carry out objective audits in order to determine if the QMS has been effectively implemented and maintained and conforms to ISO 9001:2000. In addition, Stingray may carry out audits to identify potential opportunities for improvement.

The audit process, including the schedule, shall be based on the status and importance of the activities and/or areas to be audited and the results of previous audits.

 Note: See also ISO 10011 Parts 1, 2 and 3 for guidance.

2. Responsibilities

Top management has overall responsibility for establishing, implementing and maintaining this activity.

3. Implementation

QP/4 – Quality Management System Review.
QP/6 – Internal Quality Audits.
QP/8 – Meetings and Reports.

8.2.3 Monitoring and measurement of processes (ISO 9001:2000 – 8.2.3)

1. Stingray policy and objectives

Stingray shall monitor and measure processes to ensure that they continue to satisfy their intended purpose.

2. Responsibilities

Top management, assisted by Section Managers, has overall responsibility for establishing, implementing and maintaining this activity.

3. Implementation

SP/1 – Compliance and Approval.
QP/4 – Quality Management System Review.
QP/6 – Internal Quality Audits.
QP/8 – Meetings and Reports.

8.2.4 Monitoring and measurement of product (ISO 9001:2000 – 8.2.4)

1. Stingray policy and objectives

Stingray shall monitor and measure the characteristics of the product to verify that requirements for the product and/or service are met.

Evidence conformance shall be documented and recorded. Records shall indicate the authority responsible for release of product (see 4.2.4).

2. Responsibilities

Top management, assisted by Section Managers, has overall responsibility for establishing, implementing and maintaining this activity.

3. Implementation

SP/1 – Compliance and Approval.
QP/4 – Quality Management System Review.
QP/6 – Internal Quality Audits.
QP/8 – Meetings and Reports.

8.3 Control of non-conforming product (ISO 9001:2000 – 8.3)

1. Stingray policy and objectives

Stingray shall ensure that products that do not conform to requirements are identified and controlled to prevent unintended use or delivery. These non-conformities shall be:

- corrected or adjusted to conform to requirements and re-validated; or
- accepted under concession, with or without correction or adjustment; or
- re-assigned for alternative valid application; or
- rejected as unsuitable.

2. Responsibilities

The Quality Manager, assisted by the Section Managers, has overall responsibility for establishing, implementing and maintaining this activity.

3. Implementation

SP/1 – Compliance and Approval.
QP/4 – Quality Management System Review.
QP/6 – Internal Quality Audits.
QP/8 – Meetings and Reports.

8.4 Analysis of data (ISO 9001:2000 – 8.4)

1. Stingray policy and objectives

Stingray shall analyse all applicable data to determine the suitability, adequacy and effectiveness of the QMS and use this to provide information relating to:

- customer satisfaction and/or dissatisfaction;
- conformance to product requirements;
- characteristics of trends and opportunities for preventive action;
- suppliers.

2. Responsibilities

Top management, assisted by the Section Managers, has overall responsibility for establishing, implementing and maintaining this activity.

3. Implementation

SP/1 – Compliance and Approval.
QP/4 – Quality Management System Review.
QP/5 – Customer Feedback.
QP/6 – Internal Quality Audits.
QP/8 – Meetings and Reports.

8.5 Improvement (ISO 9001:2000 – 8.5)

8.5.1 Continual improvement (ISO 9001:2000 – 8.5.1)

1. Stingray policy and objectives

Stingray shall plan and manage the processes necessary for the continual improvement of the QMS through the use of a system level procedure that describes the use of quality policy, objectives, internal audit results, analysis of data, corrective and preventive action and management review to facilitate continual improvement.

2. Responsibilities

Top management has overall responsibility for establishing, implementing and maintaining this activity.

3. Implementation

QP/4 – Quality Management System Review.
QP/6 – Internal Quality Audits.
QP/8 – Meetings and Reports.

8.5.2 Corrective action (ISO 9001:2000 – 8.5.2)

1. Stingray policy and objectives

Stingray shall define the requirements for:

- identifying non-conformities (including customer complaints);
- determination of the causes of non-conformity;

- evaluating the need for actions to ensure that non-conformities do not recur;
- implementing corrective action;
- recording the results of actions taken;
- reviewing that corrective action taken is effective and recorded.

2. Responsibilities

Top management, assisted by the Section Managers, has overall responsibility for establishing, implementing and maintaining this activity.

3. Implementation

QP/4 – Quality Management System Review.
QP/6 – Internal Quality Audits.
QP/8 – Meetings and Reports.

8.5.3 Preventive action (ISO 9001:2000 – 8.5.3)

1. Stingray policy and objectives

Stingray shall define the requirements for:

- identification of potential non-conformities;
- determination of the causes of the identified potential non-conformities;
- determination of preventive action needed to eliminate causes of potential non-conformities;
- implementation of preventive action;
- recording the results of action taken;
- reviewing that preventive action taken is effective.

2. Responsibilities

Top management, assisted by Section Managers, has overall responsibility for establishing, implementing and maintaining this activity.

3. Implementation

QP/4 – Quality Management System Review.
QP/6 – Internal Quality Audits.
QP/8 – Meetings and Reports.

Annex A – Stingray organisation and responsibilities

Figure 6.1.10 Stingray Management Services Ltd – organisational chart

1. Managing Director

The Managing Director is responsible for the overall management of Stingray. He is responsible for the overall and final success of all contracts undertaken, for providing guidance on all major issues and for ensuring that all Stingray's products and services are produced and delivered to the highest possible level.

The Managing Director is responsible for:

- supervising the day-to-day running of Stingray;
- the overall progress of the work with which he has been entrusted and the budget placed at his disposal;
- controlling budget, time schedules, quality plans, resources and quality within the company;
- approving changes to agreed time schedules, resources and budgets;
- ensuring that the organisation will, at all times, meet the business requirements and objectives (as stipulated in Stingray's Memorandum of Articles and Association) as well as keeping to the agreed time schedule;
- maintaining overall responsibility for all sections;
- preparing contracts for section members, in consultation with Section Managers.

2. Quality Manager

The Quality Manager is responsible for ensuring that the organisation's QMS is defined, implemented, audited and monitored in order to ensure that

Stingray's documents comply with the customers' quality standards as well as the ISO 9000 series of documents concerning 'Quality Management System'. The Quality Manager shall report directly to the Managing Director.

His tasks shall include:

- maintenance and effectiveness of Stingray's QMS;
- ensuring compliance of Stingray's QMS with ISO 9001:2000;
- ensuring the consistency of Stingray's QMS;
- ensuring that the quality message is transmitted to and understood by everyone.

3. Company Secretary

The Stingray Administration, Finance and Secretarial Office is headed by the Company Secretary. The Company Secretary is responsible for general administrative activities such as filing and distribution of Stingray documents as well as aspects of financial and contractual administration. The Company Secretary shall report directly to the Managing Director.

His tasks shall include:

- the daily running of the Stingray Office;
- issuing financial reports;
- producing monthly financial statements to the Managing Director;
- the organisation of special meetings, workshops, seminars etc. when requested to do so by the Managing Director;
- arranging (and planning) publication of documents when required.

4. Section Managers

Section Managers are appointed by the Managing Director and are responsible for the general progress of their section, the budget placed at their disposal, for organising the work of their section and distributing this work between the sectional members according to the directives, procedures and instructions making up the Stingray QMS whilst duly observing the requirements of Stingray's Memorandum of Articles and Association.

Section Managers shall report directly to the Managing Director and their tasks shall include:

- controlling the time schedules, work packages, resources and quality of the tasks allocated to their section;
- ensuring that the section will, at all times, meet the business needs and objectives of Stingray;

- directing the studies of the section with the constant aim of achieving an accelerated and sustained tempo of the studies within the scope of their own particular quality plan and individual work packages;
- the progress and time management of all sub task(s).

5. Section members

Section members shall carry out the accepted tasks assigned by their Section Manager, within the deadlines set.

6. Subcontractors and consultants

When the work/studies of a section falls outside the scope of section members, the Managing Director may authorise the temporary co-operation of subcontractors and consultants.

A contract/agreement for the subcontractor's or consultant's participation will be concluded with his company or with his parent company by the Company Secretary.

The subcontractor or consultant shall be expected to make use of his personal knowledge and experience acquired both in and outside his company without, however, in any way committing the latter. The company who provides subcontractors or consultants shall, in return, grant them the greatest possible freedom of action and initiative and shall afford them the time and facilities required to carry out whatever work/studies they might be charged with in their capacity as a member of a Stingray section.

Annex B – ISO 9001:2000 cross-check

Clause no.	ISO 9001:2000 title	Quality Manual	Quality Process	Quality Procedure
4	**Quality Management System**			
4.1	General requirements	Sections 1–2		
4.2	Documentation requirements			
4.2.1	General		SP/1 SP/2	
4.2.2	Quality Manual		SP/1 SP/2	QP/4
4.2.3	Control of documents			QP/1 QP/2 QP/7
4.2.4	Control of quality records			QP/1 QP/2 QP/7
5	**Management responsibility**			
5.1	Management commitment	Sections 5–8		
5.2	Customer focus		SP/1 SP/2	
5.3	Quality policy	Section 4		QP/2
5.4	Planning			
5.4.1	Quality objectives	Section 4		
5.4.2	Quality Management System planning	Sections 1.4, 2.1 and 2.2	SP/1	QP/2
5.5	Responsibility, authority and communication			
5.5.1	Responsibility and authority	Annex A		
5.5.2	Management representative	Annex A		
5.5.3	Internal communication			QP/9
5.6	Management review			
5.6.1	General			QP/4
5.6.2	Review input			QP/2, QP/4

Clause no.	ISO 9001:2000 title	Quality Manual	Quality Process	Quality Procedure
5.6.3	Review output			QP/4
6	**Resource management**			
6.1	Provision of resources			QP/9, QP/10
6.2	Human resources			
6.2.1	General		SP/2	QP/9, QP/10
6.2.2	Competence, awareness and training			QP/9
6.3	Infrastructure			QP/4 QP/6 QP/8 QP/10
6.4	Work environment	HSE documents		
7	**Product realisation**			
7.1	Planning of realisation processes		SP/1 SP/2	QP/3
7.2	Customer-related processes			
7.2.1	Determination of requirements related to the product		CP/1 SP/1 SP/2	QP/3 QP/5
7.2.2	Review of requirements related to the product		CP/1	QP/1 QP/3 QP/7
7.2.3	Customer communications			QP/5
7.3	Design and development			
7.3.1	Design and development planning		SP/1	QP/3 QP/6 QP/7 QP/8
7.3.2	Design and development inputs		CP/1	QP/3 QP/6 QP/7 QP/8
7.3.3	Design and development outputs		CP/1	QP/3 QP/6 QP/7 QP/8

Clause no.	ISO 9001:2000 title	Quality Manual	Quality Process	Quality Procedure
7.3.4	Design and development review		CP/1 SP/1	QP/2 QP/3 QP/6 QP/8
7.3.5	Design and development verification		CP/1 SP/1	QP/3 QP/6 QP/7 QP/8
7.3.6	Design and development validation		CP/1 SP/1	QP/3 QP/6 QP/7 QP/8
7.3.7	Control of design and development changes		SP/1	QP/3 QP/7
7.4	Purchasing			
7.4.1	Purchasing process		SP/2	QP/1 QP/10
7.4.2	Purchasing information		SP/2	QP/1 QP/10
7.4.3	Verification of purchased product		SP/2	QP/1 QP/7 QP/10
7.5	Production and service provision			
7.5.1	Control of production and service provision			QP/3 QP/7
7.5.2	Validation of processes for production and service provision	PERMISSIBLE EXCLUSION		
7.5.3	Identification and traceability			QP/1 QP/6 QP/7 QP/8
7.5.4	Customer property			QP/1 QP/5 QP/6 QP/8
7.5.5	Preservation of product			QP/1
7.6	Control of measuring and monitoring devices	PERMISSIBLE EXCLUSION		

Clause no.	ISO 9001:2000 title	Quality Manual	Quality Process	Quality Procedure
8	**Measurement, analysis and improvement**			
8.1	General			QP/6 QP/8
8.2	Monitoring and measurement			
8.2.1	Customer satisfaction			QP/5
8.2.2	Internal audit			QP/4 QP/6 QP/8
8.2.3	Monitoring and measurement of processes		SP/1	QP/4 QP/6 QP/8
8.2.4	Monitoring and measurement of product			QP/1 QP/4 QP/6 QP/8
8.3	Control of non-conforming product			QP/1 QP/4 QP/6 QP/8
8.4	Analysis of data		SP/1	QP/4 QP/5 QP/6 QP/8
8.5	Improvement			
8.5.1	Continual improvement			QP/4 QP/6 QP/8
8.5.2	Corrective action			QP/4 QP/6 QP/8
8.5.3	Preventative action			QP/4 QP/6 QP/8

Note: Other than the permissible exclusions shown in the relevant parts of the text, Stingray's Quality Manual conforms to the requirements of ISO 9001:2000.

Annex C – List of Quality Procedures

Procedure no.	Procedure title
QP/1	Document Control
QP/2	Production of a Quality Document
QP/3	Design Control
QP/4	Quality Management System Review
QP/5	Customer Feedback
QP/6	Internal Quality Audits
QP/7	Change Control
QP/8	Meetings and Reports
QP/9	Training
QP/10	Budget and Finance
QP/11	Investments

Annex D – Abbreviations and Acronyms

Abbreviation	Definition
CP	Core Business Process
DCS	Document Control Sheet
Stingray	Stingray Management Services Ltd
HSE	Health & Safety Executive (UK)
ISO	International Standards Organisation
IT	Information Technology
LMO	Large Multinational Organisation
QM	Quality Manual
QMS	Quality Management System
QP	Quality Procedure
SME	Small Medium Enterprise
SP	Supporting Process
SQP	Project specific Quality Plan
TQM	Total Quality Management
WI	Work Instruction

References

Ref.	Abbreviation	Title	Issue date
1.	ISO 9001	Quality Management Systems – Requirements	2000
2.	ISO 10011	Guidelines for auditing quality systems	2002
3.	3042940	Stingray Management Services Ltd's Memorandum and Articles of Association	1994
4.	ACP 8	Directions for the organisation and direction of work	1995
5.	ACP 9	Documentation manual (draft) for the Aircraft Industry	1995

Document Ref: S-52-029RLT05
Version: 02.02
Date: 01.01.05
Quality Management System
Part Two – Quality Processes

Stingray Management Services Ltd

Quality Management System
Part 2 – Quality Processes

These Quality Processes have been issued on the authority of the Managing Director of Stingray Management Services Ltd for the use of all staff, sub-contractors, clients and/or regulatory bodies to whom Stingray Management Services Ltd may be required to provide such information to.

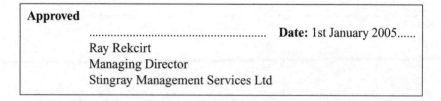

Approved

.... **Date:** 1st January 2005......
Ray Rekcirt
Managing Director
Stingray Management Services Ltd

Document Control Sheet

Abstract

The Stingray Management Services Ltd Quality Management System is divided into four parts. This document is Part 2 and describes the Quality Processes that have been developed to implement Stingray Management Services Ltd's Quality Management System. The Quality Procedures designed to meet these processes are contained in Part 3 and the details of the Work Instructions are in Part 4. Part 1 contains a complete copy of the actual Quality Manual.

Attachments

Attachment	Description

QMS revision history

No.	Chapter	Amendment details	Date
01.00	All	First published version in accordance with ISO 9001:1994	28.06.93
01.01	3	Inclusion of new chapter for customer satisfaction	05.04.94
01.02	4.2.3	Procedure for the control of documents changed	23.12.95
01.03	All	Minor editorial revisions of all sections and annexes	30.07.96
02.00	All	Second published version to conform to ISO 9001:2000	31.12.00
02.01	5	Management responsibility procedure updated to cover new (i.e. Fuels) Division	01.01.02
02.02	All	Minor editorial changes following three years' experience of ISO 9001:2000	01.01.05

Contents

List of illustrations

List of tables

1 Documentation

Stingray Management Services Ltd (Stingray) has four levels of documentation within their Quality Management System (QMS) which is structured as shown in the table below.

This document is Part 2 and describes the Quality Processes that have been developed to implement Stingray's QMS.

Table 6.2.1 Stingray Management Services Ltd's Quality System – documentation

Part 1	Quality Manual	The main policy document that establishes Stingray's QMS and how it meets the requirements of ISO 9001:2000.
Part 2	**Quality Processes**	**The Core Business Process plus the Supporting Processes that describe the activities required to implement the QMS and to meet the policy requirements made in the Quality Manual.**
Part 3	Quality Procedures	A description of the method by which quality system activities are managed.
Part 4	Work Instructions	A description of how a specific task is carried out.

2 Supporting Processes

The Stingray QMS is based on the requirements contained in ISO 9001:2000 with a common structure based on a Core Business Process model supplemented by a series of Supporting Process models.

The current list of Stingray Processes are:

Table 6.2.2 Quality Processes

Process no.	Instruction title
CP/1	Stingray Core Business Process
SP/1	Compliance and approval
SP/2	Subcontractors and suppliers
SP/3	TBA
SP/4	TBA
SP/5	TBA
SP/6	TBA

3 Core Business Process

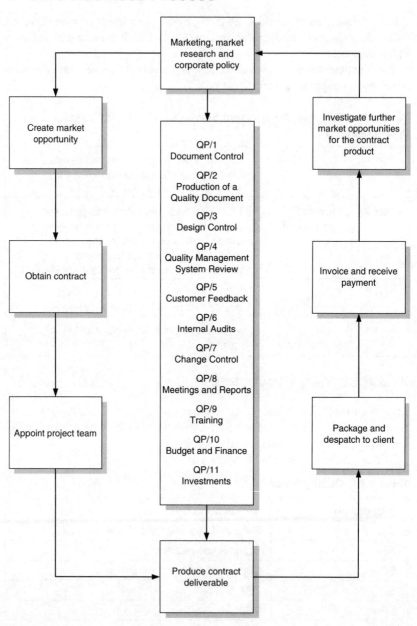

Figure 6.2.1 Core Business Process – overall

From the initial identification of the task through to the final customer satisfaction all steps in Stingray's Core Business Process are supported by Quality Procedures that ensure that all activities are fully understood, controlled and documented and that everyone knows exactly what they are supposed to be doing and how they should be doing it.

The Managing Director is responsible for managing the Core Business Process.

4 Supporting Processes

Figure 6.2.2 Supporting processes

4.1 SP/1 Compliance and approval

Figure 6.2.3 Compliance and approval

Before Stingray can tender for projects it must comply with the applicable regulations and standards. In order to achieve approval Stingray will put into practice the various steps shown in the compliance and approval chart above.

The Quality Manager is responsible for managing this Supplementary Process.

4.2 SP/2 – Subcontractors and suppliers

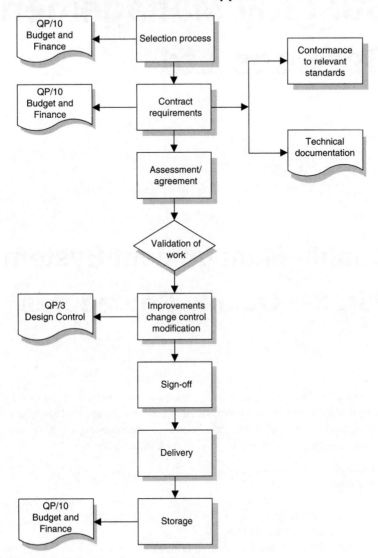

Figure 6.2.4 Subcontractors and suppliers

From the In selection process through to delivery and storage all contract requirements will be monitored and assessed for compliance.

The Managing Director is responsible for managing this Supplementary Process.

Stingray Management Services Ltd

Quality Management System
Part 3 – Quality Procedures

These Quality Procedures have been issued on the authority of the Managing Director of Stingray Management Services Ltd for the use of all staff, subcontractors, clients and/or regulatory bodies to whom Stingray Management Services Ltd may be required to provide such information to.

Approved

.... **Date:** 1st January 2005......

Ray Rekcirt
Managing Director
Stingray Management Services Ltd

Document Control Sheet

Abstract

The Stingray's Quality Management System is divided into four parts. This document is Part 3 and describes the Quality Procedures that have been adopted by Stingray Management Services Ltd. Details of the Work Instructions associated with these procedures are contained in Part 4.

Attachments

Attachment	Description

QMS revision history

No.	Chapter	Amendment details	Date
01.00	All	First published version in accordance with ISO 9001:1994	28.06.93
01.01	3	Inclusion of new chapter for customer satisfaction	05.04.94
01.02	4.2.3	Procedure for the control of documents changed	23.12.95
01.03	All	Minor editorial revisions of all sections and annexes	30.07.96
02.00	All	Second published version to conform to ISO 9001:2000	31.12.00
02.01	5	Management responsibility procedure updated to cover new (i.e. Fuels) Division	01.01.02
02.02	All	Minor editorial changes following three years' experience of ISO 9001:2000	01.01.05

Contents

List of illustrations

List of tables

1 Documentation

Stingray Management Services Ltd (Stingray) has four levels of documentation within our Quality Management System (QMS) which is structured as shown in the table below. This document is Part 3 and describes the Quality Procedures that have been designed to meet Stingray's Quality Processes.

The Work Instructions associated with these Quality Procedures are detailed in Part 4.

Table 6.3.1 Stingray Management Systems Ltd's Quality System – documentation

Part 1	Quality Manual	The main policy document that establishes Stingray's QMS and how it meets the requirements of ISO 9001:2000.
Part 2	Quality Processes	The Core Business Process plus the Primary and Secondary Supporting Processes that describe the activities required to implement the QMS and to meet the policy requirements made in the QM.
Part 3	**Quality Procedures**	**A description of the method by which quality system activities are managed.**
Part 4	Work Instructions	A description of how a specific task is carried out.

2 Quality Procedures

Quality Procedures (QPs) form the bulk of Stingray's QMS and describe how the policy objectives of the Quality Manual (QM) can be met in practice and how their processes are controlled.

QPs contain the basic documentation used for planning and controlling all Stingray activities that impact on quality and each QP is unique and contains details of procedures directly applicable to Stingray. By design, the QPs conform to the specific requirements contained in ISO 9001:2000 although (in reality) they often cover more as they are an efficient method of controlling every aspect of Stingray business.

These documented procedures can be made available and used in either hard copy or electronic format and may be used as separate documents outside the QM in places of work.

Some procedures (e.g. QP/11 – Investments) may contain data or information, the knowledge of which must remain restricted to Stingray. These procedures are not included in the QM, beyond their title and reference number. Current Stingray QPs are shown in Table 6.3.2 below.

Table 6.3.2 Quality Procedures

Procedure no.	Procedure title
QP/1	Document Control
QP/2	Production of a Quality Document
QP/3	Design Control
QP/4	Quality Management System Review
QP/5	Customer Feedback
QP/6	Internal Quality Audits
QP/7	Change Control
QP/8	Meetings and Reports
QP/9	Training
QP/10	Budget and Finance
QP/11	Investments

3 Approval Procedure

The approval procedure for all QPs is as follows:

- The Quality Manager evaluates the requirement for a new QP, researches all available information (e.g. existing work procedures, work practices, standards etc.) and produces an 'Initial Background Draft'. This is then issued, for comment, to selected Stingray staff who are directly involved in the procedure.
- The Quality Manager evaluates all comments received; co-ordinates all the necessary alterations, amendments, proposed modifications etc. and produces a draft to the Managing Director for comment.
- Upon approval (or after modification) by the Managing Director, the QP is then issued as official Stingray policy.

Figure 6.3.1 Approval procedure for Quality Procedures

QP/1 – Document Control

1.1 Scope

In conformance with the requirements of ISO 9001:2000, document control is essential for the overall efficiency and quality of Stingray and its documents.

Stingray document control procedures shall apply to all documents that are produced by and for the company, irrespective of where they originate.

QP/1 describes the document control procedures for Stingray. It details the allocation of document codes and the procedures for distributing these documents. It describes the procedures for translating (if required) and for filing (electronic and manual) these documents, how document changes are managed and the type of word-processing software and other software to be used.

The Quality Manager (in consultation with the Company Secretary) is responsible for the overall planning of document control procedures throughout Stingray.

A centralised filing system shall be retained in the main office.

Approval procedures for all Stingray documents are in section 5.24.

1.2 General

The term 'document' includes all Stingray documents, deliverables, letters, faxes, copies of e-mails, reports, minutes and contracts etc.

1.3 Document administration number

All documents which are received, despatched or processed by the main office shall receive a document administration number. A list of document administration numbers used by individual Stingray consultants shall be maintained by them. Personnel based at the Head Office shall share one book, which shall be maintained by the Company Administrator. This is also the number by which the document is stored in the company computer. The number reverts to '001' at the beginning of each year.

All documents despatched by the Office shall be entered in the 'MAIL OUT' letterbook, while all documents received shall be entered in the 'MAIL IN' letterbook (for examples see Annex A).

1.4 File numbering system

All Stingray personnel shall make use of the company filing and numbering system when originating Stingray documents, particularly where documents are to be distributed externally.

1.5 Documents produced by Stingray

1.5.1 File reference

For all documents **produced** by Stingray, the file reference (also known as the document reference) number shall be in the header, to the right, of every page (see top of this page as a typical example of this rule), regardless of whether the page is single or double sided. The format of this reference number shall be as follows:

S-XX-NNNAAAYY, where:

S	Indicates that the document is related to Stingray.
XX	Is the file reference code (see Annex B).
NNN	Is the document administration number, which provides a unique reference for a particular document.
AAA	Is the author's (or originator's) initials.
YY	Is the last two digits of the year in which the document was written.

Example:	**S-53-029RLT05**, where:
S	= a Stingray document
53	= Quality Procedures (see Annex B)
029	= Document administration number 29
RLT	= Author's initials (Ray Tricker)
05	= The year in which the document was written

1.5.2 Version numbering

To indicate the status of the document, a version number shall be included in the header underneath the Document Ref number (see top of this page as a typical example of this rule). The format of this number shall be as follows:

VV	Indicates the version number of the document – also see paragraph 5.7.1.
	Note: For preliminary or draft documents this number will always be '00'.
RR	Indicates the revision number of the document – also see paragraph 5.7.2.

Example:	**Version 02.02**, where:
02.02	= Version 2 of document 29
02.**02**	= Revision 2 of Version 2 of document 29

Changes to consecutive revisions (of versions already having a revision number), should be identified by shaded and/or strikethrough type fonts (see Annex C).

Issued documents which have changed significantly from the previous version shall receive a new version number and the revision number will revert to '00'.

1.6 Letters produced by Stingray

All letters **produced** by Stingray should be produced using the letter template available from the server. The reference number shall be in the relevant space on the first page and this number shall be repeated in the footer of every page, to the right, regardless of whether the page is single or double-sided. The format of this reference number is the same as the example in 1.5:

S-53-029-RLT05

All letters shall also have a reference indicating the person/persons, who dealt with the letter. This reference will consist of the initials of the involved persons separated by slashes (.../.../...) and shall be placed underneath the document reference number (on the front page only).

The first initials in the reference will be the person who initiated the letter. The middle initials are optional and are intended to indicate the person who actually wrote the letter. The last initials are the person who typed the letter.

Example: **MD/QM/ANO**, where:

MD   means that the Managing Director originated the document;
QM   means that the Quality Manager wrote the document;
ANO   means that the document was typed by A. N. Other.

1.7 Faxes produced by Stingray

All faxes, **produced** by Stingray, shall be produced using the fax template available for the server. The reference number need only be included on the first page of the fax.

The format of this reference number is the same as the example in 1.5.1.

1.8 E-mails produced by Stingray

All e-mails, produced by Stingray shall be produced using the e-mail template available for the server. The reference number need only be included in the subject (i.e. title) of the e-mail.

1.9 Contracts and minutes produced by Stingray

For all contracts and minutes **produced** by Stingray, the reference number shall be included in the header of every page, to the right, in small characters regardless of whether the page is single or double-sided. The format of this reference number is the same as the example in 1.5.

1.10 Documents received by Stingray

All documents, **received** by Stingray, shall have the file reference number clearly marked on the left hand side of the document, by hand, as follows:

S-XX-NNN-DDMMYY, where:

S-XX-NNN is as shown in 1.5.1 above.

DD	Is the day number of the date when the document was received;
MM	Is the month number of the date when the document was received;
YY	Are the last two digits of the year number of the date when the document was received.

Example: **S-16-1147-260504**, where:

16	= Financial (Insurance) folder (see Annex B)
1147	= Document administration number 1147
260504	= Received on 26 May 2004

1.11 Storing files on the server

In order to be able to retrieve stored files from the Stingray server, each document shall be filed within a specific directory for that particular contract/section. Each contract/section shall have a folder, with sub-folders for the various categories within each contract/section such as minutes, correspondence, reports, annexes, etc. The document numbering system shall be used. It is essential that the file reference number corresponds with the relevant part of the document number.

XX-NNNAAYY, where:

XX	is the file reference code (see Annex B) for the folder;
NNN	is the document administration number (which provides a unique reference for that particular document);
AA	is the author's (or originator's) initials;
YY	is the last two digits of the year in which the document was written.

Example: **16-1147RLT00**, where:

16	= Financial (Insurance) folder
1147	= Document administration number 1147

RLT   = Author's initials (Ray Tricker)
00   = The year in which the document was written

1.12 Filing of documents (hard copies)

Stingray file cabinets shall be located in the main office and are the responsibility of the Company Administrator.

The document reference number, as described above, indicates where the document is to be filed.

Where possible, different files concerning one particular contract or section shall be grouped together.

If a received document concerns more than one contract or section, the document reference numbers of both shall be shown on that document.

1.13 Old and obsolete documents

All documents and data relating to Stingray shall be reviewed for adequacy prior to issue with appropriate copies being made available, on an as required basis. All obsolete documents shall be promptly removed from all points of issue or use.

The Quality Manager is responsible for ensuring that at least one soft copy of any obsolete controlled document shall be retained at least for the lifetime of the product or service – as defined by the supplier.

Old and obsolete documents shall be removed from the file cabinet under the supervision of the Company Administrator. All removed documents shall be placed in file boxes, adopting the same method (used for filing documents), and shall be clearly marked as 'CANCELLED'. File boxes shall be retained in the attic storeroom.

1.14 Controlled documents

A controlled copy of each published document will be held on the server and applicable personnel notified of its publication by e-mail. The names of these personnel shall be recorded by the Quality Manager.

When a controlled document is amended or becomes obsolete, personnel will be informed of the change and instructed to dispose of any copies (printed or soft copies) they hold of the document.

1.15 Headed paper

All official Stingray correspondence shall be printed on Stingray paper using Stingray logos.

1.16 Document distribution

Approved documents, working papers, reports and documents may be freely distributed to all Stingray personnel as well as any personnel working for and on behalf of Stingray. These papers shall all be clearly marked with the file reference number, status, originator, date and a distribution statement (e.g. '**not to be distributed outside Stingray**').

When a document is being sent to someone outside of Stingray, the document or deliverable shall be approved by the Managing Director before dispatch and the cover letter shall include the Managing Director's signature: in exceptional cases the Managing Director may delegate approval of a specific document or documents to another officer (e.g. the Company Secretary).

The actual signing (i.e. per pro) of the cover letter may also be delegated to a third party (e.g. the Company Secretary).

1.17 Draft documents

All draft versions of documents shall carry the following text on the front cover of the document:

'This is a draft version and may be used for information purposes only'.

Draft documents that do not pass approval shall be removed from circulation. If such documents have to be retained, they shall be kept in files clearly marked **'NOT APPROVED'**.

1.18 Approved documents

All approved documents shall be uniquely numbered (see Section 1.5) and the main office will keep a register of all issued documents.

When a new version of an approved document is issued, copies of all previous versions shall be destroyed. This shall be covered by a statement in the covering letter to the effect that:

'On receipt of a new issue number the previous version is to be destroyed'.

1.19 Internal distribution

The Company Administrator is responsible for the distribution of all approved company documents, working papers, reports and documents within Stingray.

1.20 External distribution

The Managing Director is responsible for (and shall decide on) the distribution of all approved documents, working papers, reports and documents outside of Stingray.

1.21 Press notices etc.

The Managing Director shall decide whether Stingray approved documents, working papers, reports and documents shall be made available to the public. The Managing Director shall fix the right-of-use fee for these documents, with the Company Secretary deciding the copy price.

1.22 Software

1.22.1 Word processing

All Stingray documents, working papers, and reports shall be made and stored using Microsoft® Word version 2000 format.

1.22.2 Spreadsheets and graphics

Spreadsheets and graphics for Stingray documents, working papers, reports and documents shall be made using Microsoft® Office Professional 2000 and Visio Professional v5.

1.23 Copyright

The following shall be included on the front page of each deliverable:

1.24 Approval Procedures

1.24.1 Introduction

To achieve conformity and inter co-operation, all Stingray documents (whether these are managerial, quality related, financial or technical) require some form of approval procedure. Stingray documents shall be presented in the form of an 'official' Stingray document, which will require the approval of the Managing Director.

The following Approval Procedure details the requirements for all, management and contract-related documents within Stingray.

1.24.2 Approval Procedure

Figure 6.3.2 Flowchart showing Approval Procedure

1.24.3 The approvals list

The list of person(s) required to approve a document before it achieves 'published' status is a function of the area of the server in which the document is to be stored. For example, the approval list for documents stored in the folder 'Business Plans' may contain the Managing Director, the Marketing Manager and the Financial Manager. That for documents stored in the folder 'Expense Forms' may only require approval from the Financial Manager.

QP/1 Annex A – Examples of mail in and mail out sheets

Mail in sheet

Date	Code	From	Subject	Document admin no.	Action (by whom)	Completed (date)

Code: a letter to describe the document, i.e. F = Fax, M = Minutes, L = Letter, etc.

Mail out sheet

Date	Code	To	From	Subject	Document admin no.

Code: a letter to describe the document, i.e. F = Fax, M = Minutes, L = Letter, etc.

QP/1 Annex B – Examples of file reference codes

00–09	**Administration**
01	Accommodation – reservations, etc.
02	Internal quality audits
03	Meetings and reports
04	Office equipment
05	Stationery
06	Travel
07	Subcontractors
10–19	**Finance**
10	Audits
11	Annual Accounts
12	Budgets
13	Contracts
14	Expenditure
15	Financial Management
16	Insurance
17	Time and Expense sheets
30–39	**Public Relations**
30	Articles
31	Brochures
32	General
33	Publications and presentations
40–49	**Personnel Matters**
40	Management
41	Social and Welfare
42	Training
43	Health and Safety
50–59	**Quality Management System**
50	Quality – General
51	Quality Manual
52	Quality Processes
53	Quality Procedures
54	Work Instructions
55	Quality Plans

QP/1 Annex C – Identification of changes to a document

In addition to being ideal for controlling the quality of manufactured goods, Quality Plans are equally suited to the delivery ~~of~~ <u>processes and/or</u> services. The main requirement of a Quality Plan, however, is to provide the customer (and the workforce) with clear, concise instructions. These <u>instructions</u> must be ~~clearly~~ <u>adequately</u> recorded and be made available for examination by the customer. ~~It~~ <u>They</u> must leave no room for error but equally <u>they</u> should be flexible and written in such a way that it is possible to modify ~~its~~ <u>their</u> content to reflect changing circumstances.

QP/2 – Production of a Quality Document

2.1 Introduction

To ensure conformity of all documentation it is necessary to establish a process for the production, amendment and cancellation of all Stingray Quality Procedures and Work Instructions (collectively known as 'quality documents') covering:

- initiation;
- review;
- authorisation;
- issue;
- amendment;
- cancellation.

This Quality Procedure describes the process involved in the production of a Quality Document, from initial identification of the need for a new or amended Quality Document, through to the approval processes and the eventual publication of the final Quality Document.

2.2 Procedure

Figure 6.3.3 Production of a quality document

2.3 Initiation of a quality document

A written Quality Procedure or Work Instruction shall be required for any Stingray activity where consistency of quality output is likely to be impaired by its absence. The need for a written quality document and its scope may be identified by:

- an individual;
- the results from an internal quality audit – see QP/6;
- the results from a company biannual QMS review – see QP/4.

Development of a quality document shall be agreed and co-ordinated by the Quality Manager.

A quality document may be drafted by the Quality Manager or by an author nominated by the Quality Manager.

2.4 Drafting

Drafts shall be prepared in accordance with QP/1 – Document Control.

2.5 Quality Procedures

Quality Procedures shall be prepared using the report template available for the server.

Figure 6.3.4 Route to templates

2.5.1 Headings

The following headings are the preferred contents:

- Title Page;
- Document Control Sheet;
- Contents – if required, together with a list of all annexes and attachments;
- Introduction – a concise explanation of the specific objectives of the document together with a definition of the context and boundaries to which the document applies. Any exclusions shall also be identified;
- Detail;
- Annex(es) – if required.

StingRay

Document Ref: S-53-029RLT05
Version: 02.02
Date: 01.01.05
Quality Management System
Part Three – Quality Procedures

2.5.2 Text

The document should comprise a logical sequence of text which must be easy to:

- read;
- understand;
- use;
- remember.

2.5.3 Flowchart

A flowchart is optional. If used, it shall:

- describe the main tasks;
- include decision points and related tasks;
- include details of associated QPs and WIs.

2.6 Work Instructions

Work Instructions will normally be in the form of a flowchart. They should be prepared using Microsoft Visio and may be supported (if required and to ease understanding) by a small amount of text.

2.6.1 Flowchart

The flowchart should follow the sequence of events needed to enable the user of the Work Instruction to fulfil the task. Details should include:

- step-by-step instruction for carrying out the task;
- how to deal with problems that may arise, particularly those that may affect quality;
- measurable criteria for workmanship to ensure the required level of quality is being adhered to;
- who can carry out the procedure;
- Annex(es) – if required.

2.7 Review

In accordance with QP/1 – Document Control, each title page of a draft for review shall be endorsed with the issue number and/or current draft number (e.g. 00.01 – meaning the first draft).

For control purposes, when a draft quality document has been checked into the server it will be issued for comment, the date entry on each page shall be the date of its production.

The author shall circulate (via e-mail) the draft quality document to the Quality Manager and any other relevant members of staff for review.

When an e-mail is received by the member of staff it will show that there is a document awaiting their comment and/or approval. They should then:

- check out the document and review it;
- enter into discussions via e-mail with other staff members;
- send an e-mail to the author giving their views and/or approval.

Note: If it assists the reviewer, the draft document may be 'marked up' using the MS Word Tracker facility and reference to this made in the replying e-mail.

Upon return of the reviewed document, the Quality Manager and/or author shall:

- evaluate and assimilate the reviewers' remarks;
- resolve conflictions, by convening meetings if necessary.

Note: Final arbitration shall always rest with the Quality Manager and shall be documented accordingly:

- incorporate the comments into the revised document, dating affected page(s);
- repeat the review process if it has been necessary to make major changes to the document.

The Quality Manager shall then (with the assistance of the author – if appointed) complete the review and publish the final document.

2.8 Issue authority

A quality document shall not be issued formally until the review procedure described above has been satisfactorily completed.

Each quality document shall be issued in accordance with QP/1 – Document Control.

2.9 Amendments to a draft document

Amendments to a draft quality document shall be controlled in accordance with paragraph 2.7 above.

STINGRAY

Document Ref: S-53-029RLT05
Version: 02.02
Date: 01.01.05
Quality Management System
Part Three – Quality Procedures

2.10 Amendments to approved documents

Amendments to an approved quality document may arise from:

- an individual applying formally to the Quality Manager (with sufficient information to support the case);
- the results from an internal quality audit;
- the results from a company biannual QMS review.

Each proposed amendment shall be considered in accordance with 2.7 above.

2.11 Cancellation

Cancellation of a quality document may be proposed by applying formally (with sufficient background to support the case), to the Quality Manager.

Each proposal for cancellation shall be processed in accordance with QP/1 – Document Control.

Cancellation of a quality document shall be approved and authorised in accordance with QP/1 – Document Control.

2.12 Quality records

To ensure traceability and quality control, the Quality Manager shall retain records of all quality documents (new, revised, amended or destroyed) in separate Quality Files.

2.13 Document quality procedure

As the production of a document will normally require considerable time and effort, it is important that the documents themselves are of the required quality and reflect this.

Whilst confirming that the technical and operational content of a document is most important, it is also important to ensure that these documents are correctly formatted and their content and quality is acceptable. This can only be achieved by monitoring and confirming each stage of the document's production process, from acceptance of a task to the actual distribution of the document.

The following flowchart and descriptive table shows the various points during the production of a document that require formal approval. Formal approval is indicated by e-sign off.

In producing and finalising Stingray documents, the procedures contained in QP/1 – Document Control shall be observed, especially those concerning the layout of documents.

Figure 6.3.5 Flowchart for document quality procedure

Task	Description	Responsibility	Remarks
1	Task received and allocated for completion	Managing Director	Details of requirements, content, format and time frame received and approved by Managing Director.
	Task accepted by a Manager	Manager	Task allocated to a Working Group or individual. Work package, time plan etc. agreed.
2	Draft document produced	Working Group or individual	Initial draft produced and checked into the server, relevant staff subscribed to document and notified.
3	Re-assess and amend draft	Working Group or individual	Comments received from subscribers and comments assessed and if necessary acted upon.
	Amend draft	Working Group or individual	Draft amended and reissued for comment.
4	Authorise publication of draft	Subscribers, Managing Director	Draft accepted and authorised by subscribers and Managing Director.
5	Publish document	Quality Manager	Document published and staff notified of its publication. Any previous version to be taken out of use immediately.

QP/3 – Design Control

3.1 Scope

The primary function of Stingray is to:

- provide advice and guidance on all quality matters;
- produce either complete Quality Management Systems, Quality Manuals, Quality Processes, Quality Procedures or Work Instructions (to suit individual customer requirements);
- provide qualified advice on environmental requirements (particularly for the electronic industry) and expert advice in fuel conservation, management and safety issues.

Although this is not a design activity in the true manufacturing sense, the principles described in ISO 9001:2000 for design are, in general, also valid for Stingray Quality Procedure No. 3 which details the requirements for design control within Stingray.

3.2 Resourcing

The Managing Director shall assign system specification development responsibilities to Section Managers. Section Managers, in their turn, are responsible for ensuring completion of these tasks, for assigning the work to suitably trained and experienced specialists and for overseeing and supervising their output.

3.3 Planning

The Quality Manager is responsible for ensuring that the planning of all interfaces between the different activities is appropriate and that verification points are allocated and taken into account.

The Quality Manager shall approve the planning after each change and, where necessary, liaise with the Managing Director to ensure that more detailed plans are made in order that interfaces between the development activities are properly handled. The main objective is to see to it that the appropriate information concerning the requirements and specifications already developed and agreed on, is available to all parties – at any stage.

To facilitate this process, the Quality Manager shall use advance design planning and decision techniques (e.g. such as 'Teamwork') to control this requirement wherever appropriate.

To ensure overall task effectiveness, a time plan shall be maintained by the Company Secretary, throughout each individual contract's life and for all main Stingray activities.

3.4 Input

The input data for each stage of a contract shall (in consultation with the Quality Manager) be identified by the Section Manager, documented by the Company Secretary and agreed with the Managing Director.

For each contract the same structure shall apply and the Quality Manager is responsible for ensuring that this actually happens.

3.5 Output

All documents shall be presented in the form as described in QP/1 – Document Control.

3.6 Verification

Verification of all Stingray documents shall be in accordance with (when available) the relevant project or contract-specific Quality Plan and shall be documented.

 Note: The Quality Manager will advise the Managing Director on this subject on an as required basis.

Verification that documents are of the required format, content and quality shall be achieved via the procedures described in QP/1 – Document Control.

Approval shall be in accordance with QP/1 – Document Control.

3.7 Changes

All changes that could fundamentally influence the company scope, targets, organisation, budget, overall work breakdown structure, work packages and time plans shall be subject to the formal change control procedures described in QP/7 – Change Control.

QP/4 – Quality Management System Review

4.1 Scope

In accordance with the principles of ISO 9001:2000, biannual Stingray QMS reviews are required in order to ensure that:

- Stingray is effective in attaining its objectives as described in the QM;
- the QM remains effective and suitable for the requirements of Stingray (in other words that it 'really works' in practice);
- the requirements and rules as described in the QM remain workable and are in accordance (as far as possible) with the way Stingray personnel prefer to work – without losing the assurance that Stingray delivers quality;
- Stingray requirements are met and that the relevant rules are agreed on and are adhered to.

QP/4 details the requirements for Quality Management System Reviews within Stingray.

The Quality Manager is responsible for overseeing the operation of the QMS; for ensuring that the QM is fully and effectively implemented and for co-ordinating the writing as well as the availability of the necessary processes, procedures and instructions.

4.2 Procedure

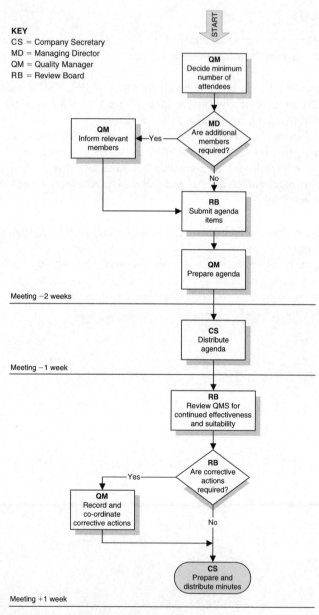

KEY
CS = Company Secretary
MD = Managing Director
QM = Quality Manager
RB = Review Board

Figure 6.3.6 QP/5 – QMS review flowchart

StingRay

Document Ref: S-53-029RLT05
Version: 02.02
Date: 01.01.05
Quality Management System
Part Three – Quality Procedures

4.3 Meetings of the Review Board

The initiative for meetings of the Review Board shall be taken by the Quality Manager. He shall prepare an agenda and provide all relevant documents (e.g. reports of internal audits, results of product reviews, etc.). If necessary the Quality Manager shall draw attention to areas where Stingray requirements are not being met or where rules are not followed. Whenever possible he will provide recommendations for improvements.

If the results of the review are such that corrective action is necessary, the Review Board shall agree on the corrective actions and suggest appropriate methods for their implementation. The Managing Director shall be responsible for ensuring the implementation of the agreed corrective actions.

The details of the review and the agreed corrective actions shall be recorded and the records shall be maintained in the company quality file.

The review shall cover all activities related to company and quality management as described in the QM, attached Quality Processes, QPs, WIs and Quality Plans.

4.4 Frequency of meetings

The Review Board shall meet every six months.

4.5 Review Board members

Permanent members of the Review Board are:

- the Managing Director (who acts as Chairman);
- the Company Secretary;
- the Quality Manager (who also acts as Deputy Chairman).

The exact number of attendees may vary according to the circumstances applicable at that time.

The Quality Manager shall decide on the minimum number of attendees for convening that meeting.

The Managing Director (in consultation with the Quality Manager) shall decide whether or not it is necessary to invite additional members and if so, who shall be involved.

4.6 Agenda

All members of the Review Board may contribute items for the agenda, but they must be submitted no later than two weeks prior to the actual date of the meeting. Such contributions shall be sent to the Quality Manager.

The Quality Manager shall prepare the agenda in consultation with the Managing Director and ensure that the relevant information documents are attached to it.

The Company Secretary shall distribute the agenda and attached information documents so that these are in the possession of all members of the Review Board at least one week prior to this meeting.

The agenda for a Review Board shall consist of:

- a review of all actions raised at the previous meetings and progressed at subsequent meetings;
- a review of minutes and actions arising from the minutes of the previous meeting;
- implementation and continued effectiveness of the QM, Quality Processes, QPs, WIs and Quality Plans;
- results of internal Stingray audits and details of the corrective actions taken;
- previous Stingray audit results;
- previous reports on all major deviations from Stingray objectives related to time, costs and quality;
- previous consequences of changes (objectives, organisation, schedules, etc.);
- previous results of verifications on major Stingray documents;
- previous results of actions agreed at previous meetings;
- customer complaints.

4.7 Meeting contents

The nature of the Review Board is such that all major issues affecting Stingray shall be considered as appropriate.

In all cases the target shall be:

- to review if the QMS is still the most effective and suitable way to reach and achieve objectives and to ensure that Stingray documents comply with the relevant quality and safety standards.
- to seek ways of improving Stingray's QMS.

4.8 Actions

- If the results of the review are such that corrective action is necessary, the Review Board shall:
  - consider solutions and agree on the corrective action(s);
  - agree on responsibility for the implementation of the corrective action chosen;

- agree on a timescale for the implementation and review of corrective action(s) taken.

The review and the agreed corrective actions shall be recorded in the company quality file by the Quality Manager.

The Quality Manager shall also be responsible for co-ordinating the completion of all corrective actions agreed by the Review Board.

All actions raised at previous meetings shall be reviewed and progressed at subsequent meetings.

4.9 Meeting records

The Company Secretary is responsible for ensuring that minutes of the meeting are prepared and distributed promptly.

The minutes shall clearly state:

- actions agreed upon;
- the person responsible for implementing these actions (i.e. the Action List);
- the agreed completion date (i.e. the Time Plan).

The minutes of the meeting shall be kept in the company quality file.

QP/5 – Customer Feedback

5.1 Scope

The successful completion of any report or specification relies on the customer commenting on the technical and operational contents of these reports and specifications.

QP/5 has been designed to ensure that any customer feedback and complaints raised against Stingray reports, documents or specifications are adequately reviewed, appropriate action is taken and trends analysed.

The Quality Manager (in consultation with the Company Secretary) is responsible for maintaining quality records demonstrating conformance to the requirements and the effective operation of the QMS.

5.2 Flowchart

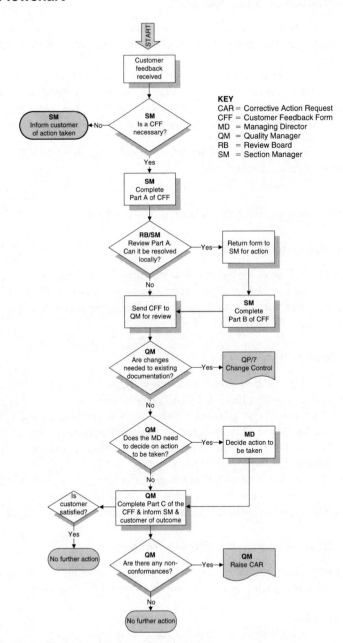

Figure 6.3.7 Customer feedback flowchart

5.3 Initiation and assessment

All customer feedback including complaints received by the company office shall (following registration) be directed to the appropriate Section Manager for assessment.

Unless the issue raised by the customer is of a minor nature (e.g. a grammatical or typographic error) or a request for information that can be dealt with directly, the Section Manager shall initiate a Customer Feedback Form (see Annex A).

The Section Manager initiating a Customer Feedback Form shall ensure that:

- there is sufficient detail in Part A for the problem to be self-explanatory;
- customer details are included;
- any related documents are attached.

The form shall then be signed, dated and forwarded for review.

5.4 Initial review

The review shall be made either by the initiating Section Manager or referred to an internal section or QMS review meeting for discussion. The review procedure shall ascertain if the problem can be resolved locally and if so, to agree the appropriate action required.

5.5 Local action

If it is agreed that action shall be taken locally, then the Section Manager is responsible for ensuring that it is carried out and the results are detailed in Part B of the Customer Feedback Form. In taking action, full consideration shall be given to the root cause of the problem and how this may be resolved.

This form shall then be signed and dated, with copies being forwarded to the Quality Manager.

If it is agreed that action shall **not** be taken locally, the original of the form shall be forwarded to the Quality Manager. Local recommendations may be made in Part B by the Section Manager if considered necessary and relevant.

5.6 Action taken by the Quality Manager

The Quality Manager shall review all forms received. Where action has been taken locally, the Quality Manager shall check that the action taken:

- is adequate;
- has no implications for other sections;
- has no implications on the Stingray QMS.

Where action has not been taken locally, the Quality Manager shall review the problem and decide if it necessitates action through a change control procedure (as described in QP/7 – Change Control) or consideration by the Managing Director.

The Quality Manager shall ensure that at all times the review considers the root cause of the problem and how this may be resolved.

Upon completion of the appropriate action, the Quality Manager shall ensure that Part B and Part C of the form are completed and that the original (or copy) is returned to the Section Manager who initiated the form.

5.7 Analysing non-conformances

The Quality Manager shall regularly review all Customer Feedback Forms to detect any trends that may have a detrimental effect on a project. When such a trend is found, the Quality Manager shall raise a Corrective Action Report (available from the Company Secretary) for review by the Managing Director.

5.8 Customer interface

The Quality Manager and/or Section Manager shall ensure that the customer, having made an enquiry, is kept informed of progress. They shall also seek comments from the customer on any action implemented.

5.9 Quality records

To ensure traceability and quality control, all records appertaining to customer feedback (and/or complaints) shall be retained by the Quality Manager in a separate quality file.

QP/5 Annex A – Customer Feedback Form

Customer feedback form

Ref No:		No of attached sheets:	
Customer:			
Related documents:			

Part A

Nature of feedback/complaint		
Input:	Face-to-face/letter/fax/phone/ e-mail (delete as appropriate)	
Signed:	Name:	Date:

Part B

Action to be taken (Section Manager/Review Board)		
Date action completed		
Signed:	Name:	Date:

Part C

Review by Quality Manager:			
Refer to Managing Director?	Yes/No (delete as appropriate)	Raise CAR?	Yes/No (delete as appropriate)
		CAR No:	
Signed:	Name:		Date:

QP/6 – Internal Audits

6.1 Scope

Although Quality Management System reviews are scheduled every six months (see QP/4), other internal quality audits shall be completed at key points throughout the company's life cycle.

These quality audits are completed so as to ensure that all activities within Stingray are carried out according to the requirements, rules and procedures provided in the QM and its associated Quality Processes, QPs, WIs and Quality Plans.

QP/6 details the requirements for internal quality audits within Stingray and describes the differences between a sectional quality audit and other internal quality audits.

6.2 Sectional quality audits

6.2.1 Frequency of audits

During each financial year, all sections shall be subject to at least three **complete** quality audits covering all relevant procedures. These audits shall be initiated by the Quality Manager and shall be scheduled at key points in relation to the status and importance of the various activities of a section.

It is the Quality Manager's responsibility to prepare (in consultation with the Section Managers) an audit schedule for the Managing Director's approval to cover the next 12 months.

6.2.2 Audit preparation and organisation

All audits shall be carried out by an audit team consisting of the Managing Director, Company Secretary and the Quality Manager (who will normally perform the function of lead auditor – but this need not always be the case).

The Quality Manager shall decide on the minimum number of attendees for convening that meeting and whether it is necessary to invite additional members and if so, who shall be involved. The exact number of attendees may vary according to circumstances applicable at that time.

In addition to agenda items, the audit team shall review, for adequacy, the Section's Quality Plan together with its associated procedures. They shall resolve all concerns where the Section Quality Plan or the section's organisation is inadequate or inappropriate to meet Stingray objectives as stated in the QM.

6.2.3 Agenda

The Quality Manager shall organise an agenda for each audit which shall include:

- scope and objectives of the audit;
- review of all actions raised at previous meetings and progresses at subsequent meetings;
- minutes of and actions arising from the last meeting.

6.2.4 Actions

If the results of the audit are such that corrective action or actions are necessary, the audit team shall:

- consider solutions and agree on the corrective action(s);
- agree on responsibility for the implementation;
- agree on a timescale for the implementation and review of corrective action(s) to be taken.

The review and the agreed corrective actions shall be recorded in the company quality file and a copy shall be retained by the section concerned.

6.2.5 Meeting records

The Quality Manager is responsible for ensuring that minutes of the meeting are prepared and distributed promptly.

The minutes shall clearly state the:

- actions agreed on;
- person responsible for implementing these actions (i.e. the Action List);
- agreed completion date (i.e. the time plan).

The minutes of the meeting shall be kept in the Stingray quality file, by the Quality Manager, with a copy being circulated to all members of the audit team plus the section concerned.

6.3 Internal quality audits

Internal quality audits are initiated by the Quality Manager and shall be scheduled in relation to the status and importance of the various activities.

When deemed necessary, an internal quality audit may be completed by invited personnel (independent of the activity being audited), such as invited specialists from other ISO 9001:2000 certified companies.

The audits and all agreed corrective actions shall be recorded and these records shall be maintained in the company quality file by the Quality Manager.

6.3.1 *Frequency of audit and audit schedule*

Internal quality audits are either scheduled by the Quality Manager or completed at the request of a company officer (e.g. Managing Director, Company Secretary, Section Manager etc.).

The Quality Manager shall organise an agenda for each audit which shall include:

- scope and objectives of the audit;
- persons having direct responsibilities for the procedure(s) to be audited;
- reference documents;
- name of lead auditor and name(s) of assigned auditor(s);
- date when audit is to be concluded;
- audit report distribution.

6.3.2 *Audit preparation and organisation*

Depending on the complexity and the size of the audit, the Quality Manager may perform the audit himself, or he can assign a lead auditor and a team of auditors.

 Note: This may be required when sections are too large, or when activities from other sections are integrated or are co-operating.

The lead auditor and the assigned auditor(s):

- shall examine all earlier audit reports on the same subject;
- shall prepare an audit check list (containing all of the topics/items to be covered and an audit programme).

The lead auditor shall report to the Quality Manager.

6.3.3 *Audit execution*

All audits shall be completed in accordance with the recommendations of ISO 10011.

An initial meeting between the auditor(s), the auditee(s) and the Quality Manager shall be held. During this meeting:

- a brief summary of the methods and procedures being used to conduct the audit shall be provided;
- the method of communication between auditor(s) and auditee(s) shall be agreed;
- the audit programme shall be confirmed.

The auditor(s) shall collect evidence via interviews, examination of documents and observation of activities. If possible information provided at interviews shall be checked for accuracy by acquiring the same information through independent sources.

If necessary (and required) changes to the audit programme may be made in order to achieve optimum audit objectives.

Auditors shall record all observations on the Audit Observation Sheet (available as a template on the server).

Auditors shall review the observations and determine which are to be reported as non-conformities.

Auditors shall discuss all observations with the Quality Manager and all observations of non-conformity shall be acknowledged by the manager (e.g. Section Manager) responsible for the activity being audited.

A closing meeting of auditor(s), auditee(s) and Quality Manager shall be held during which:

- audit observations are clarified;
- the critical significance of observations are presented;
- conclusions drawn about compliance are presented;
- system effectiveness in achieving the quality objectives are presented;
- corrective actions are agreed;
- the date for completion of the audit report is agreed.

Minutes of **all** relevant meetings, decisions and agreements shall be attached to the audit report.

6.3.4 Audit report

The lead auditor shall prepare an audit report using the Audit Report Form (available as a template on the server). The report must be signed by all members of the audit team, plus the Quality Manager, and copies sent to auditee(s) and company management as required.

Audit reports shall be retained in Stingray quality files.

6.3.5 Corrective action

After the closing meeting the lead auditor shall prepare a Corrective Action Request for each **agreed** corrective action. Corrective Action Requests (available as a template on the server) shall state who is responsible for carrying out the corrective action and the timescale for its completion.

6.3.6 Follow-up

The lead auditor is responsible for ensuring that corrective action has been carried out.

The lead auditor shall notify the Quality Manager of the status and/or completion of the corrective actions.

QP/7 – Change Control

7.1 Scope

When a contract document reaches the stage where the information that it contains is being used (or relied on) by other sections, it is imperative that any proposed changes to the original document are not completed without the knowledge of all concerned.

In order to prevent this sort of situation occurring, a decision will be made (by the Managing Director, endorsed by the Section Managers) that at a particular stage **no** further changes, alterations, modifications, insertions or deletions will be made without the Change Control procedure described below being adopted.

QP/7 details the requirements for Change Control within Stingray and is a requirement.

7.2 Procedure

All changes to Stingray documents, procedures and specifications are, in principle, subject to a formal Change Control procedure.

Changes that could fundamentally influence the scope, targets, organisation, budget, overall work breakdown structure and time schedules (in addition to changes to approved Stingray documents and other official documents), will have to be agreed by the Section Managers and approved by the Managing Director.

Proposals for changes shall be submitted to the Managing Director, in writing, using the Change Proposal Form shown at Annex A (the template for this form is available from the server).

The Managing Director will ask the Company Secretary to distribute the proposals for changes to all Section Managers for discussion. The proposal for change will have to be distributed and received by all Section Managers at least four weeks prior to the next Section Managers' meeting.

Depending on the importance and impact of the proposed change(s) the Managing Director can decide to discuss the proposal in a scheduled Section Managers' meeting or call a special meeting.

A description of the types of impact and relevant approvals are listed in Table 6.3.3.

7.3 Impact assessment

Depending on the classification of the proposed change, an 'impact assessment' may be required. The change classification (and, therefore, the need for

Table 6.3.3 Types of impact and relevant approvals

Change classification	Impact assessment	Final approval by
(A) Minor impact: No other section or from the area affected. No change in man days, time schedule and costs	No	Managing Director on advice from the Section Managers
(B) Medium impact: At least one other section or area affected. No (or little) change in man days, time schedule and costs	To be decided by the Managing Director	Section Managers' meeting
(C) Major impact: More than one other section or area affected. Significant change in man days, time schedule and costs	Yes	Management Review Board Meeting

an impact assessment) will ultimately have to be sanctioned by the Managing Director. If the time, resources and budget required for an impact assessment are expected to be significant, formal approval by the Managing Director for carrying out this assessment is required. An example of an Impact Assessment Form is included at Annex B (the template for this form is available from the server).

When the Section Managers have agreed to the proposed change it will be submitted to the Managing Director for final approval.

The Managing Director shall be responsible for implementing approved changes and shall make sure that all aspects which are affected by these changes are taken into consideration.

The Company Secretary shall be responsible for:

- incorporating the approved changes into existing technical documents;
- distributing these documents to the appropriate people;
- incorporating the approved changes into existing non-technical documents.

QP/7 Annex A – Change Proposal Form

Originator:			Section:			
File ref:		Date:			Serial No:	

Reason and description of change:			
Area(s) affected:			
Product(s) affected:			
Classification:	A/B/C	Impact assessment required?	Yes/No
Impact assessment summary (including man days, schedules, costs and risks)			
Full impact assessment attached:			Yes/No

Authorisation/ Approval	Function	Name	Date	Signature
Change preparation				
Classification approval	Managing Director			
Recommendation (submit/reject)	Section Manager			
Approval	Managing Director			

Other points:	

QP/7 Annex B – Impact Assessment Form

Originator:		Change Proposal Serial No:	

Description of proposed change:	
Impact upon (time, resources, cost, quality, etc.)	
Estimated cost of implementation of change	
Benefits:	
Recommendation	**Accept/Reject Change Proposal**
Comments:	

Signed:		Name:		Date:	

QP/8 – Meetings and Reports

8.1 Scope

QP/8 describes how Management Review Board and Section Manager meetings are convened, the proposed agenda and how minutes should be produced. QP/8 also lays down the guidelines for the reporting procedure adopted by Stingray.

8.2 Meetings

8.2.1 Management Review Board meetings

Management Review Board meetings shall normally take place twice a year in order to discuss important issues and to approve final documents. The Managing Director may convene additional meetings if required.

8.2.2 Section Managers' meetings

The Managing Director shall hold regular Section Manager meetings to discuss the methods and program to be adopted for the results, reports or other documents that have to be published. The preparation and detailed editing of reports and technical documents shall be carried out by section working groups or by small editing groups set up for that purpose.

Normally subcontractors and/or consultants shall only attend these meetings when their presence is deemed necessary by the Managing Director.

8.3 Discussion documents

The dates set for these meetings should allow sufficient time for the documents being discussed to be distributed far enough in advance of the meeting so as to enable members to consider them beforehand. In practice this means **not** later than two weeks prior to the meeting.

8.4 Agenda of meetings

In addition to those items covering technical aspects/problems, the agenda shall be established by the Company Secretary and the Section Managers (in agreement with the Managing Director) and shall contain the following points:

- approval of the minutes of the previous meeting;
- matters arising from the minutes of the last meeting;
- status report (verbal or written);
- budget and costs;
- date by which the work is to be completed;

- decision list and action list;
- place and date of the next meeting.

8.5 Guidelines for meetings

It is to be expected that a frank and objective atmosphere should prevail at all Stingray Management Review Board and Section Manager meetings, as well as with a mutual willingness to overcome problems so as to arrive, whenever possible, at a valid agreed solution.

The chair of the meeting shall direct the discussions towards a rapid solution of the problem raised without, however, sacrificing the liberty to exchange views, experience and ideas amongst the participants.

8.6 Minutes

The minutes of the Management Review Board and Section Managers' meetings shall be concise and only contain the essential points, the conclusions of the discussions and distribution of tasks between the members (i.e. the Action List).

The minutes shall, special cases excepted, normally only be sent to the Managing Director, the participants of the meeting and the Quality Manager. The minutes shall always be distributed within two weeks following the actual meeting.

8.7 Reporting

8.7.1 Company Status Report

Every six months a Company Status Report shall be written by the Quality Manager. This report will then be presented at the next Management Review Board meeting.

Following approval by the Managing Director, the Company Status Report will then be distributed to the members of the Management Review Board. These reports will contain an update of:

- overall progress;
- technical status;
- contractual status;
- financial status;
- liaison with the railways;
- liaison with industry;
- outstanding actions.

8.7.2 Financial reporting

See QP/10 Budget and Finance.

QP/9 – Training

9.1 Scope

In conformance with ISO 9001:2000, one of the requirements of a QMS is to ensure that all Stingray personnel are provided with training that will assist them in acquiring the skills and knowledge to perform effectively and to comply with Stingray Quality and Safety Management Systems.

QP/9 details the requirements for training within Stingray.

9.2 Responsibilities

Section Managers are responsible for ensuring that project tasks and activities are only assigned to staff qualified for that particular task or activity. This is on the basis of appropriate education, training and experience, in relation to staffing levels and Stingray's current recruitment policy.

Top management identifies the need for staff training to handle the expected workload where special techniques or items of equipment are involved.

The Managing Director is responsible for ensuring that appropriate training is carried out so as to ensure that all staff involved are aware of the requirements, rules and procedures to which they are to conform and against which they will be audited.

The Managing Director is also responsible for ensuring that tasks and activities are only assigned to staff qualified for that particular task or activity and that this is on the basis of appropriate education, training and experience.

9.3 Identification of training needs

A training review may be carried out at any time, as necessitated by any of the following:

- appointment of new personnel;
- new equipment or working practices;
- change of duties or responsibilities;
- as a result of an audit or management review.

9.4 Training review

The Section Manager or manager undertaking the review shall, with the post-holder:

- review training completed since the previous review;
- review and reschedule, where necessary, uncompleted training since the previous review;
- review the training needs of individual positions;

- review and identify current training requirements and ensure that the quality and safety requirements are fully covered;
- review and identify career development (where appropriate);
- ensure that the results of the review are recorded on the appropriate forms and forwarded to the Quality Manager.

9.5 Planning of training requirements

The Managing Director (with the assistance of the Company Secretary and the Quality Manager) shall budget and plan the training programme for all personnel under his responsibility. This shall also include any on-the-job training requirements.

9.6 Implementation of training requirements

The manager (e.g. Section Manager) responsible for planning training requirements may either arrange training locally or subcontract formal external courses via the Company Secretary.

9.7 Training of new personnel

The Company Secretary shall ensure that all new personnel receive a local introduction briefing as detailed in the appropriate administration procedure (being prepared).

9.8 Training of subcontractors and consultants

The manager (e.g. Section Manager) employing subcontractors or consultants is responsible for either ensuring that they are already fully competent or that they can be trained to meet the contracted specification. The manager is also responsible for ensuring that all contracted personnel are made aware and understand the local arrangements for both quality and safety.

9.9 Quality training

The Quality Manager is responsible for providing Stingray QMS induction and refresher training courses.

9.10 Training courses and records

If external training is required then it shall only be obtained from established and recognised courses for which documented course content is available.

The appropriate Senior Manager shall retain records of all training. This shall include details of attendance, achievements, course content, scope, personnel who provided the training and those who received it.

QP/10 – Budget and Finance

10.1 Scope

For all Stingray contracts, the two main resources required are finance and manpower. QP/10 describes how both of these resources shall be managed within Stingray.

Total cost management shall be computerised and controlled by the Company Secretary.

10.2 Procedure

Figure 6.3.8 Budget and finance flowchart

10.3 Financial management

10.3.1 Delegation of financial authority

The Managing Director each year approves the Stingray budget and delegates part of his authority to the Company Secretary.

The table in Annex A shows the delegation of authority for signing contracts and initiating orders, accepting deliveries (i.e. approving invoices), authorising payments and signing bank transfers. The amount each person is authorised to sign for is also indicated in this table.

Contracts, material orders or services may only be signed, or ordered, by the persons for whom an amount is listed in the columns 'Initiate orders and accept deliveries' or 'Sign contracts'. In cases where the Managing Director has to sign, the Section Manager is required to co-sign first.

Deliveries and invoices may only be accepted and approved by the persons for whom an amount is listed in the column 'Initiate orders and accept deliveries'. In cases where the Managing Director has to sign, the Section Manager is required to co-sign first.

In some circumstances a staff member's signature might be required prior to the Section Manager's signature.

Authorising payment and signing the bank transfers for invoices shall be limited to the persons for whom an amount is listed in the column 'Sign bank-transfers and approve invoices'. This action can only be completed after the delivery has been accepted.

10.3.2 Stingray budget forecast

The Stingray budget forecast shall consist of detailed financial budget planning for each contract and activity. The budget forecast shall include the following information:

- description;
- account;
- approved budget for each individual year and grand total;
- committed cost for each individual year and grand total;
- paid cost up to and including the cut-off date;
- result (i.e. difference between committed total and approved budget total);
- forecasted cost for succeeding years.

The budget forecast shall provide full details of **all** expenditures related to each contract and activity.

From the Stingray budget forecast it shall be possible to extract the financial information for any particular year. The Company Secretary is responsible for this activity and shall provide details to the Managing Director.

10.3.3 Comparison of committed costs with approved budget

The Company Secretary shall carry out a continuous check on committed costs and the actual expenditures against the approved budget.

The Company Secretary shall inform the manager concerned if the total committed costs are higher than the approved budget for their particular activity or section.

The Company Secretary shall inform the Managing Director when it becomes likely that the total committed costs will exceed the total approved budget.

10.3.4 Administrating income and expenditure

All income to and expenditure from the Stingray bank account shall be recorded by the Company Secretary in the Stingray cashbook, which shall be kept in the main office.

The Company Secretary shall be responsible for the proper administration of the Stingray bank account.

Copies of all transfer orders, bank statements and documents related to the Stingray bank transfers shall be kept in one binder in the main office.

At the end of each month the Company Secretary shall present the cashbook to the Managing Director for pre-audit.

10.3.5 Company financial audit

The Company Secretary shall, when requested, present all the required financial documents to the Company Auditor for verification.

10.4 Resource management

All manpower resources (e.g. permanent and part-time staff, subcontractors and consultants) require a separate agreement/contract. These shall be initiated by the Company Secretary and signed by the Managing Director.

10.4.1 Contracts with subcontractors and consultants

All subcontractors and/or consultants working for (or on behalf of) Stingray shall be required to agree to a contract which shall include the following elements:

- detailed task description (including documents);
- duration of the contract;
- fees;
- travel expenses and allowances;
- payment conditions;
- other terms and conditions.

The contract may be extended by mutual arrangement. Normally either party can terminate a contract by giving three months' notice.

10.4.2 Other purchases

Requests for the purchase of all other products or services (including major assets such as furniture and computers etc.) shall be submitted in writing (by the person requiring that product or service) to the Company Secretary. The Company Secretary shall, prior to requisition, obtain the Managing Director's approval.

The Company Secretary shall maintain an inventory of all capital items purchased for Stingray.

10.5 Invoices

The Company Secretary shall stamp, date and sign all invoices received by Stingray using the company stamp.

10.5.1 Subcontractors' invoices

Subcontractors and consultancies shall submit invoices for the manpower resourcing carried out and travel expenses incurred by their staff, directly to the Company Secretary for processing.

The Company Secretary shall check these invoices against the agreement/ contract previously decided. If inconsistencies are discovered, the Company Secretary shall contact the subcontractor/consultant concerned for further clarification.

Following verification by the Company Secretary, invoices shall then be sent to the Managing Director for endorsement.

Payment for invoices shall (following authorisation) be made from the Stingray bank account by the Company Secretary.

10.5.2 Filing of invoices

After payment, all original invoices shall be filed, together with the following documents:

- a copy of the order form or letter (in case of a telephone order, a handwritten note from the initiating person will suffice);
- the original delivery note and a signed receipt by the initiator or the person authorised to sign on his behalf;
- a copy of the bank transfer note or cheque.

STINGRAY

Document Ref: S-53-029RLT05
Version: 02.02
Date: 01.01.05
Quality Management System
Part Three – Quality Procedures

QP/10 Annex A – Delegation of Financial and Contractual Authority

Name	Maximum amounts			
	Initiate orders and accept deliveries	**Sign bank transfers and approve invoices**	**Sign contracts**	**Example of signature**
	Delivery as ordered	**Payment authorised**		
Managing Director	unlimited	unlimited	unlimited	
Section Managers	£6,000	£6,000	£6,000	
Company Secretary	£1,000	*	*	

* No authorisation

Stingray Management Services Ltd

Quality Management System

Part 4 – Work Instructions

This Quality Manual has been issued on the authority of the Managing Director of Stingray Management Services Ltd for the use of all staff, subcontractors, clients and/or regulatory bodies to whom Stingray Management Services Ltd may be required to provide such information to.

Approved

.... **Date:** 1st January 2005......

Ray Rekcirt
Managing Director
Stingray Management Services Ltd

Quality Management System

Part 4 Work Instructions

Abstract

Stingray Management Services Ltd's Quality Management System is divided into four parts. This document is Part 4 and describes the Work Instructions that show how a specific task is carried out.

Attachments

Attachment	Description

QMS revision history

No.	Chapter	Amendment details	Date
01.00	All	First published version in accordance with ISO 9001:1994	28.06.93
01.01	3	Inclusion of new chapter for customer satisfaction	05.04.94
01.02	4.2.3	Procedure for the control of documents changed	23.12.95
01.03	All	Minor editorial revisions of all sections and annexes	30.07.96
02.00	All	Second published version to conform to ISO 9001:2000	31.12.00
02.01	5	Management responsibility procedure updated to cover new (i.e. Fuels) Division	01.01.02
02.02	All	Minor editorial changes following three years experience of ISO 9001:2000	01.01.05

Contents

List of illustrations

List of tables

1. Documentation

Stingray Management Services Ltd (Stingray) has four levels of documentation within our Quality Management System (QMS) which is structured as shown in the table below.

This document is Part 4 and describes the WIs that have been adopted in order to carry out a specific task.

The QPs associated with these WIs are contained in Part 3.

Table 6.4.1 Stingray Management Services Ltd's Quality System – documentation

Part 1	Quality Manual	The main policy document that establishes Stingray's QMS and how it meets the requirements of ISO 9001:2000.
Part 2	Quality Processes	The Core Business Process plus the Primary and Secondary Supporting Processes that describe the activities required to implement the QMS and to meet the policy requirements made in the QM.
Part 3	Quality Procedures	A description of the method by which quality system activities are managed.
Part 4	**Work Instructions**	**A description of how a specific task is carried out.**

WIs describe how to perform specific operations and are produced for all of the relevant activities of Stingray so as to ensure that the whole company can work to the same format.

WIs describe how individual tasks and activities are to be carried out. They describe, in detail, what is to be done, who should do it and when it has to be completed. They can, for example, cover simple issues such as making travel and hotel arrangements to more complex issues such as the structure of Stingray reports.

They are produced for all of Stingray's relevant activities so as to ensure that the whole company can work to the same format.

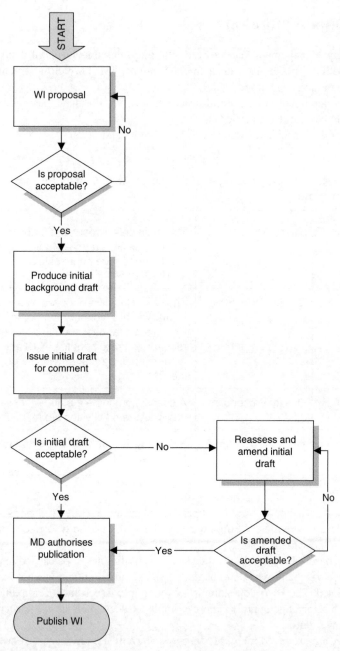

Figure 6.4.1 Approval Procedure for Work Instructions

Current Stingray Work Instructions are listed below:

Table 6.4.2 Work Instructions

WI No	Work Instruction Title
WI/1	Travel and Hotel Arrangements
WI/2	Timesheets and Expense Sheets
WI/3	Subcontractors' Invoices
WI/4	CD-ROM Distribution

2. Procedure

The approval procedure for all WIs is as follows:

- The Quality Manager evaluates the requirement for a new WI, researches all available information (e.g. existing work procedures, work practices, standards etc.) and produces an 'Initial Background Draft'. This is then issued, for comment, to selected Stingray staff whom are directly involved in the WI.
- The Quality Manager evaluates all comments received, co-ordinates all the necessary alterations, amendments, proposed modifications etc. and produces a Draft to the Managing Director for comment.
- Upon approval (or after modification) by the Managing Director, the WI is then issued as official Stingray policy.

WI/1 – Travel and hotel arrangements

1.1 Scope

This procedure defines the actions to be taken for ensuring the timely and efficient handling of all travel requests.

1.2 Procedure

When Stingray staff are required to travel away from their normal place of work for meetings etc. they shall complete a Travel Form (see Annex A), specifying the:

- name of the traveller;
- reason for the meeting(s);
- budget(s) to which the costs must be charged;
- start and end dates of the meeting(s);
- where the meeting is taking place;
- predicted departure and arrival times;
- hotel reservation and travel tickets, if required.

The Travel Form (template available from the server) will be signed by the initiator and an information copy sent to the Company Secretary.

If hotel reservations and travel tickets are required, an information copy shall also be sent to the Company Secretary Administrator, who will make the appropriate arrangements.

After the staff member has returned from the journey he/she will add the actual data to the Travel Form, sign it and then submit it to the Company Secretary for reimbursement of expenses.

An allowance for travel expenses will be given on the basis of a lump sum per absence of (or fractions of) 24 hours, as determined by the departure and in conformance with the current, published, Stingray rates.

WI/1 Annex A – Travel form

Name	
Reason for travel:	
Reservations to be made by Stingray?	Yes/No

Meeting information

Start date	End date	Where	Client to be billed

Travel information

		Predicted		Actual	
From		**Date**	**Time**	**Date**	**Time**
To					
From					
To					

Signed: (Initiator)		**Name:**		**Date:**	
Signed: (Company Secretary)		**Name:**		**Date:**	

WI/2 – Time sheets and Expense sheets

2.1 Scope and objectives

To enable Section Managers to properly account for the hours spent by Stingray staff (including Management), it is necessary for this information to be freely available to them.

WI/2 describes the procedure for keeping track of all man-hours spent and shall be used by all Stingray staff.

2.2 Time and expense sheets

The purpose of the time and expense sheets (see Annexes A and B) is to indicate the actual time spent on company and contract work as well as recording the actual travel cost (i.e. transport charges, meals, hotel and other authorised expenditure), incurred in connection with company and contract work.

During the agreement/contract period subcontractors and consultants shall (having first obtained the signature of the Section Manager concerned) send their time and expense sheets to the Company Secretary on the last day of each month.

The Company Secretary shall check the consistency of these reports **before** submitting them to the Managing Director for approval.

Note: This WI should be read in conjunction with QP/10 – Budget and Finance.

2.3 Time sheets

The time sheet shall contain the following information:

- actual office hours (hours or days, depending on what is stated in the agreement or contract);
- travel time (for official Stingray business);
- productive travel time (normally 50% of travel time).

The Company Secretary shall compare the time sheets with the budget and adjust the forecast when required.

2.4 Expense sheets

Travel costs (i.e. transport charges, meals, hotel, telephone charges and other authorised expenditure) may be charged to the company in accordance with the agreement/contract.

All costs shall be in the same currency as per the agreement/contract unless otherwise stipulated and/or agreed.

The Company Secretary shall compare the expense sheets with the budget and adjust the forecast when required.

The Company Secretary shall check and sign the expense sheets if he agrees with the contents. The expense sheets will then require approval by the Managing Director.

Personal expenditure incurred by a subcontractor/consultant is considered to be the responsibility of the subcontractor's/consultant's parent organisation. They are, therefore, responsible for reimbursing the subcontractor/consultant directly.

2.5 Time and Expense Reports

On a monthly basis, Stingray staff shall consolidate the details contained in the Time and Expense sheets into a monthly Time and Expense Report (see Annex C).

WI/2 Annex A – Time Sheet

TIME SHEET

Name	
Month:				Year:	

Day	Actual office hours	Travel time	Productive travel time	Total productive hours
1				
2				
3				
4				
5				
6				
7				
8				
9				
10				
11				
12				
13				
14				
15				
16				
17				
18				
19				
20				
21				
22				
23				
24				
25				
26				
27				
28				
29				
30				
31				

Signed:		Name:		Date:	

WI/2 Annex B – Expense Sheets

Name	
Month:	**Year:**

							TOTALS
Week No	(1)						**TOTALS**
Week ending	(2)						
Air fares	(3)						(10)
Tube & train fares	(3)						(10)
Coach fares	(3)						(10)
Taxi fares	(3)						(10)
Hotel	(4)						(10)
Meals	(5)						(10)
Entertainment	(6)						(10)
Telephone	(7)						(10)
Other expenses	(8)						(10)
TOTALS	(9)						(11)

Signed:		**Name:**		**Date:**	
Approved:		**Name:**		**Date:**	

Here follows a brief description how to use the Expense Sheet.

1) Week number.
2) Date of the Sunday of the week reported in this line.
3) Travel costs by air, train, taxi, etc.
4) Hotel costs.
5) Meal costs, if you were not at your principal location.
6) Entertainment costs for company guests.
7) Costs for official telephone calls.
8) Other costs, like material, books, software etc. (**to be approved by the Company Secretary**).
9) The total of all costs for the week concerned.
10) Total costs of your travel, hotel, meals, etc.
11) Total of all costs for the month concerned, again **except** your personal fees.

Document Ref: S-54-029RLT05
Version: 02.02
Date: 01.01.05
Quality Management System
Part Four – Work Instructions
WI/2 – Time Sheets and Expense Sheets

STINGRAY

WI/2 Annex C – Time and Expense Report

Name		
Month:		Year:

Time Card				Expenses					
Week ending	Subject	Days spent	Location	Travel expenses Train/Air fares	Hotel	Taxi	Meals	Other expenes	Totals
				Allowance:					
Totals:				Totals:					End total:

WI/3 – Subcontractors' invoices

3.1 Scope

WI/3 covers the approval procedure and payment for invoices from subcontractors.

3.2 Approval of invoices

Invoices from subcontractors shall be sent directly to the Company Secretary who shall:

- stamp the invoice and fill in the date and data as appropriate;
- keep a copy of the invoice;
- send the stamped original to the Section Manager for agreement against the planned work achievement/payment schedule as indicated in the contract.

3.3 Payment of invoices

All invoices submitted for approval must be accompanied by a copy of the approved Subcontract Approval Form.

Invoices shall be paid within one month of receipt of the invoice or of the work being completed, whichever is the latest.

3.4 Invoice records

The Company Secretary shall keep records of the invoices received and their subsequent payment.

WI/4 – CD-ROM Distribution

4.1 Scope

Stingray is frequently requested to provide copies of contract deliverables to clients, section team members and third parties. The simplest and most cost effective way of distributing this information is via CD-ROM. WI/4 describes this process.

4.2 Procedure

Section Managers and specified individuals are responsible for (and shall decide on) the external distribution of all approved deliverables, working papers, reports and documents outside the project. (Also see QP/1 – Document Control.)

Section Managers (and specified individuals) shall determine:

- the requirement (need) to distribute copies (or parts of) Stingray deliverables;
- the manner in which Stingray deliverables may be distributed to clients, project team members and third parties;
- their availability and distribution.

4.2.1 Distribution list

The distribution of all Stingray CDs shall be completed by the Company Secretary who shall maintain a distribution list, which will be updated every time a new delivery is made. The list shall include details of the person to whom the CD was distributed, its contents, the date of distribution and the selling price.

4.2.2 Updating previous distributions

Section Managers shall advise the Company Secretary every time a new version of a CD is issued and the Company Secretary shall inform all persons having received a previous version of that CD that a new version is available and (on request) provide replacement (i.e. updated) copies of that CD.

4.2.3 Price guidelines

The price charged by Stingray for a CD shall depend on:

- the type of contract;
- the method of transmitting (i.e. sending) this information to the company;

- the type and amount of information contained on the CD;
- the time spent preparing the CD.

4.2.4 CD type

All Stingray deliverables shall be distributed using electronic files formatted onto a CD-ROM which is readable by any standard CD-ROM reader.

4.2.5 CD Labelling

All CD-ROMs provided by Stingray shall be labelled. These labels shall be identified by a circular label (see example below) containing the Stingray logo and details of the contract deliverable.

Figure 6.4.2 Example of a CD-ROM label

4.2.6 Plastic case – front

The front of the CD-ROM's plastic case shall be similar to the CD-ROM label and shall contain the Stingray logo together with details of the contract deliverable and a copyright statement as follows:

Figure 6.4.3 Example of the front cover of the plastic case

4.2.7 Plastic case – back

The back of the CD-ROM's plastic case shall contain the following text:

Installation and User Instructions

This CD-ROM contains data files only. It does not contain
application software.

A PC operating in a Windows environment with a CD-ROM drive
and loaded with Acrobat Reader software is required to read the data
contained on this CD.

The Adobe Acrobat Reader is free software produced by Adobe and can be
obtained from Adobe Systems Incorporated. Details can be found on the
Internet (www.adobe.com/acrobat/).

The data files can be opened using the File Manager menu command.

- Insert the CD into the CD-ROM drive and select File Manager/Explorer
  (depending upon the version of Windows being used).
- Select the drive containing the CD (this will usually be the 'D' drive).
- From the directory structure displayed, select the **Readme.txt** file.
- From the directory structure displayed select the **index.pdf** file
  and open it.
- The index.pdf file will list the fields contained on the CD and give
  the electronic file reference. These files can be found in
  the **Contents Director**.
- Having identified the file required, select it in the directory structure
  and open in the normal way.
- To print a file, first open it and then select file and print.

Figure 6.4.4 Example of the back cover of the plastic case

4.2.8 Plastic case – spine

The spine of the CD-ROM's plastic case shall contain details of the contract
deliverable.

4.2.9 Internal matter

An optional sheet (the same size as the CD case) may be included at the discre-
tion of the Section Manager so as to include details of the deliverable, its
potential use, any limitations etc.

4.2.10 Draft deliverables

All draft versions of Stingray deliverables shall carry the following text inside the front cover of the CD case:

For example:

> 'This is a preliminary version distributed for information purposes only. It should not, therefore, be used to extract definitive information from. Neither Stingray nor its participating members are liable for any damage (including, but not limited to, claims from third parties) caused by information extracted from this preliminary version.'

4.2.11 Approved deliverables

When a new version of an approved deliverable is issued, copies of all previous versions shall be destroyed. This shall be covered by a statement in the covering letter to the effect that:

> 'On receipt of this CD, all previous versions are to be destroyed'.

Part Seven _____

Self-assessment

Assuming that by now you have your own organisation-specific Quality Management System up and running, how do you monitor its effectiveness?

Part Seven covers the often-overlooked topic of self-assessment. Methods for completing management reviews and quality audits (internal or via third party assessment) are discussed.

Also included are:

- self-assessment checklists against the requirements of ISO 9001:2000;
- examples of audit stage checklists;
- annexes listing:
  - the headings of ISO 9001:2000;
  - the likely documentation that an organisation would need to meet the requirements of ISO 9001:2000;
  - a complete index to the ISO 9001:2000 standard.

 Note: For a more comprehensive explanation about the concepts of auditing may I suggest that you have a look at my associated publication *ISO 9001:2000 Audit Procedures*.

This book follows on from where *ISO 9001:2000 for Small Businesses* leaves off and is a guide to assist auditors in completing internal, external and third party audits of all existing and newly implemented ISO 9001:2000 Quality Management Systems, as well as organisational (non-registered) QMSs. It also includes background notes for auditors as well as lots of checklists and example audit forms etc.

7

Self-assessment

7.1 How ISO 9000 can be used to check an organisation's Quality Management System

Having set up your own Quality Management System (QMS), how can you prove to a potential customer that it fully meets the recommendations, requirements and specifications of ISO 9001:2000? Indeed, how can you check a subcontractor's or a supplier's QMS?

If management have complied with the requirements for QMS standards as they have been described so far, then they will be well on their way to running a quality organisation. The requirements of QMS do not rest there, however. The organisation must continually review their QMS as to its continuing suitability and success, reveal defects, danger spots or irregularities, suggest possible improvements, eliminate wastage or loss, check the effectiveness of

Figure 7.1 Quality assurance measurements

management at all levels and be sure that managerial objectives and methods are effective and achieving the desired result. Above all an organisation must be prepared to face up to an audit of their quality procedures from potential customers.

 Note: Also see Annex 7C for ISO 9001:2000; requirements of management.

7.2 Internal audit

The purpose of an internal quality audit is to identify potential danger spots, eliminate wastage and verify that corrective action has been successfully achieved. The procedures with which to carry out these audits should always be documented and available.

Figure 7.2 Internal audit

An audit plan determines whether the QMS is effectively achieving its stated quality objectives and should be established as soon as possible. Indeed, it is a requirement of ISO 9001:2000 that an assessment is regularly completed by the organisation of all the production and manufacturing techniques that they use together with the elements, aspects and components belonging to that organisation's QMS.

The type and content of an internal audit varies with the size of the organisation. In some circumstances it can even mean going as far as having to review the statistical control methods that are used to indicate or predict the need for corrective action being carried out.

Another very important reason for carrying out an internal audit is obviously that it provides a comparison between what the QMS or Quality Plan stipulates should be done and what is actually being done.

The main aim, however, of an internal audit is to confirm that everything is OK.

This verification activity will, depending on the size and activities of the organisation, include testing and monitoring the design, production, installation and servicing processes, the design reviews and the method of auditing the QMS.

The audit should be capable of identifying such things as non-compliance with previously issued instructions and deficiencies within the QMS. In addition the audit should recommend any corrective actions that can be achieved to improve the system.

It is essential that management shall take timely corrective action on all deficiencies found during the audit. Follow-up actions should include the verification and implementation of corrective action, and reporting of results.

7.2.1 Audit plan

To be effective, an 'internal audit' must be completed by trained personnel and where possible by members of the quality control staff – provided, that is, that they are **not** responsible for the quality of that particular product.

This does not, of course, stop the management from using an outside agency (i.e. a third-party certification) if they wish to, and in so doing gain a completely unbiased view of the general success of their QMS.

The selection of the department to be audited should always be conducted on a random basis and normally these internal audits will be completed every three months or so. In an ideal world the audit should be pre-planned so that it covers all aspects of quality control within one calendar year.

There are many reasons why an internal audit should be carried out, and provided they are completed by qualified personnel, they are usually successful.

The audit plan should:

- cover all the specific areas and activities that are to be audited;
- cover the reasons why an internal audit is being completed (e.g. organisational changes, reported deficiencies, survey or routine check);

- stipulate the minimum qualifications of the personnel who are to carry out the audit;
- describe how the audit report should be finalised and submitted.

7.2.2 Internal audit program

As shown in Figure 7.3 an internal audit program normally consists of 8 separate (but interrelated) steps:

Figure 7.3 Internal Audit program

Step 1 – Audit schedule

Internal quality audits are usually planned and initiated by the Quality Manager in relation to the status and importance of the various activities of a section and/or deliverable. For large organisations, it would be quite normal for all departments and sections to be subject to at least three **complete** quality audits every year as shown in the example below.

FUNCTION/ DEPARTMENT	JAN	FEB	MAR	APR	MAY	JUN	JULY	AUG	SEPT	OCT	NOV	DEC
Administration and finance	x				x				x			
Drawing office		x				x				x		
Workshops			x				x				x	
Stores				x				x				x

Annual quality audit schedule

 Note: For smaller organisations (e.g. those only employing a handful of people) an audit every 4 months or so of selected areas would probably be sufficient.

Step 2 – Audit preparation and organisation

Depending on the complexity and the size of the audit, the Quality Manager may perform the audit himself, or (when sections are too large, or when activities from other sections are involved) he can assign a lead auditor and a team of auditors to complete the task.

The Quality Manager (or lead auditor) is then responsible for organising an agenda which will include the:

- scope and objectives of the audit;
- persons having direct responsibilities for the procedure(s) to be audited;
- reference documents;
- name of lead auditor and name(s) of assigned auditor(s);
- date when audit is to be concluded.

Audit Reference No:	File No: ....
Purpose of audit:	
Scope of audit:	
Lead Auditor assigned:	
Location(s) of audit:	
Unit or area to be audited:	
Reference documents:	
Team members:	
Date of audit:	Anticipated duration of audit: ....
Time of opening meeting:	Anticipated time of closing meeting: .....
Facilities requested:	

Internal audit plan

Following a review of earlier audit reports on the same section or the same subject, the lead auditor and the assigned auditor(s) will prepare an audit check list containing all of the topics/items to be covered together with an audit program (see example below).

AUDIT CHECKLIST	FUNCTION/PROCESS AUDITED: .... DOCUMENT REFERENCES:		AUDIT NO:....... AUDIT DATE:.......
ITEM NO	AUDIT QUESTIONS	REFERENCE	RESULT	NOTES/ OBSERVATIONS
	PREPARED BY:	PAGE ... OF ...		DATE PREPARED: ....

Audit checklist

TIMETABLE	TEAM A	TEAM B	AUDITEE PARTICIPATION
0900–0930	Opening meeting		Senior Management & Department Heads
0930–1030	Managing Director Quality Policy Management Review	Laboratory 1	Technical Director
1030–1100	Review of: Document Control Non-conformity	Laboratory 2	Department Heads
1100–1200	Purchasing	Laboratory 2	Department Heads
1200	Lunch		
1330–1500	Purchasing	Laboratory 2 (cont)	Department Heads
1500–1600	Personnel Training	Electrical Test House	Department Heads
1600–1700	Commercial/ Sales	Calibration Service	Department Heads

Audit program

Step 3 – Audit execution

An initial meeting between the auditor(s), the auditee(s) and the Quality Manager is held during which:

- a brief summary of the methods and procedures that will be used to conduct the audit is given;
- the method of communication between auditor(s) and auditee(s) is agreed; and
- the audit program confirmed.

In accordance with ISO 9001:2000 (Section 8.2.2) all organisations are required to have a documented procedure for conducting internal quality audits. Normally this procedure will distinguish between two kinds of internal quality audits, namely a 'standards audit' and a 'procedures audit'.

Note: The standards audit evaluates how well the ISO standard is being applied, while the procedures audit evaluates how effective the organisation's quality procedures, policies, plans, and instructions are.

Using the standards audit the auditor will begin collecting evidence of compliance by interviewing auditee personnel, reading documents, reviewing manuals, checking records, examining data, observing activities and studying working conditions. As the evidence is collected the auditor will answer each audit question and record his observations as either:

Yes	means that this activity is in compliance with the standard;
No	means this activity is not in compliance;
Not applicable	means that this question is not applicable in this activity's situation.

Once the auditor has completed the audit questionnaire, he makes a list of all the non-conformities (i.e. the 'No's') and summarises his evidence.

Similarly, using the procedures audit each applicable quality procedure, policy, plan and work instruction will be looked at from the point of view of *Is it documented? Is it being followed? Is it effective?* On the basis of evidence collected, the auditor will record his observation as:

Yes	means that this activity is in compliance;
No	means that this activity is not in compliance.

Auditors will record all their observations on the Audit observation sheet (see example on facing page) and all non-compliances will then be listed on a 'non-compliance worksheet' which will eventually form part of the final audit report.

Step 4 – Summarise audit results

Auditors will then meet to discuss all of their observations (particularly any non-compliances that they may have found) with the Quality Manager.

Note: All observations of non-conformity **must** be formally acknowledged by the manager responsible for the activity being audited.

A closing meeting of auditor(s), auditee(s) and Quality Manager will then be held during which:

- audit observations will be clarified;
- the critical significance of observations will be presented;
- conclusions drawn about compliance will be presented;
- system effectiveness in achieving the quality objectives will be presented;

Section or project to be audited:		
Reason for audit:		
Audit No:	Date:	
Auditor:	Sheet ... of ...	

Serial No	Observation/supporting evidence Action required	Yes/No

Circulation:	
Attached Sheets:	

Signed:		Name:		Date:	

Audit observation sheet

- corrective actions will be agreed;
- the date for completion of the audit report will be agreed.

Note: Minutes of **all** relevant meetings, decisions and agreements must be attached to the audit report.

Step 5 – Prepare audit report

The lead auditor now needs to prepare an audit report using an Audit report form similar to the one shown on p. 380.

The report must be signed by all members of the audit team, plus the Quality Manager, and copies sent to auditee(s) and company management as required.

Section or project audited:			
Reason for audit:			
Audit No:		Date:	
Auditor:		Sheet ... of ...	
Audit area(s):			
Reference document(s):			
Summary:			
Audit observation sheet number	Observation number	Comments	Corrective action requirement
Prepared:	Name:		Date:
Agreed:	Name:		Date:
Circulation:		Attached sheets	

Audit report form

The audit report will list all non-conformities discovered, observations made and discuss any conclusions drawn. It will also detail (in the summary) recommendations that should be implemented in order to correct or prevent non-conformities occurring and to make improvements.

Step 6 – Corrective action

After the closing meeting, the lead auditor will prepare a Corrective action request (similar to the example on p. 379) for each agreed corrective action.

 Note: Corrective action requests should always state who is responsible for carrying out the corrective action and the timescale for its completion.

Section or project audited:			
Reason for audit:			
Audit No:		Audit Date:	
Auditor(s):		Auditee(s):	
Audit area(s):			
Reference document(s):			
Non-conformance details:			
Signed: (Auditor)		Name:	Date:
Agreed corrective action:			
Signed: (Auditee)		Name:	Date:
Agreed time limit:			
Signed: (Actionee)		Name:	Date:
Progress		Signed	Date

Corrective action request

 Note: One sheet should be used for **each agreed** corrective action.

Step 7 – Take remedial action

The section/department that has been audited is then responsible for ensuring that the agreed corrective actions are implemented and that any observations, comments and recommendations made by the audit team have been taken into account.

Step 8 – Follow up

Finally, the lead auditor is then responsible for ensuring that corrective action has been carried out and for notifying the Quality Manager of the status and/or completion of corrective actions.

7.3 External audit

Although the supplier may have been able to convince the purchaser that their QMS is effective, it is in the interests of the purchaser to conduct their own evaluation (i.e. audit) of the supplier. This is usually done on an irregular basis.

The supplier must, of course, agree to the principle of purchaser evaluations being carried out and it is usual to find this as a separate clause in the contract.

Normally these audits are pretty simple, but – particularly when the material, product or service being purchased is complex – the purchaser will need to have a reasonably objective method of evaluating and measuring the efficiency of the quality control of the supplier's promises and be certain that the system established by the supplier complies with the laid down standards and is, above all, effective. This method is known as the 'supplier evaluation'.

7.3.1 Supplier evaluation

Part of the initial contract will stipulate that the supplier provides access to the purchaser's inspectors and sometimes even accommodation and facilities to enable the purchaser's representatives to conduct their activities and evaluations. These facilities depend upon the level of surveillance, but could require the supplier to provide:

- suitable office and administrative facilities;
- adequate work space for product verification;
- access to those areas where work is in progress or to those which affect the work;
- help in documenting, inspecting and releasing material and services;
- the use of inspection and test devices and availability of personnel to operate them are necessary.

Figure 7.4 External audit

7.3.1.1 Evaluation team

Two or more inspectors from the purchaser's organisation will form the evaluation team. These inspectors must be thoroughly skilled in the requirements of quality assurance and are normally drawn from the purchaser's own quality control section.

7.3.1.2 Pre-evaluation meeting

Before the evaluation team visits the supplier's premises they must first be given the chance to:

- meet the supplier's staff to discuss the procedures being used;
- identify the supplier's divisions that will be tested;

- decide which representatives of the organisation will be required to accompany the evaluation team during their inspection;
- agree dates and outline timetables, etc.

7.3.1.3 Study of the quality manual

The purchaser must then be given a copy of the supplier's Quality Manual. The Quality Manual will be inspected not only for its accuracy and clarity but also its position compared to national and international standards and to see that it conforms to the relevant sections of ISO 9001:2000.

When the manual has been thoroughly examined, the purchaser will then be able to send a team of inspectors to the supplier's premises to fully scrutinise every aspect of the supplier's design office, purchasing, storekeeping, manufacturing, assembly and test facilities to see that the work carried out complies with the procedures (promises!) made in their Quality Manual.

7.3.1.4 The evaluation

Having completed the pre-evaluation, the purchaser is now able to visit the supplier's premises for a complete inspection.

During the actual evaluation, the department heads will first be required to describe to the team exactly how their quality control system works. They will have to provide examples of their quality control documentation and possibly even be required to prove that certain divisions have the correct documentation and that it is up to date. The department heads will then have to show how stock is received, accounted for and withdrawn from stores, how the appropriate drawings are issued, updated and eventually disposed of.

 Note: Quite often the evaluation team will want to see the route cards and/or 'travellers' that accompany partially completed work.

The purchaser will, as part of their QMS audit, possibly carry out an evaluation of the sampling procedures used by the supplier – to ascertain whether they conform to those laid down in the Quality Plan for that particular product.

During their evaluation it is also possible for the purchaser's team to ask for a previously inspected batch to be rechecked so that they can see if a similar or comparable result is obtained.

Other aspects of the manufacturer's facilities that the inspectors might well want to look at (particularly if the supplier is an organisation actually manufacturing a product) could include:

- evidence that their test equipment and other instruments have been regularly maintained and calibrated against a known source;
- that rejected or unacceptable components and assemblies are clearly marked and segregated to avoid any chance of their accidental inclusion with other items that have already been accepted.

At the end of this evaluation, a meeting will be arranged between the evaluation team and the factory organisations to discuss their findings and to be sure that there are not any misunderstandings, etc.

The eventual evaluation report will then be formally presented at a meeting with the management. The result of this meeting could be one of the following:

7.3.1.4.1 Acceptable system control

This means that the evaluation has shown that the supplier has a satisfactory QMS, there are no deficiencies and the supplier has been able to give an assurance of quality. When this happens, there should be no reason why the purchaser should feel it necessary to demand any radical changes to the supplier's system.

 Note: But even though the supplier may have proved that they are up to a satisfactory standard, the purchaser will still have the right to (and often does) insist on making further inspections throughout the duration of the contract.

7.3.1.4.2 Weak system control

This covers the situation where the evaluation team find several significant weaknesses in the supplier's system.

If this happens, the supplier will have to take steps to overcome these failures and improve their QMS. Having done this, the supplier can then ask for another evaluation to be carried out to confirm that their quality now meets the required standards.

7.3.1.4.3 Unacceptable system control

This is the result of an evaluation team finding that the number of deficiencies – or the lack of quality discipline at the supplier's premises – mean that the supplier

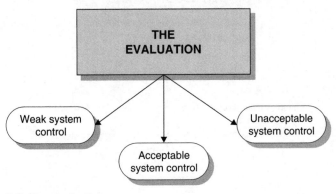

Figure 7.5 The evaluation

will have to make radical changes to improve their overall QMS before they are anything like acceptable to the potential purchaser.

When the supplier has completed the necessary changes, they will then require a second evaluation to see that their improvements are satisfactory. Unfortunately this could be as much as a year later, by which time the purchaser may well have found an alternative source or decided that the initial organisation's quality is definitely not up to standard – and virtually blacklisted that particular supplier!

Having been inspected, it is important that the records of this inspection are safely filed away in case they may be required to reinforce some point at a later stage or to provide statistical data for the analysis of a supplier's performance. This is sometimes referred to as 'vendor rating'.

In the UK, the Department of Trade and Industry (DTI) publish comprehensive lists of manufacturers and suppliers who have proved that their QMS fully satisfies the requirements of ISO 9001:2000.

7.4 The surveillance or quality audit visit

Although an organisation may well have successfully passed an initial evaluation of their facilities and the purchaser may well be satisfied that the supplier is capable of providing an assurance of quality, it cannot be assumed that the supplier will be able, or even capable of, retaining this status forever. Many things can happen to change this situation such as staff moving through promotion or natural wastage, changes in the product design that may or have been necessary, or perhaps even a new man-management philosophy.

The purchaser needs, therefore, to be informed of any changes in the organisation and personnel that might affect the overall quality of the product.

Figure 7.6 The surveillance

It is quite possible that the purchaser might also want to make irregular surveillance visits of the supplier's premises to examine a particular aspect of their QMS. These surveillance or audit visits by the purchaser will be run on exactly the same lines as the supplier evaluation and are aimed at providing the purchaser with a confidence in the supplier and an assurance that they are capable of in fact still providing the purchaser with the quality of goods that they require. The aim of these audit visits should be that all the important aspects of the quality control system are checked, in rotation.

7.4.1 Multiple evaluations and audits

It is possible that some suppliers might well be providing the same product to several different customers and it could just happen that all of these customers ask to have an audit – at the same time! This obviously cannot be allowed to happen as the manufacturer would forever have people visiting their premises and disturbing, not only the labour force, but also the production line! Thankfully there are quite a number of ways around this problem such as secondary audit or third-party evaluation.

7.4.2 Secondary audit

If a purchaser indicates that they want to carry out an audit, the supplier can offer to provide the details of another customer's audit that has recently been carried out at their premises. If this does not quite cover the problem area sufficiently, then the supplier could offer to check in more detail the appropriate points raised by the purchaser.

7.4.3 Third-party evaluation

As an alternative to the secondary audit, a third-party evaluation team (i.e. one that is not directly involved in either the supply or purchase of the article) could be employed to carry out an audit.

There are several firms that have been specifically set up to do this and these are capable of determining if a supplier's product, premises and management are capable of meeting (and still meet) the laid down standards.

Probably the most famous of these (especially for British firms) is the British Standards Institution. BSI regularly produce a certified list of all suppliers whose products meet the requirements of ISO 9000. This list is also published by the Department of Trade and Industry.

7.4.4 Conformity assessment

In these days of international markets and cross-border trading, many national regulations require that a product or deliverable is first tested for compliance with an internationally agreed specification for safety, environmental and/or quality conformance before they can be released to the market.

This sort of testing is referred to as 'conformity assessment' and in its simplest form means that a product, material, service, system (or in some cases) people has been measured against the specifications of a relevant standard – which, in most cases, will be an internationally agreed standard.

Although some conformity assessment can be completed using internal facilities, when a product has health and/or environmental implications, national legislation will probably stipulate that testing is carried out by an independent Registrar, Notified Body or specialist organisation; in other words, by a third party.

There exist many testing laboratories and certification bodies which offer independent conformity assessment services performed either as a commercial venture, or under mandate to their national government.

 Note: For details of availability in your area try the DTI website www.dti.gov.uk or perhaps one of the search engines (e.g. www.google.com).

7.5 ISO 9001:2000 checklist

Self-assessment can be a very useful tool to identify possible areas for improving an organisation's capability and ISO 9004:2000 helps organisations by providing an annex containing 'guidelines for self-assessment'. As this is an important consideration I have included a number of annexes to this chapter specifically aimed at helping small businesses complete a self-assessment of their QMS and cost-effectively work in conformance with the requirements of ISO 9001:2000. These consist of:

7.5.1 ISO 9001:2000 headings

A complete list of the sections and sub-sections making up ISO 9001:2000 requirements (Appendix A).

7.5.2 ISO 9001:2000 explanations and likely documentation

A brief explanation of the specific requirements (i.e. the 'shalls') of each element of ISO 9001:2000 together with a description of the likely documentation that an organisation would need to have in place to meet the requirements, as well as an outline of this content (Appendix B).

7.5.3 ISO 9001:2000 requirements of management

Another list of the sections and sub-sections that make up ISO 9001:2000, but this time identifying the areas that management need to address when they document their Quality Management System (Annex 7C).

Note: Most independent Registrars and Notified Bodies will use a similar 'check sheet' to determine whether an organisation's QMS complies with the requirements of ISO 9001:2000.

7.5.4 Example of an external auditor's checklist

A list of the most important questions an external Quality Auditor (e.g. BSI, TÜV, Yardely, etc.) would be likely to ask when completing an external or conformity audit. If an organisation can honestly answer 'yes' to all these questions then they would be quite entitled to say that they 'fully comply with the requirements of ISO 9001:2000' (Appendix D).

Note: Parts of these checklists could also be used when conducting internal quality audits.

7.5.5 Example stage audit checklist

Lists of the most important questions that an external Quality Auditor (e.g. purchaser) is likely to ask when evaluating an organisation for the:

- design stage;
- manufacturing stage;
- acceptance stage;
- in-service stage.

(Appendix E).

Note: These checklists could again be used for internal audits.

7.5.6 Index for ISO 9001:2000

A unique and complete index to each section of ISO 9001:2000 enabling readers to quickly access the relevant passage or sentence in the standard (Appendix F).

Appendix 7A
ISO 9001:2000 headings

4 QMS Requirements
4.1 General requirements
4.2 Documentation requirements
    4.2.1 General
    4.2.2 Quality Manual
    4.2.3 Control of documents
    4.2.4 Control of records

5 Management responsibility
5.1 Management commitment
5.2 Customer focus
5.3 Quality policy
5.4 Planning
    5.4.1 Quality objectives
    5.4.2 Quality management system planning
5.5 Responsibility, authority and communication
    5.5.1 Responsibility and authority
    5.5.2 Management representative
    5.5.3 Internal communication
5.6 Management review
    5.6.1 General
    5.6.2 Review input
    5.6.3 Review output

6 Resource Management
6.1 Provision of resources
6.2 Human resources
    6.2.1 General
    6.2.2 Competence, awareness and training
6.3 Infrastructure
6.4 Work environment

7 Product realisation

7.1 Planning of product realisation

7.2 Customer-related processes

  7.2.1 Determination of requirements related to the product

  7.2.2 Review of requirements related to the product

  7.2.3 Customer communication

7.3 Design and development

  7.3.1 Design and development planning

  7.3.2 Design and development inputs

  7.3.3 Design and development outputs

  7.3.4 Design and development review

  7.3.5 Design and development verification

  7.3.6 Design and development validation

  7.3.7 Control of design and development changes

7.4 Purchasing

  7.4.1 Purchasing process

  7.4.2 Purchasing information

  7.4.3 Verification of purchased product

7.5 Production and service provision

  7.5.1 Control of production and service provision

  7.5.2 Validation of processes for production and service provision

  7.5.3 Identification and traceability

  7.5.4 Customer property

  7.5.5 Preservation of product

7.6 Control of monitoring and measurement devices

8 Measurement, analysis and improvement

8.1 General

8.2 Monitoring and measurement

  8.2.1 Customer satisfaction

  8.2.2 Internal audit

  8.2.3 Monitoring and measurement of processes

  8.2.4 Monitoring and measurement of product

8.3 Control of non-conforming product

8.4 Analysis of data

8.5 Improvement

  8.5.1 Continual improvement

  8.5.2 Corrective action

  8.5.3 Preventive action

Appendix 7B
ISO 9001:2000 – Explanations and likely documentation

Section no.	ISO 9001:2000 title	Explanation	Likely documentation
4	Quality Management System		
4.1	General requirements	A definition of the processes necessary to ensure that a product conforms to customer requirements that are capable of being implemented, maintained and improved.	Core Business Processes supplemented by: • Supporting Processes; • QPs; • WIs.
4.2	Documentation requirements		
4.2.1	General	Documented proof of a QMS	Quality Manual. High level policy statement on organisational objectives and quality policies. Procedures. Quality records.
4.2.2	Quality Manual	A document which describes an organisation's quality policies, procedures and practices that make up the QMS	A Quality Manual containing everything related to quality controls within an organisation.
4.2.3	Control of documents	How an organisation's documents are approved, issued, numbered etc. How revisions are recorded and implemented and obsolete documents removed.	Document control procedures.

Section no.	ISO 9001:2000 title	Explanation	Likely documentation
4.2.4	Control of records	What quality records need to be kept to demonstrate conformance with the requirements of an organisation's QMS and how they are identified, stored, protected etc.	Record keeping procedures.
5	Management responsibility	Management responsibility and quality requirements.	Quality Manual.
5.1	Management commitment	A written demonstration of an organisation's commitment to: • sustaining and increasing customer satisfaction; • establishing quality policies, objectives and planning; • establishing a QMS; • performing management reviews; • ensuring availability of resources. • determining the legal and mandatory requirements its products and/or services have to meet; • continuous improvement.	High-level policy statement on organisational objectives and quality policies. A list of Government regulatory, legal and customer-specific requirements. • Procedures describing: – resource management; – contract review procedures; – management reviews; – financial business plan(s).
5.2	Customer focus	How an organisation ensures that customer expectations and needs, requirements are determined, fully understood and met.	Procedures describing: • resource management; • contract review procedures; • management reviews; • financial business plan(s).
5.3	Quality policy	How an organisation approaches quality and the requirements for meeting them, ensuring that: • They are appropriate for both customer and an organisation; • There is a commitment to continually meet customer requirements; • These commitments are communicated, understood and implemented throughout an organisation; • There is a commitment for continual improvement.	High-level managerial statement on an organisation's quality policy containing clear responsibilities, training and resources required for each organisational activity.

Appendix 7B   ISO 9001:2000 – Explanations and likely documentation

Section no.	ISO 9001:2000 title	Explanation	Likely documentation
5.4	Planning	The planning of resources, etc. to meet an organisation's overall business objectives.	Quality Manual.
5.4.1	Quality objectives	The quality objectives that an organisation expects to function achieve within each and level of the organisation.	Policy statements defining the objectives of the company and those responsible for achieving the objectives.
5.4.2	Quality management system planning	The identification and planning of activities and resources required to meet an organisation's quality objectives.	The processes and procedures used by senior management to define and plan the way that the organisation is run.
5.5	Responsibility, authority and communication	How the organisation has documented its QMS.	A Quality Manual containing everything related to quality controls within the organisation.
5.5.1	Responsibility and authority	A definition of the roles, responsibilities, lines of authority, reporting and communication relevant to quality.	Job descriptions and responsibilities. Organisation charts showing lines of communication.
5.5.2	Management representative	The identification and appointment of a 'Quality Manager' with responsibility for the QMS.	Job description and responsibilities. Organisation charts showing lines of communication.
5.5.3	Internal communication	How the requirements of an organisation's QMS are communicated throughout the company.	Team briefings, organisational meetings, notice boards, in-house journals/magazines, audio-visual and other forms of e-information.
5.6	Management review	How senior management reviews the QMS to ensure its continued suitability, adequacy and effectiveness, in the context of an organisation's strategic planning cycle.	Procedures concerning: • process, product and/or service audit procedures; • customer feedback; • process and product performance; • corrective and preventive action; • supplier performance; • record keeping.

Section no.	ISO 9001:2000 title	Explanation	Likely documentation
5.6.1	General	The requirement for management to establish a process for the periodic review of the QMS.	Management review and QMS audit procedures.
5.6.2	Review input	The documents and information required for management reviews.	Results of audits, customer feedback, analysis of process performance and product conformance, corrective and preventive action reports and supplier performance records.
5.6.3	Review output	Result of the review.	Minutes of the meetings where the overall running of the company is discussed.
6	Resource management	A description of resources with regard to training, induction, responsibilities, working environment, equipment requirements, maintenance, etc.	QPs, Quality Plans and WIs
6.1	Provision of resources	How resource needs (i.e. human, materials, equipment, infrastructure) are identified.	Quality Plans identifying the resources required to complete a particular project or activity.
6.2	Human resources	Identification and assignment of human resources to implement and improve the QMS and comply with contract conditions.	QPs, Quality Plans and WIs.
6.2.1	General	How an organisation assigns personnel on the basis of competency, qualification, training, skills and experience relevant specific tasks.	Job descriptions and responsibilities. Training records. Staff evaluations. Project plans identifying the human resources required to complete the task.
6.2.2	Competence, awareness and training	Documents showing how an organisation selects, trains and assigns personnel to specific tasks.	System level procedures for: • training; • staff evaluations; • review of work assignments; • staff assessments; • records.

Section no.	ISO 9001:2000 title	Explanation	Likely documentation
6.3	Infrastructure	How an organisation defines, provides and maintains the infrastructure requirements to ensure product conformity (e.g. infrastructure, plant, hardware, software, tools and equipment, communication facilities, transport and supporting services, etc.).	Policies, procedures and regulatory documents stating the infrastructure requirements of an organisation and/or their customers. Financial documents. Maintenance plans. Project plans identifying the human resources required to complete the task.
6.4	Work environment	How an organisation defines and implements the human and physical factors of the work environment required to ensure product conformity (health and safety, work methods, ethics and ambient working conditions).	Environmental procedures. Project plans. Budgetary and legal processes and procedures.
7	Product realisation	The requirements for process control, purchasing, handling and storage, measuring devices, etc.	Quality Manual and associated Processes, QPs, Quality Plans and WIs.
7.1	Planning of product realisation	The availability of documented plans for all product processes required to realise a product, and the sequences in which they occur.	Process models (flow charts) showing the sequence of activities that an organisation goes through to produce a product. Documented QPs and WIs to ensure that staff work in accordance with requirements. Records that prove the results of process control. Quality Plans.
7.2	Customer-related processes	The identification, review and interaction with customer requirements and customers.	Quality Manual and Quality Plans.
7.2.1	Determination of requirements related to the product	How an organisation determines and implements customer requirements.	Contract review procedures. Regulatory and legal product requirements. Formal contracts.

Section no.	ISO 9001:2000 title	Explanation	Likely documentation
7.2.2	Review of requirements related to the product	How an organisation reviews product and customer requirements to check that they can actually do the job.	Contract review procedures. Regulatory and legal product requirements. Project plans showing lines of communication with the customer.
7.2.3	Customer communication	How an organisation communicates (i.e. liaises) with their customers, keeps them informed, handles their enquiries, complaints and feedback.	Project plans showing lines of communication with the customer.
7.3	Design and development	The control of design and development within an organisation.	Processes and procedures for design and development. Design plans.
7.3.1	Design and development planning	How an organisation goes about planning and controlling the design of a product (e.g. design stages, development processes, verification and validation, responsibilities and authorities).	Design and development plans. Procedures detailing the design process and how designs are verified and validated. Risk assessment. Job descriptions and responsibilities.
7.3.2	Design and development inputs	How an organisation identifies the requirements to be met by a product.	Project Plans (detailing policies, standards and specifications, skill requirements). Specifications and tolerances. Regulatory and legal requirements. Information derived from previous (similar) designs or developments. Environmental requirements. Health and safety aspects.
7.3.3	Design and development outputs	How an organisation ensures that the design output meets the design input requirements.	Drawings, schematics, schedules, system specifications, system descriptions, etc.

Section no.	ISO 9001:2000 title	Explanation	Likely documentation
7.3.4	Design and development review	How an organisation evaluates their ability to fulfil product requirements, identify problems and complete follow-up actions.	Procedures detailing how changes are made to designs and how they are approved, recorded and distributed. Design process review procedures. Management reviews and audit procedures. Records.
7.3.5	Design and development verification	How an organisation ensures that product specifications are fulfilled and that the design and development output meets the original input requirements.	Design process review procedures. Procedures for periodic reviews. Records.
7.3.6	Design and development validation	How an organisation ensures that the design is actually capable of doing it's intended job.	Procedures for in-process inspection and testing. Final inspection and test. Records.
7.3.7	Control of design and development changes	How changes to a design are approved, together with consideration of how these changes may influence other aspects of the business.	Procedures detailing how changes are made to designs and how they are approved, recorded and distributed. Design process review procedures. Management reviews and audit procedures. Records.
7.4	Purchasing	How an organisation controls the purchase of materials, products and services from suppliers and third parties.	Documented procedures for purchasing and the evaluation of suppliers.
7.4.1	Purchasing process	The controls that an organisation has in place to ensure purchased products and services are of a acceptable standard.	Approved list of suppliers. Supplier evaluations. Purchasing procedures. Purchase orders.
7.4.2	Purchasing information	The details provided by an organisation when placing an	Approved list of suppliers. Supplier evaluations.

Section no.	ISO 9001:2000 title	Explanation	Likely documentation
		order with a supplier and the approval process for purchasing documentation.	Purchasing procedures. Purchase orders. Stock control procedures.
7.4.3	Verification of purchased product	The controls that an organisation has in place to ensure that products and services provided by suppliers meet their original requirements.	Approved list of suppliers. Supplier evaluations. Purchasing procedures. Purchase orders. Stock control procedures.
7.5	Production and service provision	The availability of a process to cover all production and service operations.	Documented Processes, QPs and WIs for production and service operations.
7.5.1	Control of production and service provision	The provision of anything required to control production and service operations.	Procedures for the provision of everything necessary for staff to carry out their work. Project plans and resources required to carry out a job.
7.5.2	Validation of processes for production and service provision	How an organisation identifies processes which cannot be verified by subsequent monitoring/ testing/inspection (including the validation of these processes to demonstrate their effectiveness).	Procedures for tasks which cannot subsequently be proved to be acceptable.
7.5.3	Identification and traceability	The means by which the status of a product can be identified at all stages of its production/delivery.	Procedures for the provision of everything necessary for staff to carry out their work. Project plans and resources required to carry out a job.
7.5.4	Customer property	How an organisation looks after property provided by a customer, including identification, verification, storage and maintenance.	Procedure for the control of customer property.
7.5.5	Preservation of product	How an organisation looks after its own products (i.e. identification, handling, packaging, storing and protecting) including authorisation of release to a customer.	Product approval procedures. Procedures which ensure the safety and protection of products.

Section no.	ISO 9001:2000 title	Explanation	Likely documentation
7.6	Control of monitoring and measuring devices	The controls that an organisation has in place to ensure that equipment (including software) used for proving conformance to specified requirements is properly maintained, calibrated and verified.	Equipment records of maintenance and calibration. WIs.
8	Measurement, analysis and improvement	The measurement, monitoring, analysis and improvement processes an organisation has in place to ensure that the QMS processes and products conform to requirements.	Procedures for inspection and measurement.
8.1	General	The definitions of procedures to ensure product conformity and product improvement	Procedures for: • product conformity; • product improvement; • statistical process review.
8.2	Monitoring and measurement	The analysis of customer satisfaction and the control of products and processes.	Procedures for inspection and measurement.
8.2.1	Customer satisfaction	The processes used to establish whether a customer is satisfied with a product.	Procedures for: • customer feedback; • change control; • customer complaints.
8.2.2	Internal audit	The in-house checks made to determine if the QMS is functioning properly, that it continues to comply with the requirements of ISO 9001:2000 and to identify possibilities for improvement.	Audit procedure. Audit schedules. Audit plans, check sheets and records.
8.2.3	Measurement and monitoring of processes	The methods used to check if processes continue to meet their intended purpose.	Audit schedules. Audit plans, check sheets and records. Approval procedures for product acceptance. Processes for failure cost analysis, conformity, non-conformity, life cycle approach, self-assessment.

Section no.	ISO 9001:2000 title	Explanation	Likely documentation
8.2.3 cont.			Compliance with environmental and safety policies, laws, regulations and standards. Procedures for testing and monitoring processes. Performance and product measurement procedures.
8.2.4	Monitoring and measurement of product	How an organisation measures and monitors that product characteristics the customer's specified requirements.	Audit schedules. Audit plans, check sheets and records. Approval procedures for product acceptance. Processes for failure cost analysis, conformity, non-conformity, life cycle approach, self-assessment. Compliance with environmental and safety policies, laws, regulations and standards. Procedures for testing and monitoring processes. Performance and product measurement procedures. Supplier approval procedures.
8.3	Control of non-conforming product	The methods used to prevent the use or delivery of non-conforming products and to decide what to do with a non-conforming product.	Documented procedure to identify and control the use and delivery of non-conforming products. Approval procedures. Quarantine procedures. Change control procedure. Corrective and preventive action procedures. Audits.
8.4	Analysis of data	The methods used to review data that will determine the effectiveness of the QMS, especially with regard to customer satisfaction, conformance to customer requirements and the performance of processes and products.	Any data or statistics produced as a result of audits, customer satisfaction surveys, complaints, non-conformances, supplier evaluations, etc.

Section no.	ISO 9001:2000 title	Explanation	Likely documentation
8.5	Improvement	How an organisation controls corrective and preventive actions and plans for ongoing process and product improvement.	Documented procedures for: • corrective action; • preventive action; • product/process improvement; • customer complaints/ feedback; • non-conformity reports; • management reviews; • staff suggestions scheme;
8.5.1	Continual improvement	How an organisation goes about continually improving its QMS.	Procedures, minutes of meetings where improvement to the organisation's business is discussed. Management reviews.
8.5.2	Corrective action	What an organisation does to identify and put right non-conformities.	Process for eliminating causes of non-conformity. Documented complaints. Complaints procedure. Staff suggestions scheme.
8.5.3	Preventive action	The proactive methods an organisation employs to prevent non-conformities from happening in the first place.	Process for the prevention of non-conformity. Documented complaints. Complaints procedure. Staff suggestions scheme.

Appendix 7C
Requirements of management

Systemic requirements

Section no.	ISO 9001:2000 title	Requirement	Explanation
4	Quality Management System Requirement	Establish your quality system	
4.1	General requirements	Develop your quality management system	• identify the processes that make up your quality system • describe your quality management processes • implement your quality management system • use quality system processes • manage process performance • improve your quality management system • monitor process performance • improve process performance
4.2	Documentation requirements	Document your quality system	
4.2.1	General	Develop quality system documents	• develop documents to implement your quality system • develop documents that reflect what your organisation does
4.2.2	Quality Manual	Prepare quality system manual	• document your procedures • describe how your processes interact • define the scope of your quality system
4.2.3	Control of documents	Control quality system documents	• approve documents before you distribute them • provide the correct version of documents at points of use • review and re-approve documents whenever you update them

Section no.	ISO 9001:2000 title	Requirement	Explanation
4.2.3 cont.			• specify the current revision status of your documents • monitor documents that come from external sources • prevent the accidental use of obsolete documents • preserve the usability of your quality documents
4.2.4	Control of records	Maintain quality system records	• use your records to prove that requirements have been met • develop a procedure to control your records • ensure that your records are useable

Management requirements

Section no.	ISO 9001:2000 title	Requirement	Explanation
5	Management responsibility		
5.1	Management commitment	Support quality	• promote the importance of quality • promote the need to meet customer requirements • promote the need to meet regulatory requirements • promote the need to meet statutory requirements • develop a quality management system • support the development of a quality system • formulate your organisation's quality policy • set your organisation's quality objectives • provide quality resources • implement your quality management system • provide resources to implement your quality system • encourage personnel to meet quality system requirements • improve your quality management system • perform quality management reviews • provide resources to improve the quality system

Section no.	ISO 9001:2000 title	Requirement	Explanation
5.2	Customer focus	Satisfy your customers	• identify customer requirements • expect your organisation to identify customer requirements • meet your customers' requirements • expect your organisation to meet customer requirements • enhance customer satisfaction • expect your organisation to enhance customer satisfaction
5.3	Quality policy	Establish a quality policy	• define your organisation's quality policy • ensure that it serves your organisation's purpose • ensure that it emphasises the need to meet requirements • ensure that it facilitates the development of quality objectives • ensure that it makes a commitment to continuous improvement • manage your organisation's quality policy • communicate your policy to your organisation • review your policy to ensure that it is still suitable
5.4	Planning	Carry out quality planning	
5.4.1	Quality objectives	Formulate your quality objectives	• ensure that objectives are set for functional areas • ensure that objectives are set at organisational levels • ensure that objectives facilitate product realisation • ensure that objectives support the quality policy • ensure that objectives are measurable
5.4.2	Quality management system planning	Plan your quality management system	• plan the development of your quality management system • plan the implementation of your quality management system • plan the improvement of your quality management system • plan the modification of your quality management system

Section no.	ISO 9001:2000 title	Requirement	Explanation
5.5	Responsibility and authority and communication	Control your quality system	
5.5.1	Responsibility and authority	Define responsibilities and authorities	• clarify responsibilities and authorities • communicate responsibilities and authorities
5.5.2	Management representative	Appoint management representative	• oversee your quality management system • report on the status of your quality management system • support the improvement of your quality management system
5.5.3	Internal communication	Support internal communications	• ensure that internal communication processes are established • ensure that communication occurs throughout the organisation
5.6	Management review	Perform management reviews	
5.6.1	General	Review quality management system	• evaluate the performance of your quality system • evaluate whether your quality system should be improved
5.6.2	Review input	Examine management review inputs	• examine audit results • examine product conformity data • examine opportunities to improve • examine feedback from customers • examine process performance information • examine corrective and preventive actions • examine changes that might affect your system • examine previous quality management reviews
5.6.3	Review output	Generate management review outputs	• generate actions to improve your quality system • generate actions to improve your products • generate actions to address resource

Resource requirements

Section no.	ISO 9001:2000 title	Requirement	Explanation
6	Resource management		
6.1	Provision of resources	Provide quality resources	• identify quality resource requirements • identify resources needed to support the quality system • identify resources needed to improve customer satisfaction. • provide quality system resources • provide resources needed to support the quality system • provide resources needed to improve customer satisfaction
6.2	Human resources	Provide quality personnel	
6.2.1	General	Use competent personnel	• ensure that your personnel have the right experience • ensure that your personnel have the right education • ensure that your personnel have the right training • ensure that your personnel have the right skills
6.2.2	Competence, awareness and training	Support competence	• define acceptable levels of competence • identify training and awareness needs • deliver training and awareness programs • evaluate effectiveness of training and awareness • maintain a record of competence
6.3	Infrastructure	Provide quality infrastructure	• identify infrastructure needs • identify building needs • identify workspace needs • identify hardware needs • identify software needs • identify utility needs • identify equipment needs • identify support service needs • provide needed infrastructure • provide needed buildings • provide needed workspaces • provide needed hardware • provide needed software • provide needed utilities

Section no.	ISO 9001:2000 title	Requirement	Explanation
6.3 cont.			• provide needed equipment • provide needed support services • maintain your infrastructure • maintain your buildings • maintain your workspaces • maintain your hardware • maintain your software • maintain your utilities • maintain your equipment • maintain your support services
6.4	Work environment	Provide quality environment	• identify needed work environment • identify factors needed to ensure products meet requirements • manage needed work environment • manage factors needed to ensure products meet requirements

Realisation requirements

Section no.	ISO 9001:2000 title	Requirement	Explanation
7	Product realisation		
7.1	Planning and realisation	Control realisation planning	• plan product realisation processes • define product quality objectives and requirements • identify product realisation needs and requirements • develop product realisation processes • develop product realisation documents • develop product realisation record keeping systems • develop methods to control quality during product realisation
7.2	Customer-related processes	Control customer processes	
7.2.1	Determination of requirements related to product	Identify customers' product requirements	• identify the requirements that customers want you to meet • identify the requirements that are dictated by the product's use • identify the requirements that are imposed by external agencies • identify the requirements that your organisation wishes to meet

Section no.	ISO 9001:2000 title	Requirement	Explanation
7.2.2	Review of requirements related to product	Review customers' product requirements	• review requirements before you accept orders from customers • maintain a record of your product requirement reviews • control changes in product requirements
7.2.3	Customer communication	Communicate with your customers	• develop a process to control communications with customers • implement your customer communications process
7.3	Design and development	Control product development	
7.3.1	Design and development planning	Plan design and development	• define your product design and development stages • clarify design and development responsibilities and authorities • manage interactions between design and development groups • update your design and development plans as changes occur
7.3.2	Design and development inputs	Define design and development inputs	• specify product design and development inputs • record product design and development input definitions • review product design and development input definitions
7.3.3	Design and development outputs	Generate design and development outputs	• create product design and development outputs • approve design and development outputs prior to release • use design and development outputs to control product quality
7.3.4	Design and development review	Carry out design and development reviews	• perform product design and development reviews • record product design and development reviews
7.3.5	Design and development verification	Perform design and development verifications	• carry out product design and development verifications • record product design and development verifications
7.3.6	Design and development validation	Conduct design and development validations	• perform product design and development validations • record product design and development validations

Section no.	ISO 9001:2000 title	Requirement	Explanation
7.3.7	Control of design and development changes	Manage design and development changes	• identify changes in product design and development • record changes in product design and development • review changes in product design and development • verify changes in product design and development • validate changes in product design and development • approve changes before they are implemented
7.4	Purchasing	Control purchasing function	
7.4.1	Purchasing process	Control purchasing process	• ensure that purchased products meet requirements • ensure that suppliers meet requirements
7.4.2	Purchasing information	Document product purchases	• describe the products being purchased • specify the requirements that must be met
7.4.3	Verification of purchased product	Verify purchased products	• verify purchased products at your own premises • verify purchased products at suppliers' premises (when required)
7.5	Production and service operations	Control operational activities	
7.5.1	Control of production and service provision	Control production and service provision	• control production and service processes • control production and service information • control production and service instructions • control production and service equipment • control production and service measurements • control production and service activities
7.5.2	Validation of processes for production and service provision	Validate production and service provision	• prove that special processes can produce planned outputs • prove that process personnel can produce planned results • prove that process equipment can produce planned results

Appendix 7C Requirements of management

Section no.	ISO 9001:2000 title	Requirement	Explanation
7.5.3	Identification and traceability	Identify and track your products	• establish the identity of your products (when appropriate) • maintain the identity of your products (when appropriate) • identify the status of your products (when appropriate) • record the identity of your products (when required)
7.5.4	Customer property	Protect property supplied by customers	• identify property supplied to you by your customers • verify property supplied to you by your customers • safeguard property supplied to you by your customers
7.5.5	Preservation of product	Preserve your products and components	• preserve products and components during internal processing • preserve products and components during final delivery
7.6	Control of measuring and monitoring devices	Control monitoring devices	• identify monitoring and measuring needs • identify the monitoring and measuring that should be done • select monitoring and measuring devices • select devices that meet your monitoring and measuring needs • calibrate monitoring and measuring devices • perform calibrations • record calibrations • protect monitoring and measuring devices • protect your devices from unauthorised adjustment • protect your devices from damage or deterioration • validate monitoring and measuring software • validate monitoring and measuring software before you use it • revalidate monitoring and measuring software when necessary • use monitoring and measuring devices • use devices to ensure that your products meet requirements

Remedial requirements

Section no.	ISO 9001:2000 title	Requirement	Explanation
8	Measurement, analysis and improvement		
8.1	General	Perform remedial processes	• plan remedial processes • plan how remedial processes will be used to assure conformity • plan how remedial processes will be used to improve the system • implement remedial processes • use remedial processes to demonstrate conformance • use remedial processes to improve quality management system
8.2	Monitoring and measurement	Monitor and measure quality	
8.2.1	Customer satisfaction	Monitor and measure customer satisfaction	• identify ways to monitor and measure customer satisfaction • monitor and measure customer satisfaction • use customer satisfaction information
8.2.2	Internal audit	Plan and perform regular internal audits	• set up an internal audit program • develop an internal audit procedure • plan your internal audit projects • perform regular internal audits • solve problems discovered during audits • verify that problems have been solved
8.2.3	Monitoring and measurement of processes	Monitor and measure quality processes	• use suitable methods to monitor and measure your processes • take action when your processes fail to achieve planned results
8.2.4	Monitoring and measurement of product	Monitor and measure product characteristics	• verify that product characteristics are being met • keep a record of product monitoring and measuring activities
8.3	Control of non-conforming product	Control non-conforming products	• develop a procedure to control non-conforming products • define how non-conforming products should be identified • define how non-conforming products should be handled • identify and control your non-conforming products

Section no.	ISO 9001:2000 title	Requirement	Explanation
8.3 cont.			• eliminate or correct product non-conformities • prevent the delivery or use of non-conforming products • avoid the inappropriate use of non-conforming products • re-verify non-conforming products that were corrected • prove that corrected products now meet requirements • control non-conforming products after delivery or use • control events when you deliver or use non-conforming products • maintain records of non-conforming products • describe your product non-conformities • describe the actions taken to deal with non-conformities
8.4	Analysis of data	Analyse quality information	• define quality management information needs • define the information you need to evaluate your quality system • define the information you need to improve your quality system • collect quality management system data • monitor and measure the suitability of your quality system • monitor and measure the effectiveness of your quality system • provide quality management information • provide information about your customers • provide information about your suppliers • provide information about your products • provide information about your processes
8.5	Improvement	Make quality improvements	
8.5.1	Continual improvement	Improve quality management system	• use your audits to generate improvements • use your quality data to generate improvements

Section no.	ISO 9001:2000 title	Requirement	Explanation
8.5.1 cont.			• use your quality policy to generate improvements • use your quality objectives to generate improvements • use your management reviews to generate improvements • use your corrective actions to generate improvements • use your preventive actions to generate improvements
8.5.2	Corrective action	Correct actual non-conformities	• review your non-conformities • figure out what causes your non-conformities • evaluate whether you need to take corrective action • develop corrective actions to prevent recurrence • take corrective actions when they are necessary • record the results that your corrective actions achieve • examine the effectiveness of your corrective actions
8.5.3	Preventive action	Prevent potential non-conformities	• detect potential non-conformities • identify the causes of potential non-conformities • study the effects of potential non-conformities • evaluate whether you need to take preventive action • develop preventive actions to eliminate causes • take preventive actions when they are necessary • record the results that your preventive actions achieve • examine the effectiveness of your preventive actions

Appendix 7D   Example checklists for auditors

Systematic requirements

Section no.	ISO 9001:2000 title	Typical auditor's questions
4	Quality Management System requirement	

4.1	General requirements	• **Has a Quality Management System been established in accordance with the requirements of ISO 9001:2000?**
		
		• **Is the QMS:**
		  • documented?
		  • implemented?
		  • maintained?
		  • continually improved?
		
		• **Does the organisation have all the documents**
		  • necessary to ensure the effective operation and control of its processes?
		
		• **Has the organisation:**
		  • identified the sequence of processes and sub-processes needed for the QMS?
		  • determined the sequence and interaction of these processes?
		  • determined the criteria and methods required to ensure the effective operation and control of these processes?
		  • ensured that information necessary to support the monitoring and operation of these processes is available?
		  • ensured that resources necessary to support the monitoring and operation of these processes is available?
		
		• **Does the organisation measure, monitor and analyse these processes?**
		
		• **Is the necessary action implemented to achieve planned results and continual improvement of the processes?**
		
		• **Does the organisation manage these processes in accordance with the requirements of ISO 9001:2000?**

Section no.	ISO 9001:2000 title	Typical auditor's questions
4.2	Documentation requirements	

4.2.1	General	• **Does the QMS include:**
		  • a Quality Manual?
		  • statements concerning quality policy and quality objectives?
		  • documented procedures?
		  • quality records?

4.2.2	Quality Manual	• **Is the Quality Manual**
		  • controlled?
		  • maintained?
		
		• **Does it include details concerning:**
		  • the scope of the QMS?
		  • justifications for any exclusion from the ISO 9001:2000 requirements?
		  • associated documented procedures?
		  • the sequence and interaction of processes?

4.2.3	Control of documents	• **Has the organisation established a documented procedure to control all of its QMS documents?**
		
		• **Does this procedure include methods for:**
		  • controlling their distribution?
		  • approving documents prior to issue?
		  • reviewing, updating and re-approving documents?
		  • identifying the current revision status of documents?
		  • ensuring that documents fulfil a useful purpose in the organisation?
		  • ensuring that relevant versions of all applicable documents are available at points of use?
		  • ensuring that documents remain legible, readily identifiable and retrievable?
		  • ensuring that information is kept up to date?
		  • identifying, distributing and controlling of documents received from an external source?
		  • ensuring that classified information is restricted to those who are authorised to receive it?
		  • the identification and control of obsolete documents that have been retained for any purpose?

4.2.4	Control of records	• **Does the organisation have a documented procedure for records covering:**
		  • control, maintenance and identification?
		  • storage and retrieval?
		  • protection and retention?
		
		• **Do these records provide evidence of:**
		  • the organisation's conformance to the ISO 9001:2000 requirements?
		  • the effective operation of the QMS?

Management requirements

Section no.	ISO 9001:2000 title	Typical auditor's questions
5	Management responsibility	

5.1	Management commitment	• **Does the organisation demonstrate its commitment to developing, establishing and improving the organisation's QMS through:**
		  • management commitment?
		  • an established quality policy?
		  • determining customer requirements and achieving customer satisfaction?
		  • a quality policy?
		  • regularly reviewing the QMS documentation?
		
		• **Does the organisation:**
		  • ensure that all personnel are aware of the importance of meeting customer, regulatory and legal requirements?
		  • establish the quality policy and quality objectives?
		  • conduct internal management reviews?
		  • ensure the availability of necessary resources to administer the QMS?

5.2	Customer focus	• **Does the organisation ensure that customer needs and expectations are recognised and established?** • **Are these customer needs and expectations converted into requirements?** • **Does the organisation ensure that customer requirements are fulfilled?**

5.3	Quality policy	• **Is the organisation's quality policy:**
		  • controlled?
		  • appropriate?
		  • regularly reviewed for continued suitability?
		  • committed to meeting requirements?
		  • communicated and understood throughout the company?
		  • capable of continual improvement?
		  • capable of providing a framework for establishing and reviewing quality objectives?

5.4	Planning	

5.4.1	Quality objectives	• **Is the organisation's quality planning documented?**
		
		• **Does it include:**
		  • quality objectives?
		  • resources?
		
		• **Has the organisation established quality objectives for each relevant function and level within the company?**

Section no.	ISO 9001:2000 title	Typical auditor's questions
5.4.1 cont.		• **Are the organisation's quality objectives measurable and consistent with quality policy?** • **Do they include:** • a commitment for continual improvement? • product requirements?
5.4.2	Quality management system planning	• **Does the organisation's quality planning cover:** • the processes required for a QMS (as mentioned in section 4)? • the identification and availability of resources and information? • any permissible exclusion (to the requirements of ISO 9001:2000)? • the requirements for continual improvement? • the requirements for change control? • **Does the organisation's quality planning ensure that the QMS is maintained during planned changes?**
5.5	Responsibility and authority and communication	• **Has the organisation defined and implemented a QMS that addresses its quality objectives?** • **Is the administration of the organisation's QMS documented?** • **Does it cover:** • responsibilities and authorities? • management representative's duties? • internal communication? • the Quality Manual? • control of documents? • control of quality records?
5.5.1	Responsibility and authority	• **Are the functions and interrelationships of all staff defined?** • **Are staff responsibilities and authorities defined?**
5.5.2	Management representative	• **Has the organisation appointed a Quality Manager who (regardless of all other duties) has sole responsibility for the implementation and management of the QMS?** • **Is the administration of the organisation's QMS documented?** • **Does the organisation's QMS adequately cover:** • responsibilities and authorities? • management representative's duties?
5.5.3	Internal communication	• **Does the organisation ensure that there are lines of communication between all members of staff to ensure the effectiveness of the QMS processes?** • **Is there a procedure for internal communication?**

Section no.	ISO 9001:2000 title	Typical auditor's questions
5.6	Management review	• **Does the organisation top management regularly review the QMS at planned intervals?**

5.6.1	General	• **Does the QMS review cover the continuing suitability, adequacy and effectiveness of the QMS?**
		
		• **Does the review evaluate the:**
		  • need for changes?
		  • quality policy?
		  • quality objectives?

5.6.2	Review input	• **Does the management review include:**
		  • internal audit results?
		  • external and third party audit results?
		  • customer feedback?
		  • process performance?
		  • product conformance?
		  • implemented preventive and corrective actions?
		  • outstanding preventive and corrective actions?
		  • results from previous management reviews?
		  • changes that could affect the QMS?

5.6.3	Review output	• **Do the outputs of management reviews include recommendations for:**
		  • the improvement of the QMS and its processes?
		  • the improvement of product related to customer requirements?
		  • confirming and establishing resource needs?
		
		• **Are the results of management reviews recorded?**
		
		• **Are the results (e.g. minutes and action sheets) circulated?**

6	Resource management	

6.1	Provision of resources	• **Does the organisation provide the resources required to:**
		  • implement and improve the QMS processes?
		  • ensure customer satisfaction?
		  • meet customer requirements?

6.2	Human resources	• **Has the organisation established procedures for:**
		  • the assignment of personnel?
		  • training?
		  • awareness?
		  • competency?

6.2.1	General	• **Has the organisation established procedures for the assignment of personnel on the basis of:**
		  • competency?
		  • qualification?
		  • training?
		  • skill and experience?

Section no.	ISO 9001:2000 title	Typical auditor's questions
6.2.2	Competence, awareness and training	• **Does the organisation:** • identify training requirements? • provide appropriate training? • evaluate the training provided? • **Does the organisation ensure that all their staff appreciates the relevance and importance of their activities and how they contribute towards achieving quality objectives?** • **Does the organisation keep staff records covering education, experience, qualifications, training, etc.?**
6.3	Infrastructure	• **Does the organisation identify, provide and maintain the necessary:** • workspace and associated facilities? • equipment, hardware and software? • supporting services?
6.4	Work environment	• **Does the organisation identify and manage the work environment (including human and physical factors) to ensure conformity of product?**
7	Product realisation	• **Has the organisation established the processes necessary to achieve the product?**
7.1	Planning and realisation	• **Has the organisation:** • identified the sequence of processes and sub-processes needed for the QMS? • determined the sequence and interaction of these processes? • determined the criteria and methods required to ensure the effective operation and control of these processes? • ensured that information necessary to support the monitoring and operation of these processes is available? • ensured that resources necessary to support the monitoring and operation of these processes is available? • **Within this sequence of processes and sub-processes, has the following been determined:** • the quality objectives for the product, project or contract? • product-specific processes, documentation, resources and facilities? • verification and validation activities? • criteria for acceptability? • required records? • **Does the organisation have a documented procedure for records covering:** • control, maintenance and identification? • storage and retrieval? • protection and retention?

Section no.	ISO 9001:2000 title	Typical auditor's questions
7.1 cont.		• **Do these records provide evidence of:** • the organisation's conformance to the ISO 9001:2000 requirements?

7.2	Customer-related processes	• **Has the organisation established procedures for the:**
		  • identification of customer requirements?
		  • review of product requirements?
		  • customer communication?

7.2.1	Determination of requirements related to product	• **Has the organisation established a process for identifying customer requirements?**
		
		• **Does this process determine:**
		  • customer-specified product requirements (e.g. availability, delivery and support)?
		  • non-specified customer requirements (e.g. those affecting the product)?
		  • mandatory requirements (such as regulatory and legal obligations)?

7.2.2	Review of requirements related to product	• **Has the organisation established a process for ensuring that product requirements have been fully established?**
		
		• **Does the process ensure that (prior to submission of tender or acceptance of contract):**
		  • all customer requirements have been defined and can be met?
		  • where no written requirements are available, that verbal customer requirements are confirmed?
		  • any contract or order requirements differing from those previously expressed (e.g. in a tender or quotation) are resolved?
		  • the organisation has the ability to meet the defined requirements?

7.2.3	Customer communication	• **Has the organisation an established process for:**
		  • providing customers with product information?
		  • handling customer enquiries, contracts or orders (including amendments)?
		  • customer feedback and customer complaints?

7.3	Design and development	**Has the organisation a process and adequate procedures for their design and development activities?**

7.3.1	Design and development planning	• **Does the organisation plan and control design and development of the product?**
		
		• **Do these processes include:**
		  • stage review, verification and validation activities?
		  • identification of responsibilities and authorities?
		  • management of the interfaces between different groups that may be involved?

Section no.	ISO 9001:2000 title	Typical auditor's questions
7.3.1 cont.		• provision of effective communication and clarity of responsibilities? • product and planning reviews? • **Are these processes adequate?**

7.3.2	Design and development inputs	• **Does the organisation have a process for developing Project Plans?**
		
		• **Does the organisation define and document product requirement inputs?**
		
		• **Do these input requirements include:**
		  • function and performance requirements?
		  • applicable regulatory and legal requirements?
		  • applicable standards, specifications, and tolerances?
		  • applicable requirements derived from previous similar designs?
		  • any other requirements essential for design and development?
		
		• **Are inadequate, incomplete, ambiguous or conflicting input requirements resolved?**

7.3.3	Design and development outputs	• **Are all products approved prior to release?**
		
		• **Does the organisation define and document their product outputs?**
		
		• **Do these critical requirements ensure that the product:**
		  • meets the design and development input requirements?
		  • provides appropriate information for production and service operations?
		  • contains or make reference to product acceptance criteria?
		  • defines the characteristics of the product that are essential to its safe and proper use?

7.3.4	Design and development review	• **Are systematic reviews of the design and development carried out at suitable stages?**
		  • evaluate the ability of the product to fulfil the requirements?
		  • include representatives from the functions concerned with the design and development stage being reviewed?
		
		• **Are follow-up actions from the reviews recorded?**

7.3.5	Design and development verification	• **Does the organisation verify that the design output meets the design and development input?** • **Are these results of this verification (and any necessary subsequent follow-up actions) recorded?**

Appendix 7D   Example checklists for auditors

Section no.	ISO 9001:2000 title	Typical auditor's questions
7.3.6	Design and development validation	• Does the organisation validate that the product is capable of meeting the requirements of intended use? • Are these results and any necessary subsequent follow-up actions recorded? • Wherever applicable, is the validation completed prior to the delivery or implementation of the product? • If full validation is impractical prior to delivery or implementation of the product, is a partial validation performed to the maximum extent applicable?
7.3.7	Control of design and development changes	• Does the organisation have a procedure that identifies the need for a design and development change? • Are these results of implementing this procedure (and any necessary subsequent follow-up actions) recorded? • Are the effects of these changes reviewed, verified and validated before implementation?

7.4	Purchasing	• Does the organisation have processes for:
		  • purchasing control?
		  • purchasing information?
		  • verification of purchased product?

7.4.1	Purchasing process	• Does the organisation have processes for:
		  • purchasing control?
		  • purchasing information?
		  • verification of purchased product?

7.4.2	Purchasing information	• Does the organisation have documentation describing:
		  • the product to be purchased?
		  • requirements for approval or qualification (i.e. product, procedures, processes, equipment and personnel)?
		  • QMS requirements?
		
		• Does the organisation ensure the adequacy of the specified requirements contained in the purchasing documents prior to their release?

7.4.3	Verification of purchased product	• Does the organisation identify (and implement) the activities necessary for the verification of a purchased product? • Are these verification arrangements specified by the organisation or its customer (particularly if verification is to be carried out at the supplier's premises)? • Is the method of product release specified in the purchasing documents (particularly if verification is to be carried out at the supplier's premises)?

Section no.	ISO 9001:2000 title	Typical auditor's questions

7.5	Production and service operations	• **Does the organisation have procedures for the control of:**
		  • production and service operations?
		  • identification and traceability?
		  • customer property?
		  • preservation of product?
		  • validation of processes?

7.5.1	Control of production and service provision	• **Does the organisation plan and control production and service operations?**
		• **Is this achieved through:**
		  • information concerning the characteristics of the product?
		  • appropriate work instructions?
		  • the use and maintenance of suitable equipment for production and service operations?
		  • the availability and use of measuring and monitoring devices?

7.5.2	Validation of processes for production and service provision	• **Where the resulting output cannot be verified by subsequent measurement or monitoring, does the organisation validate production and service processes to demonstrate the ability of the processes to achieve planned results?**
		• **Does this validation demonstrate the ability of the processes to achieve planned results?**
		• **Does the validation include:**
		  • qualification of processes?
		  • qualification of equipment and personnel?
		  • use of defined methodologies and procedures?
		  • requirements for records?
		  • re-validation?
		• **Does this validation include any processes where deficiencies may become apparent only after the product is in use or the service has been delivered?**

7.5.3	Identification and traceability	• **Does the organisation have procedures available to identify the product throughout production and service operations?** • **Is the product status identifiable with respect to measurement and monitoring requirements?** • **When traceability is a requirement, does the organisation control and record the unique identification of a product?**
7.5.4	Customer property	• **Does the organisation exercise care with customer property?** • **Does the organisation verify, protect and maintain customer property provided for use or incorporated into a product?** • **Are records maintained of any customer property that is lost, damaged or otherwise found to be unsuitable for use?**

Section no.	ISO 9001:2000 title	Typical auditor's questions
7.5.5	Preservation of product	• **Does the organisation have set procedures for the identification, handling, packaging, storage and protection of products during internal processing and delivery to the intended destination?**
7.6	Control of measuring and monitoring devices	• **Where applicable, are measuring and monitoring devices:** • calibrated and adjusted periodically or prior to use, against devices traceable to international or national standards? • safeguarded from adjustments that would invalidate the calibration? • protected from damage and deterioration during handling, maintenance and storage? • **Are the results of the calibration recorded?** • **Is the validity of previous results re-assessed if they are subsequently found to be out of calibration, and corrective action taken?** • **If software is used for measuring and monitoring, has it been validated prior to use?**
8	Measurement, analysis and improvement	• **Does the organisation define the activities needed to measure and monitor:** • product conformity? • product improvement?
8.1	General	• **Does the organisation define the activities needed to measure and monitor:** • product conformity? • product improvement? • **Does the organisation continually strive to improve the effectiveness of its QMS?**
8.2	Monitoring and measurement	• **Has the organisation procedures available to:** • ensure customer satisfaction? • control internal audits? • ensure effective measurement and monitoring of products and processes?
8.2.1	Customer satisfaction	• **Does the organisation monitor information regarding customer satisfaction?** • **Does the organisation monitor information regarding customer dissatisfaction?** • **Are the methods and measures for obtaining such information defined?** • **Is there an agreed change control procedure?**

Section no.	ISO 9001:2000 title	Typical auditor's questions
8.2.1 cont.		• **Is there an agreed customer complaints procedure?** • **Are these methods and measures utilised as part of the performance measurements of the QMS?**

8.2.2	Internal audit	• **Does the organisation conduct periodic internal audits?**
		• **Do these audits determine whether the QMS:**
		  • conforms to the requirements of ISO 9001:2000?
		  • has been effectively implemented and maintained?
		• **Are audits only carried out by personnel who are not associated with the activity or department being audited?**
		• **Are the audits planned to take into account:**
		  • the status and importance of the activities and areas to be audited?
		  • the results of previous audits?
		• **Are the audit scope, frequency and methodologies defined?**
		• **Does the organisation have a documented procedure for audits that includes:**
		  • the responsibilities and requirements for conducting audits?
		  • the method for recording results?
		  • the method for reporting to management?
		• **Does management take timely corrective action on deficiencies found during an audit?**
		• **Do these follow-up actions include the verification of the implementation of corrective action and the reporting of verification results?**

8.2.3	Monitoring and measurement of processes	• **Does the organisation apply suitable methods for the measurement and monitoring of processes:**
		  • to meet customer requirements?
		  • to confirm the process's continuing ability to satisfy its intended purpose?

8.2.4	Monitoring and measurement of product	• **Does the organisation apply suitable methods to measure and monitor the characteristics of the product at appropriate stages of the product realisation process?** • **Is there documented evidence of conformity with the acceptance criteria?** • **Are the responsibilities and authorities defined with regard to release of product?** • **Does the organisation ensure that the product is not released or the service delivered until all the specified activities have been satisfactorily completed (unless otherwise approved by the customer)?**

Section no.	ISO 9001:2000 title	Typical auditor's questions

8.3	Control of non-conforming product	• **Has the organisation defined a procedure for the control of non-conformities?**
		
		• **Does this procedure ensure that:**
		  • products which do not conform to requirements are prevented from unintended use or delivery?
		  • non-conforming products that have been corrected are subject to re-verification to demonstrate conformity?
		  • non-conforming products detected after delivery or use are either corrected or removed from service?
		
		• **Is there provision for the notification of the customer, end user, regulatory or other body when required?**

8.4	Analysis of data	• **Does the organisation collect and analyse data to determine suitability and effectiveness of the QMS?**
		
		• **Does the organisation analyse the data to provide information regarding:**
		  • possible improvement that can be made to the QMS?
		  • customer satisfaction and dissatisfaction?
		  • conformance to customer requirements?
		  • the characteristics of processes, products and their trends?
		  • suppliers?

8.5	Improvement	• **Does the organisation have procedures available for:**
		  • planning continual improvement?
		  • corrective action?
		  • preventive action?

8.5.1	Continual improvement	• **Does the organisation plan and manage the processes necessary for the continual improvement of the QMS?**
		
		• **Is the continual improvement of the QMS facilitated by the use of:**
		  • the quality policy?
		  • quality objectives?
		  • audit results?
		  • analysis of data?
		  • corrective and preventive action?
		  • management reviews?
		  • concessions and approvals?
		  • concession scheme?
		  • defects and defect reports?
		  • bonded store?

8.5.2	Corrective action	• **Has the organisation a documented procedure to enable corrective action to be taken to eliminate the cause of non-conformities and prevent recurrence?** • **Does this procedure define the requirements for:** • identification of non-conformities (including customer complaints)?

Section no.	ISO 9001:2000 title	Typical auditor's questions
8.5.2 cont.		<ul><li>determining the causes of non-conformities?</li><li>evaluating the need for action to ensure that non-conformities do not recur?</li><li>determining and implementing the corrective action needed?</li><li>ensuring results of action taken are recorded?</li></ul>
8.5.3	Preventive action	<ul><li>**Has the organisation a documented procedure to enable preventative action to be taken to eliminate the cause of non-conformities and prevent recurrence?**</li></ul> <ul><li>**Does this procedure define the requirements for:**<ul><li>identification of non-conformities (including customer complaints)?</li><li>determining the causes of non-conformities?</li><li>evaluating the need for action to ensure that non-conformities do not recur?</li><li>determining and implementing the preventative action needed?</li><li>ensuring results of action taken are recorded?</li><li>reviewing the preventative action taken?</li></ul></li></ul>

Appendix 7E Example internal stage audit checks

Design stage

	Item		Related item	Remark
1	Requirements	1.1	Information	Has the customer fully described his requirement?
				Has the customer any mandatory requirements?
				Are the customer's requirements fully understood by all members of the design team?
				Is there a need to have further discussions with the customer?
				Are other suppliers or subcontractors involved? If yes, who is the prime contractor?
		1.2	Standards	What international standards need to be observed? Are they available?
				What national standards need to be observed? Are they available?
				What other information and procedures are required? Are they available?
		1.3	Procedures	Are there any customer-supplied drawings, sketches or plans? Have they been registered?

	Item		Related item	Remark
2	Quality procedures	2.1	Procedures Manual	Is one available?
				Does it contain detailed procedures and instructions for the control of all drawings within the drawing office?
		2.2	Planning Implementation and Production	Is the project split into a number of Work Packages? If so: • are the various Work Packages listed? • have Work Package Leaders been nominated? • is their task clear? • is their task achievable?
				• Is a time plan available? • Is it up to date? • Regularly maintained? • Relevant to the task?
3	Drawings	3.1	Identification	Are all drawings identified by a unique number?
				Is the numbering system strictly controlled?
		3.2	Cataloguing	Is a catalogue of drawings maintained? Is this catalogue regularly reviewed and up to date?
		3.3	Amendments and Modifications	Is there a procedure for authorising the issue of amendments, changes to drawings?
				Is there a method for withdrawing and disposing of obsolete drawings?
4	Components	4.1	Availability	Are complete lists of all the relevant components available?
		4.2	Adequacy	Are the selected components currently available and adequate for the task? If not, how long will they take to procure? Is this acceptable?

Appendix 7E   Example internal stage audit checks

	Item	Related item		Remark
		4.3	Acceptability	If alternative components have to be used are they acceptable to the task?
5	Records	5.1	Failure reports	Has the Design Office access to all records, failure reports and other relevant data?
		5.2	Reliability data	Is reliability data correctly stored, maintained and analysed?
		5.3	Graphs, diagrams, plans	In addition to drawings, is there a system for the control of all graphs, tables, plans etc.? Are CAD facilities available? (If so, go to 6.1)
6	Reviews and Audits	6.1	Computers	If a processor is being used: • are all the design office personnel trained in its use? • are regular back-ups taken? • is there an anti-virus system in place?
		6.2	Manufacturing Division	Is a close relationship being maintained between the design office and the manufacturing division?
		6.3		Is notice being taken of the manufacturing division's exact requirements, their problems and their choices of components etc.?

Manufacturing stage

	Item	Related item		Remark
1	Degree of quality	1.1	Quality control procedures	Are quality control procedures available?
				Are they relevant to the task?
				Are they understood by all members of the manufacturing team?

Appendix 7E   Example internal stage audit checks

	Item		Related item	Remark
				Are they regularly reviewed and up to date?
				Are they subject to control procedures?
		1.2	Quality control checks	What quality checks are being observed? Are they relevant?
				Are there laid down procedures for carrying out these checks? Are they available? Are they regularly updated?
2	Reliability of product design	2.1	Statistical data	Is there a system for predicting the reliability of the product's design?
				Is sufficient statistical data available to be able to estimate the actual reliability of the design, before a product is manufactured?
				Is the appropriate engineering data available?
		2.2	Components and parts	Are the reliability ratings of recommended parts and components available?
				Are probability methods used to examine the reliability of a proposed design? If so, have these checks revealed design deficiencies such as: • assembly errors? • operator learning, motivational, or fatigue factors? • latent defects? • improper part selection? (Note: If necessary, use additional sheets to list actions taken)

Acceptance stage

	Item	Related item		Remark
1	Product performance			Does the product perform to the required function? If not what has been done about it?
2	Quality level	2.1	Workmanship	Does the workmanship of the product fully meet the level of quality required or stipulated by the user?
		2.2	Tests	Is the product subjected to environmental tests? If so, which ones?
				Is the product field tested as a complete system? If so, what were the results?
3	Reliability	3.1	Probability function	Are individual components and modules environmentally tested? If so, how?
		3.2	Failure rate	Is the product's reliability measured in terms of probability function? If so, what were the results?
				Is the product's reliability measured in terms of failure rate? If so, what were the results?
		3.3	Mean time between failures	Is the product's reliability measured in terms of mean time between failure? If so, what were the results?

Appendix 7E   Example internal stage audit checks

In-service stage

	Item		Related item	Remark
1	System reliability	1.1	Product basic design	Are statistical methods being used to prove the product's basic design? If so, are they adequate? Are the results recorded and available?
				What other methods are used to prove the product's basic design? Are these methods appropriate?
2	Equipment reliability	2.1	Personnel	Are there sufficient trained personnel to carry out the task?
				Are they sufficiently motivated? If not, what is the problem?
		2.1.1	Operators	Have individual job descriptions been developed? Are they readily available?
				Are all operators capable of completing their duties?
		2.1.2	Training	Do all personnel receive appropriate training?
				Is a continuous on-the-job training (OJT) programme available to all personnel? If not, why not?
		2.2	Product dependability	What proof is there that the product is dependable?
				How is product dependability proved? Is this sufficient for the customer?
		2.3	Component reliability	Has the reliability of individual components been considered?
				Does the reliability of individual components exceed the overall system reliability?

	Item		Related item	Remark
		2.4	Faulty operating procedures	Are operating procedures available?
				Are they appropriate to the task?
				Are they regularly reviewed?
		2.5	Operational abuses	Are there any obvious operational abuses? If so, what are they? How can they be overcome?
		2.5.1	Extended duty cycle	Do the staff have to work shifts? If so, are they allowed regular breaks from their work?
				Is there a senior shift worker? If so, are his duties and responsibilities clearly defined?
				Are computers used? If so, are screen filters available? Do the operators have keyboard wrist rests?
		2.5.2	Training	Do the operational staff receive regular on-the-job training?
				Is there any need for additional in-house or external training?
3	Design capability	3.1	Faulty operating procedures	Are there any obvious faulty operating procedures?
				Can the existing procedures be improved upon?

Appendix 7F   Index for ISO 9001:2000

Subject title	ISO 9001 element
provision of training	6.6.2b
records	4.2.4, 6.2.2e
requirements	6.2.1
Complaints	7.2.3c
Continual improvement	8.5.1
analysis of data	8.4
management commitment to	5.1
measuring and monitoring activities	8.1c
processes	5.6.3a
Quality Management System	4.1f, 5.6.3a, 8.5.1
quality objectives	5.4.1
quality planning	5.4.2a
quality policy	5.3b
Contract review	7.2.2
amendment	7.2.3b
capability to meet requirement	7.2.2c
definition of requirement	7.2.2a
differences resolved	7.2.2b
records of	7.2.2
requirements	7.2.2
supplier capability	7.2.2
Control of	
customer property	7.5.4
design and development changes	7.3.7
documents and data	4.2.3
inspection, measuring and test equipment	7.6
measuring and monitoring devices	7.6
non-conforming products	8.3
processes	4.1c
product, customer supplied	7.5.5
quality manual	4.2.2, 4.2.3
quality policy	4.2.3, 5.3
records	4.2.3, 4.2.4
Corrective action	8.5.2
determining causes of non-conformity	8.5.2b
determining and implementing	8.5.2d
documented procedure	8.5.2
evaluation of actions to be taken	8.5.2c
identification of non-conformities	8.5.2a
internal audits	8.2.2
verification of	8.2.2
non-conforming product	8.3
recording results	8.5.2e

Subject title	ISO 9001 element

Subject title	ISO 9001 element
Damage and deterioration	
protection from	7.6e
Data analysis – see analysis of data	
Data control – see document control	
Delivery	7.5.5
Design and development	7.3
change control	7.3.7
approval	7.3.7
identification	7.3.7
validation	7.3.7
verification	7.3.7
communication	7.3.1
control	7.3.1
inputs	7.3.2
essential requirements	7.3.2d
function and performance	7.3.2a
information from previous designs	7.3.2c
regulatory and legal requirements	7.3.2b
review	7.3.2
outputs	7.3.3
documentation – approval of	7.3.3
information for production & service operations	7.3.3b
meeting input requirements	7.3.3a
product acceptance criteria	7.3.3c
product characteristics	7.3.3d
verification	7.3.3
records	4.2.4, 7.3.7
review	7.3.4
evaluation	7.3.4a
follow-up actions	7.3.4b
identification of problems	7.3.4b
participants	7.3.4
records	4.2.4, 7.3.4
validation	7.3.6
records	4.2.4, 7.3.6
verification	7.3.5
follow-up actions	7.3.5
records	4.2.4, 7.3.5
planning	7.3.1
responsibility and authority	7.3.1c
stages	7.3.1a

Subject title	ISO 9001 element
control	7.5.3
design and development	7.3
control of changes	7.3.7
input	7.3.2
output	7.3.3
planning	7.3.1
review	7.3.4
validation	7.3.6
verification	7.3.5
function and performance	7.3.2a
identification and traceability	4.8, 7.5.3
information	7.5.1a
measuring and monitoring	8.2.4
measuring and monitoring devices	7.6
non-conformance	8.3
obligations (legal and regulatory)	7.2.1c
post-delivery activities	7.5.1f
release	7.5.1f
provision of facilities	7.1b
provision of resources	7.1b
purchasing	7.4
conformance to requirements	7.4.1
verification	7.4.3
quality objectives	7.1a
realisation	7
customer-related processes	7.2
design	7.3
development	7.3
measuring and monitoring devices	7.5
planning of	7.1
production and service operations	7.5
release purchased	8.2.4
requirements	7.1, 7.2.1
confirmation of	7.2.2b
customer	7.2.1a
definition of	7.2.2a
delivery and post-delivery	7.2.1a
differences resolved	7.2.2b
necessary for intended use	7.2.1b
records	4.2.4, 7.2.2
review	7.2.2
status	7.5.3
traceability	4.2.4, 7.5.3

Annex A   Documentation requirements

In addition to providing a simplified set of standards that are equally applicable to small as well as medium and/or large organisations, the main objectives behind the 2000 revision of the ISO 9000 series of standards were that:

- they would be much less prescriptive than the 1994 version of the standard;
- organisations would be allowed more flexibility in the way it chose to document its management system;
- the amount of detailed documentation that was required by the standard would be limited;
- the amount of documentation required by individual organisations would be significantly reduced – provided that it was still capable of demonstrating the effective planning, operation and control of their processes as well as the implementation (and continual improvement) of its QMS;
- the type and extent of the documentation would depend on the nature of the organisation's products and processes.

 Note: It has to be stressed that whilst ISO 9001 requires a '*Documented quality management system*', it does **not** require a '*system of documents*'!

To achieve these aims, organisations will need to document – either electronically or on paper – their quality policy, objectives, procedures, planning and operations. They will need to describe how they control quality in these areas and will also need to retain quality records to prove that these procedures have been followed (i.e. inventory control listings, travellers, work orders, signed contracts, etc.).

There are no specific requirements on the actual type or form documentation. It can differ from one organisation to another depending on size, type of activities, or complexity of processes.

A.1   The requirement

ISO 9001:2000 clause 4.1 General requirements requires an organisation to '*establish, document, implement, and maintain a quality management system and continually improve its effectiveness in accordance with the requirements of this International Standard'.*

The standard then goes on to explain that the QMS documentation shall include:

- *documented statements of a quality policy and quality objectives;*
- *a quality manual;*
- *documented procedures required by this International Standard;*
- *documents needed by the organisation to ensure the effective planning, operation and control of its processes; and*
- *records required by this International Standard;*

and that these documents may be in any form or type of medium **such as:**

- *paper;*
- *magnetic;*
- *electronic or optical computer disk;*
- *photograph;*
- *master sample.*

Note: For additional advice on documentation see ISO/TR 10013 *Guidelines for quality management systems documentation.*

A.1.1 Documented statements regarding quality policy and quality objectives

These will normally be included in the Quality Manual (see A.1.2 below).

A.1.2 Quality Manual

Clause 4.2.2 of ISO 9001:2000 specifies the minimum content for a quality manual. The format and structure of the manual, however, will vary between organisations depending on the organisation's size, culture and complexity. For example, a small organisation may find it appropriate to include the description of its entire QMS within a single manual, including all the documented procedures required by the standard. On the other hand, large, multi-national organisations may need several manuals at the global, national and/or regional level together with a more complex hierarchy of documentation. Alternatively, some organisations may choose to use the quality manual for other purposes besides that of simply documenting the QMS.

Note: The Quality Manual is a document that has to be controlled in accordance with the requirements of clause 4.2.3.

A.1.3 Documented procedures required by ISO 9001:2000

ISO 9001:2000 specifically requires the organisation to have 'documented procedures' for the following six activities:

- Control of documents (4.2.3);
- Control of quality records (4.2.4);
- Internal audits (8.2.2);
- Control of non-conforming products (8.3);
- Corrective actions (8.5.2);
- Preventative actions (8.5.3).

 Note: The term 'documented procedure' means that the procedure has to be established, documented, implemented and maintained.

By implication documented procedures should also be included for :

- Customer communications (7.2.3) – which states '*The organisation shall determine and implement effective arrangements for communication with customers*' and;
- Purchasing process (7.4.1) which states '*Criteria for selection, evaluation and re-evaluation shall be established*'.

Procedures can take any suitable form. They can be a narrative, a flow chart, a process map, or indeed any other suitable structure. As long as the procedure is effective, it really doesn't matter what it looks like.

Whilst some organisations may find it convenient to combine the procedure for several activities into a single documented procedure (for example, Corrective action and Preventive action), others may choose to document a given activity by using more than one documented procedure (for example, Internal audits). Both are acceptable.

Some organisations (particularly larger organisations, or those making use of more complex processes) may also require additional documented procedures (especially those relating to product realisation processes) in order to implement an effective QMS. This will clearly vary depending on the size of the organisation, the kind of activities in which it is involved and their complexity.

A.1.4 Documents required by the organisation to ensure the effective planning, operation and control of its processes

The two main objectives of an organisation's documentation should be to pro-vide communication of information (as a means of disseminating information about the aims, objectives and requirements for quality management) and evidence of conformity (i.e. the availability of evidence that all planned activities are being achieved in an efficient and effective manner).

Although the only documents specifically mentioned in ISO 9001:2000 are for quality policy, quality objectives and the actual quality manual itself, there are also several requirements in the standard where an organisation can demonstrate conformity by preparing additional documentation such as:

- process maps, process flow charts and/or process descriptions;
- organisation charts;
- specifications;
- work and/or test instructions;
- documents containing internal communications;
- production schedules;
- approved supplier lists;
- test and inspection plans;
- quality plans.

A.1.5   Records required by ISO 9001:2000

Records specifically required by ISO 9001:2000 are as follows:

Clause	Type of record required
5.6.1	Management reviews.
6.2.2 (e)	Education, training, skills and experience.
7.1 (d)	Evidence that the realisation processes and resulting product fulfil requirements.
7.2.2	Results of the review of requirements related to the product and actions arising from the review.
7.3.2	Design and development inputs relating to product requirements.
7.3.4	Results of design and development reviews and any necessary actions.
7.3.5	Results of design and development verification and any necessary actions.
7.3.6	Results of design and development validation and any necessary actions.
7.3.7	Results of the review of design and development changes and any necessary actions.

Clause	Type of record required
7.4.1	Results of supplier evaluations and any necessary actions arising from the evaluations.
7.5.2 (d)	As required by the organisation to demonstrate the validation of processes where the resulting output cannot be verified by subsequent monitoring or measurement.
7.5.3	The unique identification of the product, where traceability is a requirement.
7.5.4	Customer property that is lost, damaged or otherwise found to be unsuitable for use.
7.6 (a)	Basis used for calibration or verification of measuring equipment where no international or national measurement standards exist.
7.6	Validity of the previous measuring results when the measuring equipment is found not to conform to requirements.
7.6	Results of calibration and verification of measuring equipment.
8.2.2	Internal audit results and follow-up actions.
8.2.4	Indication of the person(s) authorising release of product.
8.3	Nature of the product non-conformities and any subsequent actions taken, including concessions obtained.
8.5.2	Results of corrective action.
8.5.3	Results of preventive action.

There is, of course, no restriction on an organisation developing other records that may be needed to demonstrate conformity of their processes, products and/or quality management system.

A.2 Control of documents

'Proper control of documents' is required by the standard which means that you need to ensure that all your QMS documents have been correctly identified, reviewed, authorised, issued and distributed. You need to take care that old (i.e. obsolete) documents are not being used and that they are stored in a secure location if they are required for future reference. You also need to make sure that any external documents that you use in your QMS are identified within your system and that the access to these documents is controlled.

A.3 Software programs for document control

With the acceptance of ISO 9001:2000 as the principal standard for integrated management has come the requirement to see the business in process terms.

One method of achieving this is to use a process mapping software tool which not only describes the organisation's business processes (through a series of multi-layer maps) but also provides direct access to existing documentation sitting below the process maps. This enables staff to have immediate access (i.e. through an intranet desktop PC) to the relevant documents, rather than having to cope with searching through a forest of printed documents. It also ensures that only the latest issues of these documents are available to staff.

The benefits of using software to manage your documentation and processes are numerous and is the reason why more organisations are now turning to an IT solution whose advantages include:

- ease of use
- error reductions
- cost savings on print, paper and distribution
- improved functionality
- space and environmental savings and
- time no longer wasted on searching for hard copies.

Annex B   Customer satisfaction

Customer satisfaction is not just a perception, it is also a question of degree which can vary from high satisfaction to low satisfaction. If customers believe that you have met their requirements, then they experience high satisfaction. If they believe that you have not met their requirements, then they experience low satisfaction.

B.1 The requirement

Section 8.2.1, ISO 9001:2000 requires an organisation to '*monitor information relating to customer perception as to whether the organisation has met customer requirements*' and requires '*the methods of obtaining and using this information to be determined*'.

As you can see, the emphasis here is on monitoring customer perception (systematic checks on a periodic or continuous basis) rather than measuring customer satisfaction during a one-off event. Whilst customers may accept a product, they may not necessarily be entirely satisfied with either that particular product or the service they have received and, quite legitimately, believe that you have not met their expectations. To overcome this possibility, you should always strive to provide a service or product that exceeds the customer's stated requirements – provided that it can be kept within budget.

Satisfied customers are always good for business for not only will they return but they will also recommend your organisation to other people. Getting your customers to tell you what's good about your products or services and where there is room for improvement, helps you to ensure that your business meets or exceeds their expectations. You obviously want your customers to be happy with the products and services that you provide and if they feel they have received good value for their money, then your business will prosper.

Market research can help you to track and monitor customer satisfaction. But first you must consider which form of market research you want to employ.

B.2 Brief overview of market research

Within market research there are two main methodologies – Quantitative and Qualitative.

Quantitative Research – is the gathering of data from a large sample group to create statistically viable data. It is the basis for monitoring customer satisfaction but needs to be completed systematically and regularly in order to monitor and track changes effectively.

Qualitative Research – is an in-depth investigation of topics using a small sample group. Although this will provide an indication of how the target market is feeling and how they will react to a given topic, it cannot be relied upon as statistically viable data.

Often both methodologies will be used in the monitoring and evaluation of customer satisfaction. Each has its place, each will deliver important and useful information but, in order to make best use of these research tools, you must have a clear idea of what you want to achieve in the first place and then use the most effective tool to deliver the results you want.

 It must be remembered that customer satisfaction surveys will only give you a status quo and an indication of what customers would like to see changed. Unless you react and respond to these customer needs, things will never change. Research can give you a quick way to see whether your changes are impacting on them, positively or negatively.

B.3 Qualitative research

In general, qualitative research is used by researchers at the beginning of a survey to give a snapshot of the general trends that may come up when they complete the main survey and which will help them to ensure that they ask the correct questions in the main survey. Qualitative research may also help to establish some possible solutions to customer issues which can then be tested in the main survey and the results evaluated before radical changes are made in the way a business is run, product produced or service undertaken.

Qualitative research can also be used in the middle stage of a research programme to re-investigate general trends, explore whether things have changed in the consumer's mind and evaluate whether different questions should now be asked. Finally it will often be used at the end of the programme to gain a clear understanding of how customers are feeling and if anything changed for them.

Qualitative research can be divided up into a number of different methodologies, but the main methodologies that you will probably encounter are:

- Focus Groups; and
- Depth Interviews.

B.3.1 Focus groups

Focus groups are effectively a brainstorming session. They are usually small groups comprising 10 or less people who are tasked to examine a particular product, service, policy or idea by 'focussing' on a comparatively short list of issues and then thoroughly exploring every aspect of it.

Focus groups are especially good at generating ideas early in the product development cycle, when it's too expensive or too complex to develop multiple prototypes. Whilst the conclusions of a focus group can sometimes be very revealing, it should nevertheless be remembered that a focus group only represents a small sample of the population and should, therefore, not be relied upon to be statistically robust.

Choice of membership of a focus group is unlimited. It can include all types of professional, managerial, as well as a working level of expertise to encourage interactive thinking and enables all aspects of an issue or problem to be investigated.

Generally speaking, however, certain people should not be asked to participate in the same focus group. These include managers and subordinates, direct competitors, family members, experts and novices, and those who hold drastically different opinions from the other participants. Members won't fully engage with the rest of the group if they're intimidated or unduly influenced by some of its members. To ensure that the participants are able to interact constructively, it is often better to choose people with somewhat similar backgrounds and/or demographics.

For most types of research it is also advisable to recruit people who do not previously know each other. This will avoid the possibility of divisions within the group and friends ganging up on others! Sounds crazy, but it happens!

Note: Sometimes strongly opposing views can be very useful in raising and discussing challenging topics. However, caution should be taken if considering a 'conflict' focus group as the moderator of the group will have to be very experienced and capable of controlling and managing the situation, which could easily get out of hand.

In order to control and manage the focus group a moderator (often referred to as the 'facilitator') is used to preside over the session. Their main task is to ensure a free-flowing discussion that continues to move in the right direction and to ensure that all pertinent details are recorded.

Moderation of focus groups is a tricky business and should be left to those with experience – it certainly isn't the same as chairing a meeting with colleagues or clients! It is, therefore, advisable to employ the services of a moderator, either through a research agency or employ a freelance moderator to work directly for you.

To avoid anybody coming to the session with preconceived ideas or a closed opinion on a topic, generally speaking participants will not be informed of the topics to be discussed prior to the start of the focus group because if they have already considered a topic, they could be quite fixed in their views. It has been statistically proven that advance research can often influence a participant's thoughts and opinions during the group discussion which will inevitably result in flawed information for the researchers. You want responses and thoughts to be spontaneous and honest.

Typical topics and lines of questioning could include:

- *What do you like about this product/policy/idea?*
- *What do you dislike?*
- *How does it compare to other products/policies/ideas?*
- *What would you change about it?*

Focus groups are generally held in a relaxed setting, with a circle of seats, coffee table in the middle, with refreshments available. All this will help to relax the participants. Participants will become comfortable with the topic and with each other and this will enable them to focus on the details.

Note: It is important not to let a focus group last more than two hours as participating in a lively discussion can consume a considerable amount of energy.

In order to ensure that all the topics and areas that need to be covered are covered, the moderator will need to have some form of agenda to work to. This is commonly known as a topic guide and it is just that, a guide. The topic guide should **not** be seen as a strict guide to be followed, however. The discussions may veer off and circle around but as long as all the topics are covered eventually, then that is fine.

Note: If the moderator was to stop the participants mid-flow and pull them back to their agenda this could embarrass them and maybe stop them from speaking out again.

In normal circumstances a moderator will not make any notes themselves as this will only act to stop the free flow of the discussions, and can remind the participants that the moderator is noting down everything they are saying. Nevertheless, some form of record should be kept of the meeting and this can be either a manual record or some form of electronic means. Nowadays focus group's discussions are almost always recorded using audio recorders and/or video camera as they are particularly useful for recording the emotions, opinions, interactions and 'hot topics' that the group uncovers.

In order to ensure that you achieve a good mix of your customer sample, a number of different focus groups may be required and your customer base will need to be split accordingly. This could include doing focus groups separately for men and women, old and young, regionally or nationally to ensure that no biases exist, and if they do, you will discover them.

B.3.2 Depth interviews

Depth interviews follow the same pattern as focus groups (i.e. they are in a relaxed setting, they use a topic guide, they are recorded etc.), but they are carried out with smaller numbers of people. Generally a depth interview will be a one to one discussion between a moderator and a selected individual and can be used in cases where you either have a small number of very important customers to interview, or where the topic is of a confidential or sensitive nature and participants would not open up in a general conversation. In all other ways depth interviews follow the same pattern as focus groups.

B.4 Types of quantitative survey

Quantitative (often known as 'Quant') surveys are probably the best way of gathering vital information on customer satisfaction. There are many different Quant methodologies that can be employed, but of these, the main ones are:

- postal/e-mail;
- telephone;
- on street;
- house to house; and
- mystery shopping.

Some of these will be more appropriate to your market and customer base than others; all have their advantages and disadvantages and below are the key pros and cons to each methodology.

B.4.1 Postal and telephone surveys

Sometimes these two methodologies are referred to as 'impersonal surveys', because by their nature they have less of the human touch to them. Postal surveys are, however, recognised as being the most impersonal of them all, as you are asking your customer to go through the questionnaire completely alone. With a telephone you do at least have a member of your staff (or an agency working on your behalf) interacting with the customer. The main benefits to both of these methodologies are the relatively low cost per response.

Postal (and e-mail) surveys are cheap to produce, with only printing costs, postage and reply postage to consider before you get to the point of analysis.

In addition a postal or e-mail survey can be an ideal way of communicating with your customer base if you have a wide spread of customers across the UK (Europe or the world) and where face-to-face work would not be cost effective.

In general terms, apart from the set up and form of delivery, most of the pros and cons of a postal survey will hold true for an e-mail study too. An added benefit, however, is that as you are conducting an electronic survey, you can thank everyone who responded by only having to send **one** multi-addressed e-mail!

 Note: Currently there are a wide number of specialist software packages and specialist research companies who can assist in the setting up of an e-mail survey (for details try one of the search engines such as www.google.com or the Market Research Society www.mrs.co.uk).

The main things to remember when compiling a postal/e-mail survey is that the questionnaire itself must be very user friendly and self explanatory and mustn't be too long or you will not get your customers to even consider answering the questions. In addition, as with all postal marketing activity, the response rate to a postal survey could be very low indeed and in general times you should only anticipate a 5–10% response rate to this type of survey. Some types of businesses may well get a better response than this, especially where businesses have a very good and close relationship with their customers, or where their product or service is of vital importance to them. In these cases, customers will **want** to contribute, but if your product has low importance to a consumer, is a commodity or service that is seen as the norm, then you will probably get a very apathetic response.

Postal surveys can and will take time to complete as they have to be posted out (anticipating potential delays in delivery!), then you have to allow customers time to complete and send back their survey forms (again allowing time for the post) before any analysis can commence. E-mail surveys, on the other hand, are increasingly being used as they have two distinct advantages over the old traditional postal surveys, response time (i.e. e-mail surveys can be turned around in days if not hours) and ease of completion. E-mail surveys are also much easier to complete and less confusing than paper questionnaires which often include advice (i.e. routing) such as '*if answered YES go to Qxx*' and '*if answered NO go to Qx etc*'. An electronic survey, on the other hand, will automatically route the respondent in the correct way, ensuring that they answer fully and correctly. More information on routing and single and multiple response questions etc. are explored in Section B.5 Writing a questionnaire.

Another consideration with this type of survey is that they are, of course, self selecting in nature. You have no control over who responds, thus you cannot ensure that you achieve a good and representative sample of your customer demographics. This sort of problem does not occur with telephone surveys.

B.4.2 Telephone surveys

Telephone surveys are not dissimilar to the postal or e-mail route discussed above. The main difference of course is that they are conducted over the phone by a member of your staff or a person employed by you to complete the survey.

The three main advantages to this type of survey over postal are the speed of response, accuracy of response and control of the sample profile.

By using a telephone methodology you can ensure that you get to the right people at the appropriate time, but it is important that you target them in the right place and at the right time. For most general customer surveys, this means that calls should be made in the evening, in their home, when they are available and where they will be in a (hopefully!) relaxed atmosphere and more responsive. The opposite of course applies if you are contacting them about a business related product or service, then you can get them at their office during working hours.

Secondly, accuracy of response can be assured. By using trained staff to fill in the survey with the customer you can ensure that all the right questions are answered and explanations given are relevant – as far as possible that is, because you will always get some people who will start a questionnaire and then get bored and just hang up half way through! This is especially true if you are employing a research company who will no doubt use a computerised system of recording the information called CATI (Computer Assisted Telephone Interviewing) which like e-mail ensures that all the correct questions are asked and answered. Again the data is automatically captured and analysis can begin immediately, in fact some analysis can be done 'on the fly' during the research to give you an emerging picture.

Thirdly, and this is very important to ensure your data is statistically viable, by controlling those who answer your survey you will ensure that you get the correct cross sample of customers answering the questions. This will ensure that the results you get give you the correct indicators and directions for your business. This is explored further in Section B.6 Sample profile.

B.4.3 On-street or house-to-house surveys

On-street or house-to-house surveys (often referred to as 'face-to-face' surveys) are to all intents and purposes, one and the same thing. It is just the location that changes! The most appropriate methodology will depend on the type of product or service you offer, who your customer is, how easy is it to find these people on the street or in a specific location, town, road, estate, etc. In addition, this kind of survey will be necessary if you need to show your customers something.

Whereas postal, e-mail and telephone surveys will be ideal if you have a customer base that is widely dispersed, on-street and house-to-house are more relevant if you know your customers are easy to find and/or you can be in one spot and get them as they pass you by. You will need to consider if this is the case before you go for the on-street or house-to-house option, because if you get it wrong and find yourself chasing for days to get one or two people to answer your questions, then costs will soon mount up.

One of the main advantages of on-street and house-to-house surveys is that you can generally have a longer survey. This is more true of house-to-house, when you can sit down and chat to the customer over (possibly!) a cup of tea!

As previously described, quantitative studies are a way of discovering what customers may want in the future. If you discover that they would like an additional service, revised packaging etc., then a pictorial representation of this (called a show card) will help the customer to understand what you are suggesting and therefore help them to make a more informed decision on the possible benefits of this (a picture is worth a thousand words!).

Being face-to-face with the customer may or may not be an advantage, depending on your product or service and the relationship customers have with it. Customers may want to tell you face-to-face, however some may be embarrassed to. Even if you employ a third party company to complete the research for you, customers will often consider that they represent your company. Again you should know your customer and be able to judge whether this will be an advantage or a disadvantage.

The main disadvantage about on-street and house-to-house surveys is the time and expense of carrying it out. Fieldworkers (i.e. the staff to carry out the interviewing) need to be organised and their locations agreed.

 Note: If you are carrying out on-street interviews in shopping centres, high streets etc., permission may need to be sought from the council or centre management.

Surveys need to be sent out to fieldworkers along with all their instructions, show cards and so on. Fieldworkers then need to be given time to familiarise themselves with the survey before they go out. Then the fieldwork (i.e. the survey itself) is then carried out, usually over the space of a few days to ensure that a correct sample is obtained. After this, the surveys need to be posted back to the research company before analysis can begin. Again some of the larger research companies will have automated systems for collecting data which is then downloaded, but these do come with a price tag attached – and let's not forget the fieldworkers' travel and subsistence expenses!

The following flow chart and accompanying table describe a typical procedure for this process.

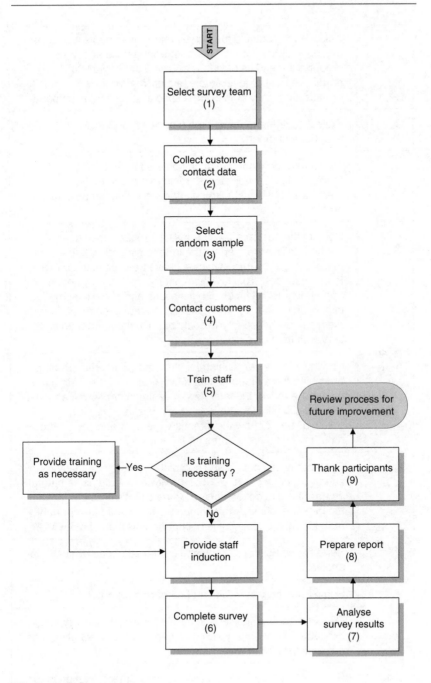

Figure B.1 Survey process

1	Select and assemble the survey team (use people who have a good telephone manner, are knowledgeable about the organisation and its business and who are capable of remaining neutral at all times), either from your own organisation or by employing a specialist research company.
2	Collect customer contact data (i.e. name, address, telephone number).
3	Select a random sample of customers for the survey (geographical as well as according to the size of the customer's business) using quotas – see section B6 Sample profile.
4	Contact the customers (via e-mail is probably the cheapest method) telling them about the forthcoming survey, the reasons for the survey, why they have been selected and ask for their support. This is a nice thing to do, but may not be appropriate for all types of businesses and could in some instances have a detrimental effect on the outcome of the main survey, because you could put people off from doing the survey in the first place.
5	Provide interviewer training for staff and volunteers. (Prior to beginning the telephone interviews, team members should review the role of the interviewer, explore interview scenarios, review fall back statements and role-play an interview to obtain a 'feel' for how the interview will work **and** review the record keeping procedures for the survey.)
6	Contact the customers and complete a Customer satisfaction survey for each person. (The interviewer should be as natural as possible. Do not apologise for the call; it's better to make the person feel they are contributing to something important rather than suggesting it is unimportant with an apology.)
7	Send the completed survey and call sheets to an evaluator for analysis.
8	Summarise survey results and prepare a report.
9	Consider communicating the key findings of the survey in an executive overview to your customers. This may not always be necessary or indeed appropriate.
Finally	Review the process to see where improvements can be made for future surveys.

Note: A customer satisfaction index or ACSI (American Customer Satisfaction Index) uses data obtained from customer interviews, to produce an independent measure of performance that is useful to economists, investors and potential customers. It is frequently used in North America, Sweden and Germany.

B.4.4 Mystery shopping

Although not strictly a tool to measure customer satisfaction, mystery shopping is a revealing way to experience the reality first hand. Mystery shopping is where someone impersonates a customer on behalf of the organisation, paying close attention to product or service quality. The undercover customer's findings are often very beneficial and frequently reveal patterns about the effectiveness of the organisation's processes.

The mystery shopper can be an employee of the organisation or someone hired specifically for this sole purpose and should focus on the organisation's system, processes and procedures. The sort of areas that could be investigated include:

- courtesy of personnel;
- degree of knowledge;
- accuracy of information received;
- adherence to organisational policies;
- timeliness of service;
- efficiency of processes;
- conformity of the final product;
- past results.

There is no set rule to the type of questioning that can be used by a mystery shopper. Generally there will be a questionnaire of sorts, but this will be completed after the mystery shop is over as obviously writing up notes whilst in the shop would give the game away somewhat! Generally the mystery shopper will be given a 'scenario' (or story) of why they are there and this scenario will allow them to ask all the relevant questions required.

Whilst the mystery shop is normally unscripted, the data is generally captured on predefined questionnaires with some elements of free text to allow them to include any exceptional information. This is again relayed back to the research company for analysis.

Mystery shopping is an expensive but valuable tool in the quest to fully gauge the reality of the service you are offering. Expensive because a statistically robust sample must be achieved in the same way as with any other Quant study, and seasonal and regional variations also need to be considered.

 Note: This technique is widely used in the retail industry (e.g. restaurants, hotels, mail order businesses and car dealerships) and can produce some very interesting results!

B.5 Writing a questionnaire

There are a number of considerations that must be made when setting out to write a questionnaire.

Firstly you must be very clear what your objectives are. What do you want to find out, what are you going to do with information once you have it. How will you judge whether you are succeeding or failing? It sounds simple, but until you know what you want to find out, there is no point moving on.

Next create yourself a logical question plan. Start with the general and get more specific as you move through the questionnaire. It may be that you do not want your customer to know it is you asking the questions and, therefore, you will need to start with general questions about your marketplace before getting down to the specifics of your product and service later. It can help to remain anonymous and leave it to the customer to work it out. In this way they can have no preconceived ideas of how they 'should' answer the question and will respond more honestly, and not answer how they think you will want them to answer.

Types of questions are vital. In the majority, the questionnaire you should keep to closed questions and avoid open questions. With closed questions you will ensure that all customers answer exactly the same question, if you give 100 people an open question you will probably get 100 different answers and how will you be able to analyse that?! By all means let your customers have their say, but in a controlled way (i.e. by including an *'any other comments'* after each section of questioning).

Example of open and closed questioning:

Closed question – *'Do you agree or disagree with the following statement'* .....
Open question – *'How do you feel about the following statement'* ....

The length of the questionnaire is also important. There is no such thing as a short survey that is too short but there is such a thing as a survey that is too long! However is there any point in only asking one or two questions? You have, after all, a captive audience so why not ask them at least 10–12 questions?!

A survey that is too long is a waste of time from a postal point of view because many people will look at it and not even bother to start, or they may start but then give up half way through.

Whether the customer is expected to answer the questionnaire on their own or with the help of a researcher, the questions should be easy to understand and logical. Avoid unnecessary use of jargon (you may understand it, but will they?).

B.5.1 Routing

Routing is a vital part of any quantitative survey. This allows you to have all eventualities covered. If they say *'yes'* to a question, then ask them more, if they say *'no'* to a question, move them on to the next section (we've all seen it on tax returns!). Routing is very usual but it is essential to get it right.

You don't want to confuse your customers and you want all the relevant people to answer all the relevant questions, not miss swathes out of important parts of the questionnaire by a previous routing error. This is why planning of the questionnaire is vital, and why starting with the general and honing into the specific is key.

B.5.2 Rating scales

For many closed questions (and in order to gauge levels of agreement to statements) rating scales are important. There will be very few questions which you will want just a yes/no answer as opposed to a lot of maybe/sometimes answers! Rating scales will allow you to capture this information. There are a number of schools of thought on the rating scales, how many levels should you allow, should you have an odd or an even number of scales. In general terms the answer will fall to you to decide what is best for your particular company, but it is most normal to see an even number of levels in a rating scale usually of 4 or more. Again this will depend on what information you expect to find out and what you will do with that incremental information. Odd numbers are generally avoided as this would allow people to choose the middle number to sit on the fence. Below is an example of a rating scale question and how you could use the information.

Q – On a scale of 1–10 (where 10 = agree completely and 1 = disagree completely) would you agree that the service that company X offers is better than the competition?

Say you asked 10 people this question, you may get the following data:

1 person said '1' – disagree completely;
3 people said '4';
1 person said '7';
4 people said '8';
1 person said '10'.

That would mean that 60% of people agreed to some degree with the question, of that 50% agreed to some degree (e.g. they rated it 7–9), and 10% of people categorically agreed, whilst 40% disagreed to some degree and 10% categorically disagreed.

This information is giving you degrees of agreement. If you did not have the scale how would those who answered '4' have answered, if they could only choose agree or disagree? This could have skewed your data all of a sudden and you would have had 40% disagreeing with your statement, instead of only 10% strongly opposed, with a 30% wavering.

B.6 Sample profile

Sample profiles are a complex issue and are only described here in the briefest and most broad brushstroke of ways. Sampling, at its most complex, is a highly sophisticated process of statistics and demographic profiling. However there are some basics that we should look at.

Essentially the sample profile is a definition of your customer base. The sample should be a direct representation of the breakdown of your customer base, in all aspects (for example to reflect the split of male to females, old to young, home-owners to those who rent properties etc.). When national polls are undertaken they don't ask every member of the population, but a representative sample of that population.

Although sample profiles should cover all elements of your customer base don't try to get too sophisticated with it, stick to exploring the views of the majority not the minority. When establishing the profile you will want to set broad 'quotas' for each of your main profile groups – for example you may need to achieve 70% male and 30% female respondents to reflect your customer base.

 Note: Some quantitative methodologies (i.e. such as postal surveys) will not allow you to control the quota and you should consider whether this will pose an issue for you. If the majority of your customer base is broadly the same, then this will not be an issue at all. If, on the other hand, you have a wide diversity in your customer base then you need to be able to control the sample.

Whilst undertaking your research, the sample breakdown should be monitored to ensure you are covering all of the vital groups and so that a plan of action can be put in place if you find you are missing a vital group at this stage – it is difficult to do this later on.

B.7 Areas suitable for analysis

The possibilities for analysing customer satisfaction can vary from one organisation to another but probably the three most important areas are:

Type of analysis	Reason	Type of data
Conformance to customer requirements	Targets should be established for product conformity as a measure of achievement. Data needs to be collected and analysed for all products in order to determine whether these objectives are being achieved.	Data generated whilst monitoring and measuring the characteristics of a product as well as data generated during design, purchasing, production, installation and operation, and data collected from customer feedback.

(continued)

Product and process characteristics	Opportunities for preventive action may arise when the trend in a series of measured values indicates deterioration in performance and if the deterioration were allowed to continue, non-conformity would result.	Variation in product characteristics such as dimensions, voltage, power output and strength.
Supplier data	Information relating to suppliers concerning their performance regarding product and service quality, delivery and cost.	Suppliers are a key contributor to the performance of an organisation and therefore information on the performance of suppliers is necessary to determine the adequacy, suitability and effectiveness of the management system.

B.8 Analysis of customer satisfaction data

Customer satisfaction is not something one can monitor directly by simply installing a sensor. One has first to collect the data and then analyse it in order to draw conclusions, to identify the key areas where action is necessary and where major opportunities for improvement are indicated. This data can be collected from a number of sources (see table below) and the results can then be used as the basis for business and process development plans for current and future products and services.

Type	How collected	Result
Repeat orders	From the order process.	Whilst the number of repeat orders is not necessarily a measure of whether a customer is completely satisfied, it does show loyalty and provides useful data when analysing customer satisfaction.

(*continued*)

Competition	This data is more subjective and results from market research.	Monitoring the workload of competitors is an indicator of your success or failure.
Referrals	From sales personnel during the transaction or later on follow-up calls.	When you obtain a new customer you should try to find out why they chose your organisation in preference to others. It could be that one of your existing customers referred them to you, which is a sign of that customer's satisfaction.
Demand	From sales trends.	Monitoring the actual demand for your products and services relative to the predicted demand is also an indicator of success or failure to satisfy customers.
Effects of product transition	From sales trends following new product launch.	When you market a new product or service, it is important to gauge whether you still retain your existing customers – or do go elsewhere?
Surveys	From survey reports.	A customer satisfaction survey is one way of gathering this vital information and there are two main types of survey that can be used, the impersonal form and the personal form.
Focus meetings	From the meeting reports.	A focus meeting is another form of personal survey where a meeting is arranged between people from within the customer's organisation and people internal to your own organisation (e.g. Marketing, Purchasing, Quality Assurance, Manufacturing departments etc.).

(continued)

Annex B   Customer satisfaction

Complaints	From complaints recorded by customers or by staff on speaking with customers.	Complaints relating to fitness for purpose, delivery deadlines, product information, conditions of sale, use of personal data, after-sales service and guarantees are an important method for capturing customer feedback (see note below).
Compliments	From written compliments sent in by customers or by staff on speaking with customers.	Compliments can vary from a casual remark during a conversation to something included in correspondence. These are usually unsolicited remarks and a sure sign of customer satisfaction.

When analysing your customer satisfaction data you can compare your data with industry norms to evaluate whether your company is performing above or below the norm for your sector. This is achieved through a Customer satisfaction index or ACSI (American Customer Satisfaction Index) which uses data obtained from customer interviews, to produce an independent measure of performance that is useful to economists, investors and potential customers.

 Note: ISO10002 (Quality Management, Customer Satisfaction – Guidelines for complaints handling) is part of a forthcoming trio of international best practice codes of conduct (the others being ISO 10001 for complaints handling and ISO 10003 for an external customer disputes resolution system) which are currently working drafts scheduled to be published as International Standards in 2006. This new standard will provide guidelines for handling complaints in a way that will not only benefit the organisation but also the unhappy customer. In addition to meeting the requirements of ISO 9001:2000, ISO 10002 will also be capable of being used as a stand-alone process in support of other quality management and customer satisfaction tools such as Customer Relation Management, Six Sigma and the EFQM Models.

B.9 Other considerations

- Make it easy for your customers to complain – customers who are dissatisfied tell ten times as many people about it as those who are happy with your service.

- Respond to complaints quickly and courteously – a speedy response can add 25 per cent to customer loyalty.
- Resolve complaints on the first contact – reduce the cost of unnecessary additional contacts.
- Use your computers to develop a database of complaints – an electronically compiled customer complaint system enables an organisation to better align their services and products to meet customer expectations.
- Recruit and hire well motivated, front-line employees, to deal with customer complaints – it is important that all personnel who come into contact with customers should have a non-intrusive method for conveying to the customer that the compliment is appreciated and will be passed on to the staff involved.
- Be sure to keep your customers informed about any change in procedure that you have introduced because of the survey.
- Document and follow up on all the comments you receive. If you have to change a procedure, then you need to ensure that everyone involved in that procedure is aware of the changes.
- Advertise the fact that you are doing things differently and in a more qualitative manner.
- Above all the survey process needs to be free from bias, prejudice and political influence.

Annex C   Guidance on non-conforming products

By definition, a non-conforming product is a product that does not conform to the agreed product requirements when subjected to a planned (or unplanned) verification and which fails to meet:

- specified customer's requirements;
- intended usage requirements;
- stated or implied needs;
- customer expectations;
- the organisation's own requirements.

 Note: A product that becomes damaged or fails at any other stage is normally considered unserviceable.

C.1 Identifying non-conformities

Identifying and controlling non-conforming products is a fundamental quality control discipline whose purpose is to prevent unacceptable items or services from reaching customers in the first place.

This discipline is covered by ISO 9001:2000 clause 8.3 which states that *'The organisation shall ensure that a product which does not conform to product requirements is identified and controlled to prevent its unintended use or delivery'*. In simple terms this means that an organisation must identify products that don't conform to requirements and probably the most common method of carrying this out is just to stick a label to the product warning people of this fact, but there are other ways such as:

- fixing barcodes, or other means of electronic identification, to the product;
- using coded markings on the product (e.g. paint spots);
- writing remarks directly on the product;
- fixing tags, signs or stickers to the product;

- wrapping tape or ribbon around the product;
- storing the product in specially marked areas (e.g. quarantine areas).

 Note: Whilst products are often capable of operating even though they do contain certain non-conformities, a service is usually withdrawn once the non-conformity has been detected (no matter how trivial the fault) and this is usually achieved by using notices such as '*Out of Order*' or by announcements such as '*Normal service will be resumed as soon as possible*'.

C.2 Controlling non-conforming products

The prime aim for any organisation, of course, is that they should prevent any non-conforming products from reaching the customer in the first place and to remove the root cause of non-conformance. Whilst the most obvious way of achieving this aim is to actually scrap or destroy the product, it might also be possible to eliminate the non-conformity by amending an existing procedure or to repair (or rework) the offending item. This process would, of course, have to be covered by a specific documented procedure which would include requirements for:

- defining responsibilities for the control and maintenance of these documented procedures;
- training employees on the use of these procedures;
- segregating non-conforming products from conforming products;
- securing non-conforming products in locked or protected areas.

C.3 Documented procedures

In addition to section C.2 above, a documented procedure will have to be written for the control of a non-conforming product should specify:

- the responsibilities for authorising a product (or service) as a non-conformity, where this is to be recorded and what information should be provided;

   Note: This should also include:
  - who can identify non-conforming products?
  - who can move or handle non-conforming products?
  - who can authorise remedial action to deal with non-conforming products?
  - who is responsible for completing this action?

- how the product should be scrapped or recycled (together with the forms to be used and the authorisations to be obtained);

- the various repair procedures that should be used (and how they should be produced, selected and implemented);
- how modifications should be defined, identified and implemented;
- how production permits (deviations) and concessions (waivers) should be requested, evaluated, approved or rejected;
- products should be returned to its supplier (the forms to be completed and any identification requirements etc.);
- how regrading a product is to be carried out (product markings, prior authorisation and acceptance criteria etc.);
- the records that must be maintained.

C.4 Dealing with non-conforming products

When a product is found to be non-conforming there are three decisions that should be made based on the following questions:

- can the product be made to conform?
- if the product cannot be made to conform, is it fit for use?
- if the product is not fit for use, can it be made fit for use?

In clause 8.3, ISO 9001:2000 suggests that one of the following methods should be used to control non-conforming products:

• By taking action to eliminate the detected non-conformity.	Such as repairing, reworking or reprocessing.
• By authorising its use, release or acceptance under concession by a relevant authority and, where applicable, by the customer.	If a product non-conforms to the organisation's internal specifications but conforms to the customer's specifications, then a concession (i.e. an agreement to use, release or accept a product) can be issued by the organisation.
	If the product non-conforms to the customer's specifications, then the concession must come from the customer.
• By taking action to preclude its original intended use or application.	Such as scrapping, recycling, reprocessing or regrading.

If you need to recall a product that is suspected as being defective you will need to devise a Recall Plan, specify responsibilities and time-scales and put the plan into effect.

 Note: Product recall is a remedial action not a corrective action because it does not prevent a recurrence of the initial problem.

C.5 Records

ISO 9001:2000 requires *'that records of the nature of non-conformities and any subsequent action taken, including concessions obtained, shall be maintained'*.

These records should contain:

- a description of the non-conformity;
- action taken (usually referred to as 'disposition');
- action taken to re-verify the non-conforming product after it has been corrected;
- details of any concessions made or given.

C.6 Re-verifying non-conforming products

When non-conforming products are corrected, they must be re-verified before being delivered to the customer. This re-verification should be completed using the original (or a modified version of the original) and the records must include:

- evidence of conformity (i.e. actual measurements or observations);
- identification of the person authorising the release (i.e. the person performing the verification or responsible for seeing that the task is carried out).

C.7 Non-conformities detected at a later date

Occasionally non-conformities will be detected after delivery or after the customer has used the product and in these cases ISO 9001:2000 requires that the organisation *'shall take action appropriate to the effects or potential effects of the non-conformity'*.

Normally this is achieved by the organisation having a procedure to cover a returned goods process. This procedure will include:

- Identifying the non-conforming product (see section C.1 above);
- Initiating corrective action is initiated to determine and eliminate the root cause of the non-conformity (see section C.4 above).

C.8 Corrective action

ISO 9001:2000 states that *'The organisation shall take action to eliminate the causes of non-conformities in order to prevent recurrence'* which basically means that all non-conformities will be submitted for corrective action and that this corrective action should be appropriate to the type of non-conformity found.

Action to remove the detected non-conformity is a remedial action and can include the completion of operations, rework, repair or modification.

References

Standards

Number	Date	Title
93/42/EEC	1993	European Community Council Directive concerning medical devices
94/408218 DC	2000	Draft for Comment on ISO 1005
A 137.1	1988	Ceramic tiles
ANSI 90 series		American quality standards
BS 0	1997	A standard for standards – guide to the context, aims and general principles
BS 0:–1	1991	A standard for standards – guide to general principles of standardisation
BS 0:–2	1991	A standard for standards – BSI and its committee procedures
BS 0:–3	1991	A standard for standards – guide to drafting and presentation of British standards
BS 3934	1965	Specification for the dimensions of semiconductor devices and integrated electronic circuits
BS 4778–1	1987	Quality vocabulary
BS 4778–2	1979	Quality vocabulary – international terms, national terms
BS 4778–3.1	1991	Quality vocabulary – availability, reliability and maintainability terms – guide to concepts and related definitions
BS 4778–3.2	1991	Quality vocabulary – availability, reliability and maintainability terms – glossary of international terms
BS 4891	1972	A guide to quality assurance
BS 5701	1980	Guide to number defective charts for quality control
BS 5703	1980	Guide to data analysis quality control using cusum charting
BS 5750 series	1987	Quality systems – principal concepts and applications

Number	Date	Title
BS 5750–1	1979	Quality systems – specification for design, development, production, installation and servicing
BS 5750–2	1979	Quality systems – specification for production and installation
BS 5750–3	1979	Quality systems – specification for final inspection and test
BS 6001	1999	Sampling procedures for inspection by attributes
BS 6002	1993	Sampling procedures for inspection by variables
BS 6143–1	1992	Guide to the economics of quality – process cost model
BS 6143–2	1990	Guide to the economics of quality – prevention, appraisal and failure mode
BS 7850–1	1991	Total quality management – guide to management principles
BS 7850–2	1992	Total quality management – guide to quality improvement methods
BS 7850–3	1994	Total quality management – guidelines for quality improvement
BS 8800	1996	Guide to occupational health and safety management systems
DEF STAN 13–131/2	1997	Ordnance Board safety guidelines for weapons and munitions
DIS ISO 9000	1999	Quality management systems – fundamentals and vocabulary
DIS ISO 9001	1999	Quality management systems – requirements
DIS ISO 9004	1999	Quality management systems – guidance for performance improvement
EN 29000	1987	Renumbered as ISO 9000/1
ISO 8402	1995	Quality management and quality assurance – vocabulary
ISO 9000		Quality management and quality assurance standards
ISO 9000	2000	Quality management systems – fundamentals and vocabulary
ISO 9000–1	1994	Quality management and quality assurance standards – guidelines for selection and use
ISO 9000–2	1997	Quality management and quality assurance standards – generic guidelines for the application of ISO 9001, 9002 and 9003

Number	Date	Title
ISO 9000–3	1997	Quality management and quality assurance standards – guidelines for the application of ISO 9001:1994 to the development, supply, installation and maintenance of computer software
ISO 9000–4	1993	Quality management and quality assurance standards – guide to dependability programme management
ISO 9001	1994	Quality systems – model for quality assurance in design/development, production, installation and servicing
ISO 9001	2000	Quality management systems – requirements
ISO 9002	1994	Quality systems – model for quality assurance in production and installation
ISO 9003 ISO 9004	1994	Quality systems – model for quality assurance in final inspection and test Superseded by ISO 9004–1
ISO 9004	2000	Quality management systems – guidance for performance improvement
ISO 9004–1	1994	Quality management and quality system elements – guidelines
ISO 9004–2	1991	Quality management and quality system elements – guidelines for service
ISO 9004–3	1993	Quality management and quality system elements – guidelines for processed materials
ISO 9004–4	1994	Quality management and quality system elements – guidelines for quality improvement
ISO 10005	1995	Quality management – guidelines for quality plans
ISO 10011–1	1990	Guidelines for auditing quality systems – auditing
ISO 10011–2	1991	Guidelines for auditing quality systems – qualification criteria for quality systems auditors
ISO 10011–3	1991	Guidelines for auditing quality systems – management of audit programmes
ISO 10012–1	1992	Quality assurance requirements for measuring equipment – metrological confirmation system for measuring equipment
ISO 10012–2	1997	Quality assurance for measuring equipment – guidelines for control of measurement processes
ISO 10013	1995	Guidelines for developing quality manuals

Number	Date	Title
ISO 14001	1996	Environmental management systems – specifications with guidance for use
ISO 14010	1996	Guidelines for environmental auditing – general principles
ISO 14011	1996	Guidelines for environmental auditing – auditing procedures – auditing of environmental management systems
ISO 14012	1996	Guidelines for environmental auditing – qualification criteria for environmental auditors
ISO TR 10013		Guidelines for quality management systems documentation
ISO TR 10017	1999	Guidance on statistical techniques for ISO 9001:1994
QS 9000	1995	Quality system requirements (for the automotive industry)
TR 9000		Quality system requirements (for the electronics industry)

Other references

Title	Author	Publisher
BS 5750/ISO 9000:1987 – a positive contribution to a better business		BSI pamphlet
Crusading for quality		International Management, July/August 1989
Letter for Oslo – voice of the other Europe	Fossli, Karen	Management Today, May 1989
Operating degradations during the in-service stage	Tricker, R.L.	StingRay Management Consultants, 1999
Quality – its origin and progress in defence procurement	Drew, H.E.	Paper to the Institution of Production Engineers, 1971
Quality assurance	PSA	HMSO, 1987. ISBN 86177:143.53

Title	Author	Publisher
Quality counts – developments in qualities and standards since 1982	White paper	HMSO
Quality Management Handbook (BSI)		BSI
Selling to the single market	DTI	June 1989
Setting the scene for European standards, testing and certification post 1992	Strawbridge, Geoff	BSI
Standards, quality and international competitiveness	DTI	October 1986
Standards, quality and international competitiveness	White paper	Cmnd 8621, July 1982
Statistical Process Control, 5th edn	Oakland, John	Butterworth-Heinemann, 2002
The History of Quality Assurance and EQD	Tennyson, Peter	
Working for Quality		BSI

Notes

Extracts from British Standards are reproduced with the kind permission of the British Standards Institute. Complete copies of all British Standards can be obtained, by post, from Customer Services, BSI Standards, 389 Chiswick High Road, London W4 4AL.

Books by the same author

Title	Details	Publisher
ISO 9001:2000 Audit Procedures, 2nd edn	A complete set of audit check sheets and explanations to assist quality managers and auditors in completing internal, external and third part audits of ISO 9001:2000 Quality Management Systems.	Butterworth-Heinemann ISBN: 0 7506 6615 3
ISO 9001:2000 in Brief, 2nd edn	A 'hands on' book providing practical information on how to cost-effectively set up an ISO 9001:2000 Quality Management System.	Butterworth-Heinemann ISBN: 0 7506 6616 1
7.1.1 Building Regulations in Brief, 2nd edn	Handy reference guide to the requirements of the Building Act and its associated Approved Documents. Aimed at experts as well as DIY enthusiasts and those undertaking building projects.	Butterworth-Heinemann ISBN: 0 7506 6311 1

Title	Details	Publisher
Optoelectronic and Fiber Optic Technology	An introduction to the fascinating technology of fiber optics.	Butterworth-Heinemann ISBN: 0 7506 5370 1
CE Conformity Marking	Essential information for any manufacturer or distributor wishing to trade in the European Union. Practical and easy to understand.	Butterworth-Heinemann ISBN: 0 7506 4813 9
Environmental Requirements for Electromechanical and Electronic Equipment	Definitive reference containing all the background guidance, ranges, test specifications, case studies and regulations worldwide.	Butterworth-Heinemann ISBN: 0 7506 3902 4

Title	Details	Publisher
MDD Compliance using Quality Management Techniques	Easy to follow guide to MDD, enabling the purchaser to customise the Quality Management System to suit his own business.	Butterworth-Heinemann ISBN: 0 7506 4441 9
Quality and Standards in Electronics	Ensures that manufacturers are aware of all the UK, European and international necessities, know the current status of these regulations and standards, and where to obtain them.	Butterworth-Heinemann ISBN: 0 7506 2531 7

Abbreviations and acronyms

AFNOR	Association Francais de Normalisation
ANSI	American National Standards Institute
APQP	Advanced Product Quality Planning and Control Plan
AQAP	Allied Quality Assurance Publications (NATO)
ASQ	American Society for Quality (was ASQC)
ASQC	American Society for Quality Control (now ASQ)
ASTM	American Society for Testing and Materials
BS	British Standard, issued by BSI
BSI	British Standards Institution
CCIR	International Radio Consultative Committee
CCITT	The International Telegraph and Telephony Consultative Committee
CECC	CENELEC Electronic Components Committee
CEN	Commission European de Normalisation
CENELEC	European Committee for Electrotechnical Standardisation
COS	Corporation of Open Systems
CP	Core Business Process
CPPD	Critical Path Project Management
CSA	Canadian Standards Association
DCS	Document Control Sheet
DIN	Deutsches Institut für Normung (German Institute for Standardisation)
DIS	Draft International Standard
DTI	Department of Trade and Industry
DOD	(American) Division of Defence
EEC	European Economic Community
EIC	European Information Centre
EMAS	Eco-Management and Audit Scheme
EMS	Environmental Management System
EN	European Number (for European standards)
ENHD	European Harmonised Directive
EU	European Union
FDIS	Final Draft International Standard
FIIE(elec)	Fellow of the Institution of Electronics and Electrical Incorporated Engineers

FinstM	Fellow of the Institute of Management
FMEA	Failure Mode and Effect Analysis
FR	Failure Rate
HEC	Herne European Consultancy Ltd
HSE	Health & Safety Executive (UK)
IAF	International Accreditation Forum
IEC	International Electrotechnical Commission
IEE	Institution of Electrical Engineers
IQA	Institute of Quality Assurance
ISO	International Organisation for Standardisation
ISO/CASCO	OSI Committee on Conformity Testing
ISO/TC176	The ISO Technical Committee responsible for the ISO 9000 series standards
IT	Information Technology
ITU	International Telecommunications Union
LAN	Local Area Network
LCA	Life Cycle Assessment
MIQA	Member of the Institute of Quality Assurance
MIRSE	Member of the Institution of Railway Signal Engineers
MOD	Ministry of Defence
MSc	Master of Science
MTBF	Mean Time Between Failures
NATO	North Atlantic Treaty Organisation
NoBo	Notified Body
NQIC	National Quality Information Centre
NSA	National Supervising Authority
NSO	National Standards Organisation
OSI	Open Systems Connection
PF	Probability Function
PPAP	Production Part Approval Process
QA	Quality Assurance
QAI	Quality Assurance Inspector
QC	Quality Control
QM	Quality Manual
QMS	Quality Management System
QP	Quality Procedure
QSA	Quality System Assessment
SCEEMAS	Small Company Environmental and Energy Management Scheme
SP	Supporting Processes
SQP	Section Quality Plan
TQM	Total Quality Management (e.g. BS 7850)
UK	United Kingdom
VDE	Verband Deutsch Elektrotechniker
WI	Work Instruction

Glossary of terms

As international trade increases, it is becoming more important than ever to know the exact meaning of some of the basic definitions when referred to the quality of a product or service – especially when used in the vernacular! To overcome this problem an international standard (ISO 8402:1994 – Quality management and quality assurance – vocabulary) was published in three languages (English, French and Russian).

ISO 9000:2000 was then developed within ISO/TC 176. It was developed by first screening existing quality standards (e.g. ISO 8402:1994) and publications that were available to determine the quality terms that could be included and then producing internationally acceptable definitions of them. Because of this "international acceptability" many of these definitions and terms have specific meanings and applications as opposed to generic definitions that are normally to be found in dictionaries.

1st party – The original equipment or component manufacturer.

2nd party – A subcontractor or supplier under a direct contract to the main contractor, both for manufacture or services, and for installation, repair and maintenance.

3rd party – A party completely independent of the 1st and 2nd Party, e.g. an independent 3rd Party Certification Body (e.g. BSI, NQA).

4th party – Term, sometimes used to describe an independent but approved agent, e.g. a company who is authorised by a computer manufacturer to repair computers returned directly from the retailers under guarantee and then invoice the computer manufacturer directly, is called a 4th party repairer.

Accreditation – Certification, by a duly recognised body, of facilities, capability, objectivity, competence and integrity of an agency, service or operational group or individual to provide the specific service/s or operation/s as needed.

Audit – Systematic, independent and documented process for obtaining evidence and evaluating it objectively to determine the extent to which audit criteria are fulfilled.

Audit client – Person or organisation requesting an audit.

Audit conclusions – Outcome of an audit decided by the audit team after consideration of all the audit findings.

Audit criteria – Set of policies, procedures or requirements against which collected audit evidence is compared.

Audit evidence – Records, verified statements of fact or other information relevant to the audit.

Audit findings – Results of the evaluation of the collected audit evidence against audit criteria.

Audit plan – A chart showing the areas to be audited during a specific audit of an organisation, including the timing and names of the auditors involved.

Audit programme – Set of audits to be carried out during a planned time frame.

Audit report – A factual account of the results of the audit including the good points, extent of compliance, non-conformities, conclusions, recommendations and corrective actions.

Audit scope – Extent and range of a given audit.

Audit team – One or more auditors conducting an audit, one of whom is appointed as leader.

Auditee – Organisation being audited.

Auditor – Person qualified and competent to conduct audits.

Bonded store – A secure place in which only supplies that have been accepted as satisfactory by the inspection staff are held.

Business process – A series of operations that are an essential part of a business.

Calibration – The operation that is required to determine the accuracy of measuring and test equipment.

Capability – Ability of an organisation, system or process to realise a product that fulfils the requirements for that product.

CE marking – CE marking is the manufacturer's or supplier's self-declaration symbol to indicate that the product has undergone all the necessary evaluation procedures and is in conformity with the minimum requirements of the relevant European directives (also see *Kitemark*).

CEN (European committee for standardisation) – European equivalent of ISO.

CENELEC (European committee for electrotechnical standardisation)
certification body – An impartial body who have the necessary competence and reliability to operate a certification scheme.

Censored test – A test carried out on a number of items which is terminated before all the tested items have failed.

Certification – The procedure and action by a duly authorised body of determining, verifying and attesting in writing to the qualifications of personnel, processes, procedures, or items in accordance with applicable requirements.

Certification audit – An audit performed for the purpose of certifying a product, process, person or organisation.

Certification body – An impartial body, governmental or non-governmental, possessing the necessary competence and reliability to operate a certification system, and in which the interests of all parties concerned with the functioning of the system are represented.

Certification system – A system having its own rules of procedure and management for carrying out certification.

Check list (audit) – A list of topics or questions that guide an auditor conducting an audit. An aid to memory rather than a list of all questions to be asked.

Chief inspector – An individual who is responsible for the manufacturer's Quality Management System (also referred to as the Quality Manager).

Company – Term used primarily to refer to a business first party, the purpose of which is to supply a product or service.

Compliance – The fulfilment of a Quality Management System or quality procedure of specified requirements.

Concession – Authorisation to use or release a product that does not conform to specified requirements.

Concession/waiver – Written authorisation to use or release a quantity of material, components or stores already produced but which do not conform to the specified requirements.

Conformance – The fulfilment of a product or service of specified requirements.

Consignment – Products (or goods) that are issued or received as one delivery and covered by one set of documents.

Continual improvement – A set of activities that an organisation routinely carries out in order to enhance its ability to meet requirements. Continual improvement can be achieved by carrying out internal audits, performing management reviews, analysing data, and implementing corrective and preventive actions.

Contract – Agreed requirements between a supplier and customer transmitted by any means.

Contract review – A set of activities that an organisation carries out in order to make sure that customer orders and contracts specify all the requirements that must be met, and in order to establish that the organisation can actually meet these requirements.

Corrective action – Action taken to eliminate the cause of a detected nonconformity or other undesirable situation.

Customer – Ultimate consumer, user, client, beneficiary or second party.

Customer complaint – Any written, electronic, or oral communication that alleges deficiencies related to the identity, quality, durability, reliability, safety or performance of a device that has been placed on the market.

Customer dissatisfaction – Customer's opinion of the degree to which a transaction has failed to meet the customer's needs and expectations.

Customer organisation – Customer organisation or person that receives a product.

Customer satisfaction – Customer's opinion of the degree to which a transaction has met the customer's needs and expectations.

Defect – Non-fulfilment of a requirement related to an intended or specified use.

Design and development – Set of processes that transforms requirements into specified characteristics and into the specification of the product realisation process.

Design authority – The approved firm, establishment or branch representative responsible for the detailed design of material to approved specifications and authorised to sign a certificate of design, or to certify sealed drawings.

Design capability – The ability of a manufacturer to translate a customer requirement into a component that can be manufactured by their particular technology.

Design failure – A failure due to an inadequate design of an item.

Design review – A formal documented, comprehensive and systematic examination of a design to evaluate the design requirements and the capability of the design to meet these requirements and to identify problems and propose solutions.

Design validation – A process whose purpose is to examine products and to use objective evidence to confirm that these products meet user needs.

Design verification – A process whose purpose is to examine design outputs and to use objective evidence to confirm that outputs meet input requirements.

Document – Information and its support medium.

Effectiveness – Measure of the extent to which planned activities are realised and planned results achieved.

Efficiency – Relationship between the result achieved and the resources used.

Environment – All of the external physical conditions that may influence the performance of a product or service.

Environmental condition – The characteristics (such as humidity, pressure, vibration etc.) of the environment in which the product is operating.

Equipment – Machines, apparatus, fixed or mobile devices, control components and instrumentation thereof and detection or prevention systems which, separately or jointly, are intended for the generation, transfer, storage, measurement, control and conversion of energy for the processing of material and which are capable of causing an explosion through their own potential sources of ignition.

Evaluation – The systematic evaluation of the effectiveness of a contractor's Quality Management System.

Failure – The termination of the ability of an item to perform a required function.

Failure mode/fault mode – One of the possible states of a failed (faulty) item, for a given required function.

Failure mode and effect analysis (FMEA) – A qualitative method of reliability analysis which involves the study of the failure modes which can exist in every sub-item of the item and the determination of the effects of each failure mode on other sub-items of the item and on the required function of the item.

Failure mode, effect and criticality analysis (FMECA) – FMECA together with a consideration of the probability of occurrence and a ranking of the seriousness of the failure.

Failure rate (instantaneous) – The limit, if this exists, of the conditional probability that the instant of time of a failure of an item falls within a given time interval to the length of this interval, when given that the item is in an up state at the beginning of the time interval.

Failure tree analysis (FTA) – The study, with the use of diagrammatic algorithms, of the possible sequence of events leading up to the failure of a product.

Fault – The state of an item characterised by inability to perform a required function, excluding the inability during preventive maintenance or due to lack of external resources or other planned action.

Fault tree – A logic diagram showing how a given fault mode of an item is related to possible fault modes of sub-items or to external events, or combinations thereof.

Fault tree analysis – An analysis in the form of a fault tree in order to determine how a stated fault mode of the item may be the result of the fault modes of the sub-items or of external events, or combinations thereof.

Final inspection – The last inspection by a manufacturer or supplier before delivery.

Generic – Means that the same standards can be applied:

- to any organisation, large or small, whatever its product;
- including whether its 'product' is actually a service;
- in any sector of activity; and
- whether it is a business enterprise, a public administration, or a government department.

'Generic' also signifies that no matter what the organisation's scope of activity, if it wants to establish a Quality Management System or an Environmental Management System, then such a system has a number of essential features for which the relevant standards of the ISO 9000 or ISO 14000 families provide the requirements.

Infrastructure – Buildings, workspaces, equipment, hardware, software, utilities and support services such as transportation and communication.

In-process inspection – Inspection carried out at various stages during processing.

In-progress inspections – QA Inspectors perform these on a random basis or while assisting the technician. They may also be considered as 'Training' inspections and are meant to help the technician perform better maintenance whilst actually learning about the equipment.

Inputs – Products or services others provide to a process.

Inspection – Activities such as measuring, examining, testing, gauging one or more characteristics of a product or service and comparing these with specified requirements to determine conformity.

Interested party – Person or group having an interest in the performance or success of an organisation.

Internal quality audit – Carried out by the organisation's staff to examine the elements of a Quality Management System in order to evaluate how well these elements comply with quality system requirements.

Maintenance – The combination of technical and administrative actions that are taken to retain or restore an item to a state in which it can perform its stated function.

Management – Co-ordinated activities to direct and control an organisation.

Management review – Reviews carried out by the organisation's top managers which are completed on a regular basis with the aim of evaluating the overall performance of an organisation's Quality Management System and identifying improvement opportunities.

Management system – The organisation's structure for managing its processes (or activities) that transform inputs of resources into a product or service which meet the organisation's objectives, such as satisfying the customer's quality requirements, complying to regulations, or meeting environmental objectives.

Manufacturer – The natural or legal person with responsibility for the design, manufacture, packaging and labelling of a device before it is placed on the market under his own name, regardless of whether these operations are carried out by that person himself or on his behalf by a third party.

May – This auxiliary verb indicates a course of action often followed by manufacturers and suppliers.

Measurement – Set of operations having the object of determining the value of a quantity.

Non-conforming products – When one or more characteristics of a product fail to meet specified requirements or deviates from agreed quality requirements.

Non-conformity – Non-fulfilment of a requirement.

Operational cycle – A repeatable sequence of functional stresses.

Operational requirements – All the function and performance requirements of a product.

Organisation – A company, corporation, firm or enterprise, whether incorporated or not, public or private.

Group of people and facilities with an orderly arrangement of responsibilities, authorities and relationships.

Organisational structure – Orderly arrangement of responsibilities, authorities and relationships between people.

Out-going inspections – These are performed after a job or task has been completed to verify that everything has been done correctly on a repaired equipment that is ready for return to the Customer. The Quality Assurance Inspector is normally required to check the item to see how it compares against the manufacturer's specification. Any item failing an out-going inspection has to be returned to the Technician or his Section Manager for corrective action. It will then be subject to a further out-going inspection by the QA Inspector.

Outputs – Products or services provided to others; the result of a process.

Preventive actions – Steps that are taken to remove the causes of potential non-conformities or to make quality improvements. Preventive actions address potential problems, ones that haven't yet occurred. In general, the preventive action process can be thought of as a risk analysis process.

Procedure – Describes the way to perform an activity or process.

Process – An activity that uses resources to transform inputs into outputs.

Process control – Operations with a built-in finding and adjusting step to keep a product or service in conformance with the specifications.

Process approach – A management strategy used to control the processes that make up their Quality Management System.

Product – Result of a process.

 Note: There are four agreed generic product categories:

- hardware (e.g. engine mechanical part);
- software (e.g. computer program);
- services (e.g. transport);
- processed materials (e.g. lubricant).

Hardware and processed materials are generally tangible products, while software or services are generally intangible.

Most products comprise elements belonging to different generic product categories. Whether the product is then called hardware, processed material, software or service depends on the dominant element.

Product non-conformity – When one or more characteristics of a product fail to meet specified requirements.

Project – Unique process, consisting of a set of co-ordinated and controlled activities with start and finish dates, undertaken to achieve an objective conforming to specific requirements, including the constraints of time, costs and resources.

Quality – Ability of a set of inherent characteristics of a product, system or process to fulfil requirements of customers and other interested parties.

Quality assurance – Part of quality management, focused on providing confidence that quality requirements are fulfilled.

Quality audit – A systematic and independent examination to determine whether quality activities and related results comply with planned arrangements and whether these arrangements are implemented effectively and are suitable to achieve objectives.

Quality control – Part of quality management, focused on fulfilling quality requirements.

Quality costs – The expenditure incurred by the producer, by the user and by the community, associated with product or service quality.

Quality level – A general indication of the extent of the product's departure from the ideal.

Quality loop – Conceptual model of interacting activities that influence the quality of a product or service in the various stages ranging from the identification of needs to the assessment of whether these needs have been satisfied.

Quality management – That aspect of the overall management function that determines and implements the quality policy.

 Note: The terms 'quality management' and 'quality control' are considered to be a manufacturer/supplier (or 1st party) responsibility. 'Quality assurance' on the other hand has both internal and external aspects which in many instances can be shared between the manufacturer/supplier (1st party), purchaser/customer (2nd party) and any regulatory/certification body (3rd party) that may be involved.

Quality management system – System to establish a quality policy and quality objectives and to achieve those objectives.

Quality management system review – A formal evaluation by top management of the status and adequacy of the Quality Management System in relation to quality policy and new objectives resulting from changing circumstances.

Quality manager – A person who is responsible for the manufacturer's Quality Management System (also sometimes referred to as the Chief Inspector).

Quality manual – Document specifying the Quality Management System of an organisation.

Quality plan – Document specifying the Quality Management System elements and the resources to be applied in a specific case.

Quality policy – The overall quality intentions and direction of an organisation as regards quality, as formally expressed by top management.

Quality procedure – A description of the method by which quality system activities are managed.

Quality records – Records should provide evidence of how well the Quality System has been implemented.

Quality requirement – A characteristic that an entity must have. For example, a customer may require that a particular product (entity) achieves a specific dependability score (characteristic).

Quality system – The organisational structure, responsibilities, procedures, processes and resources for implementing quality management.

Quarantine store – A secure place to store supplies that are awaiting proof that they comply with specified requirements.

Receiving inspection/incoming inspection – Inspection by a customer (or department) of materials and manufactured products as received.

Record – Document stating results achieved or providing evidence of activities performed.

Reliability – The ability of an item to perform a required function under stated conditions for a stated period of time.

Repair – Action taken on a non-conforming product to make it acceptable for the intended usage.

Requirement – Need or expectation that is stated, customarily implied or obligatory.

Review – Activity undertaken to ensure the suitability, adequacy, effectiveness and efficiency of the subject matter to achieve established objectives.

Risk – The combined effect of the probability of occurrence of an undesirable event, and the consequence of the event.

Sample – A group of items or individuals, taken from a larger collection or population that provides information needed for assessing a characteristic (or characteristics) of the population, or which serves as a basis for action on the population, or the process that produced it.

Shall – This auxiliary verb indicates a course of action that must be followed by manufacturers and suppliers.

Should – This auxiliary verb indicates that a certain course of action is preferred but not necessarily required.

Specification – The document that describes the requirements with which the product, material or process has to conform.

Supplier – The organisation that provides a product to the customer [EN ISO 8402:1995].

- Note 1. In a contractual situation, the supplier may be called the contractor.
- Note 2. The supplier may be, for example, the producer, distributor, importer, assembler or service organisation.
- Note 3. The supplier may be either external or internal to the organisation.
- Note 4. With regard to MDD the term supplier is **not** used. The directive instead refers to 'manufacturer'.

Supplier evaluation – Assessment of a supplier's capability to control quality.

Supplier rating – An index related to the performance of a supplier.

Top management – Person or group of people who direct and control an organisation at the highest level.

User requirement – The documented product or service requirements of a customer or user.

Validation – Confirmation and provision of objective evidence that the requirements for a specific intended use or application have been fulfilled.

Verification – The act of reviewing, inspecting, testing, checking, auditing or otherwise establishing and documenting whether items, processes, services, or documents conform to specified requirements.

Work instruction – A description of how a specific task is carried out.

And finally – 'The ISO Glossary'!

BISON – Official ISO mascot.

ISOAP – Detergent used to clean up before the Registration Audit.

ISOB – The shedding of tears resulting from receiving too many audit non-conformances.

ISOCIAL – A party thrown to celebrate passing an ISO audit.

ISODA – Beverage served at an isocial.

ISOHAPPY – The pure joy of conformity!

ISOLATION – How the management representative feels when introducing the new system.

ISOMETRICS – Used to measure quality objectives.

ISONO-NO – Activity leading to a non-conformance.

ISORE – Eye strain resulting from writing procedures and work instructions.

ISORRY – Response to a corrective action request.

ISO-SO – Not a full blown non-conformance; something that's just getting by.

Useful addresses

American National Standards Institute (ANSI)
1819 L Street, NW
Washington, DC 20036, USA
Tel: 00 1 202 293 8020
Fax: 00 1 202 293 9287
e-mail: ansionline@ansi.org
website: http://www.ansi.org

American Society for Quality Control (ASQ)
611 East Wisconsin Avenue
PO Box 3005
Milwaukee WI 53201–3005, USA
Tel: 00 1 414 272 8575 or 800 248 1946
Fax: 00 1 414 272 1734
e-mail: cs@asq.org
website: http://www.asq.org

British Standards Institution (BSI)
389 Chiswick High Road
London W4 4AL
Tel: 020 8996 9001
Fax: 020 8996 7001
e-mail: info@bsi.org.uk
website: http://www.bsi.org.uk

Comission Europeen de Normalisation (CEN)
36, rue de Stassart
1050 Bruxelles, Belgium
Tel: 0032 2 550 08 11
Fax: 0032 2 550 08 19
e-mail: infodesk@cenclcbel.be
website: http://www.cenorm.be

European Telecommunications Standards Institute (ETSI)
Route des Lucioles – Sophia Antipolis – Valbonne
06921 Sophia Antipolis, France
Tel: 0033 4 92 94 42 00
Fax: 0033 4 93 65 47 16
e-mail: infocentre@etsi.fr
website: http://www.etsi.org

European Committee for Electrotechnical Standardisation (CENELEC)
35, rue de Stassart
1050 Bruxelles, Belgium
Tel: 0032 2 519 68 71
Fax: 0032 2 519 69 19
e-mail: general@cenelec.be
website: http://www.cenelec.be

European Organisation for Testing and Certification (EOTC)
Egmont House
Rue d'Egmont 15
1000 Bruxelles, Belgium
Tel: 0032 2 502 4141
Fax: 0032 2 502 4239

ILI (Infonorme London Information)
Index House
Ascot, Berkshire
SL5 7EU, UK
Tel: 01344 636400
Fax: 01344 291194
e-mail: databases@ili.co.uk
website: www.ili.co.uk

ILI (America)
60 Winters Avenue
Paramus, NJ 07652, USA
e-mail: sales@ili-info.com

International Electrotechnical Commission (IEC)
Rue de Varembe 3
Case Postale 131
1211 Geneva 20, Switzerland
Tel: 0041 22 919 0211
Fax: 0041 22 919 0300
website: http://www.iec.ch

International Standards Organisation (ISO)
Case Postal 56
1222 Geneva 20, Switzerland
Tel: 0041 22 749 0336
Fax: 0041 22 734 1079
website: http://www.iso.ch and http://www.iso.org
 Iso/TC 176 – http:www.tc.176.org
 Iso/TC 176 subcommittees – http:www.bsi.org.uk/iso-tc176-sc2

National Center for Standards and Certification Information
US Department of Commerce
Building 820, Room 164
Gaithersburg, MD 20899, USA
Tel: 00 1 301 9754040
EU Hotline: 00 1 301 921–4164
Fax: 00 1 301 926 1559

Office of the European Union and Regulatory Affairs
US Dept of Commerce – Room 3036
14th & Constitution Avenue, N.W.
Washington, D.C. 20230
Tel: 00 1 202 482 5276
Fax: 00 1 202 482 2155

Office of the Official Publications Of the EC
2 Rue Mercier
2144 Luxembourg
Tel: 00352–29291
Fax: 00352 292942763
e-mail: infor.info@opece.cec.be
website: http://www.eur-op.eu.int

VDE-Verlag GmbH
Bismarkstrasse 33
10625 Berlin, Germany
Tel: 0049 30 348001–0
Fax: 0049 30 3417093
e-mail: service@vde.com
website: http://www.vde.de

Index